March 7, 2025

THE BEGGAR LAMA

To my beloved professor,

Your wisdom and kindness have shaped my journeys in ways beyond words.

With deepest gratitude for your parently love and guidance, I wish you all the best!

With love,

Tenzin

The Beggar Lama

THE LIFE OF THE GYALRONG KUZHAP

Tenzin Jinba

Columbia University Press
New York

Columbia University Press
Publishers Since 1893
New York   Chichester, West Sussex
cup.columbia.edu
Copyright © 2023 Columbia University Press

Library of Congress Cataloging-in-Publication Data
Names: Tenzin, Jinba, author.
Title: The Beggar Lama : the life of the Gyalrong Kuzhap / Tenzin Jinba.
Description: New York : Columbia University Press, [2023] |
Includes bibliographical references and index.
Identifiers: LCCN 2023011146 (print) | LCCN 2023011147 (ebook) |
ISBN 9780231209342 (hardback) | ISBN 9780231209359 (trade paperback) |
ISBN 9780231557894 (ebook)
Subjects: LCSH: Ngag-dbang-tshul-khrims, Btsan-lha. | Tibetologists—Rgyal-rong—Biography. |
Lamas—China—Rgyal-rong—Biography. | Tibetans—China—Rgyal-rong—Social conditions. |
Tibetans—Biography. | Rgyal-rong (China)—History—20th century. | Rgyal-rong
(China)—Biography.
Classification: LCC DS786.3.N43 J56 2023 (print) | LCC DS786.3.N43 (ebook) |
DDC 951.505092 [B]—dc23/eng/20230502
LC record available at https://lccn.loc.gov/2023011146
LC ebook record available at https://lccn.loc.gov/2023011147

Printed in the United States of America

Cover design: Milenda Nan Ok Lee
Cover image: The Okzhi Palace, photo by Wilson, Ernest Henry, 1876–1930,
American, English, 1908-06-26; see https://images.hollis.harvard.edu/permalink/f
/100kie6/HVD_VIAolvwork287201

For my late mother, Khandro, and my daughter named after her grandma

CONTENTS

CONTENTS

ACKNOWLEDGMENTS

I have never doubted how lucky I am to be acquainted with the Gyalrong Kuzhap, the protagonist of this book. This is more than a book for me: it represents a milestone in my life trajectory and intellectual journey. The Gyalrong Kuzhap and his stories recounted here help me see hope and something good in desperate situations. He shows me the power of humility, forbearance, and resilience as a "trivial" person when many around us are carried away by the surging tides of insatiable material desire, formidable political power, division, and animosity. Overall, focusing on positive values like meaning, hope, well-being, and strength, as reflected in this life story, is instrumental in advancing my research agenda and projects revolving around the notion of the good, especially in times of suffering and hardship. I cannot thank the Gyalrong Kuzhap enough for that influence.

Many others have significantly impacted my life and career, eventually making this book possible. My parents, especially my late mother, Gyelbo Khandro, had a nearly religious belief in the power of knowledge. They made a somewhat unusual choice by permitting me to pursue a college dream and, finally, a Ph.D. in the United States. My mother's strong sense of justice and compassion shaped my attitude so that associating with the peripheral and minorities became a natural and right thing for me to do. She told me weeks before her sudden death that she was proud of me. It was the first time she had said something like this, and it meant more than she or I could have expected. These simple but powerful words gave me the strength to move on in my dark moments. What's more, my mother first told me about the "miraculous birth" of the Gyalrong Kuzhap and inside stories about him. Thanks to her acquaintance with some of his family members, relatives, and friends and her bedtime stories, I better understood the source of my intense interest in the Gyalrong Kuzhap's life history, ultimately contributing to this book.

My daughter, Serkhyung Khandro, who has just turned seven and has a compassionate heart like her grandma and mother, has enlightened my life in multiple ways. As she knew this book was dedicated to her and my mother, she periodically asked, "Daddy, have you finished the book for Grandma and me?" She proudly told her playmates, "My daddy is writing a book for me." Moreover, when I tried reading some paragraphs of the Gyalrong Kuzhap's childhood experiences to my daughter as bedtime stories, I was amazed that she was so mesmerized that she asked me to recount these stories again and again. Her questions and absorption were an extra incentive to complete the book and write in a more accessible way. Although I am unsure whether this book is suitable for younger children, my daughter's curiosity and perspective reminded me of the power of stories and "plain language." I was also reminded of problems with "esoteric language" in academic writing, rendering it virtually incomprehensible to those outside a particular field. Although there must be legitimate reasons for using complex abstract academic language in various disciplines, I hope to write more intelligibly to reach general audiences and "ordinary people." This book focuses, above all, on "ordinary" everyday experiences.

Next, I am grateful to my Boston University teachers, especially Fredrik Barth (1928–2016), Robert Weller (Rob), and Charles Lindholm (Chuck), for helping turn a curious but confused amateur into a scholar. I had a very tough time in the first two years of Ph.D. study because of my limited training in anthropology and social theory. With extraordinary trust in my potential, these teachers helped me acknowledge my self-worth and sense of accomplishment. Some of my cohorts might have seen their attention to me as favoritism. If there was anything like favoritism in how they treated me, I used extra diligence, optimism, and gratitude to justify and earn their special attention. This attention continued after my Ph.D. as I discussed my present book at its different stages with Rob and Chuck, seeking their feedback. No words can fully express my gratitude to these great teachers, especially considering that Chuck has experienced serious health issues in the last few years. Furthermore, I received more than special attention from two extraordinary teachers during my MA study at Beijing Foreign Studies University, John G. Blair and Jerusha McCormack, who are now living their happy retirement lives in Dublin. Since my encounter with this couple, we have become one another's honorary family members. We had an annual ritual to visit until the COVID-19 pandemic started. I plan to give them a copy of this book as my special present at our anticipated next meeting. They have witnessed and celebrated each major transition and breakthrough in my life and career over the last decade. I know how proud they are of me, and I am truly grateful. I thus use this book to pay tribute to all my outstanding teachers who have transformed my life.

I profoundly thank Gray Tuttle, who has had a tremendous impact on me, though I met him only once years ago. As I sought guidance and suggestions from him through e-mails during my Ph.D. study, I saw him as a role model for being sophisticated, intelligent, humble, diligent, sincere, and altruistic. Moreover, he has played a crucial role in shaping this project. Thanks to his advice, I cut the original manuscript into two parts and turned one into this present book. Apart from sheer length, he helped me see the problem of two parallel conflicting narratives and themes in the original manuscript (the other focused on humanistic interventions). He also encouraged me to submit my book prospectus and manuscript to Columbia University Press for review. This outcome might not have been possible without Gray's advice and support. I also thank Stéphane Gros. While I was working for a European Research Council-funded project that he led ("Territories, Communities, and Exchanges in the Kham Sino-Tibetan Borderlands," 2012–2016), Stéphane sponsored my fieldwork on a Gyalrong revolt in the early twentieth century. The hub of the revolt happened to be the monastery—Sönamyak Monastery or Senggé Trashi Chöling—that later recognized the Gyalrong Kuzhap as their reincarnate lama. I have used my then-collected ethnographical and archival data in this book.

Moreover, I thank others who have contributed to this book through their comments, critiques, and intellectual inspiration. I am grateful to the anonymous reviewers for recognizing its value and helping me enhance it through constructive comments. I would also like to acknowledge individuals who provided valuable input and inspiration through their works or conversations. This list includes Henrietta Harrison, Benno Weiner, Emily T. Yeh, Wang Xiuyu, Zhao Dingxin, Wang Mingke, Liang Yongjia, Sun Yanfei, Tian Geng, Wang Juan, John Bray, Max Oidtmann, Hans Steinmüller, Janet Gyatso, Yudru Tsomu, Andrew Quintman, Samten Karmay, Erik Mueggler, James C. Scott, Tenzin Gyurmé, Drayang, Tenzin Tsondru, Tseyung, Namkha Tsültrim, and Temur, among many. In addition, I am fortunate to be part of a collegial and intellectually stimulating community at the NUS. Numerous conversations with colleagues in my department (sociology and anthropology) and others, including in the engineering and science departments, inspired me to think beyond my comfort zone. This book is also an outcome of these conversations.

I am also grateful to my wife, Arten Métok, who I sometimes jokingly call "my beautiful wife" because of her beauty both on the outside and on the inside. She moved to Singapore with me to support my choice to live as an ordinary person and scholar, despite her homesickness for the vast Yugurs grasslands in northwestern China, where she grew up. I especially thank her for her emotional support while writing this book. Additionally, I thank many others who have shown their moral support from this book's conceptualization to its writing, in one way or another, including my father, brothers, in-laws, relatives, friends, and students. Two of my friends deserve special mention: Ma Liyuan and Mei Shenyou, the cohorts in my M.A. program. We have seldom been in touch with one another, but they hold a special place in my heart because of their beautiful souls and noble humanity. I know that they will be cheering for this book, as they always do for all significant stages in my life.

I would like to extend my special thanks to my team of exceptional editors, who have each played a vital role in shaping my work. My first language editor, who prefers anonymity, provided invaluable assistance in refining my language early on. My talented and uplifting copyeditor, Leslie Kriesel, has worked tirelessly to perfect my prose, and I am deeply grateful for her contributions. Last but not least, I thank Caelyn Cobb and Monique Laban, excellent editors at Columbia University Press, for their patience, kindness, and support.

NOTE ON TRANSLITERATION

I use the University of Virginia Tibetan and Himalayan Library (THL)'s Simplified Phonetic Transcription of Standard Tibetan to transliterate Tibetan-Gyalrong names, places, and terms in the main text. Tibetan pronunciations and spellings are diverse and complex across Greater Tibet and the Himalayas. For instance, the linguistic classification of various Gyalrong dialects (as part of the Tibetan or other language families) remains controversial. Some Tibetologists argue that the Gyalrong dialects (e.g., Situ or Tsanlha dialects) retain ancient Tibetan spellings, sounds, and pronunciations. Therefore, I use the phonetic transcription system mentioned above, which is based on modern and standard Tibetan, to simplify this complication and avoid further confusion. It is the most plausible solution, although not perfect.

I apply other transliterations when needed, for instance, Gyalrong (not Gyelrong), Gyalrongwa (not Gyelrongba), Tsanlha (not Tsenlha), Ngawang (not Ngakwang), and so on, to adhere to the approach I have adopted regularly. I use THL's Extended Wylie Transliteration Scheme for the bibliography to assist readers, especially Tibetologists. However, in applying this scheme, I choose to capitalize only the first letter of the first word in my cited works and the authors' names, regardless of whether it is pronounced or not. For instance, I use "Rgyalrong" or "Rgyal rong" instead of its common transliteration, "rGyalrong" or "rGyal rong" (its first letter *r* is silent). I use pinyin in transcribing Chinese terms.

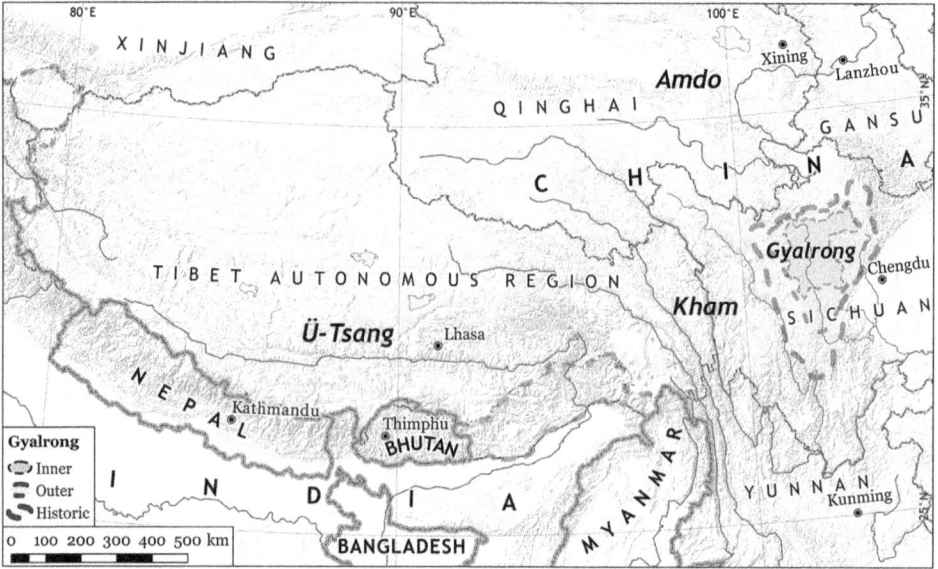

MAP 1. Gyalrong in Greater Tibet and China. Digital cartography by Mark Henderson

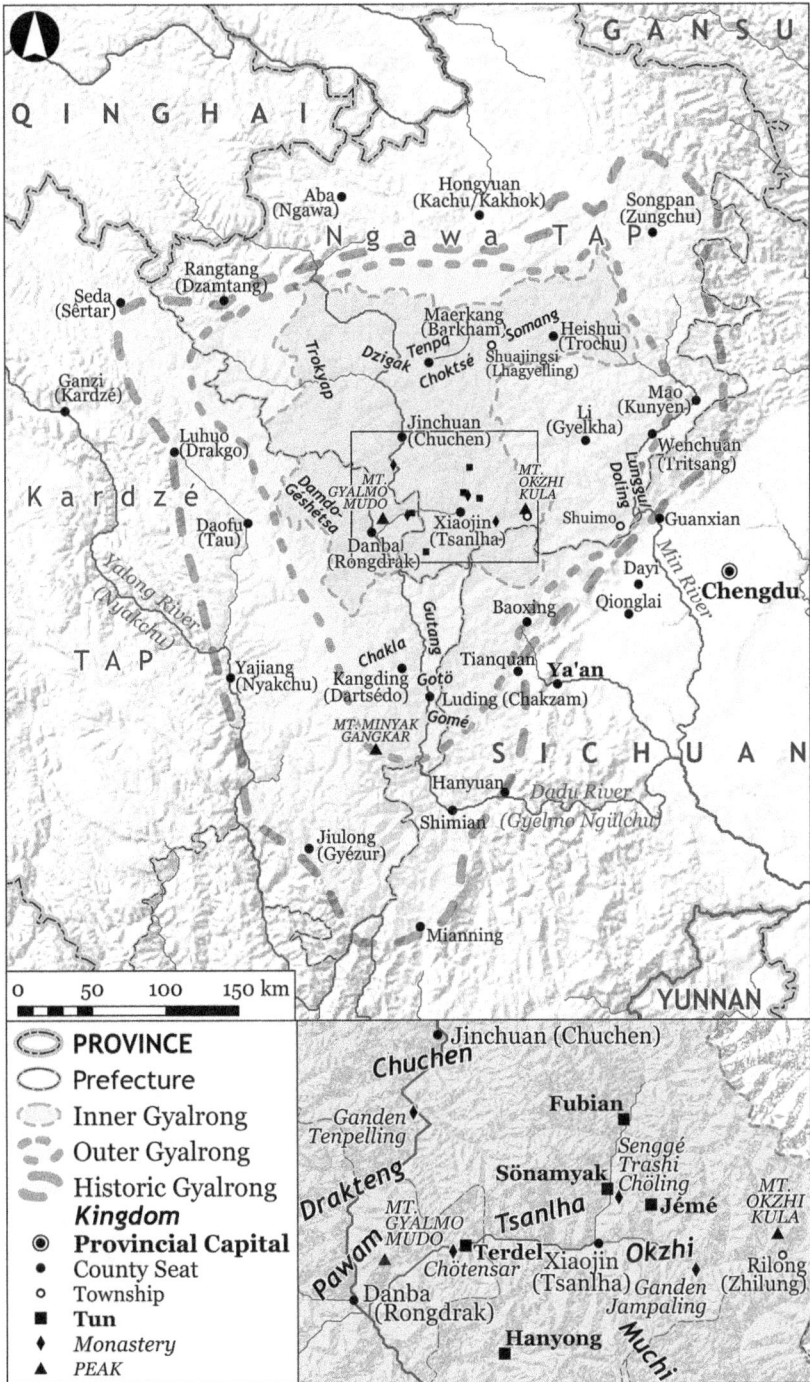

MAP 2. Gyalrong Until the Mid-Twentieth Century. Digital cartography by Mark Henderson

Main map labels:

QINGHAI
GANSU
G A N S U
Q I N G H A I

Aba (Ngawa)
Hongyuan (Kachu/Kakhok)
Songpan (Zungchu)
N g a w a   T A P
Rangtang (Dzamtang)
Seda (Sêrtar)
Maerkang (Barkham)
Somang
Heishui (Trochu)
Trokyap
Dzigak
Tenpa
Choktsé
Shuajingsi (Lhagyelling)
Li (Gyelkha)
Mao (Kunyen)
Ganzi (Kardzé)
Luhuo (Drakgo)
Jinchuan (Chuchen)
Wenchuan (Tritsang)
K a r d z é
Damdo-Geshetsa
MT. GYALMO MUDO
MT. OKZHI KULA
Lungwu Doling
Daofu (Tau)
Danba (Rongdrak)
Xiaojin (Tsanlha)
Shuimo
Guanxian
Yalong River (Nyakchu)
Dayi
Chengdu
Baoxing
Qionglai
T A P
Gutang
Yajiang (Nyakchu)
Chakla
Kangding (Dartsédo)
Gotö
Tianquan
Ya'an
Luding (Chakzam)
Gomé
MT. MINYAK GANGKAR
S I C H U A N
Min River
Hanyuan
Dadu River (Gyelmo Ngülchu)
Shimian
Jiulong (Gyézur)
Mianning
YUNNAN

0   50   100   150 km

Legend:

PROVINCE
Prefecture
Inner Gyalrong
Outer Gyalrong
Historic Gyalrong Kingdom
Provincial Capital
County Seat
Township
Tun
Monastery
PEAK

Inset map labels:

Jinchuan (Chuchen)
Chuchen
Ganden Tenpelling
Fubian
Drakteng
Sönamyak
Senggé Trashi Chöling
Jémé
MT. OKZHI KULA
Pawam
MT. GYALMO MUDO
Tsanlha
Terdel
Chötensar
Xiaojin (Tsanlha)
Okzhi
Ganden Jampaling
Rilong (Zhilung)
Danba (Rongdrak)
Hanyong
Muchi

NOTE ON THE MAPS

Drawing maps of Gyalrong is a challenging task. The notion and boundary of the region have been historically inconsistent and fluid. I divide Gyalrong into three layers (Inner, Outer, and Historical) to showcase this fluctuation. These maps are primarily for illustrative purposes, not for historical or geocultural veracity. "Inner Gyalrong" refers to Gyalrong's core cultural area, where most locals identify themselves as the Gyalrongwa (people of Gyalrong). "Outer Gyalrong" refers to Gyalrong's peripheral area adjacent to Han Chinese, Kham, or Amdo Tibetan cultural areas. Despite the strong influence of these powerful political-cultural entities, most Outer Gyalrong natives identified themselves with Gyalrong to varying degrees up until the 1950s. However, from the 1950s onward, the situation began changing. For instance, Chakla royal lineage descendants and the native population in this previously Outer Gyalrong kingdom started renouncing their "in-between" status associated with Kham and Gyalrong and reasserted themselves solely as Khampa (Tibetans of Kham).

I will not discuss the particular reason here due to a different focus. Those interested in delving further into this issue may refer to my book *In the Land of the Eastern Queendom* (cited in this book) and the discussion therein on the shifting identity of a local community (Suopo) in Rongdrak (Danba) that had been a constituent of the Chakla kingdom. This specific circumstance suggests that similar to Chakla, other Gyalrong kingdoms straddle Inner and Outer Gyalrong, notably Choktsé, Somang, and Trokyap. These three kingdoms have been classified traditionally as part of Inner Gyalrong. The nomadic and seminomadic areas under their administration, which have spread today to Ngawa, Sêrtar, Drakgo, Dzamtang, and Kachu/Kakhok, are, however, usually viewed as part of Outer Gyalrong. This complexity highlights the fluid Gyalrong identity and its shifting boundaries throughout history, and hence the difficulty of showing such complex shifts on static maps.

"Historical Gyalrong" identifies a broader Gyalrong area (circa eighth to eighteenth centuries). The historical records on this boundary have been primarily collected in my coedited *Gyalrong Tibetan History and Culture Series* (2017), frequently cited here. However, many records provide somewhat ambiguous, if not confusing, information. I have collected folktales about Historical Gyalrong. The written documents and oral accounts imply that the area was much more expansive than delineated on these maps. In other words, Historical Gyalrong's boundaries as drawn here are an outcome of my relatively cautious stance toward the existing historical records and accounts. Even so, this delineation can still be quite controversial. Again, these maps were not created for their historical accuracy but rather to provide a rough idea about Gyalrong's relative locations in Greater Tibet and its historical fluidity.

Map 2 is mainly based on the status quo of the mid-1950s, when all the remaining Gyalrong kingdoms were receding from the historical stage due to unprecedented political restructuring under the new Communist regime. For the purpose of illustration, this map includes Chuchen and Tsanlha, the two kingdoms the Qing court officially abolished at the end of the eighteenth century, and all the other Gyalrong kingdoms, although most also had been officially abolished by 1911. Except for a few cases (Chakla, Gotö, and Gomé), most kingdoms' de facto territory and influence remained intact by the early 1950s. This book sheds light on that situation.

INTRODUCTION

This book focuses on the life history of the Gyalrong Kuzhap (Tsanlha Ngawang Tsültrim, 1930–), a reincarnate lama or *tulku* in Tibetan. He is also
an ex-Communist official and a retired professor of Tibetan studies. Based
on local tradition, a *tulku* is more frequently referred to as *kuzhap* than by
the standard honorific title "Rinpoche" (precious one) found in other cul-
turally Tibetan areas. Additionally, because of his regional-cultural solid
identification with Gyalrong, I use the title "Gyalrong Kuzhap" to identify
him in this book. He was born in Tsanlha, part of the broader Gyalrong
region at the easternmost fringe of the Tibetan Plateau. Gyalrong's Tibetan
status is often contested due to its unique political, cultural, and linguistic
traditions (further discussed below; see also chapters 1 and 14). The Gyalrong Kuzhap believes that defending Gyalrong's Tibetan status is crucial
in safeguarding Tibetan civilization from perishing and for Tibetan cultural survival in China. It is no exaggeration to say that this defines his life
purpose after retirement. Therefore, although "the Gyalrong Kuzhap" may
be singular in standard Tibetan usage, I have decided to use it.

To gain a better idea of the Gyalrong Kuzhap's life purpose, it is important to understand the unique role of Gyalrong in Greater Tibet and its
ambivalent status within broader Tibetan history and identity. This specific status involves Gyalrong's convoluted political, cultural, and religious
histories in relation to the Tibetan Empire (seventh to ninth centuries),

Central Tibet (Ü-Tsang in Tibetan; roughly today's Tibet Autonomous Region or TAR, with Lhasa as its capital), and other parts of Greater Tibet (mainly the Amdo and Kham regions, spread across today's Sichuan, Qinghai, Gansu, and Yunnan provinces), as well as to the Chinese (and Mongol and Manchu) empire.[1] This complexity is to be unwrapped in the book's main body to varying extents, such as in chapters 1, 4, and 14. For now, it is important to point out that this ambivalence has much to do with one vital issue: even though Gyalrong was Tibetanized step by step no later than the seventh century, this does not automatically mean that the Gyalrongwa (Gyalrong natives) are unproblematically Tibetans.[2] It is not totally certain that they have been acknowledged by other Tibetans as such throughout history, or that they considered themselves a Tibetan subgroup by the eighteenth century, a crucial moment that redefined the region's historical trajectory. There are no definite answers to these questions or Gyalrong's Tibetan status.[3]

This situation is further complicated by the concurrently unfolding processes of Sinicization (becoming Han Chinese)[4] and (Central) Tibetanization (becoming Lhasa-Gelugpa institutionalized) after a redefining historical moment, namely, the Qing's subjugation of the two rebelling Gyalrong kings in its two massive Jinchuan Campaigns (1747–1749, 1771–1776).[5] The Qing court dispatched Han officials directly (and trustworthy Gyalrong nobles) to rule the Gyalrong locals and introduced economic incentives to mobilize Han Chinese migration. Meanwhile, the Qing court granted Lhasa and the Gelugpa regime led by the Dalai Lama the privilege of taking a chief role in local religious affairs after enforcing the Gyalrong natives' religious conversion from Bön (an indigenous Tibetan religion), thereby formalizing Gyalrong monks' training in Lhasa (see a more thorough discussion of this religious transition and broader repercussions of the Jinchuan Campaigns in chapter 4). As a result, Gyalrong strengthened political and religious ties with the Qing and Lhasa Gelugpa regimes, becoming Sinicized (in terms of Han migration and cultural assimilation) and (Central) Tibetanized (in terms of the Lhasa-Gelugpa regime's influence) simultaneously.

The political restructuring at the end of the Qing was characterized by the radical reforms of Zhao Erfeng (1845–1911), popularly known as "Zhao the Butcher" for his brutal suppression in Kham, to absorb the Sino-Tibetan borderlands into the Chinese administrative system. This substantially changed the power balance between the relatively equally matched Chinese and Tibetan political and cultural(-religious) entities in Gyalrong.[6] Consequently, the people and political and religious institutions there were subjected to even more vigorous effects from and constant tensions between these two formidable forces. This tendency was enhanced during the Republican era (1912–1949) when Han migration sped up and the Republican governments (the Beiyang regime from 1912 to 1928 and Chiang Kai-shek's Nationalist government from 1928 to 1949) implemented more direct, though not always more effective, control over Gyalrong (chapter 7). After Gyalrong and other Tibetan regions were incorporated into Communist China, various political movements undermined Gyalrong's Tibetan religious tradition and cultural heritage to the point that they couldn't be restored or revived properly in the Reform era (chapter 11). As a result, the Sinicizing process in Gyalrong has gained unprecedented momentum and speed compared to most other ethnocultural Tibetan regions. This process is not always smooth, as periodic frictions and antagonisms attest. For example, while many Gyalrongwa have distanced themselves further from the Tibetan nationality, especially since the 2008 Tibetan unrest, the Gyalrong Kuzhap and many other Gyalrongwa have chosen an opposing path, staunchly defending Gyalrong's authentic Tibetan status. Notably, some Gyalrong subcommunities have chosen to disintegrate from Gyalrong and declare their (non-Gyalrong) "real Tibetan" status.[7]

The story of the Gyalrong Kuzhap's life reveals such effects and tensions to varying degrees, and these have boiled down to his life purpose and urgent mission after retirement. This mission is represented by his endeavor to open Tibetan language classes in Gyalrong and re-educate the Gyalrongwa and other Tibetans about Gyalrong's "authentic" Tibetan past and its historical and continued significance for the integrity and survival of Tibetan civilization (chapter 14). The significance of this is self-evident to the Gyalrong Kuzhap because Gyalrong has been a critical cultural frontier of Tibetan civilization for at least 1,300 years. Moreover, the region has produced some of the most prominent scholars and lamas in Tibetan history. Within the Gelugpa alone, more than seven Ganden Tripa ("Holders of the Ganden Throne" or abbots of the Gelugpa tradition) from Gyalrong and multiple Gyalrongwa tutors and assistant tutors to different Dalai Lamas since the eighteenth century, including the two assistant tutors of the present (Fourteenth) Dalai Lama (chapter 5). Therefore, if such an important Tibetan cultural frontier collapses and becomes a Han Chinese region, other Tibetan regions may follow, typifying the domino effect. This critical circumstance has devasted the Gyalrong Kuzhap. The following episode addresses his anguish and hopes.

During a casual conversation in the summer of 2019, I asked the Gyalrong Kuzhap, "Have you started to consider your next reincarnation? If so, where do you want to be reborn?" He replied, "I have had little control over my present life, not to mention my next life. However, if I could choose, I wish to be reborn in Bhutan." In his eyes, Bhutan is the only place on the planet where a relatively authentic version of Tibetan culture remains intact and true happiness resides. Against the odds of material scarcity (as seen in economic GDP and subsistence standards), how the Bhutanese express happiness is believed to be consistent with the teaching of Tibetan Buddhism that most Bhutanese follow, emphasizing spiritual enrichment by downplaying the role of earthly materials or instrumental rationality in well-being. According to the Gyalrong Kuzhap, the whole world can learn an essential lesson from Bhutan: techno-scientific and material progress do not automatically bring happiness or translate into human spiritual development. An unbridled desire for material goods would lead to humankind's disaster or even destruction, e.g., the 2008 Sichuan earthquake, the COVID-19 pandemic, etc. This idea is broadly reflected in his life experiences this book records.

Even so, we may still ask: Why Bhutan in particular? For anthropologists, Tibetologists, and most scholars, the image of Bhutan often represents a typical example of the "invention of tradition" and the making of Shangri-La (an imagined pure land or paradise on earth with unbounded happiness, unfeigned innocence, and lasting harmony).[8] Such image making typifies our contemporary era, being closely associated with a growing global market for authenticity and nostalgia to address such negative consequences of high modernity as alienation, rationalization, anxieties, and commercialism.[9] In short, Bhutan is an antidote to high modernity and the present in the popular imagination. Therefore, the Gyalrong Kuzhap's response does not appear to be unreasonable. Even so, many, especially those with knowledge about Tibetan culture and identity and the Gyalrong Kuzhap's status, may find his answer somewhat unexpected, if not unacceptable. For most Tibetans, Lhasa has long been the most sacred city and the hub of Tibetan civilization. Under this hierarchical imagination of

Buddhist civilization, a place such as Bhutan used to occupy, or remains in, a lowly and peripheral position. Traditionally, Bhutan and its neighboring Himalayan regions and tribes were identified as Mön in Tibetan, literally, "land of darkness." Thus, how can the Gyalrong Kuzhap, one of the last living Tibetan Buddhist polymaths of his generation in China, reverse this hierarchical order and willingly represent Bhutan as a new and probably the only existing center of Buddhist civilization?

This is not unique to the Gyalrong Kuzhap; many Tibetans based in China have similar convictions, especially since the 2008 unrest. This book is intended to resolve this puzzle. In the eyes of the Gyalrong Kuzhap and many Tibetans, the Bhutanese image is in stark contrast to the immensely Sinicized ("becoming Han") and "spiritually contaminated" regions of Greater Tibet facing growing challenges to the survival of the Tibetan nationality and culture. In invoking the romanticized image of Bhutan as a critical foil to the desperate present status quo in Greater Tibet, the Gyalrong Kuzhap expresses frustration with what Greater Tibet, especially his hometown of Gyalrong, has become today. But he also remains hopeful that Tibetan nationality and civilization will not quickly die out due to the great worth of Tibetan traditions, or "spiritual civilization," in this increasingly materialized and rationalized world. The paradoxical coexistence of his desperation and hope exemplifies multiple contradictions in his life experiences and roles, such as his polarized positions and seemingly incompatible roles as both a quasi-aristocrat and a beggar, as reflected in the book title, *The Beggar Lama*.

On several occasions, people from Lhasa conveyed to me that during their first encounters with the Gyalrong Kuzhap, they were amazed to find that he possessed the elegance of a Lhasa aristocrat from subtle signs in his verbal and body language and his etiquette. During his monastic training in Lhasa in the 1940s, he cultivated the tastes of the Lhasa aristocrats through close interactions, convinced that the aristocrats in Lhasa possessed much more elegant, elaborate, and sophisticated manners and rituals than their Gyalrong counterparts, thanks to the role of Lhasa as the primary hub of "high" Tibetan culture (chapter 6).[10] These high tastes are manifested in manners, music, art, food, dress, and speech patterns, among other things. An aristocratic taste cannot, however, be mistaken for aristocratic status, which in Greater Tibet is a hereditary rank.[11] Despite his supposedly superior status as a spiritual leader, his aristocratic playmates in the local magistrate's household referred to him as the "Beggar Lama" (Tib. *archo lama*) during his childhood due to his low family background and dependency on the nobles for survival (chapter 3).

The Gyalrong Kuzhap is satisfied with this title, believing it captures his simultaneously paradoxical roles and dramatic ups and downs in life during different periods. This book casts fresh light on those roles and events that tend to alternate between "heaven" and "hell," the metaphors he likes to use to describe his life's vicissitudes and the underlying volatile sociopolitical environments (see, for instance, act III, chapters 7–11). I am aware that leaning toward these dramatic experiences can be incomplete or reductive, if not seriously biased, in terms of the objective to provide a complex and multidimensional portrayal of the Gyalrong Kuzhap's life story and its entangled sociopolitical histories. Indeed, it is almost impossible to capture an inclusive portrayal of the Gyalrong Kuzhap. Thus, this book focuses mainly on certain of his major roles and key life episodes to provide insights into the unprecedented sociopolitical changes in Gyalrong, Greater Tibet, and China over the past hundred years or so.

DEFINING THE AGENDA: THE AUTHOR'S INTERVENTION

To define what this book is intended to achieve, it is necessary for me first to explain why and how I decided to take on this work. Doing so addresses this project's nature and objectives and reflects my role and positioning as its author.

I am originally from Tsanlha in Gyalrong, the same hometown as the Gyalrong Kuzhap. During my childhood, I heard a lot from my mother and others about the miraculous birth of their *tulku*, the Gyalrong Kuzhap, which was said to have been accompanied by a rainbow emerging over his village and house, among other auspicious signs (chapter 1). Therefore, in my mind, he was a saintly being with an awe-inspiring presence and patronizing, if not superior, manners. The desire to meet with this "holy man" and experience his specialness began to emerge and grow stronger during my college years in the late 1990s. I was troubled about whether I should kneel before him when I met him. This standard ritual shows reverence for a *tulku* or great lama in the Tibetan religious tradition, but I was "modernized." I didn't feel comfortable with the idea of performing such an extravagant, or even ostentatious, ritual toward a total stranger, despite his prominent religious status.

Around 2001, I finally gathered my courage and went directly to meet the Gyalrong Kuzhap at his residence at the Southwest Nationalities University in Chengdu, where he had retired but continued to live. Referring to the Gyalrong Kuzhap as "Rinpoche," I presented a *khata* (a ceremonial scarf commonly used on religious and social occasions in Tibetan and Mongolian regions and beyond) while still wondering if I should kneel. He rescued me with, "Don't call me 'Rinpoche.' I am not a *tulku*. If I am a *tulku*, you are also a *tulku*." His somewhat teasing remarks perplexed me to the point I didn't know how to respond. Over the years, I realized what he meant. Rebirth or reincarnation is considered a natural and inevitable process after passing away, unless the deceased is enlightened or has achieved buddhahood. The *tulku* system is founded upon such a premise, and Tibetan Buddhism applies the idea of reincarnation creatively to its institution of lineage succession. Eminent masters and leaders of a particular lineage are said to return again and again through rebirth and go on to resume their duties as lineage holders and masters.

The best-known *tulku* lineage in Tibetan Buddhism is that of the Dalai Lama in the Gelugpa tradition, which has had fourteen reincarnations. The oldest Tibetan reincarnate lineage, the Karmapa, the leader of the Karma Kagyu, is now in its seventeenth reincarnation. However, the Gyalrong Kuzhap argues that the reincarnation system is seriously flawed with an inherent hierarchical nature that is subject to manipulation and infighting among the different interest groups it represents (chapter 6).[12] In particular, he is highly critical of the growing popularization of Tibetan Buddhism among the Han. However, he sees the inevitable appeal of Tibetan Buddhism to the Han and others in this increasingly materialized and rationalized world.[13] The process of his criticism accentuates the flaws and manipulation inherent in the *tulku* system. For instance, a number of real or fake *tulku*s have been actively, if not shamelessly, seeking money, reputations, and other benefits from their Han disciples.[14] In the Gyalrong Kuzhap's own words, "They [*tulku*s] and other Tibetan monks have turned tantric teachings into cabbages to be sold at [a Chinese] market." Tantric teachings are core to Tibetan Buddhism and have rigorous rules for transmission and practice (chapter 5). Hence, in the eyes of the Gyalrong Kuzhap, this state of being highlights an inherent problem in the hierarchical and mystified *tulku* system and the general decadence of Tibetan Buddhism. The Gyalrong Kuzhap considers himself an inauthentic *tulku* partly because of his uncle's potential strategizing during his recognition (chapter 1) and his self-proclaimed average intelligence and talents (chapter 2).

The Gyalrong Kuzhap's self-effacing attitude appealed to me greatly, and I immediately sensed a unique type of elegance: a combination of his looks, attire, way of speaking and walking, and so on. I first took for granted that this had to do with his *tulku* status and his position as an intellectual and professor. However, after encountering many other *tulku*s and Tibetan intellectuals, I realize that this sort of elegance is uncommon. Only recently did I learn that it was associated with the Gyalrong Kuzhap's cultivated high tastes and refined manners as someone strongly influenced by the aristocratic code of conduct, which was most pronounced in Lhasa before 1959, as noted above (see more in chapter 6).

My first visit to the Gyalrong Kuzhap was inspired by curiosity, and I obtained much more from it than I had expected, which partially explains the beginnings of this book. His sense of urgency struck me in his dedication to rescuing Tibetan history and memory in Gyalrong. He has been collecting Tibetan language manuscripts throughout the region for his own Tibetan manuscript project on Gyalrong history intended for publication. This urgency mainly stemmed from two factors. First, Gyalrong has become the most Sinicized region in Greater Tibet due to the dilution of Tibetan culture and the natives' assimilation into the Han culture and way of life. Second, the Gyalrong Kuzhap is probably the only individual in Gyalrong and Greater Tibet equipped to embark on such a vast and comprehensive manuscript project, thanks to his training in classical and modern Tibetan, his knowledge of the Gyalrong dialect/language and culture, and his sense of mission and purpose.

Gyalrong produced numerous eminent lamas and scholars in history, as noted earlier. Unfortunately, few Tibetologists have emerged out of the region since Liberation compared to many other parts of Greater Tibet.[15] This has everything to do with Tibetan language programs never being fully established in Gyalrong schools. The Gyalrong Kuzhap elaborates on this issue in chapter 14. To put it simply, this situation is influenced by linguistic and other observable cultural differences that lead to the Gyalrongwa not being categorized as "real Tibetans" by the state, by other

Tibetans, and even by many Gyalrong locals. This represents the repercussions of a large-scale ethnic identification project in China that began in the early 1950s.[16] The state has created and reinforced boundaries among various officially identified ethnic groups and communities of a particular ethnic group. Gyalrong's marginalized identity as a political-cultural entity straddling the Sino-Tibetan borderlands, as well as its regional cultural features, do not fall into the ideal type of what a "Tibetan" is, as acknowledged and codified through the state's "official Tibetans" (*Zangzu*) category.[17]

In short, the Gyalrong Kuzhap is one of very few Tibetologists from Gyalrong. The several others are preoccupied with their work or do not necessarily share the Gyalrong Kuzhap's endeavor to preserve the Tibetan past and memory of Gyalrong. As a result, the Gyalrong Kuzhap has become a "lone fighter" for this mission. Besides his Tibetan manuscript project on Gyalrong history, this includes his ambition to convince local governments to endorse and establish Tibetan language classes in schools. Due to his advanced age, he feels the need to make the best use of his "last breaths" on this massive, if not impossible, two-pronged effort (chapter 14).

Since our first encounter, I have visited the Gyalrong Kuzhap at least once or twice annually (disrupted during the COVID-19 pandemic in 2020, 2021, and 2022). We had casual but great conversations together for a few hours each time. In addition to his mission and work, he shared with me some of his life experiences, which eventually became the main thrust of this book. Initially I had no plans to write a book about him. It was not until 2008 that the idea to record the Gyalrong Kuzhap's life story began to emerge. That year I started conducting fieldwork in Gyalrong for my Ph.D. dissertation. As a result, I had the opportunity to engage with the Gyalrong Kuzhap more regularly and intensively. More important, it was a time when many of his narratives and life principles started to make much greater sense to me personally. My reflection on this was, however, deeply entangled with the repercussions of two catastrophic events that also occurred in 2008.

First, in mid-March of that year, large-scale unrest erupted in Lhasa and other Tibetan regions. Somewhat unexpectedly, Ngawa County, under the jurisdiction of the Ngawa Tibetan and Qiang Autonomous Prefecture of Sichuan (hereafter Ngawa Prefecture), became a hub of the unrest. Most parts of Gyalrong, including the Gyalrong Kuzhap's and my shared hometown of Tsanlha, are located in Ngawa Prefecture. Moreover, much of Ngawa County was ruled by various Gyalrong kings throughout history, particularly the Somang and Choktsé chieftains. Ngawa County is where the first instance of self-immolation occurred on February 27, 2009, and is where the most cases have since taken place.[18] When I asked myself how this happened, I realized that the answer could already be found in the Gyalrong Kuzhap's experiences and narratives. For instance, the Gyalrong Kuzhap shared with me how the well-respected Ngawa chief (the Megyal king) Meu Pelgön Trinlé Rapten (1916–1966) had assisted the new Communist regime in the Democratic Reform in the late 1950s. He finally had little choice but to commit suicide by jumping into a river at the start of the Cultural Revolution, due to profound frustrations with how the regime had betrayed him (chapter 10).[19] The Gyalrong Kuzhap's experiences with the Chinese Communist Party (CCP) echo such despair (chapter 11). He once mentioned that officials in Ngawa Prefecture referred to the written Tibetan language as the "Dalai Lama's language" (chapter 14). In this sense, the 2008 Tibetan unrest, as well as the status of Ngawa County as the hub of turmoil, is not unexpected.

Second, an 8.0 magnitude earthquake struck Ngawa Prefecture, Chengdu, and other neighboring regions in Sichuan on May 12, 2008. Its epicenter was in Wenchuan (Tib. Tritsang), also within Ngawa Prefecture's jurisdiction. Much of the Wenchuan region was formerly ruled by one of the Gyalrong kings, the Wasi (Tib. *doling*) king. This devastating earthquake caused over 69,000 casualties, nearly 18,000 missing, and destroyed thousands of homes and cultural objects, such as ancient and old-style buildings. Although this catastrophe was overwhelmingly portrayed as a natural disaster, it is not unreasonable to see it as a human disaster, at least in part. Hundreds of dams and hydroelectric plants of varying sizes have been built on the various rivers and their branches that run throughout Ngawa Prefecture, including in Wenchuan, which has a relatively fragile geological structure.[20] According to an established geologist based in Chengdu whom I spoke with, these projects catalyzed the earthquake, even if they may not have caused it directly. This again reminded me of my conversations with the Gyalrong Kuzhap. He often made sharp critiques of contemporary materially driven development models in China and other parts of the world at the cost of the natural environment and (mental-)spiritual developments (e.g., happiness or well-being). Based on this logic, the Sichuan earthquake can be seen as a form of nature's inevitable revenge inflicted upon humankind for their avaricious acts.[21]

More than that, I also began to gain a much deeper understanding of his reiterated urgency in preserving Tibetan memory and Gyalrong history before he dies, which realistically could happen at any time. Wenchuan is undoubtedly the most Sinicized Gyalrong region due to its proximity to the Chengdu basin, a predominantly, if not exclusively, Han Chinese region.[22] During the summer of 2012, I accidentally encountered a few Wenchuan locals who could speak the Gyalrong language/dialect, my native tongue. I was utterly shocked because it was the first time I had met Gyalrong dialect-speaking locals in Wenchuan. In theory, this county had an "official Tibetan" population of nearly 20,000, among whom most were Gyalrongwa. While I was chatting with these native speakers, they told me they knew no more than ten other Gyalrongwa in Wenchuan who could also speak their native tongue. Although there are probably more, this demonstrates that most Gyalrongwa in the area were no longer different or distinct from the Han in terms of their language, cultural practices, and way of life even before the earthquake. The earthquake destroyed most of the remaining artifacts of the Gyalrong/Tibetan past, e.g., Gyalrong-style architecture. According to the Gyalrong Kuzhap, other Gyalrong regions will follow Wenchuan's example sooner or later and become fully Sinicized. This motivates him to use his "last breaths" to accomplish the Tibetan manuscript project on Gyalrong history, to remind future generations about their Tibetan and Gyalrong pasts.

As I began to better understand this wise man's life story, philosophy, and mission, I saw its greater significance and broader implications. Therefore, I decided to record some of our conversations, with his consent. From 2008 to 2019, I would stay with him in his apartments in Chengdu and Barkham (the capital of Ngawa Prefecture) for two weeks to two months yearly. The "official" reason for my extensive stay with the Gyalrong Kuzhap was to assist him in his manuscript project on Gyalrong history. Sometimes we stayed alone, and at other times others, including his family members, students, assistants, and collaborators for his various book projects, were present. Routinely, every morning we had an "endless" breakfast with tea and *tsampa* (roasted barley flour, a typical and traditional Tibetan food), among other things, which often took over an hour and occasionally about two hours.

We talked about almost *everything* over these long breakfasts, from a hegemonic discourse about progress (materially-scientifically driven), the relationship between sexuality and civilization, the future destiny of humankind, the role of scientists in developing weapons of mass destruction, American imperialism, the rise of China and the ironic coexistence between "uncivilized" and "ungrateful" images of Tibetans[23] and the popular portrayal of Tibetan Buddhism as a most humanistic religion among the Han, Tibetans' irreversible Sinicization, prospects for the Tibetan culture and nationality, and finally to the Gyalrong Kuzhap's family disputes. Such conversations continued during lunch and dinner and breaks from our work (manuscript analysis, writing, editing, etc.) and often after dinner. We probably had at least two to four hours of conversation each day. This book is built upon our hundreds of hours of conversations over the last decade.

I was challenged to convince the Gyalrong Kuzhap of the "significance" of this book and to share his personal experiences and narratives. In a way, his attitude toward my book plan and writing was discouraging until I began reading the whole manuscript draft back to him in December 2018 and April 2019. He would say, "There's little value in writing about a person as insignificant as me. Don't waste your time on this." When I asked, "If you had no choice but to produce your autobiography, would you write the same way I have?" His answer was, "Definitely not." He feels I have written and captured many "trivial" and "meaningless" pieces of information about him, and he would never write something like this about himself. As a result, he emphasizes, "This is not my autobiography." So how can we define this book?

To better understand his perspective, this statement should be contextualized in the Tibetan literary tradition of *namtar* or sacred biography.[24] In this tradition, there exist three genres of biographies: *namtar* (biography), *rangnam* (autobiography), and *tokjö* (panegyric, or hagiography).[25] My book appears to fall into the *rangnam* (autobiography) category, revealing one's inner feelings and secrets or serving as a confession.[26] As the Gyalrong Kuzhap reiterates clearly, this is not a true *rangnam* because traditionally, the *rangnam* must be composed by the narrator, despite the Gyalrong Kuzhap's profound revelations about his inner feelings and struggles shared with me as his listener and author. Thus, this book is best seen as *namtar* (biography). The Gyalrong Kuzhap is also not comfortable with this classification because the *namtar* tradition is generally oriented for use with accomplished individuals, especially religious masters. He sees himself as neither a religious figure nor an established scholar. Instead, he argues that he is an ordinary and insignificant individual or someone situated in the sociopolitical and cultural peripheries in China and Greater Tibet (discussed later). Although his somewhat unenthusiastic attitude toward his life story and this book project could be detrimental at times, I gained a better understanding of his perspectives about biographies, including his own, situated in the classical Tibetan *namtar* tradition.

As a result, I had to keep reminding the Gyalrong Kuzhap that this notion does not always hold in new circumstances. First, on a global level, biographies of all sorts by "ordinary" people have emerged because of the flourishing of social memory and oral histories. I introduced *My Tibetan Childhood* by Naktsang Nulo, one of the best-known (auto)biographies by an ordinary Tibetan (a retired civil servant) in the past two decades.[27] Through personal accounts of his childhood experiences, the author recalls dramatic changes that occurred for his family and fellow Tibetans in the 1950s, when his hometown in Qinghai (Amdo) was integrating into Communist China. This biography struck a chord with the Gyalrong Kuzhap regarding the atrocities committed by the new regime and the "naivety" of most Tibetans (e.g., belief in the regime's promise of justice and equality). Second, even biographies by renowned masters like the Fourteenth Dalai Lama may not easily fall into any of the traditional *namtar* categories. That is, the Fourteenth Dalai Lama's autobiographies (authored by himself), such as *My Land and My People* (1962), *Freedom in Exile* (1990), and *My Spiritual Autobiography* (2012), exhibit the internal strength and intelligence of the Dalai Lama as well as that of the Tibetan nation.[28] This contradicts the more classical version of *rangnam* (autobiography), in which the author usually reveals their inner thoughts that are not otherwise known to others, say, secrets or weaknesses. For instance, in the Fifth Dalai Lama's autobiography, he claimed that he was neither a real incarnation nor as capable and accomplished as others assumed.[29]

I have made every effort to persuade the Gyalrong Kuzhap that this book is not about him exclusively, especially his accomplishments, but rather about the social and political history of Gyalrong and Tibetans at large since 1930 and earlier. My approach to conveying this idea is informed by a now discarded notion of second-wave feminism, "the personal is political," and equally by the idea that "the political is personal," as argued by Gail Her-shatter in her seminal study of transforming gender relations and women's roles in socialist China.[30] The dynamic relationship between "the personal" and "the political" can be applied to contexts far beyond gender relations or feminist scholarship. This framework helps in considering how personal destiny and experiences are deeply entangled with our political environment and social transformations.[31] Such entanglement can be understood as two inseparable processes: how political waves shape an individual life trajectory and how individual choices and actions simultaneously reshape the political. This book is characterized by a mutual embedding of "the personal" and "the political," including an investigation of personal history in close juxtaposition with broader social and cultural milieus. Therefore, it is intended to examine how the personal and political interlock and participate in each other through the Gyalrong Kuzhap's life story.

I utilized this reasoning to at least partly convince the Gyalrong Kuzhap that his experiences are neither trivial nor lackluster as he might claim, nor simply personal (or individual-focused). As noted, his self-effacing attitude is embedded in his upbringing in the Tibetan Buddhist tradition (e.g., the doctrine of "no-self" or *dakmé*) and also in his humble birth and the special education that he received in childhood, including being deserted by local nobles during times of desperation in fleeing the Red Army in 1935 (chapter 2). Thus, even having the Gyalrong Kuzhap partly convinced is the best result I could have imagined, because it means that he endorses my book project in his way. After recounting and rehearing his own life story, which I then spoke back to him word by word using this complete manuscript in draft form in 2018 and 2019, he said, "This is much better than I had expected." The working manuscript allowed the Gyalrong Kuzhap to understand my point about the deeply intertwined relationship between "the personal" and "the political" illustrated compellingly.

Nevertheless, the Gyalrong Kuzhap insists that this book should not be seen as his autobiography in the strictest sense because he did not author it directly. This, in and of itself, is not just an issue of being stubbornly adherent to the Tibetan *namtar* tradition; it is also his concern about the book's possible political repercussions regarding his not altogether positive experiences with and critiques of the CCP. This has become part of my ethical dilemma as the exclusive author. I would nevertheless claim that the book is probably as much about the Gyalrong Kuzhap as about myself, although

"I" (the author) appear not to be present in his narratives directly. I, the author, do not simply play the role of a passive listener but act as an active interlocutor directing or redirecting some conversations and accounts through my endless questions and numerous doubts expressed to the Gyalrong Kuzhap.

For instance, my interest in the role of women and gender in Tibetan and Gyalrong societies led me to ask the Gyalrong Kuzhap to address relevant questions, including the assumed subjugation of women in Tibetan Buddhism and culture (chapter 8); the role of women, especially political activists, in the sociopolitical transition in Greater Tibet during the 1950s and 1960s (chapter 10); and perceived gender difference in academic performance (chapter 12), as well as the political role of female leaders in Gyalrong like the queen of the Okzhi Kingdom and the acting magistrate of Sönamyak (chapters 1 and 7). Moreover, I am keen on the destiny of the Tibetan nationality and culture, especially the role of "traditional" and modern Tibetan intellectuals, so I asked the Gyalrong Kuzhap to share his views on these matters and the relevant experiences of several of his close teachers and associates. For example, I asked about accounts and "rumors" I had heard about Döndrup Gyel, his classmate and friend from the Central Nationalities Institute in Beijing (circa 1978–1981), such as the latter's attitude toward religion and the future of the Tibetan nationality, his conflicts with Han Chinese Tibetologists at the Institute, and his eventual tragic death, which is assumed to have been a suicide (chapters 12 and 13). Next, I asked the Gyalrong Kuzhap to directly compare his two illustrious teachers, Mugé Samten (1914–1993) and Dungkar Lozang Trinlé (1927–1997), concerning their intellectual work, life trajectories, and political destinies (chapter 13).

The Gyalrong Kuzhap would not have otherwise gone into the level of detail necessary if he had considered some of these issues in his account. These are three of the multiple examples of how the Gyalrong Kuzhap's narratives are tailored to my inquiries and concerns. This also simultaneously accounts for the Gyalrong Kuzhap's reluctance to consider this book his autobiography, meaning that the way his life trajectory unfolds is distinct from his agenda and priorities. In sum, there is a piece of me and my identity in this (auto)biography of the Gyalrong Kuzhap. Furthermore, his story about his peripheral position, as well as his heightened anxieties about cultural survival and the moral decline of the Gyalrong and Tibetan societies,[32] resonate deeply with my life trajectory and experiences with ethnocultural dilution and political repercussions (e.g., the 2008 Tibetan unrest) in the Sino-Tibetan borderlands and Greater Tibet as a whole.[33] Therefore, I would like to share a few episodes from my own life.

At age six, I left my village for the predominantly Han county seat of Tsanlha (Ch. Xiaojin), part of Gyalrong, and stayed there for about ten years. My entire family was frequently referred to as "barbarians" (Ch. *manzi*) by Han neighbors and residents in this Han-dominated town.[34] I was made to believe, both consciously and unconsciously, that the label of "Tibetans," or *Zangzu* (the officially acknowledged ethnic category for Tibetans in China), is the equivalent of "barbarian." My school education is also closely related to this. From primary school to high school, local schools used standardized Chinese textbooks identical to those used in the Han Chinese regions of Sichuan. I received zero Tibetan language education and learned little about Tibetan history at school. The only "official history" that we learned about Tibet was that without the CCP as their great savior, Tibetans would remain in a state of horrendous and "barbaric" serfdom. In this way, I grew up in a highly Sinicized environment, and even worse, I internalized these images about Tibetans and felt ashamed to identify myself with this "barbaric" nationality from time to time.

This shame accompanied me until I was in graduate school in Beijing in the early 2000s, a time when my Tibetan identity, or more accurately, my pride as a Tibetan, was gradually ignited because of my increasing intellectual exposure to Tibetan history and culture. It also grew from my interactions with Tibetan teachers and students from different parts of the Tibetan Plateau at the Central Nationalities University, located next to my graduate school. Before completing my master's degree in Beijing, I decided to go to Lhasa and work as a volunteer teacher at a local college, in search of my Tibetan roots. I didn't expect that this would prove transformative. While teaching in Lhasa, I began to sense a chauvinistic (moral-cultural) superiority among some of my Han colleagues. For instance, one said, "Many of my Tibetan students are too slow-witted," while another challenged me suddenly on a bus to southern Tibet by asking, "Can you explain why you Tibetans do not like us Han? We have built great highways like this and many schools for you." Even having endured such condescending and hurtful remarks, I was even more irritated in realizing that my local Tibetan students, colleagues, and acquaintances in Lhasa didn't appear to fully acknowledge the dependent economy that Lhasa (and, more generally, Central Tibet) had cultivated with Beijing.[35]

The stark reality is that Lhasa's economy relies mainly on Beijing's fiscal transfers and other provinces' financial and various other forms of aid. Although this boosts the local GDP, I started to see the downside, namely that locals lost their incentive or initiative to build up Lhasa on their own due to the constant flow of "free" money. This situation automatically reinforces the Party-state paternalistic policy and self-righteous attitudes of the Han toward Tibetans. Such realization heightened my sense of anxiety about the survival and future of Tibetan culture and nationality. Based on my impressions, which I acknowledge could be pretty subjective and not impartial, as well as interactions I have had with Tibetans in Sichuan, Gansu, and Qinghai, especially the educated youth, all seem to have become more aware of this jeopardy. Many of them shared my uneasiness. The 2008 Tibetan unrest proved to some extent that my impression was not solely figurative, because most of those who became directly involved in the unrest and subsequent self-immolations were from Eastern Tibet or the Sino-Tibetan borderlands, where Tibetan cultural erosion and ethnic tensions were more discernible. Ngawa County was one such place, and much of this county once constituted part of broader Gyalrong (ruled by Gyalrong kings or chieftains).

After my year of teaching in Lhasa, I returned to Beijing to resume my graduate school courses. Meanwhile, I began planning to pursue my Ph.D. in the United States. This decision had much to do with my exasperation about my Han colleagues and others' assumed "moral superiority" toward Tibetans, as noted above. In China at that time, great prestige was associated with having a degree from the United States. At some level, I wanted to prove that we Tibetans aren't dimwitted and dependent (in reference to reliance on the state support and Han "mercy") as they imagined. I chose anthropology because the notion of cultural relativism (where no culture is superior to other cultures and each culture must be understood on its terms) had great appeal.

Thus motivated, my Ph.D. study had a special mission: I would "prove to the whole world" that the Gyalrongwa were "real Tibetans," as the Gyalrong Kuzhap hoped. However, to his disappointment, I gradually deviated from this plan even though I was probably the first and the only Ph.D. student from the Gyalrong heartland studying overseas at that time. More seriously, I seemed to detach myself further from Gyalrong and Tibet. My approach to Gyalrong's Tibetan status is a significant departure from that of the Gyalrong Kuzhap, who sees it as a given that the Gyalrongwa are authentic Tibetans due to Gyalrong's historical, cultural, and linguistic links with (Central) Tibet. I see their status mainly as a constructed fact or even an "invention," hence a *problem*. The Gyalrong Kuzhap would indicate that my perspective derives from having been "brainwashed" by Western anthropological and social theory via ideas about the "invention of tradition" and "imagined communities."[36] In this way, my anthropological lens of identity and authenticity distances me from the Gyalrong Kuzhap's agenda and from Gyalrong and Tibet, positioning me as a stranger or even a curious outsider.

Moreover, we have very different views about the role of oral history. The Gyalrong Kuzhap sees little value in it due to his deep-seated doubts about the authenticity of oral accounts and the (in)significance of anecdotes and "trivial acts." This attitude explains some of his skepticism about the anthropological approach to research subjects (fieldwork, interviews, and attention to "little things"). To some degree, this simultaneously gives context to his reluctance in endorsing my writing about him and in acknowledging his role as this book's coauthor (because of its focus on seemingly "casual" conversations and on "unimportant stuff").

This has, however, not prevented me from putting myself in the Gyalrong Kuzhap's shoes to make sense of his choices and concerns. Usually, I don't have to try very hard, because I share his concerns and anxiety over the survival of the Tibetan nationality and culture in China. In our conversations, he is my audience as I am his. I also confide my intimate thoughts and episodes in my life, including my childhood, my experiences in Lhasa, and my frustration with Han chauvinistic and paternalistic attitudes toward the Tibetans, the Uyghurs, and ethnic minorities in general. The Gyalrong Kuzhap almost always empathizes with my concerns. For instance, one day, I shared with him an episode of a former Han colleague, a professor of sociology, asking me, "It is said that the Dalai Lama has increased the bonus up to 100,000 yuan (roughly US$15,000) for those willing to commit self-immolation. Is that true?" The Gyalrong Kuzhap replied that he had heard a similar rumor. Outraged, he said, "I just want to ask these people (my ex-colleague and other rumormongers), 'Would you like to burn yourself if I give you that amount of money?'" We are both frustrated with how little the state and Han Chinese, including even well-educated individuals like my former colleague, know about Tibetans, and their tendency to interpret ethnic conflicts and the "Tibet issue" as fundamentally an "economic problem" (uneven economic development).

This material-driven logic, along with the CCP's official stance of atheism, has sidelined the significance of religious-spiritual values for the Tibetans, the Uyghurs, and others. When the CCP realizes its economic incentives are not working as well as planned, the state immediately looks to the army, police, and other forces to tighten its control over these peoples and regions. Worse, this materially driven model has infiltrated people's daily lives in China, including those of many Gyalrongwa and Tibetans, who are becoming increasingly inclined to view material success as an end in itself and ignore their spiritual traditions and cultural values. Having seen and experienced this firsthand, both the Gyalrong Kuzhap and I have little hope of ameliorating the present status quo. However, in general, the Gyalrong Kuzhap remains hopeful about the unique value of Tibetan culture and its "spiritual civilization" in this overmaterialistic and rationalized world (chapter 14). Such moderate optimism has significantly influenced my perspective on Tibetan nationality and culture prospects.

According to the Gyalrong Kuzhap, the Sinicization of the Gyalrongwa and Tibetans is irreversible. Still, he is hopeful that at least some of these Sinicized people and their descendants, say, in several hundred years, will be able to rediscover the value of Tibetan cultural traditions, particularly those that attach great importance to humanity (e.g., karma or good deeds, compassion, etc.) and spiritual enrichment (as contrasted to an exclusive focus on material gain). I see myself as one of those Sinicized people who have been reawakened or re-Tibetanized to whom he refers. With his encouragement, I started learning written Tibetan from him, in order to explore Tibetan history and culture better using Tibetan language materials. He invited me to be his assistant and coeditor on a Tibetan manuscript project on local history and culture in Gyalrong. This manuscript primarily uses Tibetan language materials and archives from the late nineteenth century.[37]

In this way, the Gyalrong Kuzhap has played a crucial part in the metamorphosis of my attitude from a reluctant association with the *manzi* (barbarian) and Tibetan identity to a now eager embrace of the Tibetan nationality and culture. I assume such a reawakening is not unique among many Sinicized Tibetans and others, although each case and transformative experience probably has its particularities. As a result, I gained a better sense of the Gyalrong Kuzhap's hopefulness and optimism about Tibetan culture and tradition and empathized even more with his agenda. This inspires me to find new directions and meanings in life and research. Consequently, there is a lot of "me" in this book, not merely in relation to the Gyalrong Kuzhap's life story but also reflecting my experience and critical standpoint.

It would be a far stretch to claim that this book is my quasi-autoethnography. While not a conventional ethnography, it is ethnographic in nature, like a historical ethnography or ethnographic memoir. My intensive interactions with the Gyalrong Kuzhap over nearly two decades can be understood as fieldwork and participant observation. Although I cannot go back in time to observe and examine what was happening in the Gyalrong Kuzhap's life as it took place, I conducted necessary ethnographic research. In addition to accessing archival research and relevant historical and other texts, I revisited a number of key sites where many of the Gyalrong Kuzhap's life events occurred and conducted intensive interviews with people connected to those instances when possible. More important, I engage the Gyalrong Kuzhap's story through the lens of an ethnographer, with particular attention to ethnographical contexts in various chapters. Specifically, I play the role of a critical and curious observer, as if I were present to observe all the scenes (who, what, how, where, when, etc.).

To make a long story short, if I must define this book's nature and agenda, I am inclined to see it as an experimental *critical memoir*. As demonstrated, it is *critical* on multiple fronts, including, for instance, the Gyalrong Kuzhap's critical perspectives on both Tibetan and Chinese (religio-)political institutions (to engender delicate Tibetan/Chinese politics) and an interrogative approach to "the personal" and "the political" in biographical writing. A vital part of the book is the author's intervention through interspersion of shared rumination on the Gyalrong Kuzhap's life story as a critical interlocutor and inquisitive ethnographer, such as the dynamic relationship between "the personal" and "the political," the Sinicizing process and cultural survival in Gyalrong and Greater Tibet, and so on. Nonetheless, my intervention does not stop here. I must admit that I recount the whole story on the Gyalrong Kuzhap's behalf and in so doing, play the role of the first-person narrator/author for the Gyalrong Kuzhap.

To clarify this somewhat unusual circumstance, the Gyalrong Kuzhap is reluctant to be my coauthor for this memoir due to his self-identification as an "insignificant" person, concern for political repercussions, and role as a narrator rather than a cowriter (hence, the book does not qualify as a *rangnam* or autobiography based on Tibetan biographical tradition), as discussed earlier. Therefore, although the Gyalrong Kuzhap should be my de facto coauthor, I have become the single author and his life's first-person narrator. Although one may interpret this circumstance as some form of compromise and constraint, this constraint is a rare opportunity for me— an opportunity to write the way I have hoped, although it is not unproblematic. First, I hope to make my writing as explicit, simple, and forthright as possible due to this book's nature as a memoir. Second, thanks to my anthropological training, I hope to use something ordinary or even "trivial" (in the eyes of the Gyalrong Kuzhap) to convey important messages. My new role as the single author and the first-person narrator has allowed me to implement these plans. As a result, this book is different from the Gyalrong Kuzhap's idea of the traditional Tibetan biography (*namtar*) and autobiography (*rangnam*) that are supposed to focus on "important" matters, even though he has gradually acknowledged the value in my "everyday" approach to his life story.

Lastly, I hope to make the best use of this book and my role as the single-author and first-person narrator to convey a multivalent and unique account of unprecedented sociopolitical transformations in Gyalrong, Greater Tibet, and China, distinct from the often polarized "mainstream" narratives and literature found in China and the Tibetan exile community. A typical portrayal of social changes in Greater Tibet in China focuses on the demonization of the feudal and hellish "Old Tibet" and eulogization of the irreplaceable role of the CCP in liberating ordinary Tibetans from this inhuman system.[38] In contrast, a prevailing depiction of Greater Tibet under CCP rule in the exile literature and among liberal overseas (e.g., Western) scholars focuses on the CCP's coercion, repression, and controls and the Tibetan people's resistance and agency.[39] People may interpret the Gyalrong Kuzhap's life story in diverse ways. Still, many will not miss an important message in it: the images of Greater Tibet presented in both China and the exile community (and in the West) tend to be partial and biased. A multidimensional representation of Greater Tibet and China is hence badly needed.

Notably, although the Gyalrong Kuzhap does not approve of either of these polarized images, he refrains from saying this aloud on his own, especially through a formal publication like this memoir. I know he wants me to say it on his behalf, although he has never expressed this explicitly. I cannot fully explain this, but thanks to our close bond and mutual trust, I can figure out relatively quickly what he wants and hopes for. The Gyalrong Kuzhap mentions to me from time to time that he managed to survive the Democratic Reform and Cultural Revolution because of his political reticence (not being too vocal about political matters). However, he also feels an urgent need to utter his concerns at a critical time when the survival of the Tibetan nationality and culture has become a principal source of increasing anxieties among Tibetans, as exemplified by an appalling number of self-immolations.

Here is a recent episode. In a telephone conversation in late 2019, the Gyalrong Kuzhap told me that he was on his way to completing his *rangnam* (autobiography) authored by himself. I was more than surprised at this news because he had told me repeatedly that he would not consider writing an autobiography on his own despite my multiple requests. He explained that many people (his students, acquaintances, and Tibetan scholars) had repeatedly asked him to do so. That explains a lot because, in traditional Tibetan biographical writings, these repeated "ritualistic" requests usually play a crucial role in a master or saint's initial consideration of writing an autobiography or entrusting a disciple with this task. However, during his writing, he encountered tremendous difficulty in explaining many things clearly, such as his attitude toward the Democratic Reform and the CCP's Tibetan policy, because doing so would undoubtedly "touch the red line" (Ch. *chupeng hongxian*; the bottom line for political tolerance). We see considerable irony here. Although the Gyalrong Kuzhap does not view my authored memoir as his real autobiography, this account turns out to be a much more truthful representation of his real thoughts and intentions than his self-written autobiography.[40]

This illuminates to some extent the legitimacy of my role as the first-person narrator for the Gyalrong Kuzhap's memoir, although it does not fully justify that role. I want to add more to the story. I stayed with him from 2008 to 2019 for two weeks to two months each year, and we had at least two hours of conversation daily, as I have described. He has told and retold me his various life episodes and experiences, as recorded in this book, more than a dozen times. Such a high level of repetition happens mainly because of his aging and fading memory. Consequently, I often ended up listening to the same story he had shared a few days earlier. His aging compromises his short-term memory but not his long-term memory. He may fail to recall what he did and said a few days ago, but he can remember his childhood and early years in a highly consistent and precise manner—all the details match perfectly. This repetition familiarizes me with his life experiences to the extent that I have little difficulty as a first-person narrator recounting most of the episodes precisely regarding the details, narration style, and tone.

To avoid errors and misinterpretations, I resorted to the notes and recordings I made during my writing and frequently confirmed various details with the Gyalrong Kuzhap. To further warrant these accounts' accuracy, I would read him parts of my draft from time to time. After completing the whole book manuscript draft, I spent more than a week reading everything (translating word by word) back to him in April 2019. I revised and updated, based on his feedback, for about three years (late 2019–late 2022). Despite this, I have gradually noticed limits to my role as a first-person narrator; I may still have misinterpreted or mistranslated his original ideas and accounts. Many of his original accounts, especially those on religion like the tantric training and debates (chapter 5), are extremely difficult to follow for a broader audience (including me) with little or limited knowledge of Tibetan Buddhist philosophy and terminology. Hence, I often find it hard to put them in a much simpler, concise, faithful, and "lay" language even after multiple rounds of fact checks and requests for reclarification with him.

This exemplifies the promises and pitfalls in my becoming a first-person narrator in this memoir. This state of being has much to do with various constraints and opportunities of the following concrete conditions: the political circumstances, the author and protagonist's different perspectives about what constitutes an autobiography (*rangnam*), and prolonged intensive interactions and participant observation (over one decade). The broader methodological and ethical implications are not something that I can address here. Therefore, I would like to leave this question to interested readers for your interpretation. Still, I see my first-person narrator's approach as an integral part of a new and *critical* memoir that I experiment with. At the least, it is because this memoir is a *critical* engagement with various constraints (e.g., authoritarianism) and the opportunities they provide. More accurately, it is about how to turn the constraints into opportunities.

CONCLUDING REMARKS

As will be further showcased in the book, the standpoint for the Gyalrong Kuzhap's life journey is unequivocally the present: his narratives are founded upon his observations and thoughts about the current situation. These observations include digressions on the limited progress in psycho-spiritual well-being as opposed to scientific-technological innovations, rampant materialism, destructive models of development in China and the rest of the world (such as ecological degradation), instrumentalized religions in contemporary society, and hegemonies and power politics in international relations. They also include Han-centric narratives in China about Tibetan and Chinese history, the rapid Sinicization of Tibetan and Gyalrong societies, a rigid attitude toward sex in various civilizations and modern society, and so on. Overall, the Gyalrong Kuzhap is critical of what he sees as "social ills," especially the dilution of Tibetan culture and increasingly "materialized" mindset or aggravated "Sinicization" among Tibetans in China. Nonetheless, he is hopeful because he believes that Tibetan spiritual civilization is urgently needed in the contemporary world and will be even more desired in the future when materially driven models in social development bring about even more disastrous effects.

The Gyalrong Kuzhap has never explicitly associated my Sinicization or Westernization ("brainwashed" by Western theory and ideas) with my limited knowledge of Tibetan culture and history. He has not said directly that this kind of drift would not have happened if I had had a solid foundation in Tibetan literacy and tradition. However, he made this idea plain to me in his critique of Alai, a Gyalrong native and one of the most acclaimed writers in China, who is known for having attacked Tibetan religion and written language for their "backwardness."[41] The Gyalrong Kuzhap contended that Alai's ideas only demonstrate a shallow knowledge of Tibetan religion, literary tradition, and Gyalrong history due to his serious Sinicization, like many other Gyalrongwa. As a Sinicized Gyalrong native and Tibetan, I believe that I understand the source of Alai's comments. His points of view on Tibetan religion and language are not uncommon among a number of educated Gyalrongwa. I could have been an Alai, relentlessly mocking Tibetan culture and religion, not because of expertise in Tibetan literary traditions but due to superficiality. However, my life has taken a different turn because I identify with the Gyalrong Kuzhap in his endeavor to preserve Tibetan memory and history in Gyalrong and underscore the humanistic value of Tibetan spiritual civilization in this increasingly materialized and instrumentalized age.

In sum, this book is about the Gyalrong Kuzhap and my life journey. I see it as a shared story of "insignificant people" lamenting the fast vanishing of cherished cultural traditions and the disintegration of the Gyalrong Tibetan community as it merges into the world of mainstream Han Chinese and "modern" society. We remain hopeful about the dignity and worth of humanity in this fast-changing world. It is thus no accident that the Gyalrong Kuzhap is the book's protagonist for his life story and a mirror reflecting my own life, and a reminder to be persistent in the pursuit of determining what connotes humanity and the value of life as a Gyalrong native, a Tibetan, a scholar/anthropologist, and above all a human being. More important, I see this as a "common book" for anyone in sociopolitical and cultural peripheries struggling to create meaning out of their otherwise challenging life circumstances and with limited resources available.

The notion of the periphery or "insignificant people," with which the Gyalrong Kuzhap and I tend to identify ourselves, may be disturbing to many, especially since we may appear to hold an "elite" status. As ethnic Tibetans, a unique category of "internal others" in China, the Gyalrong Kuzhap and I are marked as "others" through various tropes and stereotypes, e.g., being less civilized or uncivilized, exotic, noble, spiritual, ungrateful, rebellious, and so on, depending on different contexts. I have also had intense, if not profound, experiences being external to others (e.g., racism) when studying and working in North America, Western Europe, and Southeast Asia. This partly explains why I identify with the marginal. I simultaneously acknowledge my privilege as a Ph.D. holder and faculty member at one of the most prestigious universities in Asia. For instance, such privilege became even more apparent during the COVID-19 pandemic. While migrant workers in the prosperous city-state in Southeast Asia where I work and live were exposed to a highly vulnerable environment conducive to infection (due to overcrowded living quarters and the unsanitary conditions there, but above all, because of government negligence), I, as well as my family, benefit from stable salaries, excellent housing, and a safe and clean living environment. The Gyalrong Kuzhap is also in a privileged position in multiple ways as a retired professor and well-respected academic. Even though he has been a marginal figure in various ways, such as his denigration as "Bönpo Lama" by high-ranking Gelupga *tulku*s due to his call for a reevaluation of the role of Bön in Tibetan history and culture (chapter 14), his *tulku* status places him in an advantageous, if not superior, position in Tibetan contexts. For that reason, both my and the Gyalrong Kuzhap's marginality and privilege must be contextualized.

All things considered, the Gyalrong Kuzhap's life is best interpreted as a story about hope against all odds and simultaneously about struggle and agency. These struggles are revealed in his often single-handed effort to rescue Tibetan culture and memory on the Sino-Tibetan borderlands, as exemplified by his large-scale Tibetan manuscript project on Gyalrong. Undoubtedly, the Gyalrong Kuzhap is exceptional in his determination and accomplishments, but this does not mean that other people necessarily fall short compared to their struggles with agency. As identified in James C. Scott's work on agency, or more precisely, everyday forms of resistance, *The Weapons of the Weak*, poor peasants, or subalterns (people from below) in general, are always able to devise and act out various subtle methods to circumvent and undermine the dominant sociopolitical arrangements, such as foot-dragging, dissimulation, false compliance, and so on.[42] These methods, which appear to be trivial acts at face value, can produce, little by little, far-reaching impacts on the existing social structure that are unmatched by even more direct and confrontational forms of resistance, including revolutions.

I contend that this sort of Western liberal notion of resistance is not unproblematic in its interpretations of "Tibetan politics" or Tibetans' relationship with the Chinese nation-state. For instance, should we interpret the Gyalrong Kuzhap's life trajectory and experiences primarily as an act of resistance against the state? Or, since it has become increasingly difficult to "speak up" in that particular system because an inquiry of internal hegemony can easily be interpreted as "touching the red line," should my choice to work on this book also be seen as a form of resistance? On multiple occasions, both Westerners and non-Westerners have expressed their "admiration" for my "courage," "bravery," and "determination" concerning my straightforward manner of both speaking and writing about Tibetan politics, including my critiques of the Han and Party-state's paternalism and chauvinistic attitudes toward Tibetans. I should not, therefore, exclude the possibility that some readers may see either or both of our stories as a form of resistance against state hegemony. I hope to bring their attention to the fact that there are multiple Tibets (and multiple Chinas) and that Tibetans encompass a rather diverse range of experiences and opinions toward the CCP, Liberation, and the Party's modernization and development agenda, as manifested in the Gyalrong Kuzhap's accounts and my reflections.

ACT I

Childhood (1930–1941)

Chapter One

BIRTH AND RECOGNITION

In 1930 I was born into a household known as Polo-o at a place called Gogo (also known as Gakgo). It was a small village with only seven or eight households.

Gogo lies at the foot of Mount Okzhi Kula in the district of Zhilung within the Okzhi Kingdom in Tsanlha, part of the Gyalrong region in western Sichuan. This mountain is well known among Chinese and overseas tourists today, having risen in popularity as a tourist site starting in the late 1990s, especially after being listed as a UNESCO World Heritage site in 2006.[1] Many tourists are amazed by the spectacular landscape and the mountain's snow-capped crown. In Tsanlha and Gyalrong, however, Mount Okzhi Kula is acknowledged not for its rugged terrain and beauty but because it is a sacred mountain, generally known, in terms of the hierarchy of holiness, as one of the three major holy mountains under Mount Gyalmo Mudo, the most sacred mountain in Gyalrong, straddling the Tsanlha and Rongdrak (Ch. Danba) regions.[2]

"Gogo" literally means "guarding gate" in Tibetan, highlighting the role of Zhilung as a gateway between Gyalrong and Chengdu (the capital of Sichuan Province) and a crucial route for goods and personnel circulating between Tsanlha and Chengdu. Because of its importance, the Okzhi kings maintained a lesser palace there. According to tradition, successively, one of the king's brothers would be dispatched there to rule Zhilung on behalf of the king. Meanwhile, kings would stay at the Gogo palace from time to time to deal with lawsuits and other bureaucratic matters for Zhilung. Before I was born, however, these activities were relocated to a new palace on higher ground nearby, closer to the route from Tsanlha to Chengdu. Even so, for much of my life, an imposing stone blockhouse about twenty stories tall stood at the original palace site until it was pulled down during the Cultural Revolution.

The Okzhi Kingdom, with sixteen divisions or villages (Tib. *déshok*) under its jurisdiction, was a part of the broader Gyalrong region.[3] Referred to as the Eighteen Kingdoms of Gyalrong (Tib. Gyalrong Gyelkhak Chogyé), it was made up of a dozen little kingdoms or chieftaincies. Additionally, its location on the easternmost fringes of Greater Tibet made Gyalrong an essential juncture linking the Tibetan and Chinese cultural worlds. This largely explains why the Qianlong Emperor (1711–1799) launched two large-scale wars against Gyalrong rulers, known in Chinese history as the two Jinchuan Campaigns. The campaigns began with internal strife and warfare among various kings in Gyalrong, especially between the two allied Jinchuan kings, Chuchen (Ch. Dajinchuan) and Tsanlha (Ch. Xiaojinchuan), and other kings. The Qing court dealt with such conflicts through direct intervention because of the potential for these disagreements to destabilize their newly conquered frontiers on the expansive Sino-Tibetan borderlands. Since the Okzhi king was bullied by the Tsanlha king and assisted the Qing army in their campaigns, the Qing court allowed the Okzhi Kingdom to continue to exist after the wars. In contrast, as part of the Qing policy known as "substituting chieftains with state-appointed civilian officials" (Ch. *gaitu guiliu*), the Tsanlha and Chuchen kingdoms were abolished, and a number of magistratures were established in their former territory.

Sönamyak was one of these magistratures. It was my second hometown, as it was where my family migrated after I was recognized as its *tulku* and where I grew up. The first magistrate of Sönamyak appointed by the Qing was Druktar (eighteenth to nineteenth centuries), a Gyalrong noble relocated from neighboring Gyelkha (Ch. Lixian). The Qing appointed him as a reward for his assistance in their second campaign against the two Jinchuan kings. In this way, Druktar, along with the other new magistrates, was absorbed into the Qing's civilian-military system and hence was obligated to fulfill military and other services for the court whenever commanded.

Druktar and his men were, for instance, dispatched to Taiwan from 1787 to 1788 to subdue a revolt there and to Central Tibet to fight the invasion of the Gurkhas from Nepal during the second Tibet-Gurkha war in 1791–1792.[4] Since the position of magistrate was hereditary, the successive Sönamyak magistrates were Druktar's direct descendants. Because magistrates wielded just as much power as kings or chieftains in this system, they enjoyed the same high status. Intermarriages were commonplace between the two ruler types, for example, between the families of the Okzhi kings and the Sönamyak magistrates.

In addition to this unique political history, Gyalrong is well suited for agricultural production compared to many parts of Greater Tibet that have higher altitudes and harsher climates. This is highlighted in Gyalrong's full name, Shar Gyalmo Tsawarong, literally the "agricultural region in the east with mild weather under the supreme Queen of the Universe—Sipa Gyalmo."[5] Gyalrong is recognized as a *rongchenzhi* or one of the four major agricultural regions of Greater Tibet. There is only a tiny population of nomads. My parents farmed on a piece of land owned and allocated by the Okzhi king, so they were required to provide corvée labor (Tib. *ulak*) and perform other duties for the king.

According to legends and historical records, successive kings from the ancient Zhangzhung kingdom, which was once centered on the western and northwestern Tibetan plateau but exercised loose control over the whole plateau and its neighboring regions, dispatched their princes and soldiers to Gyalrong to rule and guard this frontier on behalf of the Zhangzhung court as early as nearly four thousand years ago.[6] Okzhi was one of the local kingdoms that descendants of these Zhangzhung princes established. Meanwhile, during the Tibetan Empire (seventh to ninth centuries), various kings and generals were dispatched from Central Tibet to reign over Gyalrong. Due to this history, the kings in Gyalrong usually traced their lineages back to the Zhangzhung and Tibetan royal families. This emigration pattern was not exclusive to the royalty. As a general practice in Zhangzhung and the Tibetan Empire, subordinates, soldiers, and their families moved with their commanders during military expeditions. These migrants intermarried with the local population and became ancestors of today's Gyalrongwa.

As a result, in various Gyalrong dialects, especially in my native dialect (popularly referred to as the "Situ dialect" among Tsanlha locals and the most widely used dialect in Gyalrong), despite having a more significant proportion of ancient Tibetan, our vocabularies include many words from Zhangzhung and indigenous Gyalrong languages.[7] In the wake of the two Jinchuan Campaigns, many loanwords were adopted from the Sichuan Chinese dialect. Encouraged by the Qing court, large numbers of Han Chinese from the Sichuan Basin and elsewhere began migrating to Gyalrong and built communities in the late eighteenth century.[8] The Han, however, were not ruled by the local kings or chieftains but by county mayors, appointed by the Qing and later by the Kuomintang. Nonetheless, a small number of Han migrants chose to become subjects of the Gyalrong rulers, with the Qing's permission, and promised to fulfill all necessary duties to these native lords. Therefore, many of these Han were gradually absorbed into the local Gyalrongwa community through marriage and acculturation.

A small number of Muslim Hui people also migrated here.[9] Most Han migrants farmed, but the Hui typically engaged in farming and commerce. Several Hui households with the surname Cai resided in Zhilung, for example, and were among the wealthiest families in this district. They traded herbs, game meat, and daily necessities such as tea, salt, and cloth, and ran hostels. Therefore, they could afford properties in Guanxian (today's Dujiangyang) and Chengdu, and some of their family members became civilian officials and military officers of the Kuomintang. My father descended from such a migrant family. His family name was Liu, and I was given the Chinese name Liu Mingde. It was common for the Gyalrongwa in Tsanlha and Chuchen, including kings and nobles, to adopt Chinese names, as the Qing court imposed this custom after suppressing local unrest.[10] However, the surname that I inherited, Liu, came from my father's grandfather, who migrated to Okzhi from Shuimo in Wenchuan County toward the end of the Qing. Shuimo was part of the territory of the Wasi king (Tib. *lungguam doling gyelpo*) east of Okzhi and Tsanlha. Because Wasi was the most Sinicized Gyalrong kingdom, with a sizeable Han population due to its proximity to Dujiangyan and Chengdu, I am unsure whether my father's grandfather was originally from a Han or Gyalrong family.[11] Nevertheless, his offspring all married local Gyalrongwa and became assimilated. Both my and my father's lineage are, however, quite twisted. My father's biological father was not of the Liu lineage, as he was the illegitimate son of a Hui man in Okzhi surnamed Cai. Similarly, the man I called father was not my biological father. Nevertheless, we were still biologically related because I was also the illegitimate son of another Cai family member.

My (foster) father returned home only once or twice a year. He was said to be a hired gun for Wang Yonglu, an influential gang leader (*duobazi*), head of the *paoge* or Gown Brothers, a gangster organization from Shuimo in Wenchuan County, who came to Tsanlha frequently to trade opium. There were many Gown Brothers factions of various sizes throughout Tsanlha, and their strong presence had to do with the growing poppy production and opium trade.[12] The members were mainly Han, but native participants included people like my father, who enjoyed roaming about. However, they were entrusted by their kings and nobles with the task of spying on the Gown Brothers. During my father's absence, my mother, in her early twenties, had to take care of the crops, livestock, house chores, and their first child (my elder brother) by herself. A boy of fifteen or sixteen years old from the Cai household followed her wherever she went, and they ended up sleeping together. My mother became pregnant with me as a result. When my father came home and learned this, he threatened to punch my mother's abdomen to induce a miscarriage. My mother pleaded for mercy until my father said, "I'll let it go now and allow you to give birth to this bastard. But the moment it is born, I'll throw it into the river." I was born in a cowpen because, in keeping with Gyalrong tradition, women were prohibited from giving birth within the house's living quarters. Delivery was considered filthy and contaminating, so women often gave birth in a cowpen on the house's ground floor. Despite his anger, my father did send for a midwife to help my mother. Before the midwife arrived, I was born as a *pakto* (a newborn cocooned in a fetal membrane). Seeing this, my father screamed, "It's a monster!" grabbed me from my mother, and was about to step outside to throw me away. At that moment, the midwife's call at the door startled him, and he dropped me on the floor, where I began to cry hard. My mother said, "Please give me the baby and let me look at him before you discard him." My father complied, and she held me tightly, would not give me to him, knowing he would dispose of me after the midwife left. He gave in but said, "Watch out. Someday I will get rid of this bastard." Afterward, my mother carefully guarded me.

I was born on the tenth day of the seventh month of the lunar calendar. In those days, few locals, especially commoners, were accustomed to the idea of remembering and commemorating one's birthday. But mine was always remembered since it fell on the date of an annual mountain pilgrimage when many people climbed high up a mountain and made offerings to mountain deities by burning juniper, presenting butter and *tsampa*, hanging prayer flags, and so on. That year on the day of the annual pilgrimage, they saw a rainbow appear right above our Gogo village. When the news spread that a boy was born in the village as a *pakto*, a connection was made, making my birth unusual and auspicious. At that time, two search teams happened to be looking for their respective *tulkus*. The *tulku* of Sönamyak Monastery (Senggé Trashi Chöling) had passed away while he was studying in Lhasa, and the monastery and magistrate were searching for his reincarnation. Tawé Monastery (Ganden Jampaling) in Okzhi was also seeking their *tulku*. It was said that an erudite lama from Qinghai, Jamyang Damchö, had recently visited the monastery's hermitage at the foot of Okzhi Kula, known as Kula Ritrö. This hermitage site was supposedly visited and blessed by Vairotsana (circa eighth to ninth centuries), one of the most influential Tibetan Buddhist masters and translators in history.[13] Jamyang Damchö was said to have been so impressed with its superior organization and learning environment that he vowed to return there in his next life. The search for his reincarnation began after his death. Upon hearing of my miraculous birth, both search teams began to inquire into it.

In the meantime, the steward of the recently deceased Sönamyak Tulku in Lhasa entrusted my uncle with the task of keeping a watch on newborn boys for signs of reincarnation, since my uncle was going to return to his homeland after years of study at Drepung Monastery in Lhasa. The steward consulted the oracle for signs indicating the whereabouts of the "soul boy" or new reincarnation. The oracle described the specific surroundings of a place where the soul boy could likely be found. When my uncle returned, he claimed that the setting of our house and village matched the description perfectly. This was subsequently acknowledged and endorsed by the Sönamyak search team. I was then recognized at age three as the correct reincarnation for their *tulku*, the fourth reincarnation in the line. This was likely part of my uncle's deliberate long-term plan to establish a household for himself. According to local practice, monks could find a woman to live with and produce offspring without declaring a formal marriage, although many monks remained celibate. It would therefore be unsurprising if my uncle had such an arrangement. To make this happen, though, he needed his own house and land. If my family were to leave, he could legitimately take our house and land and build his own family. This was against the Gelugpa school's precepts but was generally practiced in local society, a custom resulting from a compromise among local monasteries, kings, and magistrates.

The secular powers wanted checks on the growth of the monasteries, as their expansion increased the power of the monastery and its *tulku*s and increased the number of monks, thereby decreasing the secular labor force and subjects directly under secular authorities. This monk household practice also benefited monasteries because the monastic population would still grow, so it was tacitly accepted because it contributed to maintaining the power balance. The importance of this compromise cannot be separated from the aftermath of the two Jinchuan Campaigns. Most native populations, especially young men, were killed during the wars. Consequently, this practice was instrumental in restoring local secular and monastic populations. As my uncle had expected, after my recognition, my parents decided to move to Sönamyak with me because I was too small to take care of myself in the monastery and because the Sönamyak magistrate had promised to look after our family.

Once I was "found," the magistrate and the monastery sent people to help me and my family move to Sönamyak. I rode a horse or was carried on people's backs along the way. My uncle also accompanied me on this trip and used the opportunity to instruct me on the etiquette and manners appropriate for a *tulku*, for instance, how to behave properly when people came to pay homage to me. Halfway up the mountain to our destination, we were stopped by people sent by the Okzhi king. Our party was asked to return to Okzhi immediately to meet with the king, who was hesitant to give up a *tulku*, especially one born in his territory, to Sönamyak without immediate benefit. This was despite Sönamyak magistrates and Okzhi kings having had stable marital exchanges over many generations. Furthermore, the acting magistrate, Zungchen Drölma, was the king's paternal aunt.

There already was a *tulku* at Tawé Monastery in Okzhi, although the people did not hold him in high esteem. He had been sent to Lhasa to study but was not interested in learning. He soon fled and returned to Okzhi, where he led a debauched lifestyle, drinking, smoking, and having love affairs. Despite the king's unhappiness with their *tulku*, this or any other *tulku* couldn't easily be replaced once formally recognized, as such status was typically a lifetime recognition. Moreover, this *tulku* was considered the reincarnation of a former female chieftain[14] and thus the Okzhi king's family member. The king nevertheless hoped to enthrone another, more promising *tulku* to balance out the negative influence of the incumbent. With this in mind, he endorsed the Tawé Monastery's search for the reincarnation of the above-mentioned Qinghai lama, Jamyang Damchö. Although I was said to be a likely candidate, Sönamyak Monastery had moved more quickly to recognize me as their *tulku*. Despite this—and the fact that one generally cannot have two souls in one body and can therefore only be the *tulku* of one line of lamas—the Okzhi king also wanted to identify me as their *tulku* anyway.

After negotiations, the Sönamyak magistrate and monastery agreed to share my *tulku* status with Okzhi. Therefore, I was obliged to return annually to Tawé Monastery in Okzhi for its most important annual religious gathering, the Great Prayer Festival (Tib. Monlan Chenmo), held right after a similar festival at Sönamyak Monastery during the Lunar New Year period. During the assembly, I was seated right next to the Tawé *tulku*. However, his subordinates would remove layers of cushion from my seat, subtly recognizing my lesser status and more submissive role relative to their main *tulku*. Despite this, the Okzhi king negotiated better terms for my family by urging the acting Sönamyak magistrate to approve my parents' elevation from the rank of "taxpayers" (Tib. *trelpa*) to "free peasants" (Tib. *rangzépa*), which entitled them to land and exemption from duties.[15] The king did this to show that I was also their *tulku* and that he would ensure my family, his previous subjects, were treated fairly by the Sönamyak magistrate. The Okzhi king and queen continued to show concern for my family, especially me, sending for me from time to time, and I would stay in their palace for ten to twenty days. They treated me with warm hospitality and great respect. Because my mother's side was remotely related to the queen, originally from a low-rank noble family, the queen treated me like family, so I developed close bonds with the Okzhi royal family. In 1941, before I left for Lhasa to study, the king and queen promised to allot a new piece of land in Zhilung to my family, and eventually kept their promise. In the late 1940s, after serious confrontations with Sönamyak bullies, my brother fled to Okzhi to take refuge with the queen and became her bodyguard.

After Okzhi and Sönamyak agreed on my and my family's statuses, our team resumed our journey to Sönamyak. We were warmly welcomed by hundreds of locals and monks from all eighteen *déshok* (divisions/villages) of Sönamyak, who had lined up to celebrate my arrival. As we approached, cannons were fired nine times, an honor reserved only for a *tulku*, king, or magistrate during their visits. Sönamyak Monastery, formally known as Senggé Trashi Chöling, had been relocated from Sumdo, about 50 kilometers to the north, where it was known as Sumdo Monastery. Sumdo was the birthplace of Tsakho Ngawang Drakpa (circa fourteenth to fifteenth centuries), one of the earliest and closest disciples of Tsongkhapa Lobzang Drakpa (1357–1419), the founder of the Gelugpa school. Tsakho Ngawang Drakpa became the first Gelugpa master in Gyalrong and the first to spread its teachings in this area. It was said that he built a total of 108 Gelugpa monasteries throughout Gyalrong, including those converted from the Bön tradition such as Sumdo. Bön, an indigenous Tibetan religion, had been the predominant influence on nobles and commoners before Tsakho Ngawang Drakpa returned to Gyalrong from his Gelugpa training in Lhasa.[16] However, lightning later struck the monastery, which was destroyed by the resulting fire. Circa 1785, during the rule of Druktar, the first magistrate of Sönamyak, the monastery was relocated to its present site near the official residence of the Sönamyak magistrates in a mountainous valley called Nakyo.

Senggé Trashi Chöling was the largest monastery in Tsanlha and one of the largest Gelugpa monasteries in Gyalrong. It housed five hundred monks at its height in the late Qing period. In 1917, when it still sheltered over three hundred monks, a monk-led uprising against the Beiyang regime erupted[17] and the monastery was burned to the ground. Most monks were killed or fled. Dozens of monks went to Lhasa and studied at monasteries there. Among my companions who traveled back to Sönamyak with me from Lhasa in 1948, two had participated in that revolt and gone to Lhasa afterward. The Han county government confiscated the monastery's properties to punish it, and the magistrate mortgaged its land to Han gangsters to compensate the county for the extensive damages. When I first arrived at Sönamyak as their new *tulku* in 1932, the monastery was in the process of recovering but still in miserable shape. Only a tiny portion was restored. While there were some thirty monks in total, most stayed home and would only come for religious events due to the lack of residential chambers. There was not even a chamber for the *tulku*, so I stayed with my parents, who moved into an old unused monk's residence allocated by the magistrate.

The acting magistrate at that time was Zungchen Drölma, who was in her sixties. Originally from the Okzhi royal family, she was the mother of

Yong Heling (1898–1970), the acting magistrate of Terdel (one of the four magistrates in Tsanlha) and the first mayor of Tsanlha (Xiaojin County) after Liberation. Her daughter was married to the magistrate of Sönamyak, Mu Jiguang, who was Zungchen Drölma's nephew and an Okzhi prince but had been adopted by the former Sönamyak magistrate, who was childless. That is, Mu married his cousin, but she died not long after the birth of their daughter, the Sönamyak princess, Mu Lanfen. Following his wife's death, Mu Jiguang left Sönamyak for Okzhi because of his unpopularity with the locals stemming from his collusion with the Han mayor and the Beiyang regime to subdue the 1917 rebellion. Consequently, Zungchen Drölma was invited to take on the role of acting magistrate. An extraordinary individual proficient in Tibetan, well-read in Buddhist scriptures, and knowing some Chinese, she was also highly regarded for her fair and just adjudications of local disputes. While caring for her granddaughter, the Sönamyak princess, she fulfilled her duty as the de facto ruler of Sönamyak.[18] Zungchen Drölma arranged for my recognition as their *tulku* and our subsequent relocation to Sönamyak from my hometown in Okzhi.

Zungchen Drölma treated me respectfully and would invite me to her magistrate's residence once or twice a month. When I arrived, she and her family would kneel to greet and welcome me. I was even honored with a seat higher than her and the other nobles. She also required all others, including my parents, to respect me in the same manner. She entrusted my parents with the duty of taking great care of me until I was old enough to separate from them and move into the magistrate's residence. Zungchen Drölma made this arrangement because I was their *tulku* or spiritual leader and because I was viewed as a family member, given the fact that the first Sönamyak Tulku, also known as Gyélek Chödzé, was born into the magistrate's family.[19]

In a way, my parents became my servants. They were required to speak to me using honorifics, a part of the language characterized by great politeness and respectfulness when used by commoners toward nobles and lamas. However, not all commoners knew how to speak using this language, especially those below the *rangzépa* (free peasant) rank my parents had recently been assigned. Therefore, they had to learn it from scratch. My parents were also told to cook special meals for me, separate from theirs. My foodstuffs were provided for by the magistrate, including high-quality flour, *tsampa*, butter, yak meat, fresh vegetables, and other delicacies. My mother usually cooked for me, though she was not allowed to do so during her menstrual period because, religiously speaking, that was contaminating. My father or a male servant dispatched by the magistrate would cook for me during those times instead. All the while, if other people were around, my parents had to treat me even more dutifully, including kneeling before me while passing things to me. Also, when I was still breastfeeding, my mother had to kneel before me to breastfeed me when we were in the magistrate's residence.

Such upbringing inculcated in me a sense of being superior to those around me, especially commoners. This, however, ended abruptly when I was six years old during a historical event of such magnitude that it transformed not only my destiny and that of Tibet but also the destiny of all of China for years to come.[20]

Chapter Two

SPECIAL EDUCATION

Throughout my life, I have been told that I am easygoing and approachable. Many also say I am talented, with considerable skills in different areas. Both assertions are overstated because, in their eyes, I am a *tulku* with naturally endowed prestige and gifts. In people's imagination, I am supposed to act as if I were superior to others, and people presume that I should be more accomplished than others. They are dead wrong. I am not an authentic *tulku*, and I believe the search team must have made a colossal mistake. I did not inherit supernatural powers; I was just born as an ordinary child from an altogether ordinary impoverished family. Therefore, as an ordinary person, how could I not see others as my equals and treat them fairly and respectfully? Like anyone else, I had to acquire various life skills through learning and practice. However, I should probably concede that I am unique in some ways and very fortunate in receiving a special education during my childhood that has benefited me daily. This education derived from my experiences in fleeing the Red Army, my parents' grumblings about the nobles' betrayal, and most important, my uncle's mentorship.

The comfortable life provided by the magistrate nearly led me to believe that I was a real *tulku* and deserved to enjoy these privileges. I even began to display contempt toward my elder brother, who was always dirty-looking and unkempt. In this way, I cultivated a self-centered outlook. However, this didn't last long. In 1935 when I was around six years old, the Red Army passed through Sönamyak and Tsanlha during the Long March.[1] Locals had little idea about who they were. We only heard that the demon-like Red Han would come killing, pillaging, burning, and so on, sending most people fleeing and hiding. The magistrate Mu Jiguang initially joined the neighboring Jémé magistrate to fight against the Red Army. Even my father was recruited, but the far more powerful Red Army quickly crushed the local forces.[2] Subsequently Mu Jiguang fled to Chengdu with his family, including the acting magistrate, Zungchen Drölma. I, however, their precious *tulku*, was left behind. The Okzhi royal family also made their way to Chengdu without me. Later I learned that they had undergone enormous hardships along the way. The king even went insane due to the tremendous humiliation he suffered in fleeing. Other principal nobles also went to Chengdu or elsewhere. Most locals fled, hiding in nearby forests from time to time. This situation lasted about a year, until the Red Army completely pulled out of Tsanlha (from June 1935 to July 1936). Others, including monks, survived by escaping. My parents also took my elder brother and me to the forest to hide. When things quieted down a bit, we would return home for a few days and then hurry back to the woods at any news of the Red Army's approach. As our monastery and neighboring villages were located along the steep and deep Nakyo Valley, the soldiers arrived briefly only twice before our family decided to set off for Zhilung to seek refuge after about six months of hiding in the forest. In contrast, the Red Army frequented villages farther down the valley or simply occupied them until departing.

My mother and I narrowly escaped when the Red Army first arrived at the monastery early in the morning, before we had eaten breakfast. I cannot remember exactly where my father and brother had gone, but they weren't at home. Suddenly, someone screamed, "[They are] approaching!" The other villagers and we knew that this screaming woman was referring to the Red Army. My mother and I ran out as fast as we could as dozens of soldiers appeared, chasing us and yelling "Do not run!" in Chinese. We rushed down toward a mill on a stream bank, hiding in a ground-floor corner. The soldiers arrived there soon after. One of them even looked around our hiding place, but he didn't spot us in the dim morning light. Finally, they left. We heard several gunshots afterward, and a short while later, we saw some locals come out of the woods where they had been hiding. One monk was groaning, his hands covering his face. It turned out that a bullet shot by the Red Hans had grazed his face, leaving it bloodied. Nonetheless, no one was killed or seriously hurt. The Red Army came again after a while, and this time they killed villagers. My family hid deep in the forest above the monastery, and we didn't see or hear the soldiers. News of the killings soon spread. On hearing this, my father decided to go with several other men to check its veracity. When they got there, they found nine people murdered on the spot, with blood spilling everywhere. One of the terrifying scenes they saw was a girl in her early teens who had a stick shoved into her vagina before her death.

It was not until Liberation that I learned some of the history of the Red Army and the Long March. I then assumed that the first mob of soldiers my mother and I had run away from belonged to the Central Red Army, led by Mao. In contrast, the second murderous mob was part of the Fourth Front Army, led by Zhang Guotao (1897–1979), Mao's foremost rival. Mao's Central Red Army maintained principles such as no unprovoked killings and no looting, and even wrote IOUs to locals from whom they took grain and other things. According to the IOUs, they would return someday and return what had been taken. The locals didn't believe this would ever happen, and because they were concerned that they could be accused of colluding with the Red Hans, most of them discarded or destroyed those IOUs. When the successor of the Red Army, the People's Liberation Army (PLA hereafter), returned to Tsanlha in 1950 and asked for the IOU documents to pay back their loans, few locals could provide them. This fair-minded act of handing out IOUs might suggest that the Red Army appeared trustworthy in the eyes of our local population. However, the truth is that most viewed the Red Han negatively because of the atrocities Zhang Guotao's Fourth Front Army soldiers committed. After all, how could we villagers distinguish one faction of the Red Army from another? So when the PLA soldiers arrived and told people that they were the successors of the Red Army, they didn't anticipate how fearful the villagers would be, let alone that their return would trigger a rebellion against them.

On this foundation of distrust, recurring accounts of violence against locals, rumors about the Red Hans' atrocities, and the intense fears they inspired kept sending us back to the forest. Consequently, we all became exhausted and experienced starvation. In the forest, we would come across others who were also hiding. Still, at that unsettled time, the people prioritized the interests of their own family over others, including their *tulku*. Sometimes people did offer me a little food, like a potato or some bread, but overall, we, especially my parents, were left to our own devices. Due to their unfamiliarity with the area, my parents struggled to find a suitable place to take refuge. Ideally, we would come across a relatively flat spot, easy to sleep on and sheltered from the wind. My mother gave birth to my sister in the forest under these difficult circumstances. When my baby sister cried, my father would shout to my mother, "Hand the kid to me, and I'll break her neck (to avoid attracting the attention of the Red Army)!" but my mother refused and held my sister tight in her arms. My parents thus felt frustrated and helpless because the magistrate, nobles, and people at Sönamyak had deserted their *tulku* and his family. My parents decided to return to Zhilung, where at least we had relatives and friends who would help us. Even though my uncle had taken over our house and land there, my father believed that his brother would not be cruel enough to turn us away. So we embarked on our journey back to Zhilung, taking our few belongings with us. Walking out in the open could attract attention from the Red Hans, so we had to leave the walking paths and disappear deep into the forest whenever we heard unfamiliar noises. In this way, we trekked in and out of the woods.

After two or three days, we arrived at a place called Jiangjunbei (literally "general's stele" in Chinese) at Dérongkyo (Muyaqiao in Chinese), within the Okzhi territory. It was named after a stele said to commemorate a Qing general killed there during the Jinchuan Campaigns.[3] We saw Kuomintang troops passing by, heading toward Tawé (where Tawé Monastery is located) and Zhilung. These soldiers would soon encounter the Red Army, and a battle broke out between the two sides. Defeated, the Kuomintang soldiers started to scuttle away in retreat.

Seeing this, my parents hurried my brother and me into the bushes above the path, instructing us to keep our heads low. From there, we climbed quickly to higher ground and quietly hid for a little while to observe the situation before climbing farther up. We hid and climbed in turn until we reached halfway up the hill. We then waited until we saw other travelers emerging on the pass, heading downhill again. Uncertain about the situation, my parents decided to go toward a deep valley at Muyaqiao instead and stay there until the path back to Zhilung had cleared and was safe.

When we reached the end of the valley, we found a community of about ten households. Some monks also lived there, so we approached a better-known lama first.[4] However, this lama's family was not very welcoming, so we turned to another monk for help, whom I called Atro Gélong (hereafter Atro).[5] He and his family received us warmly. Atro even gave me a thick sheepskin jacket that he had brought from his time in Lhasa. I was fond of this jacket and took it to Lhasa with me later because I could use it as clothing and sleep on it, thanks to its comfort and large size. We stayed with Atro and his family for about half a year. Then we heard that the Red Army had left but that the Okzhi king and Sönamyak magistrate had not yet returned to town. Despite this, my parents decided it was time for us to depart. My father still wanted to return to Zhilung, but Atro suggested we return to Sönamyak. According to Atro, our previous lands at Zhilung were now in the hands of my uncle, and our return would likely bring about a confrontation. Although we had no relatives or friends at Sönamyak, we could still rely on our land for survival. My father took his advice, and we went back to Sönamyak. It had already been difficult for my parents to make ends meet before the Red Army's arrival, and fleeing only exacerbated our already precarious situation. When we came home, we didn't have much to eat, so we supplemented our meager meals with wild berries, roots, and anything else we could find.

This entire episode transformed my life completely. It was a heavy blow, and I was so frustrated and hurt. I began reflecting upon my tragic experience and compared it to living in heaven only to plunge into hell. I used to be worshiped by the magistrate, king, and nobles, but I still had become a helpless refugee and undesirable beggar with my family. These sentiments were reinforced through my parents' constant laments, complaining to me about the untrustworthy and coldhearted magistrate and king. My mother frequently reminded me that these manipulative nobles were the root of our hardship: "The nobles see you as their *tulku* during peaceful times but won't hesitate to turn their backs on you in troubled times. You are no more than their instrument. Common people look up to you only because they see their nobles treating you this way. Therefore, when the nobles start to abandon you, they will shrug you off too." This intensified my dislike for the aristocratic system, although I was too young to know exactly what was wrong with it. In the meantime, I came to see the precariousness of my *tulku* status and was conscious of the cruel fact that I was just an ordinary person like anyone else, and no one would rescue me in difficult times. I had to depend on myself in all circumstances. My previously cultivated sense of superiority was gone entirely. I started to play with other kids, and we would engage in squabbles and fistfights as all ordinary kids do. After all, none of my playmates now treated me as a *tulku*.

I learned about this new reality through the dramatic Long March experience and from my uncle. He had many unique, even unconventional, ideas and practices, profoundly influencing me since my early childhood. It is no exaggeration to say that he was the most influential mentor in my life. I'm not sure exactly where his original thoughts came from, but I assumed they stemmed from his extensive travels. During his study in Lhasa, he traveled to India, Nepal, and other places abroad and encountered new and strange customs. Such experiences convinced him that the outside world was changing fast and that Tibetan society also needed to transform. Therefore, my turning into an orthodox *tulku* like most others was the last thing he wanted. He made every effort to cultivate a somewhat atypical disposition in me. To do so, he came to Sönamyak every two to three months and stayed for four or five days to instill his views and principles in me. Above all, he particularly emphasized self-reliance. According to him, life was full of uncertainties and sudden changes in fortune. I was a *tulku* today, but I might be nobody tomorrow. It didn't take much to convince me of this, as I'd learned this lesson all too well during my family's desperate flights from the Red Army. He asked me to learn as many skills as possible and be open to new ideas. In his opinion, to be self-reliant, I had to be resourceful in terms of skills and ideas because in combination, they would help pull me through even my worst days.

We started my training with more manageable tasks like building a fire together. My uncle was thorough, teaching concrete steps and techniques for different situations, for instance, how to use firewood, what to do if the firewood was wet, how to start a fire with flint when no matches were available, and how to effectively extinguish a fire. After learning these skills from my uncle, I began to apply them by asking people to allow me to build fires for them whenever there was a chance, so that I could practice. Later I also learned how to plow, and cut, stack, and haul firewood, among many other things. I knew how to harvest opium poppies by the time I was around ten. Poppies were widely grown in Sönamyak and Tsanlha at that time. About one-third of our family's land was reserved for them. During the harvest season, I went to the poppy fields and closely observed people working. Some skillful harvesters collected more than others, so I approached them and asked how they could do that. They explained that making and grinding the cutting blades in a particular way was crucial, as was making the incision on the pods. It had to be an exact measure that was not too deep or too shallow so that the pods would produce more sap. I learned these skills quickly, volunteered to grind blades for others, and begged my brother to allow me to help him collect sap since the other adults usually dismissed my requests. My skill at collecting sap soon exceeded his.

I also learned to shoot guns when I was ten or eleven. At that time, Tsanlha was known for having the "three many"—many poppies, many guns, and many bandits. Tsanlha was an opium production hub in Gyalrong and northwestern Sichuan. Seeing the vast profit margins available, many people, especially the Gown Brothers and bandits, were deeply involved in opium-related transactions. Skirmishes, raids, and gunfights occurred so frequently that many locals, even if they weren't in the poppy trade, purchased guns to protect themselves. I also bought a handgun with the pocket money I received from the magistrate, nobles, my family, and others. I began to practice shooting in the forest and quickly became very good at it. My uncle learned this by accident but didn't scold me as I expected; he only told me to be cautious with guns. I assumed that he considered it necessary to be able to handle guns skillfully in an era of turmoil. Still, he didn't say it explicitly until the magistrate and monastery decided I should be sent to Lhasa to study there. My uncle told me, "It would be great for you to keep a gun for self-defense. If somebody tries to rob you (on your way to Lhasa), you could use it." So I bought a handgun and took it with me.

I was more interested in shooting for fun than in self-defense. I was excited to discover how the gun worked and studied it closely by dissembling it, examining each part, and then reassembling it. Besides guns, all kinds of machinery fascinated me. In the 1930s, Sönamyak and Tsanlha had few modern machines, but I did discover an intriguing device in the magistrate's residence and several other wealthy households nearby—the gramophone. I would often go to their houses to listen to it. I curiously pondered how I could learn more about the mysteries of sound and music. Where did the sound come from? Was it because of the bouncing needle? One household gave me their old gramophone because it so fascinated me. I listened to it every day, trying to figure out answers to my questions, but it soon broke. Before long, the gramophone in the magistrate's home also no longer worked, so I asked them to give it to me. Wondering if I could repair it, I took both machines apart using a screwdriver. Closely examining the different parts of these machines, I focused on the broken parts, removed them from one device, and replaced them with the working parts of the other gramophone. Finally, one gramophone could produce music again thanks to my repairs.

One day around 1936, a plane flew above Sönamyak. It was the first time most people had ever seen an airplane. They were so taken back by this amazing thing that they could only understand it using supernatural or religious explanations. While many were kowtowing to the flying machine, I wondered why this big chunky device didn't fall out of the air. I asked everyone around me but received little helpful feedback. Few people had any idea what it was. I realized that I needed to learn the Chinese language to be able to learn about the new world and ideas, such as the mechanisms of planes, guns, and gramophones. The two girls my age in the magistrate's family were learning Chinese with a Han teacher they had hired. Hearing them chanting, "People at birth are naturally good. They are similar in nature but dissimilar in nurture,"[6] I was attracted to this beautiful language and tones. Yet I wasn't allowed to join the class because the magistrate disapproved. As a *tulku*, I was supposed to focus on Tibetan exclusively, and the time for me to embark on the long journey to Lhasa was approaching.

My eagerness to learn Chinese and explore the unknown world around me was also a direct outcome of my uncle's influence, his broad knowledge of the outside world, and his concern for the destiny of humankind far beyond the small communities of Sönamyak and Okzhi. My uncle told locals that Zhilung would be full of blue-eyed, yellow-haired people one day. Locals had no idea what he was talking about, and many thought he was out of his mind. However, about sixty years later, his seemingly insane statement became a reality. Mount Okzhi Kula has attracted many Western visitors since it became a renowned tourist destination at the turn of the twenty-first century. How could my uncle have predicted this? Was it a coincidence? Had his encounters with Westerners in India inspired his imagination? I had no clue. Nonetheless, his instructions on keeping an open-minded attitude toward other parts of the world and social change have benefited my outlook on life until today.

For as long as I remember, I have been eager to learn new skills, facts, and ideas and was curious about the new and broader world far beyond Tsanlha and Gyalrong. This was probably part of my nature, but also because of my uncle's influence. I was inclined and always wanted to understand all kinds of things. My uncle would compliment me on this habit and encourage me to dig deep enough until I reached the bottom of these things. On top of that, he stressed that the ability to think critically and make my own decisions was foundational for self-reliance. According to him, independent thinking meant I shouldn't follow others blindly, whether they were the magistrate, the king, my parents, or even my teachers. He told me that I shouldn't lose the ability to question and consider alternatives in any circumstance and always do thorough research on claims before reaching a conclusion. I did develop such an attitude. I wouldn't easily or unwittingly simply accept others' opinions. Over time, this led me to challenge the veracity of Buddhist scriptures and teachings. In my opinion, Tibetans were too trusting of famous lamas. The people followed their instructions literally and superficially. The monastic institution took advantage of this to exert strict control. My later withdrawal from monastic life was partly because of my disappointment in this situation.

Having said this, I do believe that Tibetan Buddhism has made unique contributions to our understanding of the nonmaterial world. One of the most important centers on the notion of death. No matter how advanced we are in science and technology, humans will continue to ask the same types of questions as earlier humans. For instance, does the soul exist? What happens when people die? Does the soul leave the body after death? If it does, where does it go? Will it become a ghost? Will there be a rebirth? What is the intermediate stage between death and rebirth? Different religions endeavor to resolve these mysteries and make their interpretations. Since I survived numerous near-death incidents during my childhood, these experiences helped me gain unique perspectives about death that were also influenced by Tibetan Buddhism's accomplishments in this field. My thinking on this topic was also subject to the teachings of my uncle about making judgments through independent thought and thorough investigation.

Let me start by exploring ghosts, since it informed my intrinsic interest in the ideas of death and the soul. Spirits were prevalent in the stories I heard throughout my childhood. Whenever I stayed in the monastery or the magistrate's residence, monks and escorts would share many ghost stories at night. Some people even claimed to have seen ghosts. So, after hearing so many stories, I wondered whether they were true and what ghosts would look like if they did exist. Locals believed that a field below our monastery was full of roaming spirits, and some even claimed to have seen them, so few people dared to go there after sunset. At this site, hundreds of people were said to have been slaughtered and buried after the suppression of the rebellion in 1917. Determined to investigate, I snuck out of the monastery alone one night and went to the field. I wanted to see with my own eyes if there were ghosts. I took the handgun I had purchased to give me courage on my excursion. I stayed there quietly for a while but didn't see any ghosts. On another night, I left the monastery again with several escorts. After sending them away for some errands at a nearby household, I stood in the field waiting for ghosts to emerge. It was dark, and I could only hear a few dogs barking and the wind whistling, but I saw nothing like a ghost.

Later when I consulted my tutor about ghosts, he was adamant that they existed. Like humans and animals, ghosts had souls and were sentient beings. They were reborn as ghosts due to evil deeds in previous lifetimes. My tutor's confirmation only enhanced my curiosity. When I pushed further, asking what they had done to be reborn as ghosts, my tutor said, "There is no point in your digging into this issue now. You can figure out the answers when you go to Lhasa and study there." This perfunctory dismissal puzzled me even more. Would people not become ghosts right after their death? If not, where did their souls go? How was the soul of a dead person different from that of a spirit? In any case, these questions captivated my wildest imaginations about death and the soul. Before long, I underwent the separation between soul and body, not only once but twice.

When I was nine or ten years old, I returned to my parents' house one day to stay for the night. My mother put me to bed, and I soon fell asleep. Then I heard indistinct fighting that sounded like it was happening far away. I wanted to open my eyes, but I couldn't. Suddenly a flash of red appeared in front of my eyes, and then I was shrouded in it. I experienced a sense of lightness and felt no pain. I thought, *Isn't it supposed to be dark at night? Why red?* Soon I felt rain pouring all over me. I felt so comfortable but thought, *Why is it raining? Am I not inside the house?* Next I felt a few kicks land on me and was eager to find out why. "I" (my soul) was then suddenly standing at the end of my bed, seeing my parents reaching out their hands to grab something on the bed, but "I" didn't pay much attention to this. Instead my attention was focused on a wooden gun, my favorite toy, by my pillow, and "I" was worried my parents would throw it away. Such awareness (the separation of the soul from the body) was gone soon after this. Next I heard people talking and monks chanting, but the voices still sounded far away. I remained shrouded in red and felt so relaxed that I didn't want to leave it. Finally I woke up and saw people surrounding me and my mother smiling down at me. I thought regretfully, *Why did you wake me? I felt so at ease and peaceful amid red.* Later I realized that I had been at an intermediate stage between life and death. The emergence of red and the sense of coziness that I had experienced in its depth was probably what people experienced at the moment of death.

My mother told me what had happened afterward. It was a cold winter, so she had built a charcoal fire for me in my room before I slept. She closed all the windows and doors to keep me warm, left my room, and found my father, who was drunk. Whenever he got drunk, he acted crazily. This time was no exception, with him complaining to my mother again that I was the source of my family's misfortune. I was why they had come so far to this strange place where they suffered. My family had been living in hardship at Sönamyak. Despite the fertile land, we never produced enough grain to adequately support ourselves. Worse, my father was addicted to opium, which certainly didn't help him farm productively. He had expected that my *tulku* status would bring more significant benefits to him and the family and was dismayed that this didn't happen in the way he had wished. That night my father said to my mother, "Isn't your bastard son a *tulku*? I will pee on him to see what he can do about it." They started to quarrel, and before my mother realized it, he came into my room and peed on me. I was asleep and felt like it was raining. I didn't move, so he started kicking me. When I continued to lie in bed, he shouted to my mother, "Be quick. Your bastard son is dead!" Hearing this, my mother hurried in. At that moment, "I" (the soul) left my body, and I saw my parents standing at the end of my bed.

It turned out that upon finding me unconscious, my mother desperately tried to wake me, but to no avail, so she started screaming for help from our neighbors. Most of our neighbors were monks, so several came and began reciting prayers for me. An elderly monk soon arrived and told them to open a window, probably due to stale air in the room from the people and smoke from burning juniper. Fresh air came in through the open window, and I soon regained consciousness. I was struck by what had happened during my unconsciousness, so I asked my mother to explain it. However, she could only reflect that my experience was likely due to the fire she had built for me. Even so, she and others didn't understand its mechanisms in those days. It was only many years later that I learned that I had likely suffered carbon monoxide poisoning generated by burning charcoal in a tightly sealed space. Without this knowledge, my mother struggled to resolve my questions about the red I saw and the state of ecstasy I had experienced.

Before I learned more about these types of experiences, a similar instance occurred while I was staying with the Pawam Tulku at Pawam Monastery in Rongdrak/Danba on my way to Lhasa. I was twelve years old then, and I made friends with a few of his aides at the monastery there. They often went to the river below the monastery to swim. As my uncle had instructed me to learn as many skills as possible before leaving for my trip, I learned to swim from them. One day, we arrived at the riverbank, and the others started to drink liquor, despite the monastery prohibiting alcohol. I also asked for some liquor before getting into the water. Emboldened by the effects of the alcohol, I swam to deeper water, which I typically avoided. Without solid swimming skills, I started to sink. I tried desperately to get out of the water and scream to my friends for help, but I swallowed too much water to yell a second time. I thought that at least they had heard my first scream. At that moment, the red again appeared in front of me, just like I had experienced at my parents' house. I thought, *Am I not in the water? Why am I in red?* Afterward, something hit me, and I thought that my companions had come to rescue me. I lost much awareness in those moments, but I sensed being shrouded in red. A feeling of lightness seized me. I felt like I was floating and when I looked down, I thought, *I just went underwater. Have my companions succeeded in getting me out of the water?*

Then I saw someone carrying a person on his back, heading toward the monastery. I realized that the person on his back was me, so I thought, *Why am I simultaneously here in the air while I am on someone's back?* After that, pressure on my chest increased. It turned out that my mouth was pressed on the carrier's back, making it hard for me to breathe. I wanted to shout, "Don't press your back against my mouth. I can't breathe!" But obviously, I couldn't make any sound. The sensation of floating in the air was gone, but I remained in the red and entered a blurry state of mind. Feeling warmth emanating from the carrier's back, I told myself, *I should be fine soon.* I was told later that I was subsequently carried to a monk's chamber, and I could feel my body being put to bed. I could also hear indistinct voices in the distance. My companions were talking about fleeing to Lhasa before Pawam

Tulku discovered what had happened. After all, the drowning of a *tulku* was not a small thing. They then started cooking a meal and packing up before taking off. I thought, *Why would you flee? I will soon wake up.* When they were finally ready to leave, I thought, *I don't even know where I am now. They cannot leave me alone like this. If they flee, what am I supposed to do?* Then I heard a loud sound like a window opening, relieving much of the heaviness that had been sitting on my chest. I felt a sense of comfort, so I told myself I must move. I was also silently shouting and trying to open my eyes. One of my companions came by and yelled, "Look. His eyes are rolling." Finally, I opened my eyes, but I could say nothing right away because the sense of heavy pressure on my chest was not gone completely. When I could speak after some moments, the first words that popped out were, "Remove that thing from me. I can barely breathe." They replied, "What are you talking about?" Then I looked about, but I found nothing on me.

These experiences convinced me that the body and soul can separate from each other. Tibetan Buddhism maintains that one can enter a state called the *bardo*, an intermediate stage between death and rebirth.[7] I was in this particular state while experiencing these two near-death circumstances. Therefore, it seemed logical that rebirth or an afterlife was possible. Nonetheless, something still perplexed me. As a so-called *tulku*, I couldn't remember anything about my past life, although it was believed that a *tulku* could usually recall something that had happened in their previous lives. Was this because I was a fake? Did true *tulku*s possess some supernatural powers to remember their previous lives, and probably other powers too? In any case, I believe that the reincarnation system is primarily a political rather than a religious practice, so it will not undermine Tibetan Buddhism's contributions to our understanding of death and rebirth. Because of these experiences, I became accustomed to thinking twice about the accounts and ideas I heard from others and read in books. If an idea interested me, I examined it closely before reaching conclusions. Of course, not all things can be tested, such as Buddhist philosophy, but I would remain unconvinced until I understood their essential logic and reasoning. Although my uncle asked me not to believe anyone unquestioningly, I completely trusted him. He was probably the only one in the world I felt this about, for the simple reason that he kept prodding me to become a curious learner and an unconventional thinker.

I also learned many other things from my uncle. He used the general Buddhist notions of the "ten virtues" (Tib. *gewa chu*) and "ten nonvirtues" (Tib. *migewa chu*), such as no killing, no stealing, no lies, and so on, to instruct me how to become virtuous. In particular, he taught me to treat all people fairly, to refrain from taking sides, and not to lie. He also made me fully aware of the importance of reciprocity. According to him, I must give something back to others whenever I received a gift or help from them. He said that people respected me as a *tulku*, but this was simply because of my status, not because of my own merits as a respectable person. Therefore, I should not confuse their kowtows requesting my blessings, their nods, and repeated, "*Lak so, lak so*," (yes, yes) as earned deference. These were all superficial. People would show proper reverence for me if I treated them with respect, justice, and honesty. This revelation influenced how I interacted with others. Even the magistrate reminded me a couple of times that I should stop becoming too close to my servants or subordinates because, in her eyes, they didn't deserve my attention. I took this as a compliment, though, as it meant that I had won true friendship and mutual respect from those around me.

Additionally, my uncle taught me to be prepared for such bitter moments in life as homelessness, famine, and war. He emphasized the hardships I would go through during my future trip to Lhasa and in my subsequent study there. I would be left alone to deal with life's difficulties, e.g., raids, hunger, overwork, stress, and bullying. Although I had already experienced some bitter moments fleeing from the Red Army, it was at a time when I was too young to have prepared myself for life vicissitudes ahead. To start serious preparations, I thought of training myself to endure, so one day I decided not to eat to see what hunger was like and whether I could withstand it. I even tasted a gallbladder to see what bitterness was like. Although this kind of bitterness was remote from the unavoidable bitter life ahead that my uncle had referred to, I still felt the value in trying new and unexplored things, just as he constantly instructed. I also learned to save money, as my uncle urged, to allow myself to have resources available whenever needed. Even during the Cultural Revolution, I managed to keep some pocket money with me. This became a lifelong habit.

I want to use one case to illustrate my uncle's profound impact on my life. I owed my survival through various political movements after Liberation to my uncle's teachings, especially his instruction on listening to different opinions and not taking sides. During those turbulent times when many people spared little effort to expose and condemn each other's vices, I was pretty much left alone. In contrast, many of those who chose to side with certain factions suffered far more than I. Without my uncle's earlier teaching and training, I probably would have acted in the same way and might have been thrown in prison or killed in fighting or by torture.

Chapter Three

JUST A KID

People may have different things to say about my childhood. The magistrate and others thought that I was rebellious and uncontrollable. My scripture tutor may have felt that I was intelligent and curious but had difficulty focusing. My mother saw me as her adorable child who needed constant care, especially protection from my vengeful father. My brother and childhood friends considered me a regular playmate. Nonetheless, in most people's eyes, despite my young age, I was still their venerable lama and probably had magical powers. If I were asked to describe my childhood, I would say that I generally was cheerful and carefree, despite the bitter moments I experienced. Although the ritualistic *tulku* role constrained my freedom to some extent, I was able to break away and find pleasure when I could. After all, I was just a kid.

The magistrate's family returned to Sönamyak two years after having fled from the Red Army in 1937. They resumed treating me like a great *tulku* and their distinguished guest. Soon I was asked to move into their residence. Although I was provided with the best food and clothing, I didn't feel content while staying with them. I remained dismayed that they had abandoned me when I needed their protection the most. Hence, even though they were reverential in their deference, their attention felt hypocritical and insincere.

Moreover, the acting magistrate, Zungchen Drölma, expected me to behave in a way compatible with my status as a *tulku*. This meant I had to act as if I were superior to others, especially commoners. I wasn't supposed to interact with the servants in the magistrate's home as though they were my equals. I was also not to play with kids from ordinary families, so the only playmates I had were Zungchen Drölma's two granddaughters. I would frequently get into fights with one of the girls, Mu Lanfen (hereafter the Sönamyak Princess), who was the daughter of the magistrate Mu Jiguang. These two girls had many toys, like wooden and cloth dolls and balls, but Zungchen Drölma hadn't prepared any for me. When I asked to share their toys, the Sönamyak Princess refused. I would then grab their toys and we would quarrel. The Sönamyak Princess would call me "Beggar Lama" because I was from a needy family and the magistrate provided for me; I was no better than a beggar in her view. This was extremely hurtful, so I retorted immediately, "I am not a beggar. I have been invited to Sönamyak with cannons fired nine times," as my parents had taught me to respond to taunts.[1] Our fights were frequent, and I often ran from the magistrate's residence and hid in the bushes above the path between the residence and my parents' house. The magistrate's family sent people to search for me everywhere, and sometimes my mother and brother came and also looked for me. When others weren't around, I would call out to my mother or brother from behind the bushes and tell them that I was all right and would soon return by myself. They then pretended not to have found me and went back home. When the coast was clear, I immediately left my hiding place and returned to my parents' house. I was usually allowed to stay with them for two or three days before being sent back to the magistrate. During my stay at home, my parents repeatedly complained about their hardships and the Janus-faced magistrate and nobles. Their grumbles reinforced my own unpleasant experiences with the magistrate's family. Although I was typically unwilling to return to the magistrate's residence, my parents, especially my mother, would force me to go back. My whole family's destiny depended on me. If I stopped playing the *tulku* role, everything we had at Sönamyak, our land and our house, would be gone.

I repeatedly escaped from the magistrate's house and returned home after fights with the Sönamyak Princess. Finally Zungchen Drölma couldn't tolerate it. She believed that I should be disciplined. After discussing my situation with the monastery, she decided to appoint a tutor to teach me written Tibetan and scriptures and discipline me. The tutor she found, Ngakrampa Talatö Lama, was a learned elderly monk who had returned to Sönamyak from Lhasa.[2] I was eight or nine years old then. A *tulku* was supposed to have started the training process at about five or six years old, but my training had been delayed because I loved playing and due to my frequent fights with the acting magistrate's grandchildren. My scripture lessons started in the magistrate's home and my conflict with the Sönamyak Princess continued. Zungchen Drölma next decided that my tutor and I should move to my parents' house to study. However, I still wanted to play and have fun, not learn. My parents urged me to study hard and reminded me that if I achieved little, there would be no end to their suffering. Thus, I felt obliged to learn a little, but I couldn't focus for long and frequently snuck out of the house to play with other kids.

Consequently Zungchen Drölma believed that my family was a bad influence and that I should be kept away from my parents to more effectively control me. She asked my tutor to take me to his own home for training. My tutor had his own family with a house high up in the valley of Nakyo, a one- or two-hour walk from the monastery. I found paradise there. There were several children my age in the tutor's home, and every morning they went to the pasture to herd their cattle. I wanted to go with them, but my tutor didn't allow this, telling me to focus on my studies instead. On their way to the pasture, these children were joined by other kids and livestock from different households and would start singing together. While I was reading my scriptures, I was also shedding tears, desperate to become part of this group of young herders. My tutor was so kindhearted that he would say, "One day, you will go to Lhasa and study there, so just go play with the other kids." But he also added, "You must return the moment you see the red robe hung in the courtyard, or we both will be in big trouble (if the acting magistrate found out)." From time to time, Zungchen Drölma would dispatch someone to bring me something and inquire about my studies at the tutor's home. My family and others also came to visit me. The tutor's house was situated at the higher end of the valley, and anyone heading toward us was easily spotted from far away. Not many people resided in this part of the valley, so everyone knew each other, and an outsider's identity could be deduced quickly. Therefore, my tutor could alert me if any visitors were coming for me by hanging his red robe in the courtyard. Seeing this, I would run home immediately, arrive before the visitors, and pretend to study. Once the visitors left, I wasted no time returning to the pasture to continue playing with my friends.

We called one of my favorite games "wedding." To start, we each took out food we had brought from our homes, usually bread and potatoes, and divided it into equal portions. Although my lunch included bread made from high-quality wheat flour provided by the magistrate family, I never minded sharing it with the other kids and never complained about the food they shared with me. Then we would place our portions on a slate before us that served as our table. This was our imaginary wedding banquet. Then, escorted by the best men and bridesmaids, the "bride" and the "groom," with flowers decorating their heads, would enter the "room" to be received and greeted by their "guests." Usually I played the role of the groom while a pretty girl I liked was the bride. However, a girl from my tutor's household would be jealous and say, "If you love that girl, why don't you go stay in her house?" I was ten or eleven at this time and fascinated with the issue of sexuality and attempted to explore it. My playmates, who were mostly around my age, both boys and girls, were also interested in playing sex-related games. The wedding was simply a more subtle version of such games. At times, we would play an intercourse game. My playmate in this particular game was the girl from my tutor's household. While the two of us were alone in the forest, I would ask her to play this game with me. She would lie down with her vagina exposed. Although my penis seemed to become erect, penetration was never fulfilled. Sometimes my brother would join us. He was also unable to penetrate her, although he was two years older than me. Other boys and girls would play too, but the boys of my age were unable to accomplish penetration. I assumed this was because we hadn't yet reached puberty.

Living like this, I had a wonderful time in my tutor's home village. However, Zungchen Drölma eventually heard that most of my time was spent playing instead of studying, as she suspected. She believed that my tutor was too lenient and unable to keep me under control due to my innate wildness. Therefore, the acting magistrate called us back. My tutor and I were made to stay at the monastery, and I had to study with him daily. However, as he was still unable to restrain me effectively, I had much freedom and greatly enjoyed playing with my brother and other kids and chatting with others, especially strangers. People would come from time to time to ask for my blessing. In particular, during the Great Prayer Festival in Okzhi and

Sönamyak in the first lunar month, many people would bring me gifts of bacon, beef, sweets, fruits, and grain. However, the gifts did not interest me. The best part of their visits was listening to their accounts and stories. I would keep asking questions until I was satisfied or the speaker had nothing more to share. Hearing them, I was inclined to make connections between the different anecdotes they told.

Interestingly, this habit helped someone find a missing bull by coincidence. While wandering outside the monastery, I met a traveler. We began our "ritualistic greetings" (Tib. *khamdri*),[3] a local custom used to exchange greetings, news, and gossip when people come across each other on their journeys. As it was not common to see strangers passing by, I found this an exciting opportunity to learn about this traveler's experiences and knowledge of nonlocal affairs. This traveler said that he was from Jémé, a neighboring magistrature. He thought he had seen a deer in one of the valleys on the other side of the mountain that day. Something flashed before it disappeared deep into the forest, so he wasn't entirely sure it was a deer. I also wondered whether he had seen a deer. After this exchange, the Jémé man said farewell and left. Then, later that afternoon, someone came to see me requesting divination about the whereabouts of his missing bull that was used for plowing and crucial to his farm work. I declined to do the divination because I didn't know how. This person kept asking me to try. At that moment, the conversation I had just had with the traveler came to my mind and I speculated that the animal the traveler had seen might be the livestock the owner was looking for. So I told this man to look in the place where a "deer" had been seen. He then found his bull in the same valley on the other side of the mountain that the passenger had mentioned. Ironically, this accident convinced many that I had some sort of divine power.

I always eagerly anticipated the annual visit to Okzhi during Tawé Monastery's Great Prayer Festival because I would see and hear many new things and meet my friends again during the visit. The Okzhi king would send for me with an escort of some twenty people, and the acting magistrate of Sönamyak and her entourage were also invited to join. Altogether, our horde of about a hundred people, with dozens of horses and donkeys, would pick our way along the narrow, zigzagging mountain paths. Our caravan stretched several kilometers and was quite a spectacular sight during the two days it took us to reach the Okzhi palace. When we were set to arrive, the king and queen would come and greet us at the main gate. The royal family treated me cordially, and I felt more at home with them than I did in Sönamyak. As the queen was a distant family relative, she was nice to me and even taught me how to shoot a gun when I was ten. It was also in Okzhi that I bought my first handgun, as I mentioned.

Once back in Sönamyak, I felt restrained again. The animosity between the Sönamyak Princess and me was growing. The monastery and the magistrate's family each had a lion dance team during the New Year festival. Our monastic squad, with my prodding, would compete with the royal squad and sometimes even resorted to fistfights with them. Seeing this intense situation, the acting magistrate, Zungchen Drölma realized she could no longer deal with me and met with the monastery's abbot (Tib. *tripa*) and disciplinarian (Tib. *gékö*). They discussed my resistance and defiance and agreed that I should be sent to Lhasa to be disciplined. I was not even twelve years old at the time. My childhood would end very soon, but before it did, I still had a few months of happy times at Sönamyak and then at Pawam in Rongdrak, where I was sent first.

ACT II

The Lhasa Trip and
Monastic Life (1941–1948)

_____

Chapter Four

ON THE ROAD

Not long after the New Year in 1941, when I was twelve, I left Sönamyak for Rongdrak with a large group. From there, I would continue my journey to Lhasa after being hosted by Jamyang Tenzin (1892–1959), the *tulku* at Pawam Monastery, for two months. In this way, my trip to Lhasa was made up of two parts, from Sönamyak to Pawam and from Pawam to Lhasa.

The Pawam Tulku was originally from Tsanlha, and his hometown of Mipham (part of the Jémé magistrate) was next to Sönamyak. Our magistrate and monastery requested that he help arrange my trip. He had excellent knowledge of what the Lhasa trip would entail and had myriad functional connections with various kings, chieftains, merchants (Tib. *tsongpön*), and monasteries in Kham. I was tasked with learning some scriptures at his monastery to prepare for more formal training in Lhasa. Even though I had already heard so much about the hardships of the Lhasa journey and course of study, I wasn't apprehensive. First, I was probably too young to consider all the adversity ahead of me. Second, I was confident that I wouldn't starve or freeze to death along the way if my companions abandoned me on the road. Tibetans are generally compassionate and will help travelers in need. Third, I was emboldened by having a handgun that I could use to defend myself in case of raids or assault. As a result, I was excited about traveling to Lhasa and starting a new life there. I had already found much pleasure in my trip to Rongdrak, as I was finally free from the magistrate's control and able to experience different places, people, and things.

Starting in Tsanlha on the road to Lhasa, I was told that seventy-two bridges had to be crossed and eighty-two mountains had to be climbed (via the Southern Route, to be discussed below). A local saying goes, "Those who will take a trip to Lhasa have smiling faces but hearts that cry." Travelers, primarily pilgrims, smiled because they were supposed to be excited about the prospect of reaching Lhasa, a holy city.[1] The trip was nonetheless full of difficulties and uncertainties. Starvation, banditry, landslides, snow-storms, sickness, and death were not uncommon. Physical tiredness was considered the least challenge. Travelers understood it was possible they might never reach their destination, leaving them with tears in their hearts. Due to such hardships, it was unusual for someone as young as me to travel to Lhasa from Gyalrong. People in Gyalrong typically wouldn't embark on such a risky journey until they were wholly independent and capable enough—at least seventeen or eighteen years old. I probably wouldn't have been forced to go if the magistrate and my monastery hadn't given up on disciplining me effectively. Despite all the risks, it turned out to be an enjoy-able and memorable trip.

Because of the perceived hardships, in those days, it was predominantly monks, including *tulku*s, from Tsanlha and the heartland of Gyalrong, not laypeople, who made the trip to Lhasa. Occasionally merchants and nobles would go to Lhasa for trade or pilgrimage, but I encountered none arriving from Tsanlha and Gyalrong during my eight years in Lhasa. Gyalrong monks went there because Lhasa was the hub of Tibetan Buddhism, espe-cially the Gelugpa school, but also because studying there was a necessary step to enhance their status in their home monasteries. According to the general practice in Tsanlha, an eight-year stay in Lhasa was a minimum qualification to be a "lama" before returning to their hometowns. Those who returned before the eight years were up were referred to as "Gélong," a status considered inferior to "lama." This tradition was part of the legacy of the Qing's two Jinchuan Campaigns. Until the Second Campaign (1771–1776), Bön was the primary religion in Tsanla and Chuchen. As Bön leaders allied with the local kings in their failed rebellions, the Qing court abol-ished the Bön monasteries and practices and replaced them with Gelugpa institutions. Meanwhile, local monks in all these formerly Bön, now Gelugpa, monasteries were required to go and study in one of the three major Gelugpa monasteries in Lhasa (Drepung, Sera, or Ganden) for a number of years.

Without these learning experiences in Lhasa, a monk had minimal status in their home monastery. As a result, nearly all eligible Gelugpa monks in the two Jinchuan regions were obliged to travel to Lhasa to study and understood that if their stay there was too short, they would not earn good prestige back at home. This requirement was essential in checking the growth of monasteries in local society. Since attaining the status of "lama" would require more than eight years of study and hardship in Lhasa, many parents were reluctant to send their sons to the local monasteries, effectively stifling the monasteries' growth.[2] This was a clever move by the local kings and magistrates to keep monasteries under control. Without such an impediment, many more boys would likely enter monasteries, whose subsequent expansion would potentially impinge on the interests of these secular authorities. However, this practical concern was also necessitated by the fact that most locals, especially eligible young men, had been killed during the Jinchuan Campaigns. Consequently, restoring the local population and agricultural production was the top agenda for both local secular leaders and the Qing.

To enroll in a monastery in Lhasa, a monk first had to apply for an official introduction letter from either the Chötensar in Tsanlha or the Ganden Tenpelling in Chuchen, leading monasteries in those places. I stopped at Chötensa on my way to Pawam to request this letter and was issued one. Chötensa was located within the Terdel magistrature, not far from the Terdel magistrate's residence. Hearing about my trip, the magistrate sent for me and invited me to stay in his residence for two days. His daughter, the Terdel Princess, with whom I had made friends back in Sönamyak, also returned home around that time. We were overjoyed to see each other again and at the time of my departure for Pawam, we were reluctant to separate. We even exchanged gifts. I gave the princess a silver pendant that I had removed from one of my rosaries. Something special appeared to exist between us, partly friendship and partly affection. When I gave her my gift, she said she would wait for me, and I nodded in agreement. But by the time I returned eight years later, she had married and was the queen of the Drakteng king, Wang Shouchang (1917–1990).

Just before our band arrived in Pawam, we encountered something amusing: local girls were wearing dresses that from the waist down were made up of a number of linen strips in the front and back that swung back and forth as they walked, exposing their bare legs. The strips in the front converged in the middle to cover their genitals when they sat and rested. We couldn't help but laugh at the sight. When we reached the monastery, we asked about this strange custom. The Pawam Tulku explained that according to local legend, because Pawam faced Mount Gyalmo Mudo, the most sacred mountain in Gyalrong, it was convenient for its mountain deity to come down and "enjoy" these unmarried girls. I was amazed by this custom, and I was also impressed with the distinctive dialect the locals spoke that I initially barely understood. Sönamyak and Tsanlha were not very far from Pawam, but the customs and language differed.[3] As far as I was concerned, this was one of the fun parts of travel, bringing exposure to many interesting new things.

The Pawam Tulku was an influential and well-respected figure in Rong-drak and beyond. He had extensive connections with various key figures in secular and sacred sectors including kings, chieftains, religious leaders, merchants, Han officials, and others in Gyalrong, Dardo, Kham, Lhasa, Chengdu, and even Nanjing, the then national capital of Republican China. Thanks to such prominence, Liu Wenhui (1895–1976), the governor of Xikang Province, thought highly of him and appointed him as a provincial representative in the National Assembly in 1947.[4] Likewise, the CCP made him the first mayor of Rongdrak in 1951 after its Liberation in 1950. Despite his high status, the Pawam Tulku was even-tempered to people. He was kind and lenient to me as well. Before I departed for Lhasa, I was expected to study in Pawam under his strict supervision. However, I was not keen on learning and wanted to leave my scriptures behind and play with my friends. The Pawam Tulku didn't force me to study, saying instead, "Have a great time here before your ordeals in Lhasa start."

I did have enormous fun exploring the new environments of the monastery and Pawam and spending much time with my new friends there, Loktar and Tenzin, both trusted assistants to the Pawam Tulku. Loktar, who spoke the Gyalrong (Situ) and local dialects (Eastern Horpa), was responsible for passing on the *tulku*'s messages to people in various villages. Loktar was extremely humorous and told many jokes. I asked him to take me along when he was dispatched to convey messages. In this way, I went to many different villages and other places in Pawam, and Loktar would tell me many local legends and stories on the way that made our trips entertaining.

He and Tenzin would also often take me to swim in a local river. As a new but eager learner, I became so addicted to swimming that, as I related earlier, I nearly drowned once when swimming while intoxicated.

Tenzin was a nephew of the Pawam Tulku and was in his twenties at the time; he took charge of the monastery's internal and external affairs on behalf of the Pawam Tulku. Simultaneously, as the *tulku* was the acting king of Pawam, it was again Tenzin who oversaw the chieftaincy's administrative matters. He was entrusted with the enormous task of building and maintaining connections with various authorities for the Pawam Monastery and its chieftaincy. While I was having so much fun in Pawam, Tenzin also made the necessary arrangements for my trip to Lhasa. First, he arranged the deposit of my money with a firm in Dartsédo, which often served a bank's role. As it was unsafe to take along too much money on the trip to Lhasa, travelers would typically keep their funds at one of several firms in Dartsédo that had branches in Lhasa and elsewhere.[5] The firm would provide a receipt that one later produced to collect the deposit at the Lhasa branch. Second, Tenzin made arrangements with that same firm in Dartsédo, which was operated by a merchant from Béri Monastery (hereafter Béri) in Kardzé, for me to join their caravan that was also heading to Lhasa. The firm asked me and my cohorts to arrive at Béri at a particular time so we could begin our trek together. Third, Tenzin arranged for a few letters in the name of the Pawam Tulku, addressed to monasteries, kings, chieftains, and acquaintances along our route, to bring along with us on our way to Béri. In those days, safety was not guaranteed during travel. Assaults on passing travelers were common, and the perpetrators were usually locals. Therefore, these letters requested that the Pawam Tulku's local connections, all of whom had due influence within their respective communities, provide for us when needed and, more importantly, shelter and protect us.

The two major routes from Tsanlha to Lhasa are the Northern and the Southern Routes. The Northern Route ran through Rongdrak, Dartsédo, Tau, Drakgo, Kardzé, Dégé, Kyégudo, Nakchu, Damzhung, Penyul (Penpo), and Lhasa. The Southern Route passed through Rongdrak, Dartsédo, Nyakchu, Litang, Batang, Chamdo, Kongbu, and Lhasa. The Northern Route went through vast rolling pastures but fewer settlements and local inhabitants. In comparison, those going along the Southern Route experienced a more significant number of large mountains and rivers and more settlements. If traveling in a small band, most people would take the Southern Route because it tended to be more convenient when traveling on foot. It also provided more opportunities for travelers to seek accommodations and replenish their provisions in local settlements, despite running through more difficult mountain passes. For a caravan with horses and mules, the Northern Route was often a logical choice because of pasture availability for the pack animals. In my case, the Northern Route had been chosen because of my status and age. The magistrate and monastery prepared several mules and one horse for me to ride. More importantly, traveling with a caravan like this one meant enhanced safety, reducing the likelihood that we would be robbed or get lost, which was common in the wild terrain, and increased our chances of surviving natural disasters.

Finally, I, together with the treasurer (Tib. *chakdzö*) for the trip, a monk himself, and three other monks from Sönamyak departed from Pawam. As the treasurer had previously studied in Lhasa and was familiar with the routes and passes, the magistrate and monastery made him our guide and charged him with arranging our accommodations on the road. Like me, the other three monks were going to study in Lhasa. We had two horses and three mules for our luggage and for me to ride. According to the original plan, several monks from Tawé Monastery would join us. However, due to miscommunication regarding the trip schedule, they went directly to Dartsédo and subsequently took the Southern Route. Thus, the Pawam Tulku had two men, one monk and one layman, accompany us to Damdo Monastery along the narrow, ascending Géshétsa valley. I was excited to see wild walnut trees in the valley—I had never seen so many walnut trees before. The walnut meat was delicious but difficult to extract. The locals had a thick needle for this exact purpose. There were flocks of parrots flying about that also fed on walnuts. I also saw bear cubs playing with and chasing each other on high cliffs from time to time. It took us two or three days to reach the monastery, and they hosted us for two nights.

Then, the monastery coordinated with the king of Damdo-Géshétsa to dispatch two guards on horseback with shotguns to escort us to Tau, on the other side of the mountain. This passage was notorious for frequent raids by locals, so few people chose to take it. Traveling with two armed native guards guaranteed our safe passage because locals would not assault their people, especially those with guns. The guards were very familiar with the difficult passes on the way and rode ahead to check and ensure the passes were clear before we followed. After we finished climbing the mountain pass and entered Tau territory, I was amazed to see rings of steaming hot springs scattered along the valley floor. Some of these springs were used by people, immersing themselves in the water for its curative effects. We also pitched our tent for more than two nights by hot springs, enjoying the warmth they provided.

Upon arriving at Tau, we were entrusted to a local monastery called Nyatso Gönpa. The monastery soon found companions for us to travel with to Drakgo. Traveling was becoming easier as the landscape from Nyatso Gönpa onward began to change from predominantly deep and narrow mountain valleys to wider and flatter pasture areas. Next, when we reached Drakgo, a local monastery (Drakgo Gön) again found us companions for the next leg of our journey, to Kardzé. On our way, we passed by villages where we were hosted by locals for the night once or twice. But most of the time we stayed in our tents because we felt constrained under others' roofs. We usually chose to keep our distance from villages and settlements when we camped to avoid harassment from locals. Even with our precautions, rocks were thrown at our tents in the middle of the night. The treasurer or other companions would yell at the top of their voice, "Just come! O-he-he!" I asked him to lower his voice and stop shouting to prevent retaliation from the attacking party. Still, he answered that we weren't supposed to show any fear because any sign of unease on our part would likely invite another attack and being robbed by locals. Nonetheless, all of us were prepared for possible assaults by people or animals, usually dogs, which were not uncommon on the way to Lhasa. I had my handgun, and all my companions were armed with spears. The spears could be used both in defense against human and animal attacks and as walking sticks to ease the difficulty of travel.

It took us more than ten days to go from Tau to Kardzé, where we were told our destination of Béri was near. Therefore, we decided to go to Béri on our own, although we could have first gone to Kardzé Monastery and asked for their coordination and help, as Pawam Tulku had arranged. The Tsongpön of Béri, known as Gönpoling Chödzé, was our guide to Lhasa and received us with great hospitality. Alhough a monk at Béri Monastery, he was responsible for conducting trade on behalf of the monastery. The Tsongpön owned a massive house, its first floor packed with sacks of goods.

Except for tea, I didn't know what was in those sacks. We were told that the caravan would not set off for Lhasa again for another ten days, so we stayed at the house of another monk, who prepared beef momo (dumplings) and butter tea for us. The following day, our Sönamyak crew visited the monastery. It was not very large, and I only saw a few dozen monks. I am not sure whether any other monks were staying there or elsewhere. For the next two days, we watched a Tibetan opera performed in a nearby pasture, where the actors were primarily monks. I've forgotten which opera it was, but I remember that the pasture was filled with people and tents. Several thousand people came and put up their tents and stayed there for a few days to celebrate this local festival. Moreover, I was invited to have meals at the Tsongpön's residence several times and saw so many of his crew busy packing and unpacking goods there. A caravan from Dartsédo arrived shortly after ours, and they also were preparing for the trip to Lhasa.

Finally the caravan was ready to take off again. It was made up of dozens of people with long rifles strapped to their backs, horses, and some 300 mules loaded with tea, tents, food, and other baggage and goods. The Drungsa Kyapgön (hereafter Kyapgön) and his crew joined a few days later.[6] His crew included more than 20 people, both monks and laymen, and dozens of horses and mules. All the laymen also carried guns. The Kyapgön was a major *tulku* from Kardzé Monastery in his forties or fifties whom the Tsongpön had introduced to us. The Kyapgön had previously studied in Lhasa, so this was his second or third trip there. We didn't go very far the first day, probably traveling only one or two hours. The Tsongpön wanted to reorganize all the caravans concerning the positioning of the tents, mules, horses, and our personnel arrangements. In doing so, he assigned each tent and animal to a particular spot relative to one another, which was to be strictly followed each day. Likewise, everyone, especially the Tsongpön's subordinates, was expected to perform a particular duty.

First, the Tsongpön pinpointed spots for his tent to be pitched and locations for the two tents on either side of it. He subsequently determined where the remaining tents would go. All together, the dozen or so tents formed a big circle. The Tsongpön and his bodyguards shared a large tent, which was also used to hold leather sacks of goods after they were unloaded from the mules at the end of each day's travel. Five to eight people were then assigned to share a tent, depending on its size. Our Sönamyak crew stayed in our tent. Next, the Tsongpön designated an area where horses and mules were kept in rows in the middle of the campsite. Each row, under the charge of one person, was composed of ten to twenty animals, and the distance between rows was fixed. Mules are clever, and most learned to maintain their respective positions and line up in an orderly manner within just a few days. These animals roughly followed the same order while traveling on the road. Furthermore, the Tsongpön assigned people to manage the livestock, pitch tents, and take on other responsibilities. He also made every tent a basic dining unit. Each prepared its cooking utensils and bellows, and everyone in the unit had their specific role in the cooking process, such as building a fire pit, making tea, cooking, and so on. As a teenager and *tulku*, I was not assigned any duties in the caravan or within our Sönamyak unit. However, I couldn't stay put, so I helped with things like pitching tents, building fires, etc.

At daybreak, the Tsongpön would clap his hands to wake us up. People would awaken and begin their respective work—building fires, making tea, loading mules, collecting tents, etc. Meanwhile, we quickly drank our tea and ate our *tsampa*. The entire process was fast, taking no more than half an hour. Then the caravan started, spearheaded by seven or eight lead mules adorned with colorful strips of fabric on their heads and necks. These mules were among the strongest, largest, and most experienced. They would stop at crossroads and move into a line to block the way, preventing the other animals from passing. They moved again only after being directed by the Tsongpön or one of his assistants to the right path. Occasionally, due to rain, snow, or landslides, the trails would disappear. The Tsongpön would then rely on a compass he had brought and his experience on the trail to determine the right direction to follow. The leading mules went on to lead the way after that.

Moreover, these mules and the most seasoned horses played an important role in leading the pack animals to cross large rivers. Most horses and especially mules have no difficulty crossing a stream or a relatively shallow river since they have a natural gift for swimming. Some stronger and more experienced ones can cross while carrying a person on their back in addition to their standard cargo load. However, the situation was much more difficult when trying to cross a broader and deeper river. The Yangtze was the largest river that we encountered during our trip. While we were trying to cross from Kamtok Drukha (the Port of Kamtok), a dividing line between Xikang and Central Tibet, most of the animals were afraid to step into the water and desperately tried to return to the shore after being driven into the river. The packmen told me that the animals would occasionally turn and swim back to the original riverbank once they reached the middle of the river, fearing the rough and deep water there.

Under this circumstance, the leading mules and the most seasoned horses were badly needed to lead the way and guide all the pack animals. The experienced mules would choose the best and shortest route across the water and were brave enough to finish crossing in one committed effort. Several hundred loaded pack animals crossing a river is an impressive scene. With only their heads emerging out of the water and their bodies floating with the current, they resembled Tibetan noodles dropped into boiling water one after another, rolling all together.

The Tsongpön and the Kyapgön typically dined together. They took their time drinking tea and eating breakfast after the caravan took off at daybreak. Since the caravan moved slowly, the Tsongpön, the Kyapgön, and their attendants would quickly catch up and ride past all of us. The Tsongpön would then find an ideal place for camping before noon. His tent would be erected, and his band of travelers would begin to drink tea, relax, or play games. When the rest of the caravan arrived about an hour later, they would position their tents accordingly and perform the duties they had been assigned from the first day. I was sometimes invited to drink tea and dine with the Tsongpön and the Kyapgön. If this invitation happened in the morning, I was pleased that I didn't have to hurry to leave with the rest of the caravan and could sip my tea leisurely. Our food stock, composed chiefly of butter, *tsampa*, meat, and cheese, was replenished every ten or fifteen days. The Tsongpön would announce the timing in advance, and we then rationed the amount of food accordingly. We often stopped at a local village or settlement to purchase food and barter with nomads. When nomads saw us passing by from a distance, they would ride toward us. Our Sönamyak crew had prepared salt, thread, and needles, the nomads' favorite objects for bartering.

I supplied all the food my small crew ate from the budget for my living expenses in Lhasa, given by the Sönamyak magistrate and the Okzhi king. This arrangement was because my companions served as my attendants during the trip. Nonetheless, in our small group, there were two separate sacks of *tsampa*—one for me and one for the rest. My *tsampa* was more refined and tasted better. However, I could only consume an amount strictly allocated by my treasurer, who oversaw our whole crew's food rations; I couldn't eat to my heart's content. Then something surprising happened. I got lucky in terms of my food and newly acquired privileges. About half a month into our journey, a mule collapsed, falling to the ground. People assumed that it was going to die. While I was still on the back of my mule, the Tsongpön requested my blessing for this mule's rebirth. One of his subordinates borrowed my rosary and placed it on the forehead of the dying beast. When we were about to depart, the mule moved again slightly and attempted to stand up. It got up after a few minutes, with the help of several people. Word spread that I had rescued the mule from death with my blessing. After that, the Tsongpön treated me exceptionally well. He asked me to ride one of his horses and join him and the Kyapgön in dining for the rest of the trip. I had plentiful and delicious food, including a lot of meat, sweets, and other delicacies. He had a jar of Sichuan chili bean paste produced in Pixian (a city near Chengdu). Just a bit on *tsampa* made it so delicious that I became addicted to it. Even today, I love to eat my *tsampa* this way. Furthermore, the Tsongpön would take me with him to feasts that locals arranged for the Kyapgön thanks to his prominent religious status. My associates were also pleased with this arrangement since my original share of food could be redistributed among them, adding to their portions.

This trip remains vividly in my memory. For most travelers, especially those who took the Southern Route, the journey to Lhasa meant immeasurable hardship, but my experience was different. We didn't suffer from any natural disasters or human catastrophes. Occasionally we encountered rainfall, but the rain never created any real problems for us. We continued to move forward amid showers and our clothes dried as the sun reemerged. We only halted if the Tsongpön saw a landslide risk or when he could not trace a trail that the rain had washed away. I didn't fall ill throughout the trip. The few others who caught colds recovered quickly. No one raided us either. Our armed caravan was enormous, making it a formidable target. Still, we also evaded raids because the Tsongpön, as a frequent traveler, was an acquaintance to local communities along the way. He would prepare gifts for the tribal leaders, who consequently granted safe passage in addition to gifts of butter and cheese.

Early in our trip, I was somewhat exhausted by the hardships of traveling. We had to get up early while stars lingered in the sky and hurried to catch up with the rest of the crew, but I soon became used to it. The fatigue was gone, and I truly enjoyed this caravan trip, especially after I started getting special treatment from the Tsongpön. Each day we only traveled for four to six hours. Then we were free in the afternoon and evening. People could wash their clothes, swim in a stream or river, sing and dance, find shade to sleep in, and so on. From time to time, the Tsongpön sang the Gesar epics for us. I also joined the Tsongpön and Kyapgön in their daily chats that involved the political and religious state of affairs, mainly in Tibet, Kham, and China, as well as religious teachings. The Kyapgön mentioned that he thought Liu Wenhui, the governor of Xikang, wasn't a terrible Han politician because he was a devout Buddhist.[7] Nonetheless, what they said was often too abstract or remote for a teenager like me to grasp, so I didn't always fully understand or feel interested in what they discussed.

Furthermore, I took delight in the spectacular sights along the road. Range after range of mountains, often with snow-capped peaks shining in the sunshine, spread across a vast ocean of mist and fog. Views of the layers upon layers of rising mountain silhouettes resembled terraced fields of various sizes and shapes. Those views never ceased to enchant me. I was also struck by the demarcated strips of dried and bare trees on some high mountains, lying below the snow line and pastures but at the top end of the forests. I saw this in different places two or three times on our way. When I asked the Tsongpön for an explanation, he replied that it was because these mountains were growing taller. I had a vague understanding of his answer, but it wasn't until many years later that I realized this probably had to do with altitude. With the growth of mountains and increasing altitude, trees that once grew at the top could no longer survive. On our way, we often saw various animals, such as Tibetan gazelles, antelopes, and blue sheep. Using the Tsongpön's telescope, I saw Tibetan argali, a wild sheep with curved horns, on the edges of Mount Anyé Machen.[8] This rare animal is said to be found only around Anyé Machen. However, according to the Kyapgön, it is a pitiful beast because it may starve to death in its old age, when eating short grass with its head down becomes difficult due to its overgrown horns. Hence the Kyapgön felt sorry for the sheep and would recite prayers to bless them and relieve their suffering.

The trip excited me because I could see and meet different people and experience many different things along the way. Most of the people we came across were local villagers and nomads. From time to time, we also met pilgrims, monks, laypeople, and other caravans. Both parties would always stop and greet each other. When recognizing me as a *tulku* based on my robe, laypeople would dismount, approach me, and request a pat on their head with my hand as a blessing. Monks remained on their mounts while nodding and greeting me. Then we would chat a little before parting and going our separate ways. I began to sense that a complex political situation was at play in Kham and Lhasa. About five days after the caravan trip began, we ran into a number of bands of three to five laymen and monks passing on horseback, all armed with guns. It turned out that they were monks and their associates from Dargyé Monastery. I learned later that the monastery, with the support of Lhasa, had been in conflict with Béri Monastery, which had Liu Wenhui and the Xikang government behind them.[9] The conflict was said to have been officially resolved, but based on my observations, tensions remained high, and it felt as if battle could erupt at any time.

Next, we found that soldiers were garrisoned on both sides of the Yangtze River at the Port of Kamtok, dispatched by the Xikang government and Central Tibet. The port was not heavily guarded, though; I saw only a few guards on either side. Standing at a distance, these guards seemed not inclined to approach and examine our cargo as we passed. The Tsongpön approached and talked to them instead. He probably knew them since he was a frequent traveler, and he returned to us after having a brief dialogue. I was told there were trenches and barracks nearby, which could be reinforced at any time if the situation intensified between the Chinese and Tibetan sides and Central Tibet and Kham. The Tsongpön urged us not to walk about or look around the port needlessly while we were waiting to board a ferry to cross the river. He ensured that we left as quickly as possible after reaching the other shore to avoid attracting unnecessary attention from these soldiers. At the same place in 1950, PLA soldiers crossed the Yangtze River to take over Central Tibet, using this port because of its strategic significance as the main gate to Central Tibet.

While we were approaching Lhasa, I had the chance to meet briefly with the Reting Rinpoche (1912–1947) at Reting Monastery, along with the Tsongpön and the Kyapgön, because the Tsongpön planned to make offerings to the monastery. The Reting Rinpoche was the regent of Central Tibet from 1934 to 1941 and oversaw the selection of the Fourteenth Dalai Lama. However, his decision to endorse a reincarnation from a remote Amdo village estranged the aristocrats in Lhasa. To alleviate the political tensions that followed, he stepped down from the regent position, supposedly only for the time being, and had returned to his monastery only recently before we met him. My focus was not on their conversation during the meeting but on the tall, robust, and fearsome-looking guards at the door. A few years later, in 1947, the Reting Rinpoche experienced a complete downfall and tragic death while I was still studying in Lhasa (see chapter 6).

The next day, we continued our trip into the Penpo region (a.k.a. Penyul; northeast of Lhasa). On our way, we saw the ruins of monasteries and villages from the Kadampa period before the rise of the Gelugpa (eleventh–fourteenth centuries). Sometimes known as the New Kadampa, the Gelugpa carried on and incorporated the Kadampa teachings by the Indian master Atisa (982–1054), who played a crucial role in reviving Buddhism in Tibet after a period of suppression and destruction (the collapse of the Tibetan Empire in the ninth century). Then, about halfway to Lhasa, we passed by the ruins of another monastery. I was told that this was no ordinary monastery. It was built by a very influential master from Gyalrong and held a critical place in Tibetan history. At that young age, I didn't fully comprehend what that meant. Looking back years later, I realized that it was Nalendra Monastery, and its founder was Rongtön Shakya Gyaltsen (a.k.a. Rongtön Mawé Senggé; 1367–1449).[10] Originally from a Bönpo family in Gyalrong (Chuchen), Rongtön became one of the most illustrious scholars and masters of the Sakya School. He founded Nalendra in 1435 and soon turned it into one of the largest and most acclaimed Sakya and Buddhist learning hubs, attracting thousands of students and visitors from all over Greater Tibet.

My official treasurer, Dungma Lama, came to greet and escort me, as we were only about four or five kilometers from Lhasa. He brought a new robe and hat for me. He was also from Sönamyak and had been the treasurer of my previous reincarnation. Dungma Lama didn't return to our hometown after the latter's death but entrusted my uncle with the task of finding the next reincarnation, then became a steward (Tib. *nyerpa*) for the Dedrug Rinpoche. After saying good-bye to the Tsongpön and Kyapgön, I was invited to stay in my treasurer's house located behind the official residence (Tib. *labrang*) of the Dedrug Rinpoche (hereafter Dedrug Residence). It constitutes part of the Méru Dratsang complex northeast of the Jokhang (the most sacred temple in Lhasa and Tibet) because the Dedrug was the complex's official head. Because Dungma Lama worked for the Dedrug Rinpoche, he moved out of Drepung and stayed close to the Dedrug Residence. In the following years, my treasurer's house and Dedrug Residence would become my most frequented places during my stays in Lhasa, especially during the Great Prayer Festival and Small Prayer Festival in the first and second months of the Tibetan calendar, respectively.

Chapter Five

LIFE AT DREPUNG

I was naturally drawn to science and was particularly keen on machinery. However, I realized that I had no way to explore these interests. Therefore, I had better focus on something more attainable: becoming a learned lama. Since the people in Sönamyak and Okzhi considered me to be their *tulku* and had sent me to Lhasa to study, I resolved to honor their wishes. I also felt obliged to work hard for the sake of my parents and family. Their constant grumbles about their sufferings reminded me that I had to complete my education to acquire the necessary capacity to lift them out of their hardships. As a result, I devoted myself wholeheartedly to studying at Drepung, at least for the first few years.[1]

According to the standard admission procedure, all the new arrivals, including myself, must first find a trusted guarantor (Tib. *khakhyak gégen*) to enter the monastery. The guarantor vouched for his candidate's qualifications and took responsibility as their caretaker if something went wrong, such as delinquency. The novices were supposed to find our respective tutors too. At the same time, two house gurus (Tib. *khangtsen gégen*) at Gyalrong House were responsible for verifying the status of new arrivals, including examining our introduction letters from Chötensar or another major monastery in Gyalrong. In my case, all these things had been arranged for by my former incarnation's treasurer in Lhasa, Dungma Lama, through correspondence with Sönamyak Monastery and the magistrate before I even started my journey to Lhasa. Dungma Lama would continue to serve as my treasurer. He also arranged a guarantor for me, Lama Tupten Tarchin, a learned monk from Drakteng (part of Rongbrag) in Gyalrong. My guarantor would go on to earn Géshé Lharampa status (the highest level of the Géshé degree) in the years to come.

Lama Tupten Tarchin was also the assistant tutor to the Dedrug Rinpoche (fourth in that line; Jampel Kelzang Gyatso, 1934–2000), who was a few years younger than I. But he was Dedrug Rinpoche's de facto teacher since the latter's tutor, Dardo Tulku, a high-ranking *tulku* from Gyalrong, was busy with his teachings and other religious activities among the monks and aristocrats in Lhasa.[2] Dardo Tulku entrusted Lama Tupten Tarchin with the duty of tutoring the Dedrug Rinpoche. Lama Tupten Tarchin was a student of my tutor, Lama Jampel Samphel. They were both students at the Loserling monastic college technically, but it was not uncommon for a senior and capable student to tutor a junior one if both parties found it a great fit. Likewise, Lama Tupten Tarchin became my tutor, although Lama Jampel Samphel was my official tutor. Lama Jampel Samphel was originally from Sönamyak as well. He enjoyed an excellent reputation in our hometown due to his mastery of Buddhist scriptures. He hadn't yet taken the Géshé examination when I first arrived in Lhasa but would soon obtain Géshé Lharampa status. He became Loserling's abbot (Tib. *khenpo*) in 1950 after I left Lhasa (in 1948).

According to general practice, a disciple with *tulku* status was expected to provide accommodations for his tutor. However, this was unnecessary because my tutor had already moved in with another of his disciples, a *tulku* from Tshabarong (a traditionally Kham region located in Yunnan), known as Bachok Tulku, who was wealthy and kept a lot of meat, tea, sweets, and other delicacies in his residence. His treasurer was conducting caravan trade on his behalf. I was a typical poor *tulku* novice, so my financial burden was relieved of my tutor's living expenses and my standard of living was improved. I could also enjoy excellent meals at Bachok Tulku's residence after meeting with my tutor there.

After all of this was settled, I moved into a three-room apartment in the Gyalrong Khangtsen ("regional house of Gyalrong"; hereafter Gyalrong House) in Loserling Dratsang ("monastic college of Loserling"; hereafter Loserling College) at Drepung Monastery. Located on the second floor of a three-story building, this apartment had been the residence of my former reincarnation and was explicitly reserved for me for more than a decade in anticipation of my arrival in Lhasa. The attendant (Tib. *sölpön*), whom my treasurer and tutor had chosen, also moved in with me. Originally from Sönamyak, my attendant had been in Drepung for many years and was responsible for taking care of my daily needs. As my tutor was not living with us, the attendant was also asked to oversee my studies, although he was not interested in learning.

Thanks to my status as a "dharma student of a monastic college" (Tib. *dratsang chödzé*, hereafter *chödzé*), I was exempted from doing manual labor at the monastery. This title was not automatically conferred on all students, and in a way, it was paid for. I was supposed to make offerings, sums of money to be provided to each monk who attended the assembly and to Loserling College, to be accorded this status. Moreover, another round of offerings was to be made to Gyalrong House several days later. Such ritualistic offerings were called *chözhuk*, part of an initiation ceremony usually reserved for novices with *tulku* status and *chödzé*. I can't remember the amount given to every monk, but overall, I spent over 1,000 silver coins, which was more than half of the total I had brought to Lhasa. About forty to fifty *chödzé* studied at Loserling College, among whom about two-thirds were *tulkus* and the rest were from aristocratic and merchant families. Most monks couldn't afford expensive offerings, so they were required to perform domestic chores at the monastery such as cooking, repairing roofs, house painting, serving tea during the assemblies, and so on. Another advantage of being a *chödzé* was that a seat was always reserved for me at the assembly halls at both the monastery and the college, even when they became very crowded.

Gyalrong House, with about 400–500 residential monks, was only one of more than twenty regional houses at Loserling College. Loserling, with a total of around 5,000 monks, was the largest of the four colleges within the monastery. Each college functioned as a semiautonomous, self-financed division led by a khenpo (abbot of the college), with its own assembly halls, residential houses, and management systems. A regional house was a basic residential unit for the monks from a particular region. Gyalrong House was hence typically inhabited by monks originally from Gyalrong. Besides Drepung, there were two other major Gelugpa monasteries in Lhasa, Sera and Ganden, and each had their respective Gyalrong House. Since Gyalrong comprised different kingdoms, chieftaincies and magistratures, monks from particular jurisdictions tended to study in a Gyalrong House at a specific monastery. This tendency became a residential pattern over time. So according to tradition, new arrivals from Sönamyak and Okzhi, as well as those from Chuchen, Rongbrag, Dartsédo, and Gyelkha, usually chose to reside in the Gyalrong House at Drepung.

Our house regularly hosted Bön monks from Drakteng and elsewhere, just as we hosted their Gelugpa counterparts from the same chieftaincy. These Bön monks were there because Bön and Tibetan Buddhism were similar in philosophy and premises, although many people didn't realize that. Lhasa is a religious hub in Greater Tibet. Bön lacked a similar illustrious center after this religious institution was severely undermined and lost the patronage of local rulers in most parts of Gyalrong and Tibet.[3] The monks would continue practicing Bön once they returned to their home monasteries after completing their studies in Lhasa. Likewise, regional houses in the three monasteries could host monks from the same home region but different denominations, like Sakya, Nyingma, and Kagyu. However, this wasn't a fixed pattern, and it was not uncommon for certain regional houses to admit residents from other regions, depending on the situation. For instance, one of the most influential Gelugpa masters of our time, Pabongkhapa, a native of Central Tibet, was a Gyalrong House resident at Sera.[4] Han Chinese monks also tended to reside in the Gyalrong House at Drepung.[5] During my stay in Lhasa, the number of Han monks varied from year to year, say four to seven, as older monks departed and new ones arrived. The Han monks came to Lhasa primarily through Dartsédo, where they would study Tibetan and scriptures, sometimes for the first time. They were then able to build connections with local monasteries and monks there. They chose to reside in the Gyalrong House at Drepung because most monks from Dartsédo stayed there.[6]

The residents of the Gyalrong Houses in these three major monasteries came to be known in Lhasa for specific characteristics, sometimes of mixed desirability. Some monks said, "The Gyalrongwa have no intestines" (Tib. *Gyalrongwa la gyuma mé*), literally meaning that food wasn't digested, it was excreted. It is a recognition of how the Gyalrongwa were disparaged for acting impetuously without thinking, implying that they are short on honor and consistency. For instance, Gyalrong monks were characterized as prone to show off. Due to Gyalrong's location near Han regions, many monks could speak some or fluent Chinese. So when Chinese officials and visitors came to Lhasa during the Qing and Republican eras, the Gyalrong monks were frequently called upon to host Chinese guests and act as their interpreters. Therefore, other monks and Lhasa people thought that we Gyalrongwa felt superior to others because of these skills that could be used to foster ties with the Han. In contrast, one positive image was that the Gyalrong monks were diligent and intelligent. Even though Gyalrong is a tiny region compared to the three main traditional regions in Greater Tibet—Kham, Amdo, and Ü-Tsang (Central Tibet)—it has produced some of the most learned and influential lamas in Tibetan history.

Some of the best-known religious figures originally from Gyalrong include Yudra Nyingpo (eighth century), a principal disciple of Vairotsana as well as one of the twenty-five primary disciples of the legendary Indian master Padmasambhava (Tib. Guru Rinpoche), who introduced Tantric Buddhism to Tibet; Rinchen Pel (1350–1435), who played a crucial role in preserving and reviving the Jonang teachings in Dzamtang and Gyalrong after the school's destruction in Central Tibet during the time of the Fifth Dalai Lama (1617–1682); Nyammé Shérap Gyeltsen (1356–1415), honored as the second "Buddha" in the Bön tradition (after its legendary founder, Tönpa Shenrab Miwoche, a counterpart of the historical Buddha, Siddhartha Gautama); Rongtön Mawé Senggé (1367–1449), one of the most foundational scholars of the Sakya school; Tsakho Ngawang Drakpa (fourteenth–fifteenth centuries), one of the earliest and closest disciples of Je Tsongkhapa (1357–1419), the founder of the Gelugpa school; and Rongchen Jaknakpa Gendün Gyeltsen (1374–1450), another foremost disciple of Tsongkhapa.[7]

In addition, at least seven Ganden Tripas ("Holder of the Ganden Throne") hailed from Gyalrong and received their training in the three Gyalrong houses. One such example is Lobsang Khyenrab Wangchug (circa 1800–1873), who was a resident of Drepung's Gyalrong House and served as the seventy-sixth Ganden Tripa (circa 1853–1859), regent (Tib. *sikyon*) of Tibet (circa 1865–1872), and tutor of the Twelfth Dalai Lama.[8] He was even conferred the highest-ranking title for a lama, Khutuktu, by the Qing court, and thus he became the originator of one of the most prominent reincarnation lineages in Tibet, known as the Dedrug *tulku*. According to tradition, the Dedrug lineage has always been a part of Drepung's Gyalrong House, no matter where its reincarnations have been born or discovered. Consequently, this lineage is also popularly known as the Gyalrong Khutuktu. Likewise, as noted, a well-known lama, Pabongkhapa, a Gyalrong

House resident at Sera, enhanced its reputation as a great learning center. He passed away just before I arrived in Lhasa. Some monks sympathetically confided to me, "If you had come a bit earlier, you would have had the opportunity to meet the great Pabongkhapa in person." Lama Dorjé Chöpa (1874–unknown), another prominent lama at Drepung's Gyalrong House, also passed away some years before my arrival but still maintained vast influence. He was said to have accepted many powerful Chinese disciples, many of whom became regular sponsors of Drepung and Gyalrong House, even after their teacher's death.[9]

During my stay in Lhasa, some outstanding Géshés and scholars also resided in these Gyalrong houses. These include two of the four assistant tutors to the Fourteenth Dalai Lama, Sertsa Géshé (Géshé Losang Dönden) from Drepung Loserling College and Geshé Khyenrap Gyatso from Sera Mé College, as well as Jangtsé Chöjé (Lama Jampa Kelzang), one of the two candidates for the Ganden Tripa position. When I started my training at Drepung in the early 1940s, the reputation of my tutor, Lama Jampel Samphel, as a great scholar was growing. He earned the most prestigious Géshé Lharampa degree before I left Lhasa and became Losering College's abbot after I left. After that, he was referred to as the Gyalrong Khensur Rinpoche (emeritus abbot from Gyalrong). I learned recently from a Gyalrong lama who had returned from India that my tutor went on to train many exceptional students, including several Ganden Tripas (the 100th and 102nd Ganden Tripas, Lobsang Nyima Rinpoche and Ridzong Rinpoche) and Samdong Rinpoche (Kalön Tripa or prime minister of the Tibetans in exile) after I left Lhasa.

One may wonder why Gyalrong was able to produce so many great scholars. I believe that this had to do with the fact that many Gyalrong monks felt that it would be a shame not to focus on learning since they had experienced great trouble to reach Lhasa from the remotest fringes of Greater Tibet. Also, as noted, many parts of Gyalrong have a custom uncommon in other Tibetan regions—a monk must study in Lhasa for many years, at least eight years in the case of Tsanlha and Chuchen, to be recognized as a qualified lama. Therefore, if someone could endure eight years of hardship and dedicate themselves to learning, it was likely that they would extend their stay until they obtained a Géshé degree. This had been my original plan. The negative and positive images of the Gyalrongwa also partly explain why the Gyalrong Houses remained successful. At Drepung's

Gyalrong House, we had adequate rooms for all our monks, which wasn't always the case in the various regional houses. The house acquired two additional dwellings in the Lhasa suburbs after I left. Thus, when over 20,000 monks from the three major monasteries would flood into the Jokhang temple (in the center of Lhasa) during the annual Great Prayer Festival in the first month of the Tibetan calendar, our house monks could stay in our dwellings. In contrast, monks from other houses might have to request that local aristocrats allow them to stay at their homes. This was possible for Drepung's Gyalrong House thanks to its capacity to generate revenue.

Money is crucial to the survival and development of any regional house, monastic college, or entire monastery because it is needed to provide basic accommodations for the monks and cover other expenses, such as the construction and renovation of assembly halls and residences. Therefore, these different levels of monastic organizations must generate income. Common ways they earned money were by loaning extra money to people and purchasing land and real estate to be put up for rent. In most cases, however, securing regular patronage and donations was an equally, if not more important, means to acquire income. Drepung's Gyalrong House obtained donations and sponsorship from Han officials and merchants, Lhasa aristocrats, and others to enable its renovation and expansion. Han donors included lay disciples and sponsors of particular masters, such as the aforementioned Lama Dorjé Chöpa, as well as the relatives and sponsors of other Han monks living in Gyalrong House.

Nonetheless, due to the volatility of Sino-Tibetan relationships, it was of even greater importance to have local patrons, especially aristocratic families. The benefits were more than just economic. Their support helped settle disputes, such as when loans were not returned. From personal experience, I knew that our house had key regular patrons from aristocratic families in Lhasa, like the Shédra and the Gazhi. They regularly invited dozens of monks to chant prayers for the family's well-being. I was unsure how exactly these aristocrats became our house patrons, but I assumed it was related to our reputation for producing outstanding monks. I also learned that patronship was relatively stable once it was formed and, in these cases, had already lasted for generations. It also was beneficial for a regional house to have other alliances with aristocrats. For instance, although the Langdün family was not a formal patron of our house, they surely played a similar role. The Langdün was one of Lhasa's most prominent aristocratic families, thanks partly to having produced the Thirteenth Dalai Lama. The Dedrug Rinpoche of our house, known also as the Gyalrong Khutuktu, was from this family, and thus they were somehow obliged to sponsor and support our house.

I gathered from my master's conversations with other Géshés that our house had once had an even more prominent role at Drepung and in Lhasa because it had been closely tied to Tengyé Ling, the monastic seat of one of the most powerful *tulku* lineages in Central Tibet, the Démo Khutuktu, whose successive reincarnations had acted as regents of Tibet. However, Tengyé Ling was accused of treason for siding with the Chinese army (the Lhasa garrison of the Qing army) during fighting in 1911–12, when the Dalai Lama attempted to drive the Chinese out of Lhasa and Tibet. This monastery was subsequently demolished, and its monks were disbanded, which meant our house lost a potent ally. Even so, during my stay in Lhasa, Gyalrong House was better off economically than some other regional houses at Loserling and Drepung.

To guarantee its survival and growth, Gyalrong House, like any other house, couldn't just rely on regular donations or forecasted income but had to plan for the constant arrival of new residents as well. Despite this continuous effort, the financial situation fluctuated; sometimes Gyalrong House encountered difficulty in securing adequate income and new students. Whenever this happened, the house guru would assign a few monks to invoke the most powerful deity of Gyalrong, the mountain deity Gyalmo Mudo, through smoke offerings and prayers, to ask for help in alleviating the situation and ensuring the house's continuity and prosperity. Bluntly, the smoke offerings and prayers were made to request that the mountain deity "motivate" sponsors and Gyalrong locals to send more money and novice monks. This ritual wasn't only performed under challenging circumstances; it was performed regularly, three or four times annually, though more frequently in troubled times, say five or six times a year. Each regional house had its regional deity that could be invoked for a similar purpose.

When it came to learning, the environment wasn't drastically different from one regional house or college to another, as all enforced rigorous training, despite differences in learning procedures and focuses. Although Sera and Ganden had their respective traditions and curriculum, great importance was attached to five general subjects shared across these three great monasteries in Lhasa and the Gelugpa tradition. At Loserling, there were about fourteen grades for these subjects, based on content and an individual's study progress. Working toward the highest grade, one was to learn five general subjects for their Géshé examination: Pramana (Tib. *tshad ma*; Logic-Epistemology), Prajnaparamita (Tib. *phar phyin*; Perfection of Wisdom), Madhyamaka (Tib. *dbu ma*; the Middle Way), Abhidharma (Tib. *chos mngon par or mdzod*; Realization), and Vinaya (Tib. *'dul ba*; Monastic Discipline). Not many students were able to complete the courses, however. On entering, my class was made up of about 300 new students, but that number decreased as we advanced into the higher grades. After two or three years, probably only half remained, the others having quit and returned to their home monasteries. This shows the degree of difficulty in learning and braving daily life challenges in Lhasa. I studied for ten to twelve hours every day and rarely had time for leisure. My day was fully occupied with morning prayers, text recitation and memorization, meeting my tutor or other teachers, and debates with classmates and others. In theory, there were five to fifteen days of study break from time to time, but I rarely took breaks. Instead, I thoroughly used the time to recite and memorize texts and meet with my tutors.

My situation was not unique. This was more or less true for most students who aimed to complete all the courses necessary for their Géshé examination, so they had to live like this for over a decade. On top of that, the Géshé examination involved making offerings (meals, tea, and money) to hundreds or thousands of audience members, depending on the examination's particular level (Doram, Lingsé, Tsokram, and Lharam). This was no small expense for ordinary monks and could deter them from pursuing the degree. Because of this, talented, industrious, but poor monks might have to spend more time, even up to ten more years, completing the required courses and preparing for the examination, since they had to perform manual labor to save enough money to make the anticipated offerings. For instance, during study breaks, individuals with "dharma student of monastic college" status like myself and those from well-off families could focus on their studies or do something else. Poorer monks had to take advantage of the time to collect dried cattle dung (used as fuel for fires in many parts of Tibet, especially in nomadic regions with limited access to forests) for their use, conduct small trade, or learn another specific skill such as sewing (e.g., to make monastic robes) to make some money, and so on. Doing so affected and delayed their study and meant a more prolonged process to gather enough money for the Géshé examination offerings.[10]

I was thankfully exempted from various chores and duties at Gyalrong House and Loserling so that I could concentrate on studying. However, this didn't mean that I had a much easier life than that of ordinary monks. My attendant was ill-tempered and found fault with me quickly. For example, I was rebuked for failing to read out loud enough while reciting my sutras, for failing to memorize as many pages of texts as some classmates did, and so on. He would scold me for being lazy whenever I wanted to take just a few minutes' break from my studies. Moreover, he allowed me to eat only three spoonfuls of *tsampa* for each meal. This limit never changed during my stay in Lhasa, even though my body and appetite grew throughout my time there. This problem was partly alleviated since I was treated to at least one great meal at the Bachok Tulku's residence every other day when I went there to meet and study with my tutor.

If I spoke back to my attendant, he would become irate and beat me. He would lift me by my ear and spank my buttocks. Once, my whole right ear was nearly ripped off, and blood spurted everywhere. He just applied some salt on the torn part and never showed remorse. I provided for his accommodations while my attendant treated me like a beggar. Sometimes I would think that I was no better off than a beggar. Many beggars in Lhasa asked for food and money each day. They would often sing during the afternoons, which I heard almost every time I walked the *lingkor* (outer circumambulation route around the Jokhang) in Lhasa. They were undoubtedly impoverished regarding material possessions, but at least they were in high spirits. It was uncommon to see worried-looking beggars. In comparison, I ate like a beggar and was bullied daily.

Though my tutor was quick-tempered, he rarely scolded me since he was generally satisfied with my progress. I transferred to a higher grade after my first year of study since I was able to complete two years of learning in reasoning (Tib. *rtags rigs*) and epistemology (Tib. *blo rigs*) within one year and two basic subjects in Logic-Epistemology (Pramana/tshad ma), and did very well in memorization, debate, and examinations. I soon became the second or third best student in my entering class. Not long after, I accidentally found some fame. I defeated a much more senior student in a debate. My opponent, known as Minyag Kyorpön (*kyorpön* means monitor or head of the class, and therefore, Minyag Kyorpön refers to the monitor from the region of Minyag; the position of *kyorpön* was reserved for the best student in each class), was nearly as well-known as my tutor for his knowledge and debating skills. Scheduled to soon sit for his Géshé examination, he went around to the various regional houses challenging other students to debate, to test his limits and enhance his proficiency in different subjects. This was common practice at Drepung. Students applying for a Géshé degree, particularly those going for the highest level (*lharampa*), would do this often. Still, anyone, even a novice monk of a lower grade, could ask for this opportunity after completing a particular subject. Very few students could win every debate, and for us monks, it was natural for people, even very learned monks, to occasionally lose. However, it was somewhat unusual for someone like me, who hadn't been at Drepung for very long, even when I was in my second or third year, to defeat such a brilliant scholar and debater as the Minyag Kyorpön.

I can't recall the details of our debate, but I do remember the lively atmosphere. While I was challenging the Minyag Kyorpön, my classmates and the other monks would verbally jump in from time to time to help me. It was also common for a defender to face multiple challengers in a debate. However, I felt that my co-challengers, except my tutor, didn't help me much, as most failed to pinpoint the flaws in the defender's arguments, even if they grasped the crux of his position. I raised my voice and argued with the Minyag Kyorpön more vigorously to forestall my co-challengers' interventions. He was a skilled, eloquent debater and provided cogent arguments to defend his stance. My tutor would join me in the challenge at several critical moments when I was in danger of defeat. He would say a few words to remind me, so I could go from there to continue my role as the principal challenger. Finally the Minyag Kyorpön was no longer able to defend himself. He took off his hat and nodded at me, the standard way to admit one's loss in a debate.

I, a junior student, would not have been able to defeat the erudite Minyag Kyorpön by myself. My tutor knew Minyag Kyorpön's argument's weaknesses and logical loopholes and advised me to challenge this defender in particular ways to emphasize his weak spots. In the meantime, my tutor was able to anticipate possible justifications and counterarguments, then instruct me on how to reinforce my stance. Based on my tutor's instructions, I prepared myself for this debate thoroughly by thinking over the specific techniques and arguments necessary to deal with such a powerful opponent. Still, some other people felt that I had done it all on my own. As a result, people began to speak highly of my argumentative skills after this lucky triumph. This event highlights the results of the unique training system in the Gelugpa tradition. I have been notoriously inquisitive ever since my childhood. This inclination went very well with the monastic training system because the ability to question, challenge, and reason was a prerequisite for becoming a sophisticated learner.

My two near-death experiences during childhood gave me the motivation and insight to imagine the likely existence of previous and next lives. Therefore, I was eager to discover why and how such metaphysics was possible. Through my training in Lhasa, I eventually figured out the logic behind the continuity of life. The present life is a transition point that connects the previous and subsequent lives. Specifically, according to the notion of karma (Tib. *légyudré*), or the logic of cause and effect, the nature of one's present life is an inevitable consequence of one's deeds in the body (actions), speech (words), and mind (thoughts) that were accumulated during one's previous lives. Therefore, the past and present lives are simultaneously the fundamental cause of the nature of one's next life. This implies that an individual doesn't live just one single life. Furthermore, people must be responsible for their deeds and consider such actions' consequences for their future lives. For instance, someone may have a wealthy and happy life today. This circumstance has everything to do with their accumulated merit and good deeds performed in their previous lives.

Nonetheless, such effects and merit can be used up during this current lifetime, and one may suffer in their next life if they stop performing good deeds. This engenders the concept of "a little is enough" in Tibetan society, meaning that people should refrain from overindulging themselves in material and sensual pleasures now to avoid exhausting their accumulated merit before their next life. Moreover, in addition to performing other good deeds and cultivating compassion, individuals must reduce and eliminate their bad karma by experiencing and enduring suffering, such as through pilgrimages, to increase their merit for the next life. This kind of philosophy profoundly influences the Tibetan outlook and way of life. If the truth be told, Tibetan aristocrats and some well-known lamas have exploited and oppressed people. The CCP has even demonized the old Tibetan system by portraying it as hellish and fiendish. However, compared to Han Chinese feudal lords, most of the ruling class throughout Greater Tibet paid greater attention to their karmic acts and the well-being of their subjects.

Through this reasoning, I realized the immeasurable worth of Tibetan Buddhist teachings and their supreme logical approach in conveying these ideas to people. Therefore, I was deeply drawn to such teachings. Having said this, I should emphasize that I had these revelations only because of the distinctive training system in which I was immersed. The uniqueness of this system comes through at least three interlocking aspects. First are the stages of learning, which are referred to as the Three Stages of Listening, Contemplation, and Meditation (Tib. *thö sam gom sum*). Particular emphasis is put on this step-by-step learning process. To gain a thorough understanding of a topic being studied, we must proceed through different stages: first listening to teachers and reading texts, then ruminating on what we have learned, and finally going through undistracted meditation and practice to gain deeper insight into the nature of the phenomenon at hand. All the steps are interconnected and should not be viewed as separate from one another. In many instances, all three stages are performed simultaneously.

Ideally, these steps should be incorporated into a practitioner's daily activities, even when walking or eating. I confess that my accomplishments rested mainly on the first stage, "listening," as I did only a bit of "contemplation" and even less "meditation." My inclination to challenge and question nonetheless found fertile intellectual ground. I wouldn't readily accept whatever the texts and masters would say. Instead, I asked them and searched for answers and solutions on my own. These three stages enhanced my understanding of death, the soul, and karma. Only after I was exposed to modern schooling and education systems in 1977 did I see more clearly the comparative merit of this learning approach. Modern college curricula were designed in a way that insufficiently motivated students to dive deeply into the topics they were learning and quickly forget what they had already learned (see chapter 12). In contrast, even today, I can still remember many of the texts and teachings I learned more than seventy years ago because what we studied then was deeply ingrained in our minds thanks to these successive stages of learning.

Second, debates are a significant part of Gelugpa training.[11] This method is closely related to the three stages of learning since it is a crucial means and instrument to foster the trainees' critical perspectives, logical reasoning, and argumentative skills. Nearly every day, our classmates were engaged in debates. Moreover, there were many monastery-wide and inter-monastery debates held regularly.[12] The content focused on what we learned from the texts and our masters. If one failed to understand the texts and specific ideas well enough, one was easily defeated. This also suggested that despite the great importance of memorization and recita-tion in Tibetan Buddhism, a debate would become mechanical parroting if the debaters failed to comprehend the texts they had memorized and recited so many times. This motivated many classmates and me to study as assiduously as possible. Undoubtedly, this kind of pressure also eventu-ally sent many novices back to their home regions, which is why each year, the student number shrank as the grade level increased. I had incentive to participate in the debates because they helped me enhance my under-standing of specific texts and ideas and strengthen my reasoning and argumentative skills. My "accidental" success during the debate with Min-yag Kyorpön boosted my morale to continue participating in this kind of mental exercise.

Finally, there is a unique type of teacher-student relationship in monas-tic training. Lama Jampel Samphel was my primary tutor. However, I also had many other teachers who taught the same or different texts and sub-jects. Whenever my tutor or other monks suggested, I would seek out a new potential teacher and request that they tutor me on a particular subject based on their expertise. For instance, I asked Lama Para Pema Gyeltsan (later the abbot of Loserling) to help me with Prajnaparamita (Perfection of Wisdom). Not all our teachers necessarily held Géshé degrees; they also might be more senior students. However, because these more senior monks had reputations as erudite scholars, junior monks like me might go and learn from them as well. For example, Lama Jampel Samphel and Lama Tupten Tarchin, the former's disciple and another of my primary teachers, had not finished their monastic training when I began studying with them.

Another type of teacher-student relationship was more ritualistic but still necessary. One of my tutors of this kind was Lama Sertsa Géshé (Losang Dönden; assistant tutor to the Fourteenth Dalai Lama). I would visit him in the city of Lhasa once or twice yearly. These visits and our teacher-student relationship in general were largely ritualistic. I was a *tulku* from his home-town, Okzhi, and his original monastery, Tawé, so he felt obliged to care for me. The Géshé acknowledged me as one of his disciples, but he had little time to spend tutoring me since he did not stay at Drepung and was busy with his role as the Dalai Lama's assistant tutor. Nevertheless, I requested his teachings when I visited him, and he showed concern for my studies. He even considered offering me financial support to continue my stay and study in Lhasa when I faced severe financial constraints and was planning to return home after seven years at Drepung.

This didn't mean that we, the students, were learning unfamiliar and new subjects each time we learned from a different master. In actual practice, like my classmates, I tended to study the same subjects or texts with more than one teacher. This arrangement was typical because various teachers had strengths in and unique insights into specific subjects. Learning the same texts from different scholars helped us deepen our understanding and apply their wisdom to other subjects. This type of learning frequently happened because it was relatively easy to establish teacher-student relationships in the monastic tradition. To present a prospective teacher with a *khata* was sufficient to begin. To decline someone's request for learning was rare, and I have never encountered this situation or heard about it happening to someone else. Some teachers were more popular than others, which can be judged based on their class sizes. Some classes I attended had thirty to forty students in total, while others had only a few.

This wasn't all. My learning experience was enriched with various empowerment rituals and tantric teachings. An empowerment ritual is conducted when participants are initiated into a tantric practice associated with one or more tantric deities through a highly enlightened guru (master). Such a ritual empowers one to access tantric teachings and practices through this specific guru, who is hereafter considered your root guru and worthy of your complete reverence and devotion. Therefore, without such empowerment from a root guru, one is not allowed to practice tantrism. Even if someone studied or practiced it by themselves, they would fail to understand it without a guru's guidance due to its esoteric nature, so there was no merit in doing so. I was initiated in a number of empowerment rituals with some of the most prominent masters in the Gelugpa school, such as the (third) Trijang Rinpoche (Lobsang Yeshe Tenzin Gyatso; 1901–1981),[13] one of the assistant tutors to the Dalai Lama at that time; the Mokchok Rinpoche, an esteemed yet modest master from Drepung's Deyang College; and the (sixth) Ling Rinpoche (1903–1983), the principal tutor to the Dalai Lama.[14]

The rituals I attended typically admitted a small number of participants, ten to twenty, each time. My relatively easy access to these rituals had everything to do with my tutor, his eminence as an outstanding scholar and his subsequent connections with prominent religious and secular figures. Nonetheless, other monks had similar opportunities from time to time. Empowerment rituals were conducted frequently at Drepung and elsewhere, although usually on a small scale. When someone, usually a *tulku*, a relatively better-off monk, aristocrat, trader, or another individual, planned to ask a tantric master to perform an empowerment ritual, they might share this news with their internal circle. All the monks at the college related to each other in one way or another as friends, hometown fellows, and so on. So any monks associated with the ritual sponsor, directly or indirectly through friends, would have the chance to participate.

Tantric practices (Vajrayana) are seen as a shortcut or the fastest vehicle to enlightenment, through which one could reach buddhahood in just one lifetime.[15] In contrast, Theravada and Mahayana are said to be slower vehicles to enlightenment, requiring a number of lifetimes. However, they still must be complemented with tantric practices. In sum, such practices are considered an unavoidable method or path to reach buddhahood. Practicing tantrism has very rigorous criteria and is not easy. For example, as a fundamental prerequisite, the practitioner should acquire bodhicitta (Tib. *jang chup sem*; "enlightened mind"), namely, great compassion for all sentient beings.[16] To acquire bodhicitta is not quite as simple as making a vow to have compassion for others. One must go through different stages to acquire it and again focus on the three stages of the learning process (listening, contemplation, and meditation), mediated through scriptural learning and instruction from masters. *The Great Treatise on the Stages of the Path to Enlightenment* (Tib. *Lamrim chenmo*) by the founder of the Gelugpa, Tsongkhapa, is the fundamental text for trainees. It elaborates on the concrete stages necessary to cultivate not only bodhicitta but also wisdom.

This training and instruction by masters begin when the participants see all sentient beings as their mothers and gradually foster their aspirations to become enlightened and reach buddhahood. To start, they must repay their mother's kindness and love by vowing to liberate all sentient beings from their suffering. To become enlightened, one must cultivate bodhicitta while working to acquire wisdom. Only when the two processes are integrated in this way will one be able to see through the "three poisons"

(Tib. *duksum*) in life, attachment (Tib. *döchak*), aversion (Tib. *zhédang*), and delusion (Tib. *timuk*), and find a way to conquer them all gradually. Only when the problem of the three poisons is fully resolved can one reach buddhahood. While acquiring bodhicitta, the trainees may begin their tantric training under the close guidance of their tantric masters. Again, Tsongkhapa identifies concrete stages in tantric practices for the Gelugpa in his text, *The Great Exposition of the Stages of Mantra* (Tib. *Ngakrim chenmo*).

Other than attending empowerment rituals and learning from gurus about the basics of tantrism, I hadn't contemplated or meditated adequately by the end of my training at Drepung. Therefore, I accomplished little in my tantric practice. Still, I was lucky to be exposed to the gist of Buddhism and to deepen my understanding of the significance of wisdom to acknowledge the nature of things, namely, emptiness and the role of bodhicitta in enlightenment for the sake of all sentient beings.

Chapter Six

ON FREEDOM

I worked as diligently as possible during my first four years in Lhasa. Every night before bedtime, I would consider the ways I was supposed to respond to all the potential challenges that might emerge during debates the following day. Sometimes I would get up and look at my texts in the middle of the night to ensure that I was prepared for the teacher's and challenger's questions. As a result, my teachers and classmates felt I excelled in my studies and debates. I was behaving exactly the way monastic discipline required. For instance, I consciously looked at a distance of merely two arms' length ahead of me while walking to avoid looking around and becoming distracted. I also avoided looking at women directly. After that time, though, my mind began drifting away little by little, having heard, seen, and experienced many things. I began to consider more seriously: What was the true meaning of life? What was I supposed to do to fulfill a more meaningful life? And lastly, was there an alternative life path for me in which I could enjoy more freedom than an average person?

With these questions in mind, I began making closer observations of my tutor Lama Jampel Samphel to see whether it was worthwhile to follow his path and become a great lama. From time to time, I would go on meditation retreats with him. I was curious to find out what on earth he could accomplish. But first of all, I did everything he instructed me to do during meditation: visualization, controlling my breath, reciting prayers, and so on.

Nothing happened to me, however. I didn't experience anything sublime, and I wondered if my tutor experienced the situation differently. I peeked at him from time to time, and to my disappointment, I found no outward signs of elation or attainment of enlightenment. So I asked myself, if an excellent monk like my tutor appeared to accomplish little, should I wait another ten or twenty years to find out that the same thing would happen to me?

Something else puzzled me even further, namely, sexuality. Once I was on the road walking with my master and another of his students, Bachok Tulku, when suddenly something seemed to seize my master, and his body began to quiver. Afterward, he didn't say anything but quickly approached another monk walking toward us, prostrated before this monk a couple of times, and then murmured something to him. I was surprised at this scenario, so I asked the Bachok Tulku, who was a few years older than me, what was happening. He told me my tutor had experienced ejaculation because his male organ had been rubbing against his robe as he walked. So my tutor went to the other fully ordained monk to ask for absolution as a part of the Gelugpa practice of confession (Tib. *sojong*). This struck me because I had thought that such an illustrious lama like my master would have been able to suppress this kind of mundane desire. At the same time, I heard more accounts about other great lamas and their sexual explorations.

A major scandal at the time involved the Tsémönling, one of the highest-ranking reincarnations in Lhasa and among Gelugpa, as he was qualified to take on the regency. He was said to enjoy playing Tibetan mahjong (Tib. *bakchen*) with aristocrats and other players during his spare time. Through this, he became intimate with a woman from the Chakrong family and started to have "monk's sex" (Tib. *Drapéluk*; literally "monk's way") with her. "Monk's sex" was not sexual intercourse in the traditional sense. No penetration of the vagina or other orifices was involved. Instead, one simply rubbed their penis between their male or female sexual partner's crossed thighs for pleasure until ejaculation. This was a loophole in the discipline of monastic celibacy in the Gelugpa system and Tibetan Buddhism generally. This kind of informal sex wasn't considered an infringement on the monastic precepts, so the monastic institutions turned a blind eye to it. However, at some point, the Tsémönling could not hold back his urges and fully consummated the relationship with sex. After this was exposed, he was removed by the Tibetan Kashag government from his position and banished to Lhokha, where he eventually died in exile.[1]

These episodes made me wonder if the great lamas still had sexual urges and if they did, how they, and other fully ordained monks in general, were supposed to be different from laypeople. I was profoundly shocked as I came to see that monks also weren't different from laypeople in terms of sex as a primal urge in their lives. A monk could have "monk's sex" with both women and men; however, this intimacy was much more common between monks due to the relative unavailability of women for the purpose. I must confess that I was no exception. In those days, I was probably considered to be good-looking. Other monks frequently approached me for this type of amorous pleasure. I did this often with a classmate of mine, a *tulku* from Dartsédo, who was several years my senior. He was handsome and didn't dare go out alone for fear of ever-present predators, both male and female. He lived on the same floor as I did in Gyalrong House. While my attendant was out taking care of errands, he would come to my room. We would quickly complete our activity, as my attendant could return at any time. I wasn't interested romantically in men, so I did this to satisfy sexual urges. I was naturally attracted to women. My *tulku* partner said he had had "monk's sex" with nuns and added that it was a very different experience for him, because women's skin was as soft and smooth as silk. This enhanced my desire for women.

Once my master and I completed a one-month meditation retreat at Chokpori Hill, just across from the Potala Palace. The facilities were owned and lent to us by the aristocratic Shédra family, a regular sponsor of Drepung's Gyalrong House. We were invited to recite prayers by Lama Neushar Tupten Tarpa (1913–1984), a high-ranking monk-official who lived next to the Shédras and would later become Tibet's head diplomat (foreign affairs secretary). Several young nuns were also present. They were all from aristocratic families and looked very elegant. I reveled in the unique sound effect of chanting as it integrated both male and female voices. I couldn't keep my eyes on my prayer texts. From time to time I would peek at the nuns sitting across from my master and me. When my eyes met those of one nun, she gave me a sweet smile. I looked again after a little while, and her eyes met mine and she smiled again. We then made eye contact and began smiling back and forth. When she saw me step out of the room during the break, she got up and passed by me, pressing her body lightly against mine. A strange and ecstatic feeling seized me. When my tutor and I returned to our retreat after the prayers, I couldn't wait to be invited again for prayers the next day. Unfortunately, these prayers didn't happen until two days later. It was a long wait for me, but I was overjoyed to have another chance to see this pretty nun. Once again, our intimacy was conveyed through eye contact and smiles. It was fantastic.

I was also delighted to see many beautiful women in the Dedrug Residence. They included the Dedrug's sisters from the Langdün family, his cousins, and guests from other noble families. I frequented the Dedrug Residence because my tutor Lama Jampel Samphel had another disciple, Lama Tupten Tarchin, who was tutoring Dedrug. He entrusted me with assisting Dedrug as his learning mate. I also saw the woman from the Chakrong House who had gotten the Tsémönling expelled. She was beautiful, partly explaining why this high-ranking *tulku* fell for her. As a monk, I couldn't interact with these women directly, let alone initiate contact. However, some of them showed interest in me with their eyes, smiles, and little tricks. For example, when the Dedrug's sister approached to present me with oranges and other delicacies, she might take the opportunity to press her hands against mine as if by accident, making my heart pound. Once I attended a ten-day dharma teaching by Shokdruk Kyapgön at the Yutok family residence. One girl from this family gave me a pleasant smile and one day, she patted herself on the forehead with one of her hands, conveying that we should meet afterward. During the break, her male attendant came to me and soundlessly pointed to a chamber with his fingers. I entered the room, and the girl was already there. She asked me to be seated. But how could I, a monk, be seated there with a girl alone in this chamber? So I found an excuse and left immediately.

Later I shared this encounter with the young *tulku*, the same one with whom I often had monk's sex. He said that it wasn't uncommon for women to take such initiative and that it often happened to him. Some women from aristocratic families would come forward and squeeze him when no one was paying attention. Once he was even "kidnapped" by two nuns on the street whom he had previously met and taken to their rooms for "monk's sex" with both of them. I also had sexual urges and fantasies about these elegant women. When I was seventeen or eighteen, my sexual desire grew considerably. However, the principle of monastic celibacy didn't allow me to turn such fantasies into realities. With the monk's robe on, I was still trying to avoid direct interaction with women. Yet there was something else to which I was deeply attracted: the colorful life that every young man deserves.

From my observations, aristocrats knew how to enjoy their lives. They played mahjong and cards, drank, sang, and danced. I was keen on singing and dancing. Singing was one of the most popular pastimes for aristocratic youth. Some women had unbelievably beautiful voices. When they performed the *aché lhamo* (Tibetan opera) and *nangma* (a traditional form of dance music in Lhasa and Central Tibet), I was mesmerized by the rhythmic rises and falls in pitch and the euphonious melodies. Even today, I still remember the lyrics and tunes of some of these songs. Moreover, occasionally I heard a gramophone in aristocratic and senior lamas' homes, playing records from the Han region and India. Listening to them brought back memories of my carefree childhood at Sönamyak, where I played with this music machine and took it apart to see where the sound came from. These amusements helped briefly release some of the intense pressure of my studies. Many tutors would not even allow their disciples to listen to the opera, songs, or the gramophone because it was considered a distraction. Luckily, my tutor was more open-minded. Even so, my monk status meant that I was not supposed to indulge in the types of fun that laypeople were entitled to.

So I asked myself, what was the point of a monotonous monastic life? If other people could enjoy their lives fully in this way, having sex, playing games, drinking, singing, and dancing, why shouldn't I? This was not the only reason I desired to leave the monastic life. I was becoming sick of the omnipresent hypocrisy, corruption, and dirty politics in Lhasa. People in Gyalrong, like everywhere else in Greater Tibet, saw Lhasa as a holy city and thought that enrolling in one of its three main monasteries meant one would be conferred with immeasurable glory and merit. I honestly thought it was my genuine luck to make it from such a remote region as my hometown to this heavenly city. However, as time passed, I saw its unpleasant underbelly.

I lamented the pervasive sexuality in these monasteries.[2] Based on my observation and experience, at least 60 percent of the monks were engaged in such behaviors. It was not uncommon that two crowds of monks would fight over a good-looking teenage monk. This kind of competition manifested on the surface, so to an outsider, it would look like the two sides were clashing with each other over something else. Even worse, some prominent lamas seemed serious on the surface, but many also were engaged in "monk's sex." High-ranking lamas seeking sexual partners frequently approached me. Likewise, many of the government's serious-looking monastic officials (Tib. *tsédrung*) were accompanied wherever they went by good-looking young attendants, who were probably also their sexual partners. This wasn't a secret. Everyone knew about it but didn't consider it a big deal. If this was not the most notorious kind of hypocrisy, what was it?

I started to question the principle of celibacy in Tibetan Buddhism, especially in the Gelugpa tradition. The Gelugpa developed a very elaborate institution of celibacy for its monks by reiterating its significance and merits. Nonetheless, monks were all human and couldn't eliminate their biological nature, particularly sexual desires. Only a tiny percentage of the human population can cultivate a unique ability through training to leave behind their sexual urges, so celibacy should be reserved specifically for them. However, due to the practice of mass monasticism in Greater Tibet, about one-fourth of our male population became monks. I wondered, was it realistic to require these monks to be celibate and repress their sexual desires? As a consequence of this impracticable mandate, monks invented "monk's sex" to satisfy their urges and bypass the celibacy principle. What was the point in establishing such a stringent and unreasonable principle in the first place? We might even condone this kind of practice among monks for the time being. After all, we all have sexual desire, and monks must find ways to release it. However, I was told by other monks that married aristocrats would engage in homosexual activities as well. It was said that women tended to have a strange odor during the summer, so their husbands would find handsome young men to make love to during those times. How disgusting!

Moreover, I thought monks would cherish the rare opportunity to come and study in these celebrated monasteries. To my shock, most were not very interested in learning, and probably only a fifth were serious about it. A few monks from aristocratic families with the status of "dharma student of the monastic college" would surreptitiously sniff a type of tobacco imported from India during the prayer sessions in the general assembly hall. This was part of their aristocratic lifestyle. They were also well-dressed and well-fed, in sharp contrast to the ordinary monks and those of us with *tulku* status from remote parts of Greater Tibet. With such an easy life, what kind of incentive did these aristocratic monks have to learn? Next, if the monks from aristocratic families behaved like this, how could we expect lay aristocrats to act differently? I was inclined to believe that Lhasa aristocrats possessed and represented the most elegant forms of Tibetan culture in different aspects, such as their manners, speech, dress, performing arts, cuisine, and so on, because they had all the resources necessary to cultivate their high tastes. But the question became, how did they obtain these resources? The simple answer is through exploitation and corruption. How could aristocrats sustain their luxurious and comfortable life without capitalizing on the masses' sweat and suffering?

This was one of the popular topics among my tutor and other Geshés when they met for conversation. Since they were familiar with various aristocrats, they often provided concrete examples of this dirty business. These Geshés shared a lot of news and opinions on political struggles in Lhasa. According to them, the regent, Reting Rinpoche, at that time had offended the most powerful aristocrats by purposefully selecting a boy from remote Amdo as the Fourteenth Dalai Lama. Because of this, the aristocrats said that they and their monastic allies had forced the Reting to resign and imprisoned him, and that his sudden death was part of their revenge.[3] Both the Reting and his opponents were playing political games that had little to do with the sanctity of religion. When the Reting incident occurred, I was staying in Lhasa for the Small Prayer Festival (Tib. *tsokchö mönlam*) in February 1947. It had just concluded, and I was still at my treasurer's residence. Suddenly one day, a curfew was imposed, and soldiers quickly guarded all the city's key routes. Few knew what was happening initially, but we all knew something was seriously wrong. My treasurer heard that the Tibetan Kashag government had dispatched soldiers to Reting Monastery to arrest the Reting Rinpoche, who was accused of trying to regain the regency by assassinating the acting regent, the Taktra Rinpoche.

We went up to the roof of my treasurer's residence to look in the direction of Sera Monastery and see if that monastery was taking any action to rescue the Reting, since he was from Sera Jé College and its abbot (Ngawang Gyatso [1894–1968]) was his close ally.[4] Around dusk, we saw several hundred soldiers on horseback in a long queue passing by Sera on their way to Lhasa. We assumed that the Reting had been caught and was being taken back to Lhasa. We didn't see hordes of monks emerge from the monastery to intercept these soldiers. Later, I heard that Sera did arm its monks and dispatched them to intercept the Kashag soldiers on another, incorrect route to the Reting. We heard intermittent gunshots and cannon fire coming from that direction beginning the following morning and lasting about three days. We were told that Sera was being besieged and attacked by the Kashag soldiers. I was struck by this because a monastery was supposed to be a sacred place; how could the Kashag government order this assault?

The incident and the Geshés' accounts affected me profoundly, and I became aware that the monastic and aristocratic systems were contaminated and irredeemable. I also concluded that the reincarnation system was fraudulent and overly decadent. I had thought that even if I were a fake, other *tulku*s must be genuine and gifted. However, as I met and learned more about *tulku*s, I understood that some were truly dumb and mediocre, displaying no particular natural gifts. Despite the prominent role of the Dedrug lineage in Lhasa and Gelugpa, the incumbent Dedrug that I knew was one of those mediocre *tulku*s. He was said to have even been considered one of the major candidates to be recognized as the Fourteenth Dalai Lama. He appeared bright but was slow-witted when it came to study. No matter how I tried to help him understand texts, he rarely comprehended anything. As time passed, this corrupt system made better sense to me. Since the selection of the Dalai Lama was a product of political manipulation, what credibility did the reincarnation system have? This discovery made me even less willing to pretend to be a *tulku*.

What I heard and experienced convinced me that I should leave behind all this dirty business and embrace an alternative lifestyle to become an ordinary person. So I told myself that I should spend at least twenty years exploring a new life as a layperson before choosing to return to the monkhood if that was what I wished. To do so, I had to obtain freedom above all else. First I had to leave Lhasa. This dream wouldn't be plausible if I remained. My master would tighten his control over my turbulent heart and convince me to focus on monastic training. And as my attendant didn't even allow me to have adequate food, what kind of freedom could I expect from him? Moreover, practically speaking, no aristocratic women or their families in Lhasa would accept me if I took off my robe to be an ordinary person.

I was not so naïve as to imagine that there were no dirty politics back in my hometown. The chieftain and magistrate wanted to take advantage of my *tulku* status for their purposes, and they could drop me again if they found I had little value. Nonetheless, I was sure I would have much more control over my life in my hometown than in Lhasa. At least there, I had my family, relatives, and friends. While planning my return, I was enraged to hear that my brother had fled Sönamyak to Okzhi because of clashes with local bullies and that they had also beaten my father. The acting magistrate of Sönamyak, Zungchen Drölma, had promised to take care of my family before I left for Lhasa, but she broke her promise again. I decided to leave Lhasa as soon as possible, but I had to find a legitimate excuse to convince my tutor to endorse my plan. Fortunately, an opportunity popped up. The money I had brought with me to Lhasa was almost gone. I had sent letters requesting money to both the Sönamyak magistrate and the Okzhi king, but it had never arrived. So I told my tutor that I would return to my hometown to fetch the funds on my own and promised I would return in three years. As expected, he didn't agree at first, but at that time, my treasurer also wanted to return, as he was getting old. With his persuasion, my tutor acquiesced to our plan. Unexpectedly, though, Sertsa Géshé, originally from Okzhi and an assistant tutor to the Dalai Lama, intervened. He said he would provide for me financially on behalf of the Okzhi kingdom, with the condition that Sönamyak would discontinue involvement in my future training. This complicated the situation. I had to improvise a better excuse for my departure. So I said that I had left home at a young age and missed my parents. I also told them I had been working hard and wanted to take a break.

My plan was eventually approved, with my insistence and promise to return within three years. With about ten monks from Okzhi and Sönamyak, I made the trip back via the Northern Route. My desire for a new life and freedom became a possibility.

ACT III

Heaven and Hell in the New China
(1949–1976)

Chapter Seven

RESHUFFLING POWERS

On my return to Tsanlha, I was excited about the prospect of a new life. I could finally break away from the constraints in Lhasa, my cold-blooded attendant, my austere tutor, and the hypocritical monastic and aristocratic politics. Nonetheless, it wouldn't be easy for me to become an ordinary person. The magistrate and chieftain certainly wouldn't approve, and I had to seriously consider how to survive once I relinquished my *tulku* status. Therefore, upon my return in the fall of 1948, I started to take concrete steps to overcome all these possible barriers. I didn't expect, however, that I was about to become deeply involved in the newly emerging political landscape of Tsanlha and subsequently be seen by the CCP as a significant local force and potential ally.

My plan to leave the *tulku* status behind included three significant tasks and steps. First, I wanted to rebuild the monastery destroyed during the 1917 rebellion. Since the Sönamyak magistrate and people had provided for me and sent me to Lhasa, I couldn't be ungrateful to them for what they had done. But how was I supposed to return their favors? I thought the best way was to have the monastery restored for them. This was not an easy mission, or it already would have been rebuilt. I had an advantage in fulfilling this task, however. Religion played a vital role in the lives of the Sönamyak people, who would surely endorse my plan. The magistrate had no reason to oppose this idea either. The only problem was money. So I decided to use the funds from the Okzhi king and people for the reconstruction project. This money was initially collected to pay for my continued study and living expenses in Lhasa because I was expected to return in three years to finish my studies. With the thorny financial issue resolved, I made other necessary preparations like obtaining building materials, personnel, and designs. By the fall of 1949, I could assemble a large group of people to fell and haul trees for timber for the rebuilding.

About 800 trees were cut for this purpose. Transporting them back to the monastery was not a simple feat. As the trees fell on the other side of the mountain, we had to move them over the mountaintop before bringing them down to our monastery, located about halfway down the valley. More than 100 young men and about 30 monks joined in to help. Some villagers also contributed their cattle to help pull the trees. I was the leader and pioneer behind this effort. I participated in cutting the trees and moving them. Thanks to my uncle's encouragement, I had mastered these skills at a young age before I went to Lhasa. As a result, I was better at these activities than most people. The felled trees were then piled up in an open field below the monastery, but construction never began because Liberation happened soon after.

My second step to gaining freedom was obtaining a plot of land for myself to rely on for survival. The former *tulku* had a piece of land with fertile soil on a foothill. It was 30 *mu* (2 hectares), the same size each family was allocated, on average. However, after the 1917 rebellion, the land had been leased by the magistrate and monastery to a local Han gangster surnamed He, who was the head of a Gown Brothers faction. Although the contract had expired by the time I returned to Sönamyak, the gangster refused to return the land to us. I requested that the Sönamyak magistrate and the Okzhi king settle this matter for me, but the gangster dismissed their demands immediately. This refusal was what I had wanted. As a formality, I was initially obliged to ask for the local authorities' support. If they had succeeded in regaining the land, I would have been indebted to them. Since their negotiations failed, I could take back the land without their interference.

I purchased more than ten rifles and pistols for this purpose. Moreover, as almost every household owned at least one gun, it wasn't difficult to borrow more guns. The monks, their families, and my relatives at Okzhi all agreed to support me with their weapons. I was close to the teenage son of the Okzhi king, who promised to lend more than twenty rifles and a machine gun without his parents' knowledge. As a result, I gathered about eighty people, all armed, and dozens of others who would help sow the crops for me after reclaiming the land. The shooters were spread out to guard the key passes and other strategic places, and the rest were starting to uproot the opium poppies and wheat grown by the Han gangster before setting about plowing the land and sowing crops. The gangster didn't show up during this. Later I was told that he hid in a house nearby to watch what was happening. He must have been intimidated and didn't dare oppose me afterward. In this way, I reclaimed this piece of land in the spring of 1949. I asked my parents to take care of it on my behalf in 1951 when I left for Chengdu.

The third step was to find a partner. From talking with my close associates, both monks and laymen, I learned that a noble family at Drapa had two unmarried daughters. So I decided to pass by this place purposefully. Hearing about my visit, the family invited me into their home. I found that the younger sister suited me best, so I started to play little games with her, for instance, throwing small stones at her from my room upstairs when she was walking by. She got the message and began smiling back at me and dressing up whenever we saw each other. After I returned to the monastery, I sent for her. Her parents permitted her to visit Sönamyak on her own because we had come up with an excuse to convince them—that she would see her uncle, another noble, who lived near my monastery. After she arrived, I secretly kept her in my chamber at the monastery. We spent a few romantic days together before she went to visit her uncle. Unexpectedly, her uncle had seen her when she was traveling to the monastery, accompanied by the two monks I had sent to fetch her, and he questioned her until she confessed to our tryst. Her uncle told her to keep it discreet, and in a way, acquiesced to our relationship. We kept our relationship secret for another year before the new Communist state sent me to Chengdu to study Party policy and Marxism in 1951.

Even though I was on my way to accomplishing all three of my objectives, there were still substantial hurdles for me to pursue a normal life. The land I had regained still belonged to the *tulku* and the monastery. If I were to renounce my *tulku* status, the land would probably be taken away from me. This also meant that my lover's noble family would not allow their daughter to marry me, since I would be a nobody without the aura of a *tulku*. However, the CCP and PLA would soon arrive to liberate Tsanlha and Sönamyak from the Kuomintang and the old system, and unexpectedly also liberate me from these troubles.

In a way, I chose to be liberated and became a Communist ally. The political situation in Tsanlha around Liberation was chaotic, and most locals, including the nobles, didn't have a clear idea of the direction the local society was heading. Consequently, various political powers and people were making choices while evaluating their individual situations. As a *tulku*, I had influence in Tsanlha, especially at Sönamyak. Therefore, different forces, including the CCP, hoped to enlist my support. The dominant local forces included the Gown Brothers, magistrates, chieftains, and other strongmen. The chaotic political situation had much to do with the overwhelming influence of the local Gown Brothers factions. As noted earlier, Tsanlha was known as a place of many poppies, many guns, and many bandits. Before I left for Lhasa in 1941, social order was eroding. When I returned to Tsanlha in 1948, I found that the local society was in more significant turmoil, meaning that there were more guns, opium, and bandits.[1] The bandits were mainly the Gown Brothers or their allies, who constantly assaulted and raided travelers, porters, and traders. With the growing opium market and the subsequent boom in the gun trade, the local Gown Brothers were growing in numbers and power. Some of the more powerful factions had several hundred followers, having built extensive networks with gangsters in Wenchuan, Dujiangyan, and other places.[2] They frequently clashed with one another for control of the lucrative opium trade. Gunfights among the various factions were an almost daily occurrence.

Consequently, with their armed forces, the gangsters, especially the big ones, became de facto leaders of various Han communities. The successive mayors had little choice but to build alliances with these Han bullies by appointing them as government representatives to regulate local affairs. Nonetheless, the Gown Brothers usually only controlled and harassed the Han, not the Gyalongwa; we had our chieftains and magistrates. It was rare for the Gown Brothers to initiate a clash or raid against the local Gyalrongwa. The Gyalrong nobles were obligated to safeguard the security and interests of their subjects, or risk being sidelined or overthrown for being indifferent or incapable. To this end, the nobles would call together a group of people to take revenge against the Han if the latter bullied their subjects.

Accordingly, most Gown Brothers tried to avoid such confrontations. However, they became more powerful around the time of Liberation. With increasing guns and followers, some gangsters became less prudent in their dealings with the Gyalrongwa and their nobles.

I'll relate two episodes of my interactions with the Gown Brothers. First, a few Han porters, responsible for conveying baggage from my Lhasa trip from the seat of Rongdrak back to Sönamyak, were captured and robbed by Gown Brothers bandits. This was after my companions and I had left for Sönamyak, a day earlier. The Sönamyak nobles were infuriated at news of the robbery and said they would send gunmen to retrieve the baggage by force. Before that happened, the Han porters were released, and our luggage was returned when the gangsters realized it belonged to me. A second example is the case of my land dispute and the gangster who dared to ignore the mediation attempts by the magistrate and chieftain but was not audacious enough to confront me because I had more guns and people. This episode also turned out well for me.

The Gown Brothers believed in the law of the jungle and somehow saw me as someone near the top of the social food chain. Based on this understanding, they later tried to align themselves with me. As it happened, small and big Gown Brothers factions were resolute fighters against the PLA. Usually they had little choice but to go into a fierce battle with the soldiers because they knew that the Communists would never pardon their past misdeeds, which included alliances with the Kuomintang and committing mass murders. At the same time, they knew that their alliance with the local Gyalrongwa was crucial in forming a more effective bulwark against the PLA. They could enlist support from some Gyalrong nobles and their subjects in this endeavor. However, most locals took a wait-and-see approach in the uncertain political environment.

The PLA men arrived in Tsanlha in October 1950.[3] Prior to that, many Kuomintang officers and soldiers had passed through Sönamyak, typically in bands of ten to twenty. Some of these officers, soldiers, and other random Han requested a meeting with me. Since I didn't know their intentions or desire to become embroiled in an increasingly complex political climate, I dismissed these meeting requests altogether. Most of the time, my armed monk associates questioned and stopped these people at the entrance to the monastery before I had to reject them on my own. According to my associates, many of these soldiers had been defeated in their battles against the

PLA and left the area to flee elsewhere. Apart from this limited information, I had little idea what had really happened to these soldiers and where they were going. I thought at the time that this political turmoil was the exclusive business of the Han, like some sort of dogfight among themselves. Since it didn't concern us much, why should I care? It soon became obvious that I was very wrong and had to make my own political choices, both easy and difficult ones. Luckily, the CCP would say I had made the right choices.

Before I returned to Sönamyak from Lhasa, a new magistrate called Gu Longhai (hereafter Gu Junior) replaced the former magistrate. He was married to the Sönamyak Princess, Mu Lanfen, the former magistrate's daughter. You may recall she was my childhood playmate and denigrated me with "Beggar Lama." Gu Junior was one of the three sons of Gu Danchi (hereafter Old Gu), the magistrate of Jémé.[4] Old Gu was influential in Tsanlha. He had studied Chinese as a child and was later enrolled in a Republican army school. He was said to be a close associate of Deng Xihou, one of the most important warlords in Sichuan. Old Gu sent two of his sons, including Gu Junior, for training at a military academy (the Seventh Branch of the Central Army Military Academy, Guiyang Branch). Both were awarded the rank of lieutenant colonel upon graduation in the late 1940s.

However, Gu Junior didn't enjoy high standing among the Sönamyak nobles and people due to his arrogance and cruelty. Once he ordered his adjutant, a Han officer, to shoot a servant on the spot. This servant was a good-looking young man suspected of having an affair with Gu Junior's wife, the Sönamyak Princess. Nonetheless, few people knew the actual reason behind this incident. Instead, they were made to believe that this servant was killed for having put too much salt in Gu Junior's tea. People at Sönamyak were disturbed by Gu Junior's brutality for such a trivial offense, and some began to consider whether he should be deposed or even killed. Soon after, someone shot through his bedroom window one night, but he luckily survived this assassination attempt. To remove him once and for all, some people at Sönamyak believed my support was crucial because most locals respected me. Some nobles approached me and requested that I become their new magistrate. If I said yes, they said they would immediately begin a revolt to topple Gu Junior, knowing that I also didn't get along with him. When I returned from Lhasa, over a thousand people from Sönamyak, Okzhi, and Jémé came to welcome me. In contrast, when Gu Junior came to Sönamyak for his wedding, the locals didn't enthusiastically receive him, so he was jealous of me.

Once the Okzhi prince came to Sönamyak for an outing and invited me to his campsite at a meadow near the hilltop, where we had fun shooting machine guns into the sky. Gu Junior happened to be staying below the area where we were shooting and assumed I was purposely doing it to threaten him; he soon ordered his soldiers to simulate an attack on my monastery under the guise of a military drill. Inevitably, our mutual antagonism grew. Despite this, I wasn't interested in replacing him and becoming the magistrate. I was still considering whether to rid myself of the *tulku* status to live a normal life. How could I possibly complicate the whole thing even further by endorsing their plan and taking the magistrate position? I also had to consider the influence of Gu Junior's father, Old Gu. With a formidable Sichuan warlord (Deng Xihou) behind the Gu family, they could quickly raze our monastery and destroy me. So I immediately declined the Sönamyak nobles' request, which was an easy decision.

This didn't deter them from pressuring me to accept their plan. Some Gown Brothers joined the petition because they saw my potential in helping to unify all Sönamyak, which would be favorable for their schemes to consolidate their power base against the Communists. After I explicitly reiterated my stance of noninvolvement, the Gown Brothers and the Gyalrong nobles started subtly threatening me. I was told that it wasn't up to me to decide if I wanted to be the new magistrate because the Sönamyak people provided for me and warned that the Kuomintang would punish me for being unhelpful in the fight against the Communists once the Kuomintang regained complete control over Tsanlha. Many at that time assumed that the PLA would just go away at a certain point, like their predecessor, the Red Army, had more than a decade earlier, and that the Kuomintang would return.

These threats were primarily verbal, but the petitioners also hinted that they would resort to force if necessary; that never happened. I had well-armed monk aides and close associates who were a group of reckless, fearless young men. I was also young and restless and claimed no authority of a *tulku* over others. I could get along with people, especially these adventurous young men. We had a wonderful time together, drinking, wrestling, picnicking, and so on. As a result, they were very loyal and willing to risk their lives for my safety and well-being. In addition, I had allies among the

Gyalrong nobles, such as Noble Lan Shaoqing (hereafter Noble Lan), my lover's uncle, who would follow my lead. Therefore, those nobles and Gown Brothers who attempted to coerce me into following their agenda had to consider the likely consequences of their actions. Basically, they must think twice whether they could afford to become my enemy. The tensions and potential alliances between me and the others nonetheless meant little in the face of the rapidly transforming political environment. Ultimately, we were all carried away by the unprecedented titanic political tides.

Noble Lan was soon recruited by the CCP, purely by accident. When some Gown Brothers were defeated at Okzhi by the PLA and fled to Söna-myak, they robbed one native family, who were Noble Lan's subjects. In response, Noble Lan organized a retaliation squad to fight against these gangsters. While the squad was still engaged in fierce battles, the PLA men who originally came after the gangsters also arrived. The PLA officers were impressed with Noble Lan and judged he had a progressive political stance that could help them block the reactionary Gown Brothers. Noble Lan was then seen as a close ally and was later offered a key position at a governmental agency. He and some other nobles happened to make the "right choice" in this way, while others made the "wrong choice" in the CCP's view. Based on my knowledge about local Gyalrongwa's choices, especially those of the magistrates and chieftains, the so-called right or wrong choices didn't have much to do with progressive or reactionary stances. Some Gyalrongwa embraced social change, though, especially if they believed local society was becoming overly corrupt and lawless. Even so, in truth, the choices of most locals were based chiefly on pragmatic assessments of the political situation in terms of their advantages.

An example of this is the CCP labeling the Okzhi queen a reactionary enemy of the people. She was probably neither a big fan of the Kuomintang nor an absolute opponent of the CCP. She simply wanted to make the best of the opaque political situation. However, she misjudged, and the CCP executed her for making the "wrong choice." Overall, the queen was a complex manipulative figure. Originally from a low-ranking noble family, she was at first considered incompatible with the king. She could have been killed in an uprising brewing among the Okzhi people at that time if it hadn't been for the intervention of the then Han mayor. This likely contributed to her distrust of local Gyalrongwa and her great hunger for power. She actively built connections with high-ranking Kuomintang officials in

Chengdu to enhance her influence, and also engaged local Gown Brothers as her allies and associates. She gradually sidelined the king and became the actual power holder.

The queen even attended Kuomintang-organized guerrilla training (the "Central Military Academy guerrilla training for backbones, fifth term"; "backbone" here refers to foundation of the guerrilla forces) in Chengdu in November 1949, around the time of Liberation. This training was intended to motivate participants in their devotion to the Kuomintang cause against the CCP and teach specific strategies to deal with the PLA. She was received by the governor of Sichuan, Wang Linji, who armed her with weapons and ammunition for upcoming battles against the Communists. The queen went to Chengdu with more than fifty subordinates, including my elder brother. Due to a feud with a local Sönamyak household, he had fled to Okzhi to seek protection from the queen, who made him her bodyguard. However, without his or the other subordinates' knowledge, the queen provided all their names to the Kuomintang, who then enrolled them as new party members. Before long, in the spring of 1950, she and the king received the Kuomintang officers (headed by Zhou Xunyu, a vital leader of the anti-Communist base in Sichuan) who had fled to Tsanlha to establish a new guerrilla base.

This didn't prevent the Okzhi king and queen from allying with the Communists, at least on the surface. When PLA soldiers arrived in October 1950, the couple expressed willingness to cooperate with the new government. They, especially the queen, scrutinized the actions of the CCP to judge their trustworthiness and rescued and released more than twenty PLA soldiers her allies had captured during this period. However, her Han gangster allies convinced her that the new regime would show no leniency toward the ruling class once it gained complete control over Tsanlha. So that winter, she endorsed a revolt against the CCP, which the Gown Brothers initiated.[5] Her squad was soon defeated by the PLA, whose reinforcements had been transferred from Maoxian, the then capital of the newly established Sichuan Tibetan Autonomous Region. She had to hide in the forests with her guards and sneak about from one place to another to escape.

Under this circumstance, it was time for me to make a challenging choice again. The queen wanted me to arm my monk associates to help her in the revolt when needed, so she sent a message saying that she had plenty of guns and ammunition and I could ask for as much as I needed. I declined her offer, but she still sent me a machine gun through her nephew, Noble Wang Guangquan. I learned from him that the queen wanted me to take her to Lhasa if her revolt was crushed. She and her confidants couldn't speak Kham Tibetan or the nomadic Tibetan dialect; nor did they know the route to Lhasa. Moreover, she knew I had connections there and hoped to find someone like me whom she could fully trust for this critical mission. This was a dilemma. The queen had always been kind to me since childhood and took my brother in when he had to flee Sönamyak. To complicate the situation, she sent her two teenage sons to my monastery seeking protection from me. Her elder son was quite close to me and even offered his help while I was attempting to reclaim my land from the Gown Brothers. How could I turn them away? I had to host them. I discussed this matter with my associates whom I always convened to collectively decide essential issues. They said that it was risky to keep the Okzhi princes with us because we couldn't guarantee their absolute safety and we should avoid getting involved in the messy political situation. Thus, they advised me to send these two boys away as soon as possible.

A few days later, the queen sent for her sons and me and asked us to meet her at her secret place in the Sönamyak forests. We made the trip at night to avoid detection. The queen was grateful for our safe arrival and arranged a tent for me and my seven or eight associates to stay in that night. I invented an excuse, saying I had to return to the monastery to prepare for the trip to Lhasa. She consented, and my associates and I quickly returned. I was trying my best to disentangle myself from her. Later she dispatched several groups of people to urge me to flee to Lhasa with her right away, but each time I made excuses such as that I had to go to the county seat for a meeting with the new mayor.

By that time, I was interacting with Communist officials and officers and was gradually being drawn in by the CCP's refreshing ideas. However, I was concerned that the new regime would find fault with me because I had provided sanctuary for the two Okzhi princes. My associates reassured me that we hadn't done anything wrong in hosting these princes since we hadn't invited them. When the Maoxian Military Division vice-commander, Men Guoliang (hereafter Commander Men), passed through Sönamyak, he requested that we meet on May 7, 1951, at the newly established township seat in the foothills.[6] Before this meeting, Commander Men sent his greetings through a well-respected lama from Tawé Monastery, Potsachi Lama, who was not getting along with the Okzhi king and queen. His interactions with the CCP had convinced him of their sincerity. In his letter, the lama asked me to have faith in the CCP and not act against the revolutionary tides. So I went downhill with two monks and met in the township office with Commander Men, who explained the CCP policy. He said the Kuomintang had undermined ethnic unity and assured me that all people and ethnic groups would be treated equally after Liberation. He also said that in new China, people had the freedom to believe or not believe in religion. It was the first time I had heard that people had freedom to not believe in religion. I was delighted to learn this because the principle fit perfectly with my desire to have the freedom to break away from a restrained religious life. In the meantime, I was also asked to listen to their radio broadcasting in Tibetan and hear about ongoing negotiations between the Tibetan Kashag government and Beijing on the prospect of the peaceful Liberation of Tibet.[7] I was also curious to hear the revolutionary song "Tuanjie jiushi liliang" (Unity is strength) on the radio; it was also sung in Tibetan. Then Commander Men showed me to a room where intelligence was sent and received through a radio transmitter. The next day he asked his subordinate, Representative Peng (Peng Yuming), to escort me back to the monastery. Peng stayed with me for three or four days and elaborated on CCP policies.

A few days later, I was asked to attend a meeting in Fubian, the seat of the newly established Third District, one of the four districts in the county, which incorporated the previous Sönamyak and part of the Jémé magistratures. Commander Men and Mayor Wang Lezhai (hereafter Mayor Wang) chaired the meeting held in a courtyard, attended by some nobles I knew and many others I didn't. The meeting focused on clarifying various Party policies and motivating people to support the new government, such as its policies for ethnic equality, agricultural production, etc. At the end, individuals who had joined in the revolt against the CCP were publicly sentenced for their crimes. Many of them were immediately dragged out of the courtyard and executed. The convicts were all Han, including the Gown Brothers and others. No Gyalrongwa were sentenced or executed at this meeting because no revolts occurred in Sönamyak or Jémé. In most cases, the natives were subject to the orders of their chieftain, magistrate, or nobles to either revolt against or cooperate with the new regime. However, it was not uncommon for people to find ways to circumvent such an order on their own. It so happened that the Sönamyak and Jémé magistrates and people chose to cooperate with the CCP and PLA rather than revolt.

The Jémé magistrate, Old Gu, was a close ally of the Kuomintang, and it was possible that he could have been involved in a revolt against the PLA. That said, his close ally, the warlord Deng Xihou in Chengdu, had already surrendered to the CCP and sent a letter to Gu urging him to yield to the PLA. His son, Gu Junior, the magistrate of Sönamyak, also didn't organize a revolt. My noninvolvement stance may have contributed to this status quo. As mentioned, some people at Sönamyak wanted me to replace Gu Junior and be their new magistrate. If I had agreed, a fierce battle between the Gu family and my supporters at Sönamyak would have been inevitable. Although I don't know precisely what the outcome would have been, we likely would have had conflict with the PLA because the Gu family had already become new allies of the CCP, and the Gown Brothers, who had also pushed for me to replace Gu Junior, would have found a way to steer the battle toward attacking the PLA.

As the new regime scrutinized me, I was doing the same to them. In order to avoid being swayed by their potentially one-sided propaganda, I sought out other people and asked them to share their impressions and experiences with the new regime and PLA soldiers. At the same time, I kept a close eye on what was happening on the ground. The PLA officers, soldiers, and government officials I met were friendly and treated the Gyalrongwa equally. Then, when I arrived in the county seat to meet Mayor Wang, I saw him carrying firewood on his back that he had collected for the county government kitchen. I was struck by what I was witnessing. The action was worth thousands of pretty and heroic words. The kings and magistrates had servants and subordinates for this lowly job. I could hardly believe that I was seeing a mayor, with an official rank higher than even our kings and magistrates, doing something like this. I was thus convinced that the CCP's claims about equality weren't mere slogans. Since childhood, I had been uncomfortable with the old system allowing nobles to bully and oppress others. In a word, I was embracing the new society and its changes and looked forward to the day when equality among different people and ethnic groups would finally be realized.

The Okzhi queen would not give up on me, however. In a final attempt, she sent her confidant, Wang Yuanzhi. He had been a noble in Sönamyak, but due to a dispute with locals and the magistrate, he sought refuge under the queen. He was a formidable warrior, and most people feared him, including the monks and me. My monk associates could easily dismiss the queen's other messengers because we had enough weapons and manpower to fight back if they dared threaten or kidnap me. However, my associates would have had difficulty deterring Wang Yuanzhi from taking me away. Luckily, the problem was resolved when the PLA captured him on his way to my monastery. In October 1951 the queen was also taken, at Dzigak in today's Barkham, when her relatives with whom she had sought refuge betrayed her. Before long, in May 1952, the PLA executed her.

As for the Okzhi king, he fled with several bodyguards and hid in the forest, fearing the CCP's retaliation and execution. He sent a bodyguard to my monastery to ask for food from time to time. I never asked where he was hiding, but I assumed it was not too far away. Once when I was called to a meeting at the county seat, I overhead Mayor Wang discussing the king's whereabouts. I had been interacting with these officials long enough to assume that the king would be exempt from execution because the revolt was led by the queen, and especially since she had deserted him in her flight. When I told the mayor that I knew where the king was, he was overjoyed and asked me if I could find the king on his behalf. I sent an associate to meet and persuade the king to come out of hiding, and he agreed to come out of the forest in June 1951. As promised, the new regime didn't execute him and later even offered him a government position.

Many people at Sönamyak and Tsanlha hid in the forests at the start of Liberation, even though they weren't part of the reactionary ruling class in the eyes of the new regime. Most initially feared and had negative opinions of the new regime after their experience with looting and killing by the Red Army (the PLA's predecessors). Those in hiding occasionally sent people to see me at the monastery, inquiring about my interactions and experiences with the CCP. I told them what I had seen and experienced personally, including what Commander Men and Mayor Wang said and did. As a result, people began to come out of the forest gradually. Because of my help, the mayor and other officials spoke highly of my actions.

In a nutshell, the choices that I, the nobles, and others made were partly accidental and circumstantial. What if the Sönamyak magistrate (Gu Junior) had been overthrown or murdered by his opponents? Was I supposed to become the new magistrate, as many had hoped? What if Noble Lan hadn't encountered the PLA when he organized that attack on the Gown Brothers? Would he have become a "reactionary" later by joining the revolt against the PLA instead? What if Wang Yuanzhi, the associate of the Okzhi queen, hadn't been captured by the PLA on his way to get me? Would he have been able to force me to join the queen in her escape to Lhasa? Could we have made it to Lhasa successfully? What next? These accidents and circumstances, derived from my own experiences and reflections and the sociopolitical history of Gyalrong and Tibet, make these events dramatic and captivating.

Chapter Eight

NEW SOCIETY, NEW LIFE

I was frequently required to go to the county seat and attend meetings that often included CCP propaganda and concerned mobilization of local support for the suppression of bandits and rebellions, consolidation of the United Front work through alliances with local elites and activists, enhancement of agricultural production, and so on. At such meetings, I interacted with Mayor Wang, who often called me to his side and further explained the CCP agendas for me. Once Mayor Wang told me that I should travel to Nanjing and Beijing to see the tremendous social changes there; he knew that I was curious and asked many questions about the outside world. I asked him for help arranging a trip immediately. He was impressed with my eagerness and said he would start making the necessary arrangements.

I was soon informed that I would be sent to the newly established Southwest Nationalities Institute in Chengdu to study for a year. At that time, I lacked any clear idea about the difference between a visit to Nanjing and Beijing and a study trip to Chengdu and did not care. What mattered was that I could find a legitimate excuse to leave the monastery and Sönamyak behind and explore a new life as an ordinary person in the new society of Communist China. I was so anxious to leave because I hadn't yet managed to gain the freedom I desperately desired. I had planned to restore the monastery to repay the Sönamyak people's support, but this plan was aborted due to Liberation. I had taken back the land from the Han gangster, but the land would never really be mine because it belonged to the monastery. I had a lover, but it was impossible to build a new life together because I was technically still a monk. More urgently, I had promised my tutor that I would return to Lhasa in three years; that deadline was approaching, and the monastery was preparing for my departure. Under such circumstances, I wouldn't be able to liberate myself from my troubles unless I left my home region.

Mayor Wang asked me to motivate some young people with progressive ideas to go and study along with me, a task I quickly accomplished. I had many close associates, both young monks and laymen, who would follow my lead without much prodding. Many monks would follow me, not because I was a *tulku* but because they saw me as their peer and close friend. In addition, I got along exceptionally well with other restless young men. My laymen friends tended to roam about, were not keen on farm work, or had terrible relationships with their wives and family members. In contrast, the young men who tended to stay put and work diligently in the fields would have hesitated to leave home, and their families would not have given permission. However, most people in Sönamyak and Okzhi weren't very optimistic about our Chengdu trip. Someone even told me, "The tiger is keeping its mouth wide open for you, so why will you throw yourself into it?" Many people remained suspicious about the new regime's true intentions. I soon organized a group of more than twenty people, half of whom were monks. Mayor Wang disapproved and said bringing so many monks would create the wrong impression among local Gyalrongwa that the CCP was trying to prohibit religious practice. He suggested I take only one or two associates to avoid that.

Simultaneously, the government mobilized a group of young people throughout the county to attend the training in Chengdu. Most of us were Gyalrongwa, although there were probably two or three Han people. I say "probably" because these people resembled Han, but they could have been officially identified as Hui (nationality). Eventually, our band of about thirty people left the county seat in July 1951. We were all in high spirits and sang revolutionary songs en route to Chengdu. I had learned some of these songs from PLA soldiers and was excited to learn more during our trip. The county government and monastery prepared a horse for me to ride, while my fellow passengers were supposed to go on foot. Most of the time I asked two women in our group to ride my horse. Initially they resisted out of concern for their reputations as self-reliant socialist activists and didn't use the horse until they were exhausted from climbing up the mountain pass at an altitude of more than 4,000 meters. It took us about a week to reach Chengdu. Dormitories were arranged for us, we were provided uniforms, and we were assigned to different classes. In this way, my new life started.

We were among the first batch of students at the Southwest Nationalities Institute that was established in July 1950 to train ethnic minority cadres for the Party and government of New China with Wang Weizhou as the first president.[1] He was also one of the vice-chairs of the Southwest Military and Political Committee, along with Deng Xiaoping and others, and the head of its Nationalities Affairs Commission. So President Wang was quite powerful in both Sichuan and southwest China. The multiple positions he held demonstrated the great importance attached to the role of the institute in turning ethnic elites into new socialist cadres for their respective regions.[2] The institute, comprising four classes, had started officially on June 1, 1951, one month before our arrival. The class or program size differed. Some had 70 to 80 students, while others had well beyond 100. There were about 500 students in total. Each class had an organizational structure headed by one class instructor, the equivalent of a department chair, aided by assistants and other teachers. Most of the teachers were army veterans. Not everyone appeared fully literate, but they were all eloquent and had rich knowledge of Maoist thought, CCP policies, and class struggles.

There were also a number of student leader positions at different levels, from single class to the entire institute, and several divisions of each class. I was appointed vice-president of the institute's student union and acted as chair of the class life committee in charge of matters related to student life such as dining and sanitation. Since I was the only *tulku* student on campus, the institute probably made this arrangement to accommodate my special status. Most students were from the four provinces of southwest China—Sichuan, Yunnan, Guizhou, and Xikang.[3] Nearly all were ethnic minorities, with the Tibetans and the Yi being the largest groups. Overall, Yunnan and Guizhou students had a better command of the Chinese language because most of them had attended Chinese schools for some years. In contrast, most Tibetan students had limited Chinese language skills. I could speak some Chinese, but not fluently, and I had zero reading and writing skills. Some others from Tsanlha were a little better off in this respect, but not by much. Due to our limited Chinese and the fact that we started at the school one month later than our peers, we couldn't follow the teachers or our other classmates.

We made a lot of stupid but hilarious mistakes for that reason. For instance, during class, the teachers liked to say something about *kangmei yuanchao* ("resisting U.S. aggression and aiding North Korea"). Some of us had little idea what that meant. Then one day we were taken to view a street exhibition of posters on this issue. After we returned to school, someone said, "Now I know what *kangmei yuanchao* means—it is the street's name with many posters." Ultimately, the institute had to reassemble all the Tsan-lha students who had been divided into different classes to form a new class of our own so we could learn from scratch together. As a result, the institute had a total of five classes.

Apart from lectures, learning included frequent discussion sessions. Every student was asked to reflect on what they had learned from the lectures and what they thought of specific topics, such as class struggle, American imperialism, feudalism and oppression, the role of religion in the old society, ethnic equality, and so on. I originally had difficulty understanding the teachers, so our class instructor had a woman surnamed Liu sit by me to translate. Liu was probably Han or Hui and had an excellent command of Chinese. During breaks, I would ask her to explain the lecture's content to me, and then I would take notes in Tibetan. This helped me a lot, and I could contribute some sensible remarks during discussions. This impressed my teachers, and my class instructor praised me for being hardworking and intelligent. However, they didn't know that my class performance had much to do with my monastic training in Lhasa, because I had studied many similar topics during my debates and studies at Drepung. For example, we learned that the CCP's principal tenet was to "serve the people heart and soul" (Ch. *quanxin quanyi wei renmin fuwu*). The fundamental importance of this principle is why the CCP fought against imperialism, feudalism, and crony capitalism for decades before eventually liberating the people in China from these "Three Big Mountains" oppressing us. Our teachers and the Party members in general thought this tenet was unique to the CCP, but it is also an elementary principle in Buddhism referred to as the cultivation of compassion (bodhicitta) toward sentient beings. Our tantric masters in Lhasa explained the principle in this way: We all have mothers. Our mothers have been through unimaginable pain and suffering from pregnancy to our birth and raising us. Therefore, we must be grateful to them for what they have done for us. The mothers we are referring to are not just those in our present life; in fact, all sentient beings in the Six Realms of Existence have been our mothers at some point through our numerous previous lifetimes. Therefore, we should also be grateful to them and repay their kindness to us, even though many of our mothers from past lifetimes have been reborn as animals or trapped in hell or the realm of ghosts. So we are told to cultivate compassion toward all sentient beings and to vow to become a buddha to rescue them from suffering. Our masters' vivid illustrations often moved us to tears. In this way, I could easily find Buddhist examples in the CCP's principle of "serving the people heart and soul."

Furthermore, Mao's thesis, *On Contradiction* (Ch. *Maodunlun*), wasn't too abstract for me either. This theory says that things are made of two opposing sides, good and evil, life and death, etc., and that society is subject to constant change because of endless conflicts and contradictions, say between the bourgeois and working class and between peasants and landlords. Even though the Maoist approaches to class struggle and revolution contradict the Buddhist notion of compassion and nonviolence, Buddhism shares the idea that there is innate opposition in things, especially concerning constant change and impermanence. Likewise, I found similarities in Mao's famous *On Practice* (Ch. *Shijianlun*).[4] It argues knowledge is shaped through practice, which is the source and basis of knowledge. Thus, practice is a fundamental means of examining the truth. This is also found in the essence of Buddhist teachings. As noted earlier, to cultivate compassion for other sentient beings, words alone are not enough. In addition, one must always keep others' interests at heart and do good deeds to serve people.

As a result, during our class discussions at the Southwest Nationalities Institute, I contributed remarks on Mao's theories and CCP policy by making analogies using what I had learned from my masters and scriptures in Lhasa, while some of my classmates struggled to make sense of these abstract ideas. My additions to the discussions surprised my class instructor and other teachers, who asked, "How have you learned so much about Marxism-Leninism and Chairman Mao's thoughts?" In their eyes, religion was feudal and backward, no better than opium that the ruling class used to fool the masses. The teachers didn't realize that these Communist ideas weren't as original as they thought. Instead, the Buddha had illustrated some of these theses thoroughly, and Tibetan masters had been working with them for a further thousand-plus years. But how could I tell them that? Sometimes I had to make a big show of talking about religion as an opiate too, which the political climate required.

In addition to lectures and discussions, our training at the institute involved cultivating our socialist souls through action and practice. Many students were originally from noble and elite families, the so-called ruling class, compared to the poor peasants and working classes. In daily activity, we were asked to perform jobs that some thought beneath them, like cleaning filthy public toilets. As chair of the class life committee, I was once required to lead four or five male students to clean the female toilets. Some of my cohorts grumbled, "Why don't female students clean their toilets?" I didn't feel like this job was beneath me, however. For those who don't understand Tibetan Buddhism thoroughly, it can be easy to conclude that Tibetans denigrate women. On the contrary, Tibetan Buddhism looks up to females in a way unmatched by many other religions and cultures.

First, our mothers in all our lifetimes are female. Second, in many empowerment rituals, females occupy an irreplaceable role, and without their participation and support, a practitioner cannot attain enlightenment. This is a very misunderstood aspect of Tibetan Buddhism. Most people would probably consider it blasphemous in a monastery to see male and female bodhisattva images engaged in positions of sexual union and would be unaware that this is the best illustration of the perfect union between yin (female) and yang (male) in Tibetan Buddhism. I received such training in Lhasa too. As Gelugpa, we were prohibited from having consorts or female partners participate in such rituals. However, as this kind of partnership and union was crucial in many empowerment rituals, the master would ask us trainees to imagine that we had a consort sitting across our legs. This has little to do with sexual intercourse in practice. Through visualization, the master would instruct us to regulate the flow of semen around our bodies with the support of our consorts. This is a complex procedure to explain, but the fundamental point is that we (males) must view the female partners as our equals, or else enlightenment is impossible to achieve.

In any case, I did my cleaning job dutifully and diligently without complaint. I was aware that the institute and my class instructors were using this task to test me to see whether I could lower my head and be a qualified new member of a socialist society. I wasn't doing this to impress them or because of my heightened Marxist-Maoist consciousness. It was deeply embedded in my training in Buddhist philosophy. On that account, the institute and my teachers considered me to be an activist who had developed steadfast socialist beliefs. For the same reason, I was often asked to make reports on behalf of students at the institute to visiting officials and delegates concerning my spiritual transition in the wake of my encounters with the new Communist regime and Marxist-Maoist thought.

According to the institute president and officials, I had another more prominent duty to fulfill whenever necessary. They asked me to continue to perform my role as a *tulku*, one who was no longer confined to the religious establishment but was enlightened by Maoism and socialism. This created a dilemma because I was trying to leave all the *tulku* trappings in the past and completely disengage from Sönamyak Monastery. Therefore, when the monastery steward sent someone to bring me many silver coins to spend, I didn't accept a single penny. Moreover, when the steward sent repeated messages asking me how I would like to deal with my property, I replied that it belonged to all the people at Sönamyak, not me. I told him it was up to him as my steward to decide how the property should be distributed. My parents wanted it, but I urged them not to push for this. President Wang, however, reassured me that it was honorable for me to continue to perform my role as a *tulku* in certain circumstances because I could better serve the socialist state and people in this way.

What else was I supposed to do but agree? Then in December 1951 I was called to the president's office. President Wang looked me up and down, saying, "We have a special mission for you. You will be sent to Beijing to meet with national leaders. But first you must have a haircut. Have you ever seen a *tulku* with hair as long as yours? No doubt you must wear your *tulku* robe too." So I asked someone to bring my *tulku* robe to Chengdu. The unique mission that President Wang referred to was being a vice-director of the delegation to Beijing. We and three others would compose the Visiting Delegation of Southwest China Minority Nationalities. A vice-director was chosen among the delegates from each of the four provinces—Sichuan, Xikang, Yunnan, and Guizhou. A *tulku* from Yunnan held the director position for the delegation. However, the positions as directors or vice-directors were symbolic, because the actual person in charge was the vice-head of the State Nationalities Affairs Commission, Liu Geping.

There were over 200 delegates, most of whom were chieftains, nobles, religious figures, intellectuals, and other elites from dozens of ethnic minority groups.[5] The meeting with national leaders was scheduled for New Year's Day 1952. We weren't informed in advance which leaders we would meet, but I could guess they would include Chairman Mao. The day before the meeting, I was assigned a particular task concerning their security. I was to keep an eye on the Dégé Sé (a *Dégé* prince), who was acting as the vice-head of the Xikang delegation, to see if he had a knife on his person. So I went to his room to chat while observing whether he had a knife. I didn't find any, which I reported to the official in charge. On New Year's Day afternoon, they announced that no one was supposed to have knives or needles during the meeting.

A car came to pick up the five directors, and we were eventually seated around a table in a chamber to wait for the national leaders. Subsequently, Mao, Premier Zhou Enlai, Zhu De (the PLA commander in chief), and others entered the room. Mao immediately smiled when he saw me, thanks to my shaved head and colorful *tulku* robe. During the dinner following the reception, Liu Geping held his glass up, signaling me to stand and toast Mao, who was sitting at another table with other national leaders. I went directly to Mao, who shook my hand and asked where I was from. When I said I was from Maogong (Tsanlha), Mao nodded with a smile and said, "Thank the people in Maogong. I have been there. The Red Army passed there twice during the Long March."

The instant Mao stepped into the room, radiating unbounded fortune and charisma, I had felt he had an extraordinary presence. However, I never felt like shedding tears or sobbing, which was quite common when other people saw Mao. I admired him as a great leader, but he was human like all of us, still situated in the six realms of existence and not exempted from karma. I hesitated to tell people about my encounter with Mao because some might think I was unqualified to see him, given the negativity associated with religion, especially since *tulku*s were considered feudal oppressors of the people. Also, I hated showing off to others, which has been an integral part of my personality since childhood.

Still, my appointment as vice-head of the delegation and my task to spy on the Dégé Sé exhibited the trust that President Wang and my teachers had in me. Such trust was further exemplified by several other occurrences, like my appointment as director of the People's Court and vice-mayor of

Tsanlha County in early 1952, as well as approval of my membership in the Communist Youth League of China (CYLC) in September 1952 and subsequent appointment as vice-president of the newly established Sichuan Youth Federation under the leadership of the CYLC in Sichuan. I was very attracted to Communism and was convinced that the CCP was the savior for us Tibetans and others, so I planned to join. However, the institute officials advised me to join the CYLC first. I was told I was young and needed a few more years to "exercise" in society before fully joining the Party. Even so, it wasn't easy to join the CYLC. I had to consistently report my thoughts to my class instructor and his assistant until they believed that my previously corrupt soul as a religious figure had been sufficiently cleansed to satisfy the essential membership standard. My application was first thoroughly discussed at our institute's branch and then submitted to the CYLC in Sichuan for further investigation and approval.

I joined the CYLC eventually on September 27, 1952, a symbolic date that I've never forgotten, and was told to keep my membership a secret. My *tulku* status remained helpful to the United Front work of the new regime, so it would be better for me to be seen by the public as a liberal-minded ethnic elite and close ally of the CCP rather than one of its own as a CYLC member, at least for the time being. The few superiors in charge who knew about my league membership included my class instructor, President Wang Weizhou, the directors of the CYLC in Sichuan, Mayor Wang at Tsanlha, and Ren Taihe, the director of the United Front of the Sichuan Tibetan Autonomous Region. I was exempt from various meetings at the institute's CYLC, where all the other members gathered to study CCP policy and report and confess their thoughts and actions. Instead, I was asked to report my thoughts directly to a particular coordinator assigned by my superiors, depending on where I went to work.

This was not the only secret thing I did, however. I dated a classmate, Liu, from Tsanlha in a semisecret way. I say semisecret because President Wang had previously instructed me not to have a girlfriend; he explained that my *tulku* status served the CCP and people, so my continued celibacy was necessary. Moreover, my relationship with this woman never matured enough to go public. Liu helped me with my studies, we spent much time together because of our study partnership, and we became romantically involved. This happened after my relationship with my lover back in Tsanlha ended. Not long after I went to Chengdu to study, she sent me a message saying that her father had found a husband for her, the son of another noble. She asked me if she should wait for me and reject the marriage proposal. I assumed her father knew about our affair and considered her marriage to me impractical because I was a nobody without my *tulku* status. Also, my future was full of uncertainties due to the ambivalent political climate. So I replied that the decision was hers to make. Soon after, I heard that she had married.

In the beginning, my Liu would come to my bedroom to collect my clothes for laundering, a common sign of a woman's interest in a man in those days. We then started to sit next to each other at the cinema, as I was responsible for allocating tickets for these outings for the whole class. The institute organized many revolutionary movie screenings as part of our education. Sitting in the dark, sometimes Liu and I held hands, leaned our heads toward each other, and chatted in low voices. Once, while we were touching and "sticky" again, a male classmate sitting behind us yelled, "Behave yourselves." It was embarrassing for sure, and also amusing. This didn't last long, however. The head of the division Liu belonged to told me in secret that she had previously slept with a PLA officer. Confessions were an effective and popular form of socialist education then. We were supposed to confess our darkest secrets in order to advance and purify ourselves as qualified socialist members. This process was commonly referred to as "giving one's heart to the organization" (Ch. *xiang zuzhi jiaoxin*). During one of these confession sessions, Liu had revealed this affair to her division head, who told me about it.

Soon after Liberation in Tsanlha, the PLA officer involved had come to my monastery, walking about and looking around. He was wearing his PLA uniform, young, fair-skinned, and good-looking. However, he never asked for a direct meeting with me. At first I didn't know who he was, so I observed him from the shadows while he was scrutinizing the monastery. Later I learned that he worked for the secret services and that his job was collecting intelligence on nobles and monastery activities in Tsanlha and other places. After I learned about their affair, I was no longer interested in dating Liu and found excuses to distance myself from her. Soon our year of study ended, and she left for her new job. I was asked to stay behind for an additional year to learn law, to prepare myself for a new position as the director of the People's Court. Consequently, our relationship came to an end.

I hadn't planned on studying law at first. Instead I considered attending the Tibetan program. I had become acquainted with Kelzang Yéshé, a lecturer in that program. I didn't know much about his background, but I knew he was from Batang and had stayed in both Lhasa and Nanjing. He was proficient in Tibetan and Chinese and interpreted for President Wang and me because my conversational Chinese was not proficient then. Later, Kelzang Yéshé came and talked with me several times and helped me with my studies, although I wondered whether President Wang had assigned him to watch over me or if he helped me on his own accord. He said I had a solid foundation in Tibetan from my years of training in Lhasa, but I should be further trained to apply my Tibetan skills to my writings and future work. I thought that this was a great idea and agreed. The institute had a different plan for me, however. Its officials had found an inspirational role model on my behalf. I was told that my acquaintance and teacher, the Pawam Tulku, Jamyang Tenzin (the first mayor of Rongdrak/Danba after Liberation), had revealed extraordinary skill in settling complicated legal disputes. Therefore, they asked me to study law to make the best use of my *tulku* status and be like the Pawam Tulku in dealing with legal matters in my future work.

Much of what I had been taught in class about Communism was theoretical and abstract, such as the people's democratic dictatorship, the composition of the state, the use of violence, etc. My classmates and I learned only the most rudimentary facts and principles of the existing law, like the fundamental differences between civil and criminal laws. Nevertheless, I could get a little hands-on experience with legal proceedings through an internship program at the People's Court of Chengdu. Several classmates and I were assigned to study legal mediation and judgments associated with the newly implemented Marriage Law. Ironically, I never had the opportunity to practice this law, or any law for that matter, after graduation. Still, my knowledge about marital law and procedures helped me win a legal battle when I divorced my wife four decades later.

After completing my legal studies in May 1953, I returned to Tsanlha. I had been away from my hometown for nearly two years and was struck by many significant changes. The gangsters and bandits were gone, and local society had become largely stabilized. Banditry and pillaging had been rampant before Liberation. Even when I departed for Chengdu, sporadic attacks still occurred. Although the 1950 to 1952 riots complicated and intensified the local political status quo, when I returned in 1953 the riots had been suppressed and those who had participated, such as the major gangsters and the Okzhi queen, had been executed or imprisoned. Also, opium had disappeared. According to my estimation, about 70–80 percent of the land in Sönamyak and Okzhi had been used for growing opium poppies, and about 10 percent of the population in these two regions had used opium, with some users seriously addicted.[6] Consequently, it was common for there to be a shortage of food crops. Opium addiction resulted in a loss of ability to do field work because addicts easily became tired and weak. This situation continued through the beginning of Liberation, but when the full-scale prohibition of opium was fully enacted, banning the harvest, sale, and use of poppies, far fewer people starved for lack of edible crops. Additionally, the government would intervene and help anyone who didn't have enough to eat.

Old exploitative systems were vanishing, although they would linger until the Democratic Reform. This meant it was no longer necessary for commoners to provide their nobles with corvée and other free labor, and the nobles could not use their positions of power to bully and exploit their former subjects at will. Notwithstanding their downgraded status, most nobles with whom I interacted didn't develop any perceptible grudges toward the new regime. Quite the contrary, many reflected upon the injustices they had inflicted on ordinary people and understood the genuine efforts the new regime was making to integrate them into the new society. This was inseparable from United Front work and thought work focused on CCP policy propaganda and ideological education. CCP officials and cadres never tired of introducing and illustrating ethnic policies and Mao's ideas to the nobles and others. Also, these nobles, especially younger ones, were sent to Chengdu, Chongqing, Beijing, Shanghai, and other big cities to experience the brand-new world and its ideas, which brought about significant changes in the way they thought.

Equally important was the compensation the government offered the nobles as their traditional privileges were disappearing, which meant they were usually better off than others. Most elderly nobles were recruited into the CPPCC (Chinese People's Political Consultative Conference) as part of the CCP's United Front work. The CCP treated them as allies rather than enemies. They received monthly salaries and subsidies from the government, so they became government employees. As for the younger nobles, they were typically first sent to school and then offered jobs at different government agencies. Such benefits meant most nobles didn't resist social changes, and many even embraced them. Both commoners and nobles believed that Tsanlha and China were moving into a more prosperous and promising era. Morale was relatively high, as was support for the government's work. My role as county vice-mayor and director of the People's Court was to visit various places to introduce the laws and regulations to the people and motivate them to increase agricultural production. People genuinely appreciated my colleagues' and my work, so it was a relatively effortless but meaningful job.

I was also supposed to investigate the whereabouts of several notorious gangsters. One was Song Guotai, a ferocious Gown Brothers leader from Wenchuan, who was influential in the Chengdu basin and Tsanlha.[7] There were also the three He brothers, a Han immigrant family in Tsanlha who were notorious gangsters in the county.[8] Both parties had been allies of the Okzhi queen. They fled the area when the queen, her other allies, and their associates were captured and executed after their failed rebellion. No one had seen Song since then, but there were suspicions that he had fled from Wenchuan to Tsanlha. As for the three He brothers, they were spotted or encountered from time to time. Not until January 1955 was the last of these brothers captured. During the time the gangsters were fugitives, the people's support for our work was crucial, because they were the ones who reported to the PLA and government the whereabouts of the gangsters and later participated in their pursuit and capture. Close collaboration between the people and the government was a common practice. A simile to describe the relationship between the new regime and the masses in the first few years after Liberation is that the relationship was like that between fish and water. This was the kind of harmonious society I had dreamed of and the promising new life I had yearned for. Unfortunately, it was all about to change.

Chapter Nine

THE CALM BEFORE THE STORM

I stayed in Tsanlha only for a little over a year before transferring to the prefecture seat (Maoxian) when I became the president of its Youth Federation in early 1954.[1] The federation aimed to build and consolidate the United Front work among youth from different social backgrounds, such as peasants, intellectuals, religious figures, progressive former Kuomintang civilian officials and military officers, members of political parties and social organizations, the bourgeoisie, merchants, etc.[2] In practice, however, our job focused mainly on uniting the upper stratum of society, including the children of nobles from Ngawa Prefecture. In most parts of Ngawa, the nobles had enormous influence within their respective jurisdictions. Therefore, their cooperation and support of the new regime were deemed critical by the CCP for successful social transition and progress. This was especially true for the so-called Democratic Reform (chapter 10), which was expected to bring about an enormous and unprecedented storm across the regions and transform Tibetan society completely. As president of the Youth Federation, I was responsible for leading my team to mobilize young people, especially the children of nobles, encouraging them to become involved in socialist projects.

The noble youth were encouraged to attend school in Chengdu, Beijing, and elsewhere, to work as governmental employees, assist the Party-state agenda, and urge their family members, relatives, and former subjects to do the same. I organized many meetings and study tours to metropolitan cities to spark gradual changes in the way they thought.[3] The meetings involved policy advocacy, in-depth discussions, self-reflections among participants, and socializing with singing and dancing afterward. The study tours for these young nobles played a significant role in the work agenda of the Youth Federation and the United Front work in general because the CCP assumed that exposure to new ideas and modern realities would facilitate their ideological transition and support of social change.

I led these study tours four or five times in person before I left the Youth Federation in 1958. I led such trips about once a year, each taking three or four months. We traveled to Chengdu, Chongqing, Wuhan, Nanjing, Shanghai, and Beijing. It was an eye-opening experience for many group members who had never encountered nor even imagined trains, planes, factories, shipyards, museums, and department stores. Wherever we went, we were warmly received and welcomed by our local hosts, arranged in advance by officials in Sichuan. Our hosts called us "ethnic minority siblings" (Ch. *shaoshu minzu tongbao*). Many of the local people had rarely or never encountered ethnic minorities before, so we were curiously observed. We weren't offended since most of us were curious about the Han, their cities, and their working environments. The overall atmosphere was hospitable and amiable. Our tour group did feel we were their "siblings." This was a prime time of harmonious ethnic relations.

At first some noble youths didn't want to participate in these tours and found excuses to exempt themselves, such as an ill parent. However, when they heard about the positive experiences of those who had participated, they wanted to have the same opportunities. Based on my observations, the study tours greatly impacted the young nobles. They came to see the limitations of the old system and the exciting things possible in the new society. In the end, they were less resistant to the idea of studying in a Han Chinese city or taking a job in a government agency after the CCP offered such an opportunity.

I enjoyed these activities. I was a young man and loved socializing as well. Of course, in carrying out my duties, socializing was required to build connections with these noble youths and their families, but it was not the end goal. I was entrusted with observing them and evaluating their attitudes toward the new regime and instructed to report my observations to my superiors. I usually reported to Ren Taihe (Ren hereafter), the head of the prefecture's United Front Department, and to the CYLC's director, whose name I can no longer recall. They asked me to interact intensively with young and more senior nobles and to take advantage of my *tulku* status to become more intimate with the more prominent nobles and lamas, especially the "Three Giants" in Ngawa, Suo Guanying (1900–1966; the king of Choktsé; hereafter Suo), Dorjé Pasang (1909–1981; also known as Su Yonghe, the ruler of Trochu and the nominal king of Somang; hereafter Dorjé Pasang), and Meu Pelgön Trinlé Rapten (1916–1966; the king of the Ngawa region, hereafter Pelgön Trinlé).[4] Although I did approach them as a part of my work with prescribed goals in mind, I was also fascinated with this opportunity to interact with and learn from them, the elders in particular, because they all had rich and extraordinary experiences to share.

Suo was the son of Suo Daixing, the king of Wasi in Wenchuan County. The Wasi kingdom, once one of the most powerful kingdoms in Gyalrong, ruled a relatively large territory including today's Wenchuan County, part of Maoxian County, and part of Dujiangyan of Chengdu City. The successive Wasi kings were conferred various honorary titles for their loyalty to the Ming and Qing courts. For instance, the Wasi kings assisted the Qing in waging two campaigns against the two Jinchuan kings, defending Central Tibet against the invading Gorkhas from Nepal (1788–1792), and fighting the British forces in Zhejiang during the Opium War (1839–1842).[5] Since the end of the Qing, Wasi's influence had been diminishing from being near Chengdu, making it easier for the Sichuan government to exert more direct control. Also, due to its location, Wasi became largely Sinicized around the same period, and it was no longer easy to find traces of Gyalrong Tibetan culture in many parts of its territory during the Republican Era (1912–1949). Suo was born and raised there in a Sinicized environment and had a high Chinese literacy level. Later this was an essential factor in his reputation as the "chieftain for the Han" among the Choktsé people.

When Suo's father, Suo Daixing, was dying from an illness, he knew that his brother, Suo Daigeng (Suo's paternal uncle) would attempt to usurp the throne, which according to tradition should be passed on to his son, Suo. Suo's father therefore arranged for his son, then about thirteen years old, to become the future king of Choktsé. Based on tradition in Gyalrong, only those with royal lineage were considered candidates for the throne. Intermarriage was common among the various Gyalrong kings, so they were typically related to one another. Thus, if a particular lineage of a king was broken after his death, lacking direct offspring, a relative in the greater lin-eage of the deceased would be selected as the successor. This was how Suo, a Wasi prince, was eligible for a position as the new Choktsé king. After Suo's father died, his mother, from a noble family in Gyelkha, sought her brother's aid to help her son escape to Choktsé. She feared Suo's paternal uncle, Suo Daigeng, would try to eliminate him so as to legitimately inherit the throne. Fortunately, Suo succeeded in fleeing Wasi and his treasonous paternal uncle.

As Suo was too young to govern Choktsé, some prominent local nobles didn't take him seriously and tried to exercise complete control over the kingdom. Despite being officially enthroned as king, Suo ruled in uncer-tainty since he felt marginalized, humiliated, and worried that these nobles would try to assassinate him. He later met and sought the help of a power-ful head of the Gown Brothers from Jinchuan, Du Tieqiao (hereafter Du), who promised to help resolve this problem. When Du came to visit Suo, he ordered his men to create a commotion by shooting off their guns randomly one night near the palace. Hearing this noise, Suo's archenemy climbed to the roof of his house to see what was going on, and Du's subordinate shot him dead. After his strongest opponent had been removed, other nobles dared not challenge Suo's authority. Suo allied with other Gown Brothers and important Kuomintang officials and officers to enhance his power. Meanwhile, he profited from the booming opium trade by developing Choktsé as a commercial hub in Gyalrong.[6] As a result, he became an extremely influential and affluent king in Gyalrong and was undeniably significant to the new Communist regime and its United Front work. Appointed vice-governor of the newly established Sichuan Tibetan Auton-omous Region, he was also chosen to be a member of the First National People's Congress in 1954. Having these titles didn't mean that he was seen by the CCP as totally trustworthy. He had been part of the exploitative rul-ing class and had fostered close ties with the Kuomintang. I was asked to learn if he genuinely embraced social change and was loyal to the CCP. As I was a *tulku* president of the prefecture's Youth Federation, it was rela-tively easy for me to interact with Suo and other nobles. We often met and chatted at various political meetings, and I also found reasons to visit him at his residence.

Suo was exceptionally social and eloquent and gave the impression of being lighthearted, owing to his personality and life experiences. To survive and prosper in the new and complex environment in Choktsé since his relocation there in 1913, he had to build broad social networks. His eloquence and sociability contributed significantly to this goal. Moreover, I assumed that his lightheartedness wasn't feigned. This may have been related to the fact that Suo was no longer subject to the incessant contempt and insults of his foremost competitor, Dorjé Pasang, the ruler of Trochu, whose daughter, Dartso, married Suo's son, Suo Guokun (hereafter Guokun), in 1941. With her father's support, Dartso gradually sidelined Suo and her husband, Guokun, as she started to accumulate power for herself. Suo had to leave Choktsé and seek refuge in the Tenpa kingdom by marrying its widowed queen. Consequently, Choktsé became part of Dorjé Pasang and Trochu's sphere of influence. Liberation allowed Suo to regain control over Choktsé because the CCP acknowledged and reinforced his status as Choktsé's legitimate ruler, explaining Suo's better spirits and restored confidence and authority.

Suo liked to tell jokes, especially sex-related ones. He often teased me, asking if I wanted a girlfriend and if I was able to restrain my sexual urges. He said, "Young man, you should fully explore your life. Monks act as if they have no urges. That's so pretentious. Don't take them as your model," and told me a story about pretentious monks he had in mind:

A king wanted to find out whether monks could resist the temptation of women as they claimed. One day he invited a group of monks, including their *tulku*, to his residence. After they were all seated, drums were placed in front of each monk. Then many beautiful women arrived and began to take off their clothes. The drums started to make loud sounds one by one when each of the monks' penises became hardened enough to beat them. There was only one exception—the drum in front of the *tulku* never made a sound. The king was amazed and thought that the *tulku* was exceptional, as he was the only one who remained determined enough to resist this sort of temptation. After the monks left, the king took a closer look at the *tulku*'s drum and found it had a large hole. It turned out that the *tulku* had been even more aroused than the ordinary monks, and his exceedingly hard penis had punctured the drum.[7]

Afterward, we laughed heartily. This story was funny and educational by exposing the hypocrisy of sexual sins prevalent in monasteries, where homosexual acts were common. Ironically, I continued to manage my sexual urges because of my political idealism, not because of monastic taboos.

My superiors instructed me not to date anyone before the Democratic Reforms were implemented because my *tulku* status and celibacy were necessary to serve the United Front work. However, I soon realized this political idealism was another outlandish hypocrisy. In any case, interacting with Suo was entertaining. He was easygoing and always had many interesting stories to share.

Regarding his political stance, Suo took the initiative to conduct endless confessions of his crimes and demonstrate enormous gratitude to the CCP. On various occasions, he would say that he was a huge sinner and deserved to be killed a thousand times over for having oppressed people and doing many evil things before Liberation. He noted that it was only because of the great CCP's mercy that he had been spared and reborn as a new socialist member of society. Moreover, whenever activists and others questioned him about his past activities, he would always say, "*Lakso, lakso!* (Yes, yes!) It was my fault," impressing us all with his submissiveness.

Yet Suo was also stubborn and uncompromising on two things. First, he opposed the idea of establishing Barkham County. The government planned to integrate the four contiguous kingdoms of Somang, Choktsé, Dzigak, and Denpa, popularly known at that time as the "Four Chieftaincies" (*Situ*), into a single county-level jurisdiction called Barkham County. Suo proposed instead that four separate counties be established, one for each of the chieftaincies. As a result, the plan for Barkham County was not fully executed until 1956. This undoubtedly became part of his "crimes" later, as his reluctance made him appear to be trying to hold on to his old power and obstruct the CCP-led social transformation. Second, Suo objected to identifying the Gyalrongwa as a separate ethnic group. When the national and provincial nationality affairs commissions and other important officials urged him to formally declare the Gyalrongwa a non-Tibetan people, he insisted, "We Gyalrongwa have always been Tibetans. How can we possibly betray our nationality by claiming to be something else?" His foremost opponent, Dorjé Pasang, made the same claim. Eventually the central government relented and acknowledged the Gyalrongwa's official status as a Tibetan subgroup in 1954.

As part of my duties, my superiors told me to motivate Suo's wife, Lady Khopo, to leave her private domestic space and work publicly as a government employee. Lady Khopo was originally from a lesser noble family. She was well known for her elegant looks and slim figure, and Suo fell for her and took her as a lesser queen (junior wife) when she was still a teenager. Lady Khopo was shy and introverted and didn't talk much, but she was always smiling and easygoing. It was initially somewhat difficult to approach her because of her status as the queen and her introversion, but I finally found an opportunity. I was keen on singing, dancing, and playing the flute, *erhu* (Chinese two-stringed fiddle), and accordion. Lady Khopo also loved instruments and was trying to learn the *erhu* by herself. Her husband, Suo, said, "Now I have found you a teacher, and you can learn from Ngawang." So I started to teach her to play.

In this way, I had the opportunity to interact with Lady Khopo directly. I would go and meet with her even when Suo was absent. Seeing this, some people rumored that I was having an affair with Lady Khopo. Because of the nature of my mission, I wasn't in a position to explain and dispel their suspicions. Nevertheless, these rumors didn't damage our relationship. She began to share her thoughts, confiding that she wasn't sociable or capable enough to interact with strangers, let alone work in a government agency. I explained the CCP policy to her and highlighted the advantages of leaving home, including more opportunities to develop her musical interests through interaction with others who shared similar interests and with professionals. Gradually she decided to join the Women's Federation as an employee.

Moreover, I sometimes visited Guokun and his wife, Dartso, who lived in another official residence of the Choktsé king. Guokun was generally considered slow-witted or even mentally deranged, in addition to being henpecked. He reminded me of the Okzhi king, who was also said to go insane from time to time. I wonder if this was related to the fact that both of their wives were manipulative and domineering to the extent that the men resorted to feigning dumbness or insanity as a defense mechanism. Guokun didn't talk much, but he was usually nicely behaved. I did overhear him scolding a subordinate, "Don't assume that the CCP's arrival means something different for you. We (the royal family) still rule." Dartso didn't speak much, but I could tell she was unhappy with her current situation. With the support of her powerful father, the de facto king of Somang, Dorjé Pasang, she acted like the actual chieftain in charge of various affairs in Choktsé. However, she was starting to lose power since the PLA had arrived. Her subtle resentment toward social change was also evidenced through her behavior during various political meetings. Usually during these meetings, the noble youth would expose the old society's vices and express admiration for the new regime and society. Still, Dartso rarely spoke or would only say a few simple words about her political stance, like "I welcome Liberation."

As required, I would report the couple's actions to my superiors. I also kept a close eye on various activities, mainly materials and personnel flowing in and out of the Choktsé royal family. For instance, if certain of their immediate subordinates were away for an extended period, this might indicate something was afoot. Also, either directly or indirectly, listening to other people's conversations often revealed their whereabouts. One day I learned that Lady Khopo's brother, who was Suo's close aide, was gone. I assumed that Suo might have sent him to prepare something, which Lady Khopo confirmed later in casual conversation. Based on this information, I could roughly conclude that the Suo family was going to take a long trip, probably to Lhasa. I reported what I knew to my superiors, and it turned out that the family did start a pilgrimage to Lhasa in 1957. The prefectural government dispatched someone to accompany them. This person acted as Suo's assistant, but his real job was to spy on Suo and his family. It was unclear whether Suo planned to flee to India during this trip; if so, he was perhaps forced to abort his original plan because of the addition to his retinue.

I also often interacted with the Trochu ruler, Dorjé Pasang, during meetings and visits to his home. Unlike Suo, he was a man of few words with a somewhat pensive, melancholy disposition. He was very discreet, and it was hard to learn his candid thoughts. While visiting in his house, I noticed he had the habit of standing up from time to time and walking about the room while counting his rosaries and reciting prayers. I figured he did this because he was under immense pressure. He had facilitated a failed revolt against the new regime in 1952. Although the CCP had been lenient and exonerated him for his role, he assumed that someday he would be penalized for what he had done. The CCP's leniency was likely pragmatic because of his status as the most powerful native ruler in Gyalrong and the greater border region where Sichuan, Gansu, and Qinghai converged. His cooperation with the new regime was considered critical for stabilizing Gyalrong and its neighboring nomadic areas at the intersection of those three provinces.

The CCP couldn't trust Dorjé Pasang, though, as they suspected he still harbored subversive thoughts against the regime. Other kings like Suo and Pelgön Trinlé also hadn't earned the CCP's complete trust, but in comparison, they were viewed as much more reliable and levelheaded than Dorjé Pasang. The differences in how they were treated were unmistakable. Both Suo and Pelgön Trinlé were given significant official titles as vice-governors of the Sichuan Tibetan Autonomous Region and as members of the National People's Congress. In contrast, Dorjé Pasang was offered less significant positions as vice-secretary-general of the government of the Sichuan Tibetan Region, vice-chair of the region's CPPCC, and a member of the provincial People's Congress. He also was treated differently at a subtle but more conspicuous level. When CCP officials visited Suo or Pelgön Trinlé, they chatted or joked with them, but when the same officials encountered Dorjé Pasang, they only exchanged a few formal words with him. Many CCP officials and PLA officers weren't convinced Dorjé Pasang deserved to be pardoned for his revolt. He was surely aware of this, which likely contributed to his eventual flight to India.

Dorjé Pasang became talkative only about his battle experiences, perhaps the sole topic that interested him. He was born in 1909 to a lesser noble family in Trochu, a region notorious for endless warfare among the various headmen and rampant banditry and raids. Although battles and pillaging occurred in other parts of Gyalrong, the situation in Trochu was worse mainly because of the lack of a powerful king or ruler to unify the different factions. Trochu was under the jurisdiction of the Somang king, but the king's position had been vacant since 1913 because of an internal power struggle that followed the death of the last king, who was childless. In the interim, the Ninth Panchen Lama assumed the position as the nominal king from 1934 to 1937 after the Somang nobles requested his help. The Panchen Lama sent his representative, Draktong Chijikmé, who later became the director of the Panchen's Council of Khenpos, to Somang to rule on his behalf.[8] Soon after, Dorjé Pasang took the throne by force in 1937. He explained his rise to prominence in this way:

> I had no special battles skills or experience and I was illiterate. However, as my opponents pushed me into a corner, I was left with no better alternative but to fight back. Even so, I couldn't afford to fight randomly. I had to consider the situation and seize the best moment for warfare. While others would come and attack me only when they were fully prepared, I would take preemptive actions to storm their battalions and defeat them when they were off-guard.

Dorjé Pasang was only fourteen years old when his father was assassinated. After that, he began to organize battles to seek revenge and expand his territory and influence by building alliances with his siblings, in-laws, monastic establishments, Kuomintang officials and officers, and others. Meanwhile, the Sichuan warlord, Deng Xihou, attempted to mine gold and extract additional resources from the lawless and war-torn Trochu area. Deng sent expedition troops three times to subdue Trochu, but his attempts failed. Dorjé Pasang seemed to be an invincible ruler and commander, and his reputation skyrocketed among Sichuan warlords and officials. This standing was enhanced by his close ties with prominent monasteries and religious leaders, such as Labrang Monastery in Gansu and two of the most prominent *tulku* lineages, Jamyang Zhépa (the abbot) and Gungtang Rinpoche, as well as the Achok Tsenyi Monastery in Ngawa (Sichuan), the Pelyül Monastery in Qinghai, and so on. Three of his sons were eventually acknowledged as *tulkus* by different monasteries. In this way, these monasteries and religious figures made Dorjé Pasang their principal patron and guardian.

Importantly, the fifth Jamyang Zhépa and his father requested that Dorjé Pasang send troops to help them retake a subordinate tribe in upper Ngawa. This rebellious tribe had turned to Pelgön Trinlé for protection. Since the second Jamyang Zhépa's term (in the eighteenth century), the Somang kings had been entrusted with governing a large nomadic territory situated on the Sichuan-Gansu border, including upper Ngawa, on behalf of Labrang. Therefore, Dorjé Pasang, as the actual power holder in Somang, was obliged to wage war against Pelgön Trinlé to seize this lost territory. Trochu soldiers were known for being fierce, unconquerable warriors. Dorjé Pasang's army could have easily defeated Pelgön Trinlé in most circumstances, but they encountered serious setbacks this time. His army was experienced in using the mountainous landscape to their advantage, but they weren't used to battles waged on the open ground of a nomadic region. Consequently, Dorjé Pasang accepted a mediated truce with Pelgön Trinlé to avoid further defeats.

Though Pelgön Trinlé was his principal rival, Suo, the Choktsé king, was another major threat. According to tradition, Dorjé Pasang could never become a real king or marry his children into a royal family because of his low birth from a lesser noble family. However, since he had defeated all of his significant enemies in Trochu and Somang, no one could stop him from seizing the throne for himself. With the official seal of the Somang king in hand in 1937, he proclaimed himself the new king. His battles against Pelgön Trinlé were part of his responsibilities. Despite this, most nobles and subjects in the Somang kingdom outside of Trochu did not acknowledge his status as king. Nor was he accepted by other Gyalrong kings, nobles, and commoners. This may have contributed to his unsuccessful campaign against Pelgön Trinlé. According to a noble in the Naknyo family at Somang, Dorjé Pasang ordered the Somang nobles to dispatch their soldiers to assist him in the battle. The nobles didn't dare directly disobey his order, but they found an inventive way to circumvent it. The Naknyo noble, as commander of this army, took a long route to the battlefield rather than the shortest. As a result, they didn't arrive until the battle was almost over.

Dorjé Pasang attempted to bribe Kuomintang officials to formally endorse his legitimacy as king. Unfortunately for him, this dream didn't materialize until 1952, when Gyalrong had already been liberated. Chiang Kai-shek conferred the ceremonial title upon Dorjé Pasang to boost his morale to fight against the PLA on behalf of the Kuomintang. In addition, Dorjé Pasang indirectly controlled Choktsé through his daughter, who married Suo's son in 1941. Moreover, Dorjé Pasang bribed the Kuomintang officials to make his adopted son (his dead elder brother's son) Gönpo Namgyel king of Dzigak by blocking various rivals, all of whom had been competing for this position for years since the death of the childless Dzigak king. The Choktsé king, Suo, was also a major rival candidate. Dorjé Pasang was thus successful in marginalizing Suo, who had once been a predominant chieftain in the Tshakho region, or the "Four Chieftaincies," before Dorjé Pasang's rise.

I also observed the flow of personnel and materials in and out of Dorjé Pasang's residence. Since dozens of people from Trochu, mainly his relatives, allies, and subordinates, were coming and going regularly, it wasn't easy to discern what was happening at first. Gradually, though, I could see both regular and irregular patterns. For instance, some of Dorjé Pasang's aides had been away from the residence for a while, while others spreading rumors such as, "Suo Guanying has been to Lhasa for pilgrimage. Why shouldn't we go there too?" I then assumed Dorjé Pasang's associates were preparing for his trip to Lhasa and that he would flee to India once there. When I reported my findings to a key leader at the prefecture, he exploded. "If he wants to leave, just let it be. We (China) have a population of over six hundred million. What does it matter if someone like him is gone?" Before long, Dorjé Pasang submitted his application to the prefectural Party committee to go to Lhasa for pilgrimage, just as expected. Due to his prominent status, his application had to be sanctioned at the provincial level. Although I was not involved in this procedure, I assumed that the provincial officials found no real reason to reject the request because they had previously permitted Suo's and Pelgön Trinlé's earlier requests to visit Lhasa.

Oddly, no official representative was dispatched to accompany Dorjé Pasang to Lhasa, which had been the case with Suo. I do not know why. One possibility is that Dorjé Pasang was strategic and persuasive enough to dissuade the officials in charge that this was necessary. However, it is more likely that these officials believed Dorjé Pasang's flight was good for everyone. He was a potential threat to the new regime because of his lingering influence in Trochu and the surrounding regions. Imprisoning or executing him was not entirely justifiable. The same logic could be applied to the Dalai Lama's flight to India in 1959. The PLA could have prevented it if they had wanted to. However, Mao must have thought the Dalai Lama's going to India was a better solution to the Tibet problem than his remaining since he was seen as a principal barrier to Democratic Reform in Tibet and Tibet's full integration into the new Communist regime.

In this way, Dorjé Pasang and some of his remaining family members from Ngawa traveled to Lhasa in 1957 and left for India soon afterward. The Chinese government immediately labeled him as the people's enemy and a defector to forestall his potential return. Without this label, Dorjé Pasang could have claimed that he had only traveled to India for the sake of pilgrimage to Buddha's homeland. Consequently, he didn't return to China and Trochu until 1980, when he had cancer.[9]

Comparatively speaking, I had limited knowledge about Pelgön Trinlé. He was silent most of the time and would only say a few words if asked a question. Therefore, it was difficult to know his real thoughts. Unlike Dorjé Pasang, Pelgön Trinlé wasn't even inclined to talk about his battle experiences with Dorjé Pasang and others. When asked, he would say, "Let bygones be bygones. Thanks to the CCP, we are now liberated." On any occasion, he would only mention positive changes since Liberation and express gratitude to the CCP. I learned more about his personal experiences from other sources. Pelgön Trinlé had been a monk but was made to take the role of headman when his father died. He treated his subjects with fairness and justice and never assumed superiority. He didn't exploit them and would help those in financial and other difficulties. In this way, he had won enormous loyalty. Pelgön Trinlé also took advantage of Ngawa's strategic location as a critical junction between Sichuan, Gansu, and Qinghai to develop its trade and markets. This border region soon became a booming commercial hub, and some natives emerged as prosperous traders. Given his growing reputation, some external tribes defected to Pelgön Trinlé, such as the tribe mentioned above belonging to Labrang Monastery. He also seized opportunities to expand his influence and territory.

Dorjé Pasang had rarely suffered any significant setbacks in warfare, including in his battles against the invading troops of a Sichuan warlord. Still, Pelgön Trinlé succeeded in thwarting Dorjé Pasang's ambitions to further expand his territory and sphere of influence into the nomadic region. This feat contributed significantly to Pelgön Trinlé's soaring reputation as a superb commander. What's more, battles with Dorjé Pasang directly contributed to Pelgön Trinlé's initiatives to militarize his territory to prepare for future battles. He appointed officers of varying ranks to oversee different regional units and their subjects. All the people under his jurisdiction were categorized into a basic local unit, a *bakha*. Composed of about ten households, each *bakha* was led by an officer and constituted an essential dining and military unit. Every household was required to contribute in some form, whether soldiers and cooks, guns and ammunition, horses, cooking utensils, tents, etc. Everyone within a *bakha* generally understood their specific roles. As a result, this sort of unit, as well as larger units made up of multiple *bakha*, could be immediately mobilized for the battlefield whenever they were called upon.[10]

This militarization made Pelgön Trinlé a formidable regional power in the Sichuan-Gansu-Qinghai borderlands, largely explaining why the new regime attached such great importance to him. He was not, however, a generally happy person, and my interactions with him told me something weighed heavily on his mind. This was probably related to his having given protection to three important Kuomintang officers (Zhou Xunyu, He Benchu, and Wang Xufu) in 1953. He gave them refuge even though he had already publicly proclaimed his political loyalty to the CCP, and in January 1953 he had accepted the position of vice-governor of the newly established Sichuan Tibetan Autonomous Region.[11]

These Kuomintang officers weren't ordinary soldiers; they were all generals who had fled Chengdu at the time of Liberation. They were hiding in Gyalrong and the neighboring nomadic region at the Sichuan-Gansu border, waiting for the right opportunity to organize battles against the CCP. In their minds, the "right" opportunity would be the Third World War. These officers convinced Pelgön Trinlé that the war would break out at any time and that the Kuomintang would recover the mainland. Pelgön Trinlé drank blood wine with them, becoming their sworn brother by sharing blood from their fingertips. Even so, he expected the PLA would eventually learn of this disloyalty. Unsurprisingly, he was pressured to reveal their whereabouts to Tianbao (Sanggyé Yéshé; 1917–2008), a Gyalrong native from Barkham, one of the earliest Gyalrong Tibetan Communists, and governor of the Sichuan Tibetan Autonomous Region. Pelgön Trinlé agreed to hand them over to the government on condition that his role in the betrayal would be kept confidential, that the Kuomintang officers' lives would be spared, and that anyone else (like Pelgön Trinlé's subjects) involved in sheltering them from the CCP's search would be absolved. Tianbao and the PLA commander agreed to these terms, and the PLA captured the Kuomintang officers. This incident was still seen as a severe stain on his political history in relation to the CCP and had haunted Pelgön Trinlé ever since. At the same time, he likely felt guilty for betraying his sworn brothers because Tibetans take their vows very seriously.

Although I wanted to leave behind my *tulku* status and religious training, CCP officials had convinced me that I could contribute more to the new socialist state if I continued to play the role of *tulku* when necessary. This did help me a lot in my United Front work with the nobles as president of the Youth Federation. Without a *tulku*'s trappings and aura, I would probably not have been able to interact with those people in the same way. Likewise, my participation in the reception for the Dalai Lama in Chengdu during his trip to Beijing, as well as my return to Lhasa as one of the delegates organized by the CYLC in Beijing, had everything to do with my *tulku* status.

While I was working at Ngawa Prefecture's CYLC, I was called to Chengdu in August 1954 to help prepare for the Dalai Lama's visit when he stopped en route to Beijing for a meeting with Mao and the First National People's Congress. The Sichuan government took this reception seriously because of the Dalai Lama's irreplaceable role in the CCP's United Front work in Central Tibet and other Tibetan regions. Fifty to sixty people were responsible. We attended meetings chaired by Ren Jinglong, a leader of the Sichuan United Front Department, to emphasize the importance of our work. We were instructed to be extremely polite and respectful and never show contempt for the Dalai Lama and his entourage. Such instruction was necessary because many Han saw him and other religious leaders as feudal lords and class enemies. Ren emphasized that we must do everything possible to guarantee the safety of the Dalai Lama. Ren entrusted me with preparing a temporary residence for the Dalai Lama during his visit. I was taken to several official residences, some of which had been previously inhabited by Kuomintang warlords, to see which one would be best.

I recommended the residence of Liu Xiang (1888–1938; a prominent Sichuan warlord during the Republican Era), as it was relatively new and had elegant interior decor. I was also asked to give my opinion on the overall setup and the shrine, furniture, curtains, carpets, quilts, toilet, washing basin, and even bowls. Since I had frequented many aristocratic homes in Lhasa and had also seen the actual setup and design of the Dalai Lama's chambers when he had visited Drepung Monastery, I had a rough idea of what a reception room for him should be. I recommended, for instance, that yellow gold be the primary color in his room, including the curtains, as this color is considered precious and strongly associated with *tulku*s and other important lamas. The Party Secretary of Sichuan, Li Jingquan (Li hereafter), came to inspect our preparation work and asked me what else could be done to improve the residence. I saw a comb lying next to a golden yellow copper washing basin, which I had suggested, so I told Li that the comb was unnecessary. Li laughed. "Ha ha. You are right. Why would a lama need a comb at all?" and it was removed.[12]

The Dalai Lama came to Chengdu from Lhasa via the Sichuan-Tibet highway, which was under construction, so he and his entourage rode horses and occasionally rode in cars along the way. I joined the welcoming ceremony along Wuhouci Street in Chengdu as he arrived from Ya'an, the capital of the then Xikang Province. The ceremony consisted of key military and governmental officials in Sichuan including Wang Weizhou, the vicechair of the Southwest Military and Political Committee; He Binyan, commander of the Sichuan Military Region, popularly known as the one-armed general; and Li Jingquan and Li Dazhang, the Party secretary and governor of Sichuan, respectively. It also included several other ethnic minority representatives like Tibetans and Yi. I was asked to wear my *tulku* robes to welcome the Dalai Lama on behalf of Sichuan's religious community. When he arrived, he got out of his car and shook hands with the Sichuan officials and ethnic minority representatives. I presented him with a *khata* (a ceremonial scarf). He had a big smile on his young face.

The Dalai Lama, his guards, and his secretaries stayed in the warlord Liu Xiang's official residence. The rest of his entourage, dozens of other people, stayed in a Tidu Street hotel, where our reception staff also stayed. I was surprised to find an old acquaintance among the entourage. We had been classmates at Loserling, Drepung. He was from Künzangtsé, an aristocratic family in Lhasa, and had later become a monastic official in the Tibetan Kashag government. He was thrilled to see me and introduced me to other members of the entourage, most of whom were around our age: "This is my old classmate, a *tulku*. He excelled at study." We spent time together in casual conversation discussing the whereabouts of our other classmates while the others with us talked about their journey to Chengdu. We avoided speaking about political and sensitive matters. Although they treated me as one of their own, it was neither an appropriate time nor the right place to discuss such issues. The Sichuan officials were impressed when they saw me chatting with members of the Dalai Lama's entourage like old friends because they hadn't expected that I would know them so well. These officials did not know that my former classmate was the only person I actually knew, and it was only through his introduction that I could get to know the others. They took it for granted that I was well connected with the upper class in Lhasa.

Ren later explained that my future United Front work shouldn't be limited to Sichuan. Instead, my focus should be shifted to Central Tibet. I would assume that these officials would have been even more impressed if they knew that I had been familiar with the Dalai Lama's junior tutor, Trijang Rinpoche (1901–1981), who was also part of the entourage. He knew my own former tutor, Lama Jampel Samphel, well, thanks to the latter's reputation as a brilliant scholar. I had received many empowerment rituals from Trijang Rinpoche alongside my tutor during my time in Lhasa. I nevertheless tried to avoid direct encounters with the Rinpoche during his time in Chengdu because it would have been quite awkward if he had asked me directly about my own life. Because there were so many other people around all the time, I could easily sidestep him. The Dalai Lama's entourage only stayed in Chengdu for two or three days before flying to Xi'an, from where they would take a train to Beijing.

The Sichuan officials seemed satisfied with my performance during the Dalai Lama's visit and my execution of the United Front work. They then asked me to join the Central (National) Youth Delegation with dozens of delegates from different nationalities and a group of performers, singers, and dancers from the Central Nationalities Institute to attend the First Youth Delegation Congress in Lhasa in 1956. The membership of the Central Youth Delegation was primarily defined by our so-called advanced political stances and the CCP's trust in our loyalty, so this was seen as a special honor. I was one of only a few Tibetans, and my selection had everything to do with my *tulku* status. The Youth Federation in Lhasa organized this conference. The federation was directed by Losang Samten, a brother of the Dalai Lama, which evidenced the great importance Beijing and Lhasa attached to this organization. Its formal title was the Tibet Patriotic Youth Federation, with the extra word "patriotic" added in comparison to the names of its counterparts in Ngawa, Sichuan, and other places. Who were these so-called "patriotic youth"? Supposedly the CCP desired to turn all the young people in Central Tibet into "patriotic youth," but the federation primarily targeted those from aristocratic families. As in Ngawa, it organized many social events to allow the aristocratic youth to socialize. There was even a soccer team organized by the federation's socially active and charismatic vice-president, Zhölkhang Tupten Nyima (1920–1991), whom I got to know well during this visit. Usually young aristocrats loved these kinds of events because they were full of fun. Likewise, the federation mobilized them to travel to major Chinese cities. Occasionally I came across these young nobles from Central Tibet during my trips to these same cities, along with noble youth from Ngawa and Sichuan. During the Central Youth Delegation's stay in Lhasa, we mainly interacted with aristocratic youth.

These young aristocrats, especially those close to the CCP, were under enormous pressure. Many feared being stoned or beaten with sticks, or otherwise attacked by others. Therefore, they would interact with the delegates at different social events during the day but stay indoors at night to avoid attack. These aristocratic activists, who were patriotic and had advanced outlooks toward social change in the eyes of the CCP, were seen as CCP lapdogs by most people in Lhasa and Central Tibet. Most Tibetans couldn't accept the new political order under the Communist regime because they were used to being governed directly by the Dalai Lama and the Tibetan Kashag government. Even the aristocratic activists, such as Zhölkhang Tupten Nyima, expressed during casual conversations that they felt they had no other option but to ally with the new regime. They knew that the old economic and political systems would no longer work and that they had to rely on the CCP for their salaries and survival.

From the moment I arrived in Lhasa, I could sense a different atmosphere compared to the one during my studies there in the 1940s, even though everything seemed normal and calm on the surface.[13] My tutor and many great lamas, as well as most aristocrats and other people in Lhasa, naïvely believed that the geographic isolation of Central Tibet and the many powerful protective deities in Tibetan Buddhism would prevent the Chinese from taking over. It turned out that neither could stop the CCP and its People's Liberation Army. Under these circumstances, people were understandably apprehensive about the ongoing changes in Central Tibet and its uncertain political future. My old acquaintances at Drepung Monastery's Loserling who came and saw me confirmed these exacerbated tensions. One of my former teachers, Sertsa Géshé, an assistant tutor to the Dalai Lama, passed away after I left Lhasa for home. His treasurer came to see me and shared his insights about the tense environment, suggesting I had returned to Lhasa at the right time. The pro-CCP faction and advocates for "Tibet for Tibetans" were engaged in escalating constant struggles. He anticipated that the situation would soon get out of control and advised me to prepare and be ready to leave for India with him to join my tutor, who had gone to India on pilgrimage and decided to stay there. My tutor did so in part because he was offered the role of abbot in a newly established Gelugpa monastery at Bodhgaya (Dorjé Den) and due to the tense political climate in Lhasa. My tutor's absence saved me from some awkwardness. If he had remained in Lhasa, I would have had no idea how to face him. I had broken my promise to him by failing to return to Lhasa in the three years as promised, and more important, I had chosen a different path by involving myself in the CCP. My primary cause with the CCP was to transform my hometown and Ngawa Prefecture into an actual communist society in the coming decades. It would have a higher form of socialism in which injustice, inequality, and poverty would disappear. So to avoid confronting the treasurer directly, I invented an excuse to decline his offer to sponsor my trip to India, saying that I needed to return to my hometown for preparations before soon returning to Lhasa.

I didn't return to Drepung for a visit, despite receiving multiple invitations from old friends and acquaintances who came to see me in Lhasa. A Central Youth Delegation official also encouraged me to go and make offerings at Drepung, saying that all related expenses would be covered. I declined by saying I had left behind the religious life and was not interested in visiting Drepung or any other monastery. I did feel this way and saw no need to visit any religious site unless it was part of official arrangements. For instance, our delegation went to Tashi Lhunpo Monastery in Shigatse, the traditional seat of the Panchen Lama, who received us as part of the officially arranged schedule. My estrangement from religious life is indication of my loyalty toward the CCP and the Communist cause, although I was unsure if this delegation official's suggestion that I make religious offerings was a test of my political loyalty. My activist stance kept me from interacting directly with high lamas and aristocrats in private and public. Thus, I didn't visit the Dedrug Rinpoche, though we had always gotten along.

Against my wishes, however, I interacted frequently with young aristocrats in informal settings. Yéshé Tso, another member of the Central Youth Delegation, often asked me to accompany her on visits to various aristocratic families despite my protests. Originally from Kham, she became an employee at the CYLC in Beijing after completing her training at its Central Institute. She was from a merchant family with many connections to Lhasa aristocrats. Yéshé Tso seemed to know all these people and had good information about what was going on in their private lives. She was straightforward and would ask our aristocratic hosts whatever question popped into her head. Thus I could hear some of their honest thoughts, including their dilemmas. For instance, as noted above, some aristocrats felt they had to ally with the new regime for pragmatic concerns.

In a nutshell, the United Front held a peculiar place in the CCP's endeavor to incorporate various Tibetan societies into the new socialist state. Based on what I observed in Ngawa, Sichuan, and Central Tibet, the United Front played a vital role in co-opting and aligning different social and political forces in Tibetan regions to support the new regime. This success was founded on the CCP's promise to respect ethnic differences and the particulars of Tibetan cultural, political, and social realities. However, the

United Front in Central Tibet failed to accomplish as much as it did in other Tibetan regions. As highlighted by General Fan Ming (1914–2010; one of the principal PLA commanders in Lhasa and vice-secretary of the CCP Tibet Work Committee) during his meeting with the Central Youth Delegation, the cadres there encountered tremendous difficulties in reaching out to the general public and in building effective United Fronts in Central Tibet due to locals' unwillingness to cooperate.[14]

This was the truth. The Qing and the Kuomintang had left Central Tibet alone to deal with their internal affairs. In contrast, other Tibetan regions had interacted with the Chinese powers more closely throughout history. The CCP had great patience toward this situation, although aristocrats, lamas, and many others were aware that it wouldn't last forever. At that time, the CCP also exercised restraint toward the status quo in Ngawa and other Tibetan regions. Thus, the privileges of the nobles and *tulkus*, or the old system, remained largely intact in Greater Tibet until the Democratic Reform. This explains why the CCP attached great importance to the United Front regarding its potential to cultivate support from Tibetans, especially from important lay and religious figures, for more drastic reforms.

At such a historical crossroads, each person had to choose. Of the "Three Giants" in Ngawa Prefecture, Dorjé Pasang fled to India by way of Lhasa, while Suo Guanyin and Pelgön Trinlé chose to stay behind. I decided to identify with the CCP and worked for the CCP enthusiastically, genuinely believing in its capacity to rejuvenate the Tibetan nation. I believed that corrupt political and religious systems had seriously undermined Tibet's social foundations and trusted the CCP's promise to bring about equality for the different ethnicities and people from all walks of life. These choices defined our respective political destinies and personal life trajectories.

Chapter Ten

THE DEMOCRATIC REFORM

Soon after Liberation, large-scale land reform was carried out in Han Chinese regions, focusing on land redistribution to the masses.[1] However, such work, referred to as the Democratic Reform, was postponed in many ethnic minority regions, and Tibetan areas in particular.[2] The Reform in Ngawa Prefecture was not completed in one fell swoop but involved various stages. It started with the eastern part of the Min River area in October 1954 and ran roughly through the spring of 1955. Most people there were Han, although the local population included minority groups like the Qiang and Tibetans. Tibetans made up the majority in the western part of the Min River area. The Reform was carried out in its agricultural area from November 1955 to April 1956 and in its more nomadic areas from July 1958 to early 1959. Since I participated in the Reform in Ngawa and Dzamtang counties, predominantly nomadic regions, my accounts are primarily based on my experiences in those areas, but with some comparisons to the situation in agricultural regions I had general knowledge about.

The Reform in a nomadic region would typically be completed within forty to fifty days unless certain circumstances were involved, say local resistance or riots. Preparations started much earlier, probably as early as Liberation, if not earlier. The CCP sent its agents to what would later become Ngawa Prefecture to investigate local conditions before Liberation. The agents masqueraded as refugees, beggars, porters, and traders and were thus able to provide general and specific information about the local social and political systems.

Such missions were usually more successful in agricultural regions because these places tended to have a more substantial Han presence, making the agents less noticeable. In some cases, the Han had resettled there or came as traders, porters, or seasonal workers. In the wake of the Second Jinchuan Campaign in the late eighteenth century, thousands of Han had migrated to Chuchen and Tsanlha as a part of Qing policy. This trend of Han resettlement grew even more vital during the Republican Era. Many more Han migrated there to escape the Sichuan basin's endless warfare and subsequent starvation. This increasing migration and traveling was also a direct outcome of the booming poppy trade in the two Jinchuans and other parts of Gyalrong. Additionally, in many parts of the area east of the Min River, the locals became much more Sinicized or were mainly Han settlers. As a result, ethnic minority communities had been in contact with the Han and Chinese cultures, and many of them could understand or speak Chinese.

In contrast, the more nomadic region had few, if any Han migrants. Native Tibetans generally had little knowledge of the Chinese language and culture. Therefore, their resistance to the Reform was more robust than that in predominantly agricultural regions. Surprisingly, though, resistance to the PLA during Liberation in Gyalrong and other Tibetan agricultural regions in Ngawa Prefecture was stronger than in the nomadic areas. I assumed this was related to the local society's deeper involvement with the Han or Kuomintang. In the case of Tsanlha, the Okzhi queen wouldn't have joined the revolt against the new Communist regime without the prodding of the Han Gown Brothers. Dorjé Pasang and Trochu's rebellion was due partly to his deep involvement with the Han and Kuomintang. When nomads or people in seminomadic regions realized that the Han (Communists) were going to permanently settle in their native lands and profoundly transform their traditional way of life and governance, many were unable to accept it. Comparing this with the situation in Gyalrong, a relatively more Sinicized place, can help better explain it.

Many in Gyalrong expected that the Han government would eventually give up and leave them alone, just as the Qing and Kuomintang had done. Although the Qing and Kuomintang had dispatched Han mayors to Chuchen and Tsanlha, the kings and magistrates had much sovereignty over local affairs. Therefore, their subjects believed their destinies were more closely tied to these native leaders than to a faraway emperor or president. Yet the nomadic and seminomadic people were even more unfamiliar with the concept of the Han being their new rulers. Another critical factor in the nomads' stronger resistance was a much weaker tradition of hierarchical rule in nomadic society. The sedentary lifestyle of agricultural peasants in Gyalrong allowed for the full development of the chieftain system because the peasants' livelihoods were closely tied to the land that the kings or chieftains used to control their subjects. In contrast, nomads changed their pastures seasonally, traveling throughout extensive areas, which made it much more difficult for direct and rigorous administrative control to be effected. While some Gyalrong kingdoms like the Somang, Choktsé, and Trokyap had large nomadic regions within their jurisdictions, including parts of today's Kachu (Kakhok), Ngawa, Dzamtang, Drakgo, and Sêrtar Counties (the last two are located in present-day Kardzé Prefecture), the kings had to adopt more flexible and less demanding strategies to govern their nomadic populations. As a result, the nomadic lifestyle was characterized by freedom. The Communist regime, or the Democratic Reform, intended to constrain this freedom and turn locals into obedient subjects of the new socialist state. Nomads were not used to such direct rule, and many chose to resist it.[3] The revolts in the nomadic regions of Ngawa might have been much more disruptive and turbulent if it had not been for the influence of Pelgön Trinlé, the king of the Ngawa region. No large-scale revolts occurred in his territory or its neighboring nomadic areas.

As demanded by the CCP, Pelgön Trinlé urged his subjects to turn in their weapons to the government at the start of the Reform.[4] It was common practice for those living in nomadic and agricultural areas to keep guns to protect themselves from bandits and enemies and hunt wild animals. Even I kept a dozen guns at the monastery before leaving for Chengdu to study in 1951. The new regime didn't confiscate guns systematically from the public until the Reform, except for disarming the Gown Brothers and local rebels. These gangsters' and rebels' weapons were seized after their rebellions were quelled in the early 1950s. As a result, even though some of Pelgön Trinlé's subjects chose to rise against the Reform later, they failed quickly partly due to their lack of arms.

The CCP implemented a strategy critical to the Reform's success: a policy of transferring local chieftains, nobles, and other influential figures out of their territories, intended to disengage them from their previous subjects and followers. The CCP pacified the most important people by offering them critical symbolic positions at the prefectural and provincial levels. For instance, Pelgön Trinlé was offered positions as vice-governor of the Sichuan Tibetan Autonomous Region and in the Ngawa Tibetan Autonomous Prefecture. He was later relocated to Chengdu to assume a position as vice-chair of Sichuan's Chinese People's Political Consultative Conference (CPPCC). Other less important figures were offered cadre positions at the county level. Any remaining vital individuals from the local society were typically called to the county seat or other places for study sessions that were a form of house arrest; they were kept within heavily guarded and walled compounds.

Next, work teams came to instill the notion of class struggle and feudal oppression and mobilize locals to expose the vices of their nobles. Each county had a number of work teams. Typically, one team of ten to twenty members, a combination of army men and cadres, would be sent to a village or nomadic settlement of several hundred inhabitants. The cadres usually had been temporarily transferred from other counties that had already completed the Reform. When a work team arrived at its designated site, its members would go to each household to thoroughly investigate local conditions, such as property possession, circumstances of exploitation, conflicts, schisms among various people and classes, religious beliefs and practices, and so on. Strictly speaking, these investigations were more like reinvestigations that would confirm the results of similar surveys that had been going on since Liberation began, if not earlier. In Ngawa County, for example, the investigation usually took ten days or longer, depending on the size of the community or village under the Reform. It provided essential information for defining class categories, such as feudal lords, landlords or nomadic lords, and rich, middle, and poor peasants or nomads.

In theory, class classification was based on a few criteria, including land ownership, livestock, and other belongings. In actual practice, the class was often defined by more flexible standards and through a quota, making the whole process subjective and situational. For instance, based on "hard" (objective) criteria, at least fourteen to fifteen households in the Khashi community, where many were successful well-off traders, could easily have been labeled landlords-nomadic lords or rich peasants-nomads. However, only six or seven were classified as such. In contrast, not a single household in Ronggön satisfied the "hard" criteria to be labeled as feudal lords, although several individuals or households had to be "selected" for this high-class label.[5] The treasurer of a local monastery, Kirti Ronggön,[6] was consequently branded as a feudal lord since the classification system stipulated that someone from the monastery, which was considered a feudal site, had to be, though this treasurer didn't own much personal property and what he was said to possess belonged to the monastery. Most monks were classified as middle and poor peasants because they weren't said to have exploited people directly.

In other words, based on the quota system, there had to be a few households or individuals in each village or community selectively branded as members of the higher classes, above rich peasants/nomads. The people's enemies and feudal oppressors, under the classification schema, had to make up a small percentage of the society. Therefore, the mainstays of society, the poor peasants and nomads, considered the most oppressed and thus most revolutionary, would make up over 60 percent of the local population. Subsequently, depending on the varying degrees of exploitation and oppression, most of the rich's property and possessions, like their land, farm tools, livestock, clothes, and money, were confiscated by the state or redistributed among the poor. Redistribution would not happen until the completion of study sessions for the masses.

These study sessions usually took another twenty days or so in Ronggön and other places in Ngawa County. Monks were among the participants. Most monks would be expelled from the monasteries and return to their original homes. Because nomads lived in sparsely populated territories, they all had to bring their tents and set them up around the meeting ground. Everyone was mandated to attend unless they were too young, too old, or too sick to move about. In the morning sessions, work team members would propagate the significance and necessity of the Reform and then ask people to expose the vices of those in power. Initially, mobilizing people to attack their nobles and fellows was difficult. Therefore, we would encourage them to confront their enemies and oppressors and expose their unfair treatment and exploitations to the rest of the group. Once someone started, others would typically follow suit. As emotions rose, the situation might get out of control. People spit in the faces of nobles and people from higher classes, dragged them about, hit them with their fists, and so on. Work team members usually tried to restrain agitated people from assaulting others to prevent complete disruption of the study and struggle sessions.

There would be a few hours' break in the middle of the day before the sessions resumed. Usually people were divided into smaller groups to discuss and express their grievances against feudal lords and oppressors. These discussions continued again in the evening after a dinner break. Every individual was required to continually expose the old system's evils, speak highly of the CCP and Reform, express their desire to advance their political outlook, and so on. If someone hesitated to express themselves or was thought to have failed to dig deep enough into their inner thoughts, they were seen as resistant to social change or backward in their thought. These individuals would then be urged to undergo self-criticism to improve their way of thinking.

Local activists played a vital role in the Reform. Our work team emphasized the cultivation of such activists, who typically were chosen from poor families, tended to have more advanced outlooks on social change, and most importantly, could effectively influence the masses. We gauged their influence based on public acknowledgments of these candidates' skills, such as their eloquence, charming personality, fairness, and eagerness to help others. Activists were primarily young men and women, who were considered more open-minded and ready to accept new ideas. Our work team made special efforts to cultivate female activists. Gender equality was part of Communist ideals and propaganda, so it was impossible to overlook the role of women in Tibet, or any society, in socialist construction and class struggles. The female activists we cultivated were crucial in motivating other women to denounce the old system and their class enemies. To some extent, they were more politically active than the male activists, especially regarding the struggle against religious figures.

Several female activists went so far as to walk over the lamas' heads or even ride on them directly to humiliate these traditionally spiritual leaders. At the same time, they would insult the lamas by saying something like, "Aren't you able to invoke deities? Why aren't you calling your deities here to rescue you?" Or, "Aren't you capable enough to fly? Let's see how you fly." This was their revenge against the Tibetan religious institution. Religion and lamas were said to be responsible for so many restrictions and taboos for women because of their assumed unclean menstruating bodies and their supposed higher susceptibility to envy, anger, and ignorance, which were used as evidence that it was more difficult for them to attain enlightenment. In contrast, the new regime and its gender equality propaganda empowered Tibetan women to express their resentment toward their subjugation and challenge it. These female activists declared war on the religious establishment and the old system, saying, "We women were oppressed and trampled underfoot by you religious figures. It's now time for us to rise up and bring you all down."

Routinely, the work team gave only general instructions on Reform procedures, and then the local activists proceeded. For example, activists gathered monks at Ronggön, whose monastic population was about 200. They told the monks that religion was no longer necessary in the new society and that they should embrace a new outlook on life and become part of the socialist labor force.[7] In this way, nearly all the monks were dismissed from their monastic lives, with only a dozen left. Those who stayed behind in their monasteries were too old or weak to join the labor force or had no immediate family members and home to return to. The activists organized people to smash statues and other religious items and destroy monastery interiors. I rarely participated directly in the Reform work with monks and monasteries. This was done almost exclusively by activists, with only one or two work team members present.

Also, as noted, by tradition, there was a weak hierarchical structure in nomadic regions, so most nomads didn't hold entrenched grudges against their nobles and others. The activists knew how to mobilize people in their struggles against class enemies and feudal systems, thanks to their influence in and intimate knowledge of local society, including its conflicts and rivalries. During study sessions, they usually exposed the vices of the old system and tried to inflame the nomads' deep-seated resentments toward feudalism and religion. Even if there were as few as two or three capable activists, it was much easier to mobilize the locals, especially considering that most of the work team members, who were Han and spoke little Tibetan, were nearly useless in nomadic settings. Therefore, without the committed involvement of local activists, any successful execution of the Reform was practically unthinkable.

Despite the work teams' devotion and the activists' assistance in inculcating the notion of class struggle for the public, the CCP believed our efforts were insufficient in cultivating the people's adequate class consciousness. A contemporary guiding principle was Mao's idea that without violent revolution or armed struggles against class enemies, the notion of class struggle couldn't be fully realized among the masses. To achieve that goal, the CCP leadership in Ngawa Prefecture felt it necessary to instigate the upper classes to revolt so they could then be subdued in the nomadic regions. The CCP and PLA leaders devised such a strategy in Ngawa County and elsewhere. As mentioned earlier, less important figures in local societies, such as junior nobles, were called to the county seats or elsewhere for "study sessions." An example of this strategy is when inmates began digging a tunnel in a corner of their cell. The guards pretended not to notice, but when the inmates completed their tunnel, escaped through it, and fled, their actions were immediately interpreted as insurrection, and the fugitives were labeled rebels.

Not all officials approved. For instance, Ren Taihe, the director of the prefecture's United Front Department, almost had a heart attack when he heard about this outcome. He thought the strategy was imprudent and wronged those without the intention of rebelling. Unfortunately, more conscientious officials like him could do little to amend or undermine the guiding principles of the Democratic Reform among local officials, namely Mao's philosophy that "political power grows out of the barrel of a gun." Likewise, people who hid in forests because of their uncertainty about the Reform's implications were branded as rebels right away, although many had no intention of joining armed struggles against the PLA. This label left them no choice but to join. As a result, due to these involuntary rebels' prestige and lineage connections, many more locals joined them. This seriously affected the progress of the Reform on the ground, despite Mao's view of armed struggle against class enemies as an inevitable means to inspire the ordinary people's class consciousness. Our work team's operation at Ronggön was also disrupted before we began to redistribute confiscated goods, land, and livestock because more and more participants in the study sessions ran away. They were drawn to the spreading influence of a revolt led by an influential noble in the Trokyap kingdom (a Gyalrong chieftaincy), Tséwang Nor, which started in 1956.

Tséwang Nor was an influential figure in a border area between Ngawa and Kardzé Prefectures, now at an intersection between today's Chuchen, Dzamtang, Drakgo, and Sêrtar Counties. Tséwang Nor had been to various parts of China as a member of a visiting team organized for nobles and others, so he had some idea about how vast China was and how powerful the CCP was. Nonetheless, he rebelled. I didn't know much about Tséwang Nor's motives, but based on my knowledge about other nobles turned rebels, their reservations and doubts about the CCP and the Reform could be easily seen as uncooperative or counter-revolutionary. Moreover, as noted earlier, the CCP officials and PLA officers at Ngawa County's seat purposefully released their imprisoned nobles and others and subsequently labeled them rebels. Suffice it to say, the CCP could easily have implemented specific tactics to get rid of these unwanted nobles and class enemies. Tséwang Nor and some other nobles probably knew that they were unwanted and understood that the CCP would be forced to deal with them in time. So they declared war against the CCP, hoping that even if they died, they would do so as heroes. Thanks to the prestige they held in their local societies, as well as existing sentiments, suspicions, and apprehensions about the Reform that were shared by many, Tséwang Nor and his allies had a large following, likely over a thousand people. His influence soon spread to other nomadic regions, including Ngawa County.[8]

Due to the disruption of the Reform agenda at Ronggön, our work team had to defend ourselves against potential rebel attacks. Our elderly and female colleagues left for Ngawa's county seat while the brave young men stayed behind. A band known as the "armed work team" (Ch. *wuzhuang gongzuo dui*) was established, and I acted as its head. It was made up of twenty to thirty fully armed men, including local and nonlocal activists, dispatched from places where the Reform had already been carried out. At Kirti Ronggön we stayed inside the assembly hall, which was two stories tall. The monastery's perimeter walls provided a barrier to protect us from the rebels who would attack at night. During the daytime, we repaired and augmented the walls, blocked the major entrances, and took down any buildings around the monastery that had been monk quarters to prevent rebels from using them as shelter or as a garrison.

At least we had ample food. Piles of butter and barley flour, confiscated from the rich or taken from the monastery, were scattered all over the floor. We used the scriptures and wood frames from the assembly hall to build fires. Initially our only concern was the water supply. During our household visits at the start of the Reform, we learned that there had been a spring naturally running beneath the assembly hall before it was diverted with a ditch during construction of the monastery. Local activists who stayed with us knew its exact location. So we dug and found this spring, solving our water problem.

We had a telegraph transmitter-receiver to regularly report on our situation and receive instructions from our superiors based at the Ngawa County seat. The county would send reinforcements of a dozen soldiers now and then to dispel rebels and relieve us. This helped alleviate some of the pressure for short periods, but the reinforcement team stayed for only one or two days before they had to set off again to crush other revolts here and there throughout the county. While we were relatively safe in the monastery, our reinforcement team was subject to sudden attacks and setbacks from time to time.

Once our reinforcement team was ambushed by rebels. These soldiers were fighting sporadically against the insurgents on their way to the monastery where we were stationed. When the monastery was within their sight, they lost their vigilance. Seeing the monastery from a hilltop, the vanguard rushed toward it on horseback. Suddenly, dozens of rebels hiding in the bushes fired at our reinforcement soldiers, killing seven or eight. Hearing the gunshots, we realized something had gone wrong. Dozens of us ran out of the monastery and galloped our horses toward the scene. I arrived first and saw the remaining soldiers firing into the bushes where the rebels were hidden. We realized that the insurgents had planned to attack our work team members when some of us emerged from the monastery as part of our daily routine. They hadn't expected that our reinforcement team would be on its way, and in surprise they turned their guns on the PLA soldiers, receiving a more robust response than they had expected.

After this incident, we continued to hold our base at the monastery until I was called to meetings at both the CPPCC and the People's Congress in Barkham, the seat of Ngawa Prefecture, in late 1958. I left with another reinforcement team that came from Barkham. Ngawa County was short on soldiers since they had all been dispatched to different places to subdue riots. Then, before long, its new Party Secretary, Wang Zhiping (hereafter Secretary Wang), transferred me to the newly established Dzamtang County to participate in the Reform there. He said he badly needed my skills for the Reform there, which was about to begin.

Secretary Wang said he felt frustrated with the situation in Dzamtang because most of his subordinates and attendants were largely unhelpful; they mainly were Han and knew little Tibetan. There had been some Tibetan cadres, but they struggled to fully convey the Reform agenda and Party policy accurately to nomads. These Tibetan cadres hadn't mastered the Chinese language well enough to translate the agenda and policies back into Tibetan, or they struggled to effectively interpret the politically charged expressions and slogans to the public. Consequently, Secretary Wang sincerely asked for my support. I agreed with his assessment based on my own experiences. Since I had already participated in several work teams in nomadic and seminomadic regions, including Ngawa County, I had seen how most of the team members were Han and played limited roles because they could not effectively communicate with the nomads, let alone energetically mobilize them. On top of that, the work team leaders took it for granted that their Tibetan subordinates or the activists who knew some Chinese were unquestionably qualified interpreters. Ludicrous mistakes and misinterpretations occurred constantly. Here are two such episodes.

First, a Tibetan work team member interpreted the original Chinese expression of "putting up a resolute fight against the resurrection of feudalism" at a study session for the nomadic public. He mistranslated the Chinese term "resurrection" as "fox pelt" due to the words having a similar pronunciation in the Sichuan dialect—"fupi." Hence, his Tibetan translation became "putting up a resolute fight against fox pelt of feudalism." When he saw some in the audience wearing hats made of fox pelts, which was common among Tibetans, he shouted, "Have you folks not listened at all? The CCP is strongly opposed to the fox pelt of feudalism." People silently removed their hats, although they had no idea how a fox pelt was associated with feudalism.

On another occasion, the work team emphasized the significance of establishing "core leadership" (*hexin lingdao*) of CCP grassroots organizations in local society and encouraged activists to "actively move closer to the CCP" and to eventually join the Party and become part of the "core leadership." A Tibetan interpreter mistranslated "core leadership" into "black-hearted leadership" because the two Chinese terms for "core" and "black-hearted" sound very similar in the Sichuan dialect—"heixin." When activists asked the group to reflect on this principle, one looked hesitant but finally gathered the courage to ask, "I do want to join the CCP and become part of the leadership, but do I have to turn into a 'black-hearted' one?"

How hilarious! However, this simultaneously showcased the severe shortage of qualified cadres in nomadic settings, both Han and Tibetan, who could carry out effective mobilization, organization, and other work among the masses. So I felt it was a great honor to go to Dzamtang and contribute to its Reform with my bilingual expertise and hands-on experience. I first attended the Reform at Drala and Khalung, two seminomadic communities in Dzamtang, and acted as the head of the work teams there. Our work and procedures were the same as in other areas. We conducted a thorough survey of the general and specific social conditions by going door to door. In these visits, we would classify people according to different class labels, confiscate the rich's property and belongings to be redistributed among the poor, send monks home, pick out the most capable activists as our assistants, gather locals for study sessions, organize political struggles against nobles and the rich, and so on. As I was familiar with the procedure, everything went smoothly as planned.

If I were asked to evaluate the outcome of the Democratic Reform, I would say it was largely successful. The old system, characterized by inequality and exploitation, as in the chieftain and magistrate systems, was gone forever, and people were promised a better future. I, along with many others, thought that we would usher in Communism, the highest and most ideal form of human society, in another ten to twenty years. Then everyone would enjoy their fullest lives regarding equality, material conditions, and spiritual prosperity.

However, something else weighed heavily on my mind. Soon after I left Ronggön and Ngawa County, another round of the Reform was conducted there. This was called the Makeup Movement of the Democratic Reform because the CCP said the earlier Reform had not been carried out thoroughly enough. Local activists whom our work team had made every effort to cultivate were imprisoned or labeled "bad elements" (*huai fenzi*). The CCP saw the activists' superb organizing skills and influence in local society as a massive barrier to direct control by the CCP. No matter how I tried, I couldn't make sense of the Party's reasons for doing this. How could the CCP turn its back on the very activists who embraced the new regime and motivated so many others to do the same? I had been fully dedicated to the cause before, but this was the first time I started to doubt the CCP agenda.

Chapter Eleven

RIDING THE REVOLUTIONARY TIDES

Life, like rising and ebbing tides, is full of ups and downs. My experiences since Liberation were a perfect manifestation of this. At first, the CCP treated me as one of their very own. This felt like heaven, so I dedicated myself to their cause to help usher in the age of Communism. I was, however, discarded like a pair of old shoes around the start of the Cultural Revolution, which lasted from 1966 to 1976. I was plunged into hell and nearly killed myself in unspeakable desperation. Later, toward the end of the revolution, I was picked up again by local CCP officials. My life thus swung back and forth between heaven and hell. Despite my exasperation with the new regime's inconsistent tenets and practices, I realized that my experiences were not unique. I decided I would be better off adopting a more easygoing attitude about my rise and fall.

When I reflect on the best times in my life, the turbulent years spent in Dzamtang from 1958 to 1977 come to mind. The nomads inspired me to see the twilight through the dark moments. Let me explain. Heaven represents unbounded happiness. This is a constant across the diverse interpretations among different religions and people. I was so happy that my *tulku* status didn't automatically disqualify me from being identified as a valuable member of the new society after Liberation. More importantly, I earned the CCP's trust, which was a powerful, wonderful feeling, so I was willing to give up everything else, including my life, for a better society founded on equality, fairness, and justice. Besides, my happiness in Dzamtang was related to the nomads I interacted with. Overall, Tibetan nomads are the most light-hearted and wonderful people I have ever met.[1]

After the Democratic Reform, I volunteered to work in Dzamtang's nomad and seminomad sectors. Secretary Wang enthusiastically endorsed my request and praised me for my advanced political consciousness. Most cadres hesitated to work there, assuming the living conditions were horrible. Secretary Wang was, however, unaware that I made this request out of practical concerns. Above all, I anticipated that my life would be easier and more enjoyable. I had learned some Chinese, strengthened through my training at the Southwest Nationalities Institute in Chengdu and later at the Central Institute of the Communist Youth League of China (CYLC) in Beijing, which I attended from 1956 to 1957. Later, my work mainly involved direct interactions with nobles, peasants, and nomads. My Chinese language skills weren't adequate to handle paperwork, especially writing official reports, so keeping myself in an office made little sense. Because of this, I never expected to be sent to deal with administrative bureaucracy at a prefecture or county seat. I preferred a more mobile working style and enjoyed daily face-to-face interactions with people. Working in a pastoral setting was the best way to secure such a life and working style. I only stayed at the county seat or office for meetings. For most of the year, I visited nomad communities across the county one after another, supervising nomad production.

In theory, I and other cadres in our work team were there to assist nomads in their daily routines. In reality, we were pretty useless because nomad work, such as herding and milking, required skills that an outsider cannot master quickly. Apart from procedural duties as a team director, I coordinated gathering nomads for political propaganda sessions and meetings. This left me with a great deal of spare time to do whatever I wanted, so I became an expert at hunting and fishing. I had both long and short rifles. As vice-mayor and work team director, I was issued guns, so I often hunted on horseback after a political meeting. I rarely returned to my tent empty-handed and shared what I brought back with the work team members and local nomads. I also fished and caught more than we could consume in a single day. Few people had such skills that surpassed mine. I became such an expert because I wanted a simple and pleasant life. I hadn't been a bad student in Lhasa, suggesting that I was a quick learner. However, I was no longer interested in digging further into complex Buddhist knowledge and philosophy. Honing my hunting and fishing skills served me better at that time.

There is also more. I was very troubled about some actions the CCP officials took during the Democratic Reform, such as their nefarious scheme to push nomads into rebellion, unjustifiable conduct to defame innocent activists, and so on (see chapter 10). These officials' ways of doing things emboldened activists and others to follow suit. Many people went on to fabricate "evidence" out of thin air or exaggerate the degree of exploitation and oppression to incriminate the upper class. Fairness and truth gave way to political correctness and Mao's infallibility. Therefore, anyone reckless or dauntless enough to exhibit any reservation or disapproval was quickly labeled a class enemy or reactionary. The last thing I wanted to do was to wrong others by compromising my basic life principle as a just and fair-minded person under any circumstances. I was not ready to directly confront the CCP about some of its more problematic agendas. It felt like there was no way for me, or anyone else at that time, to insulate ourselves from the rising and falling revolutionary tides. Working in nomadic areas helped alleviate my plight. I poured all my talents into hunting and fishing, among other things, to entertain myself and seek peace of mind and happiness.

I had never encountered people like these nomads who knew how to enjoy their lives. Nomads had less arduous daily labor and much more spare time to entertain themselves than their counterparts in agricultural regions. They used this time to perform the epic of King Gesar, chat, joke, race horses, wrestle, and so on.[2] The nomads also enjoyed more freedom in exploring sexuality. They hadn't developed entrenched notions about chastity for women. Generally, Tibetans put much less importance on female chastity or virginity than the Han, who were said to stone unchaste women to death before Liberation. In addition, agricultural peasant communities in Tibetan regions emphasized women's chastity and sexual behavior more seriously than the nomads. As a personal example, I lost interest in my first girlfriend—the daughter of a local noble at Sönamyak—because she was not a virgin. Likewise, I began distancing myself from my female classmate, Liu, at Southwest Nationalities Institute when I learned that she had slept with a PLA officer. In the eyes of nomads, my "problem" was ridiculous. They saw sex as an essential part of life that everyone was entitled to and should enjoy.

As a result, nomads were nearly always in a good mood, which had everything to do with their mobile lifestyle and free spirit. Given this, how could they continue moving about and maintain a free spirit when the Reform established communes everywhere to confine people to their land and collectivize nomad production? The key is that collectivization was generally much less effective in nomad regions. In a farming-based society, sedentary lifestyles are essential. This means peasants are bound to their lands, houses, livestock, and other properties. Therefore, it was relatively easy for the CCP to exert tighter control over peasants and integrate their resources and production. In contrast, the nomadic lifestyle undermined the CCP's ambitious agenda. In the nomad communities I worked with in Dzamtang, people would change their pastures as frequently as every ten to twenty days in summer to graze their herds. This high level of mobility meant that the CCP and its communes were limited in their ability to curtail nomad movements effectively. Briefly, I believe that the following principle can be applied within and outside of nomad settings: freedom is the cornerstone of happiness, and happiness without freedom is nearly unthinkable. Based on my experience, it was impossible not to be strongly affected by the nomads' cheerful personalities and positive attitudes toward life through daily interactions. Everything I had dreamed about during my stay in Lhasa revolved around freedom and happiness. I nearly accomplished the goals I had set there during the intervening years between the Democratic Reform and the Cultural Revolution in Dzamtang. I say "nearly accomplished" because something still disturbed and prevented me from thoroughly enjoying life. In addition to my doubts about the aforementioned Party-state practices, I was a total failure in romance.

Although I was married then, love was elusive. My wife, a Han cadre and Party member, denigrated and regularly cursed me because of my status as a feudal lord and reactionary *tulku*. It was typical for an official or *zuzhi* (bureaucratic organization) to arrange marriages for their employees in those days, and the prefecture Party secretary had arranged ours. We had two children who were byproducts of our mutual sexual needs rather than affection. I was described as not bad-looking and was popular among young women wherever I went. However, I couldn't develop romantic relationships with any of them because, as a secret CYLC member and a CCP cadre, I felt obligated to not engage in extramarital affairs. Therefore, even though I admired the nomads and their sexual freedom, I could not follow their lead.

Despite such limitations, I asked myself, *Why shouldn't I take advantage of this time and enjoy life to the fullest like the nomads?* My pastimes of hunting and fishing partly resulted from this revelation. Unquestionably, my best times were inseparable from the freedoms I had. The pastures and forests were so expansive in nomad regions, and the population was small—no more than a hundred in a small brigade. I was pretty much left alone most of the time. This freedom was further enhanced through my frequent travel with the nomads. I also enjoyed freedom from administrative bureaucracy, a more restrained life in an agricultural setting, the inevitable consequences of collectivization, and my wife, who was transferred to Dzamtang and worked in the Education Bureau at the county seat.

I ate with the nomads, so I also had the best food one could ever have. Despite the rigid monthly rations for each cadre and nomad in those days, mainly barley and sometimes maize and other grains as well, merely 11 and 9.5 kilograms, respectively, the nomads and I had plenty to eat because our daily meals were supplemented with milk, yogurt, butter, and cheese. My diet was further enriched with game and fish. Nomads also found creative ways to obtain meat. Although there was a ration, they were never short of meat because they could claim that one of their livestock had died of a wolf attack or falling from a cliff. Since the commune cadres would rarely investigate the reason for livestock death, the nomads could then distribute and consume the meat at ease without repercussions. I was invited to enjoy this kind of extra meat with them. Everything we ate was fresh. Barley was ground every three days to make barley flour, and dairy products were regularly produced. Once, several commune cadres and I ate a meal on a pasture. Our bread was first toasted over a fire we built, and then fresh butter, still fragrant with a slight milk odor, was sandwiched between two pieces of bread. A Han who had a college degree and worked as a commune accountant exclaimed, "What on this earth could be more delicious than this?"

I reflect on my time in Dzamtang's nomad areas with immense nostalgia, though it is only part of the story. My nostalgia also has a lot to do with the nomads' outstanding personal qualities I admire, such as their true intelligence, honesty, and loyalty. The mobile lifestyle gave them much freedom, although in the late 1950s, this freedom had to be earned with extra effort because of tightened political controls. By the end of the Reform, a lower form of collectivization called "mutual-aid teams" (Ch. *huzhu zu*) was established in the nomad regions in Ngawa Prefecture, including Dzamtang. Several households formed teams to herd their livestock together as a production unit. Nomads quickly accepted this arrangement because it was in line with their traditional herding patterns. However, this type of organization was soon taken over by the highest form of collectivization, referred to as a "people's commune" (Ch. *renmin gongshe*).[3] The nomads sought effective ways to circumvent the commune's control because there was no well-grounded step-by-step transition.

The brigade was a primary productive unit under the people's commune. A Dzamtang brigade was usually composed of twenty to thirty households. The size varied according to the commune's population. The brigade and its households were normally further divided into three or four smaller units or bands, with each band responsible for herding one particular type of livestock—cows (mostly female yaks and a small number of *dzomo* or female yak/cow hybrids), yaks (male), teen yaks (male; three to six years old), and sometimes sheep—when sheep were available and plentiful (not all nomad communities kept many). Although all the households had turned over their livestock to the commune, everyone knew which animals were theirs, including newborn calves from their former cows. All the brigade members acknowledged this unspoken ownership rule.

Hence, when a brigade was required to hand in a specified number of livestock to the commune and county to be sold or slaughtered once or twice a year, the nomads would take turns providing "their" respective animals, usually two or three from several households in a band. The next time, another band would hand over theirs. People usually handed in the oldest and weakest animals in the herd. Some strong and young cattle were occasionally provided, much to the surprise of commune cadres, even when there were plenty of older and weaker cattle to choose from in the brigade's herd. The commune cadres never knew that this happened when the household whose turn it was in the rotation had only strong and young cattle left, not because of their more significant commitment to the cause.[4] Another phenomenon intrigued me. The family's size allowed each household to keep three to five cattle, typically cows, as private property. Without exception, each private cow was reported to have produced one calf per year. However, not every cow can become pregnant in a natural setting each year. It turned out that the nomads would replace a cow that hadn't given birth within their private herd with one that was "communally owned" from the brigade's herd that had given birth during that particular year. To ensure compliance with the required quota of private cattle, the cadres would count those kept near the tent of a particular household but were unaware if any of these cows had been replaced.

I also found that each household in a nomad community called Chukshül, including the local brigade Party secretary and head, would milk an additional cow from the brigade's herd for their private consumption. I saw this firsthand during my work from 1976 to 1977 after my position was informally restored. The local nomads had done this for over a decade. Why had this never been disclosed because commune cadres, especially the Han, did not understand nomad life. Also, milking one more cow isn't easily noticeable because of the vast number of livestock moving about constantly, especially for those with limited experience in nomad settings. I wouldn't have understood without being naturally curious and observant. Besides, every household was doing this. Anyone who betrayed the group by reporting it to higher officials would harm their self-interest and offend all the other brigade members. Consequently, such practices continued without the authorities' knowledge.

This shows the nomads' intelligence; however, the idea of intelligence alone cannot fully capture what they were doing. More prominently, this highlighted the nomads' true principles. They had a bottom line in their code of conduct and basic moral standards of right and wrong. They knew exactly what they should and shouldn't do. During the Reform, I found that activists and poor nomads would covertly keep some small but critical religious items, such as images and scriptures, in their homes or other safe places. Since they were said to have advanced political awareness, and because many of them had also played a role in destroying local monasteries, few would suspect them. These same people returned the objects they hid to the monasteries when religion was allowed to reemerge in the late 1970s and early 1980s. That explains why major monasteries in nomad regions today have many old precious religious objects, despite the catastrophic Reform and other movements that targeted the old systems and religion.

I had other personal experiences with these principles. I saw something unique while working as director of the work team at Khanung in Dzamtang.

An ex-monk of the Kagyü school (one of the four major schools in Tibetan Buddhism), known later as the Serkhar Lama, enjoyed an exceptional reputation among the locals. I found him making divinations for others secretly. People consulted him for decisions on various issues, including where to build a reservoir that the local commune and cadres were supposed to manage. This man had prostrated to Lhasa on pilgrimage, which was uncommon in those days due to the vast physical distance and arduous journey—the two-way trip would usually take three to four years. The Serkhar Lama also built a massive nine-story blockhouse (Tib. *khar*) on his own after returning to his hometown, as part of the new monastery construction. I did not ask specifically how long it took him to complete it, but I would assume at least four years, almost nonstop. This project was intended to commemorate and emulate the acclaimed Tibetan saint and yogi Milarepa (eleventh to twelfth centuries), whose master, the great translator Marpa (eleventh century; one of the attributed founders of the Kagyü school in Tibet) had him build, destroy, and rebuild a nine-story tower single-handedly to remove his accumulated sins (causing the deaths of many through black magic). In a word, the pilgrimage and blockhouse demonstrated this man's religious dedication and determination. However, few other work team members, except me, noticed. My religious training and knowledge of the Tibetan language and society were instrumental, so I instantly recognized such things.

Surprisingly, not a single individual or activist exposed him. After the Cultural Revolution, Serkhar Monastery was completed under his leadership, and he became one of the most influential lamas in Dzamtang. However, activists and poor peasants/nomads in Khanung behaved as if they had suffered enough from the old system and lamas and were done with religion. Their acting skills were so good that they impressed the work team members and observers with their revolutionary spirit and political awareness. In this way, they did their best to protect respected religious and secular figures. This exemplifies loyalty, one of the nomads' most prized principles and personal qualities. If someone won their trust, they would always be loyal to this person. It was politically risky to display sympathy toward higher class members and religious figures, let alone loyalty. Therefore, it was necessary to find some way to deal with this issue intelligently. That is why intelligence and loyalty tend to go hand in hand in such extraordinary circumstances.

During the Reform and the Cultural Revolution, poor nomads would beat lamas or specific individuals during struggle sessions frequently. Activists or other participants might rush to take the podium as bad actors were being attacked verbally and physically. They would take the lead in joining the beating while shouting political slogans. This turned out to be an ingenious way to protect these individuals from the enraged poor nomads. The lamas and other victims typically wore heavy robes due to the cold weather. The beatings didn't seriously injure them despite the loud *peng-peng-peng* the attackers made with their blows. In this way, the nomads used superior acting skills to masquerade as uncompromising revolutionaries and activists. Without these skills, the locals in Khanung and elsewhere would have been unable to shield the respected figures from further harm.

To clarify, this loyalty among the nomads wasn't just reserved for highly esteemed individuals within their local society. It represents their code of conduct for both friends and other people, including an outsider like me. Based on my experiences, honesty was one of the most cherished attributes among nomads. Lying was regarded as terrible misconduct. Being honest was a common virtue among Tibetans, but it was even truer among nomads. This explains why they were very frustrated with duplicitous Party officials during the Reform and rebellions broke out. This also explains why self-immolations have occurred primarily in nomadic regions since the 2008 Tibetan unrest. Qualities such as generosity, fair-mindedness, and readiness to help others play an essential role in nomad life. I admire these virtues and consider treating people with justice, fairness, and honesty and seeing others as equals to be extremely important. For this reason, I got along well with nomads and was welcomed in their regions.

When the Serkhar Lama at Khanung confided in me about his religion-related activities, I didn't tell anyone. I assumed he had done so because he knew he couldn't hide them from me, probably saw me as trustworthy, and realized I wouldn't turn him in. He would indeed have been branded a feudal lord if I had reported him. I could not betray someone's trust or believe that justice would be served if I reported him and he was persecuted as a result. Unlike the kings and chieftains who had exploited and oppressed others, the Serkhar Lama was compassionate. His reputation, including his Rinpoche title, was obtained not through his hereditary lineage but through his good deeds.

Here is another story: A nomad wanted to charge me 80 yuan for the pelt of his dog, which had recently died. This was a considerable amount of money at that time. I received only an allowance of 30 yuan for monthly expenses from my wife, who had complete control over my income. But without hesitation, I paid him the total amount because I thought this was a usual and fair price. The owner hesitated for a moment and then returned 60 yuan. He had initially planned to keep his dog pelt and was trying to scare me off from buying it by asking such a high price. He never expected that I would pay him so much. As a result, word spread in nomad social circles that I was unsophisticated, unhypocritical, and conscientious, which helped me immensely during the Cultural Revolution. Overall, I had a much easier time than many other individuals with noble or lama status. However, this revelation came sometime after my reconciliation with my political downfall.

My pleasant life with the nomads ended abruptly in 1966 when the Cultural Revolution was about to start. I was called to a meeting at the prefecture's Chinese People's Political Consultative Conference (CPPCC) in Barkham, attended chiefly by subjects being monitored by the United Front (Ch. *tongzhan duixiang*). They included twenty to thirty former nobles, religious figures, intellectuals, and entrepreneurs who were thought to have embraced the new regime with relatively progressive ideas, and whose self-transformation followed the CCP agenda. They were neither class enemies nor "the people" (poor peasants/nomads and working class). Still, they required mental and behavior modification. Before the Democratic Reform, the United Front subjects were seen as CCP allies and more closely aligned with the people's side. At that time, the CCP badly needed them to stabilize the Ngawa region. However, after the Reform, they increasingly gravitated to the enemy's side because the CCP now had complete control over this region and no longer found them useful. During the Cultural Revolution, most were labeled as "ox-headed ghosts and serpent gods." Others were reidentified as the people's enemy and sent to prison or labor camps for reform. Consequently, the CPPCC became a reform camp to transform these subjects.

When I arrived at the meeting, I immediately sensed a different atmosphere. A leading official said, "Someone is a subject of the United Front but has yet to accept this reality and willingly commit to self-transformation."

I knew he was talking about me, though he didn't identify me by name as he spoke. Other subjects of the United Front at the meeting changed how they engaged with me. Before this, I was entrusted with urging them to reform, but now they saw me as one of them. They conveyed a message of gloating through their looks and gestures: "You were too full of yourself, but now you are no better than us." I was confused and upset, so I asked a prominent leader at the prefectural Party committee about my status with the CCP. He replied that as a *tulku*, I was on the opposing side of the great masses and had been made a league member because of an earlier mistake caused by "rightist capitulation." He added that it was time to redress this colossal mistake and instructed me to devote myself to reforming my soul.

I was overwhelmed and desperate. I had removed my *tulku* robe to keep pace with the new society and Communist ideals. My loyalty and obedience to the CCP were such that in 1957 I married a Han cadre and Party member who despised me intensely because that was the "organizational will" (Ch. *zhuzhi yitu*). I felt deeply frustrated. How could the CCP make someone its ally and one of their people today but turn him into its enemy the next day? What about the CCP's credibility and its promises? I lamented that I had been naïve and unable to realize I was about to be betrayed and discarded. I had probably sensed this earlier, but my disillusionment with the CCP prevented me from coming to terms with it. Consequently, I asked myself, what was the point of continuing to live in a world with so little credibility and light? I began to consider suicide, and when I passed by a bridge in the suburbs of Barkham one day, I thought about jumping into the river. I hesitated and went back home. The following day, I was again humiliated during the CPPCC meeting, so I told myself I wouldn't hesitate. After reaching the bridge, I put one of my legs across but could not move the other. I tried a couple of times and still couldn't manage to do it. I decided to get drunk, believing this would make my jump easier. The next day, I bought a bottle of liquor and took it to the bridge. I opened the bottle and started drinking. Not feeling much at first, I continued drinking and was drunk before realizing it, and everything was spinning in front of me. I was too weak to lift my legs. I decided to return home to sleep for a few hours before returning to the bridge that evening. Somehow I got home, and threw up all over the place the moment I arrived. My sister happened to be there. After cleaning my room, she refused to leave me alone that night. The next day, I was followed by someone at a distance, whom I assumed had been dispatched by the CCP leaders after hearing a report from vigilant neighbors regarding my abnormal behavior.

I was soon transferred to Choktsé Township and taken to a reeducation camp that had been prepared for subjects of the United Front at the CPPCC. The daily routine was reading Mao's works, studying CCP documents, conducting self-criticism, and criticizing others. I was required to reflect on my "bad thoughts and deeds." A significant accusation was that I had failed to draw clear boundaries with the nobles I interacted with and purposely did not dig deeply into their private lives and thoughts. Worse, I was blamed for speaking on their behalf since I provided truthful accounts about their positive changes in my reports to prefectural leaders. Some of the other activists behaved differently, framing nobles and others for things they hadn't done. I was different, someone with a conscience. Treacherous activists disgusted me because I believe telling lies and wronging others is a severe sin, so I reported to superiors what I had seen and heard, good and bad, during my interactions with the "Three Giants" and others. I was unprepared for the CCP officials to interpret this basic human principle as a crime.

Moreover, I was accused of having not given up a *tulku*'s privileges after Liberation. This was nonsense. I had hoped to rid myself of *tulku* status since my studies in Lhasa, and this wish intensified after Liberation. However, the CCP officials made me wear the robe and play the role of a *tulku* when it served their purposes. Though I didn't want to do it, I was told it would better serve the CCP's United Front work. This had now become another of my significant crimes.

I didn't lose hope, thinking that my situation could be straightened out and my "wrongs" reassessed. However, at the same time, I prepared for the worst. I started to think about my destiny. I hadn't done anything wrong, so I didn't believe that I would be thrown into prison. The CCP would not banish me to my hometown to become a peasant or worker because at that time, being a peasant or worker was considered superior due to their status as the new ruling class in Communist China. My *tulku* status ruled out any opportunity for me to take these roles. Therefore, I took a wait-and-see attitude.

Before long, I was asked to return to Dzamtang and sent to a cowshed on the banks of the Dokhok River, which was reserved for twenty to thirty "ox-headed ghosts and serpent gods." Most of us were mid-ranking nobles and upper-class members, including several *tulku*s and other standing members of the CPPCC. The most critical and contemptible nobles and religious figures were being "reformed" at the prefectural level rather than here with us. They had been placed in the "Four Categories of Bad People" (landlords, rich peasants, counterrevolutionaries, and "bad elements") and were imprisoned or remained in their hometowns to receive "reform" and political struggle from poor peasants and nomads. In comparison, cowshed residents like myself weren't among the "Bad People" but rather subjects of the United Front. Two or three of the cadres from the county's United Front Department stayed with us to oversee our study of central Party-state documents, directing us to read *People's Daily* editorials, recite Mao quotations, sing revolutionary songs, hold sessions on self-criticism and critiques of others, and perform labor assignments such as cleaning the streets, sowing fields, and growing vegetables.

From time to time, Red Guards, poor peasants, and nomads would come to our cowshed and drag someone from our group into the street for political struggles. I was never subject to such treatment, nor were my vices seriously exposed by my cowshed roommates and fellows. I received critiques and warnings from time to time. They were usually general and broad, such as "drinking the blood of the people in old society as the ruling class" and "assuming unassertive political standing." I would be taken to the street for struggle, but always with other "ox-headed ghosts and serpent gods" and "bad people" as a part of a collective. Not a single political struggle targeted me specifically. The Red Guards were primarily teenagers from poor nomad families who didn't beat or verbally abuse me. One told me, "Don't be afraid. You're not our target." In contrast, some others in our cowshed were frequently taken to the streets alone or beaten by Red Guards, poor peasants, and nomads and would return with bloody injuries.

Occasionally my nomad acquaintances would visit me at the cowshed. Almost everyone tried to distance themselves from people like me. Even my wife admonished me to leave our son and daughter alone. Whenever I was allowed to return home and tried to interact with my children, my wife would stop me and shout, "How dare you, a stinking feudal lord, snatch the revolutionary successors and poison them with your rotten feudal thoughts. Get back to your cowshed and reform your soul!" Only the nomads didn't despise me. They still saw me as a trustworthy friend or acquaintance. In the cowshed, I was closest to Chöjor, who had been the secretary of a chief noble at Nyaklo, Gyelkha. He received more nomad guests than I.[5] An instructor at the Tibetan program at Southwest Nationalities Institute, he was sent to Dzamtang for reeducation before the Cultural Revolution. Chöjor was very popular among the nomads who were supposed to closely observe him, thanks to his kindness, honesty, hospitality, and fair-mindedness. Many visitors brought him butter, roasted barley flour, milk, yogurt, and cheese. If someone asks me what loyalty is, I will say that true loyalty can be seen in circumstances like these when even one's family and friends move away from a so-called stinking "ox-headed ghost and serpent god."

I doubted such loyal acts would happen in my hometown or other predominantly agricultural areas across Gyalrong. Mutual spying and exposure were much more common there during various movements, with activists doing everything possible to demonstrate their advanced political consciousness and loyalty to the CCP. They destroyed everything in the monasteries and badly beat religious figures and class enemies. If people visit monasteries in Gyalrong now, they will find very few relics or artifacts that date back to pre-Reform or pre-Liberation periods. Although my monastery at Sönamyak had few valuable things after the 1917 uprising, some cherished items remained by the time of the Democratic Reform, such as images, long horns, drums, *gyaling* ("Indian trumpets"), gold leaf-covered roofs, and hundreds of volumes of woodblock-printed scriptures. However, not one of these things can be found there today. They were all seized by activists or poor peasants, who never returned them. Ironically, the Gyalrongwa tended to denigrate nomads because the latter were said to be dumb and ignorant. What happened showed that the absolute idiots were the self-congratulatory peasants. The chances that religion and culture in Gyalrong could be restored, as was done in nomad regions after the Cultural Revolution, were small because the Gyalrongwa's self-destructive actions had seriously undermined the foundations of Tibetan tradition there. If I had remained in Tsanlha during those turbulent years, I would most likely have been included in one of the "Four Categories of Bad People" to be purged, a far more notorious label than that of "ox-headed ghosts and serpent gods" that I received in Dzamtang.

However, this doesn't mean that what had happened in Tsanlha didn't affect me. The so-called "Poor and Lower-Middle Peasants' Association" (Ch. *pinxia zhongnong xiehui*) at Sönamyak sent a representative to

Dzamtang to escort me back to my hometown during the Cultural Revolution. Because my past activities in Sönamyak and Tsanlha were recognized as part of the so-called "remaining historical problem" (Ch. *lishi yiliu wenti*), the Dzamtang United Front department would have had no problem letting me go as part of the political struggle in my hometown. Nonetheless, even these cadres treated me well and showed concern for what could have happened to me in Sönamyak and Tsanlha; they told me that if I chose not to return, they would dismiss the Sönamyak representative. After confirming that I would like to deal with my "remaining historical problem" back in my hometown, they allowed the representative to take me there. However, they warned him, saying, "If you dare touch even a single hair of his, we will have to square accounts with you." They demanded that he write a letter of guarantee based on Mao's principle of "struggle through eloquence rather than violence" during the struggle sessions against me. Thanks to the threatening tone of the Dzamtang cadres, this representative and the people at Sönamyak didn't use physical violence against me.

I wasn't afraid of the struggle session because I hadn't harmed people at Sönamyak. First, they knew that I had not exploited them before Liberation. Second, to repay their kindness and sponsorship during my studies in Lhasa, I had planned to rebuild the monastery for them. Despite strong objections from my steward at Sönamyak Monastery, I spent the money from Okzhi on this project. The money had been collected by the Okzhi king in the form of about six taels of opium (about 375 grams) from each household to sponsor my continued study in Lhasa. So what kind of excuse could they fabricate? Or, more bluntly, on what basis had they summoned me to Sönamyak in the first place? At the very least, the people turning their back on their harmless and innocent *tulku* shows how much peasants developed inconsistent principles of right and wrong and became more treacherous in the process.

If paradise exists, it is in a nomad region. I have interacted with people across Tibetan regions throughout my life, from peasants to nobles in Gyalrong, aristocrats in Lhasa, merchants, nomads, and others. No one ever surpassed the nomads in honesty, loyalty, being free-spirited, and happiness. I was fortunate to have had the rare opportunity to take refuge with such wonderful people during that very turbulent era. This was nearly unimaginable for others like me who had been politically condemned. Thus, when I consider the experiences of those politically significant individuals, I feel blessed to be merely a minor character in politics and life. Among the "Three Giants" in Ngawa Prefecture, only Dorjé Pasang survived the Cultural Revolution, fled to India, and later moved to Canada. Palgon Chenle followed his wife and jumped into the Min River during the Cultural Revolution. He had urged his subjects to hand in their guns and not rebel against the new regime. If he hadn't, many PLA soldiers and Party cadres would have died in Ngawa if a large-scale revolt had occurred. Despite his tremendous contribution, Palgon Chenle killed himself because of the CCP's betrayal. Likewise, Suo Guanying died during the Cultural Revolution's terror and struggles.

There are many similar examples, including among the Tibetan nobles and lamas who sided with Mao and the CCP at Liberation, such as two of the then most influential Tibetan individuals in the country, the Tenth Panchen Lama (1938–1989) and Püntsok Wanggyel (1922–2014; cofounder of the Tibetan Communist Party).[6] Even so, their experiences of betrayal and mistreatment by the CCP do not compare to what happened to some of Mao's former allies and comrades who had assisted in defeating Chiang Kai-shek and establishing new China. Notoriously, Mao didn't hesitate to purge the successor he had chosen, Liu Shaoqi (1898–1969), China's chairman.[7]

ACT IV

An Intellectual Life (1966/1977–)

Chapter Twelve

FROM COWSHED TO COLLEGE

I had never imagined that I would one day become an "intellectual." As one of the "ox-headed ghosts and serpent gods," I was better off not having dreams or illusions. However, my life took a sharp unexpected turn. Sometimes it is hard not to believe in karma, when an ordinary person like me from a family almost as poor as beggars becomes a *tulku*. I benefited and suffered because of this status. Karma again gave me an unexpected opportunity, to hone my Tibetan language skills during the Cultural Revolution and eventually become a Tibetan studies professor.

I had almost forgotten everything I had learned from my masters in Lhasa by the time of the Cultural Revolution. I rarely read anything in Tibetan after returning home because I had worked very hard during my seven years in Lhasa and wanted to enjoy a life free from monastic learning. I also didn't want to be classified as a conservative feudal individual after Liberation. The written Tibetan language could be easily labeled as a tool of the reactionary ruling class, the aristocrats and lamas. This reactionary class was assumed to take advantage of their language skills and literacy to exert absolute control over the illiterate powerless masses. Thus, when the Red Guards searched my apartment, they found nothing but a Tibetan version of Mao's Little Red Book. Under such circumstances, I could not have imagined that my Tibetan language skills would be partially restored during the chaotic era of the Cultural Revolution.

For unknown reasons, I was chosen by the Red Rebellion Headquarters (Ch. *hongse zaofan zong silingbu*; short form, *hongzong*; hereafter Red Headquarters), one of the two major Red Guards organizations in Dzamtang, to translate slogans and the central Party-state documents into Tibetan. Chöjor was selected by another major Red Guard organization, the Chengdu Workers' Revolutionary Rebel Corps (Ch. *Chengdu gongren geming zaofan bingtuan* or the short form, *chengzao*; hereafter Chengdu Corps), to perform the same duty.[1] As former secretary to a noble, Chöjor had extensive experience dealing with Tibetan records and writings. He also taught in the Tibetan Program at the Southwest Nationalities Institute until the program was disbanded in the early 1960s. Hence, he knew how to write in Tibetan. In comparison, my training in Tibetan writing was limited, despite years of study in Lhasa. Most monks, including learned Géshés, in the Tibetan monastic system, especially in the Gelugpa tradition, could not write well. We were told that established scholars in history had many great works, so we did not need to write anything. Therefore, during my stay in Lhasa, I was trained to memorize, recite, and understand texts. The advantage of such training was that I had a more comprehensive knowledge of the texts than Chöjor. I could also read some Chinese. As a result, we collaborated on translations. During this process, I learned how to write in Tibetan from Chöjor.

Written Tibetan has a complex writing system and challenging grammatical and syntax rules. Learning to write well in Tibetan takes a tremendous amount of time. In contrast, it is much easier to learn to write in Chinese. When people learn to read Chinese, most learn to write simultaneously. This explains why many foreign Sinologists can write in Chinese, but far fewer Chinese or foreign Tibetologists can write in Tibetan. Before my assigned translation work, I had never systematically studied Tibetan grammar and writing rules. While I interpreted the original Chinese texts for Chöjor, I was amazed to find that he could create elegant writings that were much better than my interpretations. When I asked how he did this, he explained that his writing style followed specific grammatical and other relevant rules. The rules I learned from him included the basics of Tibetan grammar, the *Thirty Verses* of Thönmi Sambhota, and primary rules on poetry writing.[2] We worked together for seven or eight years, and I cultivated basic writing skills through this collaboration. I say "basic" because translating the Red Guards' accusations of each other's "vices" and the central Party-state documents could not contribute much to my writing skills. Their slogans and politically charged language were homogenous, so I lost interest in repeatedly translating these dull documents. But the experience helped me regain some of what I had learned in Lhasa, such as argumentative logic.

In 1977, I was transferred to the Southwest Nationalities Institute and taught Tibetan. After the Cultural Revolution, this college resumed its regular functions as an institute of higher education, as did other colleges. Many of its programs that had been previously disbanded, including the Tibetan studies program, were restored. However, the program was seriously short of faculty members, so the institute's leaders began searching for new teachers. I had studied at the institute in the early 1950s, so some officials were familiar with my background. I had limited knowledge of Tibetan studies and lacked any teaching experience. The leadership must have had difficulty finding desirable lecturers. Otherwise, high-ranking officials like Zhang Hancheng, the vice-president of the institute, wouldn't have come to Dzamtang in person to invite me to teach in this program.

Initially, I didn't want to take this job because I was unqualified and wasn't acclimated to life in Chengdu regarding food and weather. I preferred to work in Dzamtang and Ngawa Prefecture. However, my wife urged me to take it, because she hoped to live in a Han Chinese city. When I talked to Chöjor about my dilemma, he was delighted and suggested that I accept the offer, but for a different reason. He said that I could return to Ngawa Prefecture after a few years of working in Chengdu and that my Han Chinese wife would surely not want to return, so we could more easily divorce. Due mainly to child custody concerns, we had been deadlocked for years on that issue, prolonging our turbulent marriage. Chöjor's advice persuaded me to take the job because it potentially could resolve this significant problem, so I said yes to the institute. I didn't begin teaching right away. I was allowed some time to prepare my future lesson plans and curriculum and attended many lectures in the Tibetan program to familiarize myself with the teaching style there. I discovered that many of my colleagues, especially Han, did not know the Tibetan language and culture better than I did, so I worried less about my teaching qualifications.

I had gotten lucky again. Mugé Samten (1914–1993; hereafter Teacher Samten), the then vice-chair of the CPPCC Ngawa Prefecture, was staying in Chengdu as part of a team compiling and editing *The Tibetan-Chinese*

General Dictionary, the most comprehensive of its kind at that time.[3] Teacher Samten had received his Géshé degree at Labrang, one of the six Gelugpa monasteries in Greater Tibet, and had become a teacher there. Because of his reputation as an outstanding scholar, he was generally considered one of the three most influential and learned Tibetologists of the Tibetan nationality in China. The other two were Tséten Zhapdrung (1910–1985), who was then teaching at the Northwest Nationalities Institute in Lanzhou, and Dungkar Lozang Trinlé (1927–1997; frequently referred to as Dungkar La by his students and others), who was a professor at the Central Nationalities Institute in Beijing.[4] I had known Teacher Samten since the 1950s. We had met frequently during various political meetings. I approached him and asked if I could learn grammar and writing alongside him. He immediately agreed, and I began studying at his hostel weekly. Soon after, about ten other Tibetan scholars from the institute and other organizations joined us in these weekly meetings. I relearned the *Thirty Verses* of Thönmi Sambhota from him. Unlike learning other languages, Tibetan grammar must be studied repeatedly with different teachers before the student can grasp its essence and be able to write well.

This tutoring lasted for over a year. Through this experience, I gained a better knowledge of Tibetan grammar and writing techniques, although I was still far from being a qualified scholar and teacher. Nevertheless, I had more confidence in my teaching because most of our students at the institute had limited Tibetan literacy skills due to the disruption of their schooling during the Cultural Revolution. In this way, I could get by with my teaching, but I knew my limits and was always eager for opportunities to enhance my knowledge. A rare opportunity popped up when I learned that Dungkar La was coming to Chengdu on his way back to Beijing from a stay in Lhasa. He was a *tulku* from the region of Kongpo in Central Tibet and had received the most prestigious Géshé Lharampa degree. I met him to consult about the Tibetan studies program at the Central Nationalities Institute where he taught, inquiring about the general situation of courses and teaching. I received much more from our encounter, however. First, it turned out that he was an old friend of my tutor, Gyalrong Khensur Rinpoche Jampel Samphel, and that he remembered seeing me in Lhasa when I was accompanying my master during their mutual visits. This immediately brought us closer together. Second, he shared the news that a classical Tibetan training program would soon reopen at the Central

Nationalities Institute and suggested I apply for it. All candidates were required to take an entrance examination. Dungkar La gave me specific instructions on preparing for it. I passed and was enrolled in the program in 1978.

Our class was composed of about thirty students from all over Tibetan areas, but there were only three from Sichuan, two women from Kardzé, and me from Ngawa Prefecture. Most of our classmates had had extensive work experience before joining the program. They were journalists, editors, teachers, librarians, museum staff, and so on. Nonetheless, the class's written Tibetan skills weren't very high overall. They typically learned Tibetan through school and work. They had no monastic training, so they lacked knowledge about the Tibetan literary traditions. They were also fully aware of their limitations. I indeed had and knew my limits. Although I had received a few years of training in Lhasa, I didn't study long enough to obtain a Géshé degree. Moreover, I gave up learning after leaving Lhasa in 1948 until the Cultural Revolution. At the age of forty-eight, I was the oldest student in the class. Several junior classmates were in their early twenties, around the age of my son, who was also studying at the Central Nationalities Institute. My Chinese language teacher referred to me in class as "the student who is older than I." Therefore, I was not necessarily in an advantageous position compared to my younger class-mates. We all took this learning opportunity seriously and worked hard.

We were required to take courses on religion, poetry, history, classical Tibetan, logic, and writing, and many of us attended extra courses. For instance, most of us audited a class for graduate students taught by Dung-kar La, the most knowledgeable and well-respected of all our teachers. We spent most of our time on his courses, which involved all the significant aspects of Tibetan culture, religion, and history, and his accompanying assignments. Additionally, most of us attached great importance to the classes taught by two other knowledgeable teachers, Lozang Chöjor (here-after Chöjor La) and Lozang Dorje, referred to frequently as Lodor La. Chöm jor La had great insights into Tibetan history. As an ex-monk official in Lhasa, he had a thorough knowledge of Tibetan Kashag government files and how to compose them. Nonetheless, he was better known outside academia thanks to his prominent role as the founder of Tibetan-style cross-talk (normally involving two performers engaging in a humorous dialogue filled with puns, wordplay, and social commentary).

As required, we also took courses from several other Tibetan and Han teachers, although most of our class thought we didn't learn much because they were on less comprehensive, relatively narrow, and more specialized topics, such as the *Sakya Motto* (a collection of moral precepts in verse written by Sakya Pandita in the thirteenth century) and Dunhuang documents. As a result, some of us saw these courses as less challenging, a mental break from our more intensive studies with Dungkar La. Few of us could take a break from Dungkar La's assignments and lectures because their coverage of different aspects of Tibetan literature required extensive knowledge and intensive preparation. Consequently, the study pressure became so strong that many classmates had difficulty keeping up. This proved to be a severe psychological challenge, and gender differences emerged. Although the male students encountered the same challenges, we found ways to release the pressure, such as chatting and drinking. Many female students were more reserved and felt uneasy about seeking help from teachers and classmates, and became competitive with one another, and a few of my female classmates had nervous breakdowns.

A sad example is what happened during one summer vacation when one of our female classmates from Kardzé killed herself by jumping into the river at Dartsédo, the capital of Kardzé Prefecture, just before the new semester was about to start. Although people had various interpretations of her suicide, many in our class assumed it was related to the pressures she faced, as she had shown obvious signs of desperation at school. Another female classmate from an aristocratic family in Lhasa could not fall asleep at night. To avoid her total collapse, the school sent her back to Lhasa to recuperate. She later became a prominent professor of Tibetan studies and a key official at Tibet University. Not all my female classmates reacted in the same way. Another student from Kardzé had a much more relaxed attitude and was never reluctant to ask for help from other classmates and me. For example, during an open book examination, she said to me, "Let me have a look at your answers." I replied, "This is an examination. Aren't we supposed to do our respective work?" She replied, "Don't be stingy. A quick look is sufficient for me." At other times, she would ask us for help with her homework. In this way, she didn't suffer very much from the intensive training program.

To relieve these pressures, I, acting as the class monitor, and Wangdü Tséring, the vice-monitor, organized occasional social weekend gatherings for the whole class. Some of our teachers, like Dungkar La and Lodor La, attended. We drank beer, chatted, and took turns singing and telling jokes. Many of us enjoyed activities like this, which certainly enhanced bonds among classmates. Generally, we cared about each other. Due to different dietary preferences, the male students would give our rice tickets (tickets were required to purchase rice at the school dining hall) to female students, who provided us with their bread tickets. Before these bread tickets ran out, my roommates sometimes found extra ones in a container that held our meal tickets. Often we had little idea which female classmate had come to our dorm room and dropped their bread tickets in the container. Moreover, our class members helped each other with studies and assignments. This special bond boosted our morale and helped us overcome study challenges.

I initially studied like the others by attending lectures, finishing assignments on time, and so on. However, Dungkar La thought I should adopt a more advanced approach, thanks to my previous training in Lhasa, and gave me a list of recommended texts. He asked me to read them and then ask whatever questions I had. I was allowed to meet with him once a week, which was one hour in theory but usually lasted two to three hours, to discuss my questions. He reminded me that I should keep our meetings confidential because he didn't have time to do this with all his students. This method proved productive. I read the texts extensively and prepared questions. Dungkar La was a living encyclopedia who seemed to know almost everything and had an amazing memory. He would suggest where and how I could find more specific texts and references for further inquiry. He often could remember the approximate page numbers where the information was located in those texts. I would then find these additional texts, read them, and prepare new sets of questions for him.

In this way, I read many books with him during my two years of study, gaining a clearer idea about my research field. First it was classical Tibetan. I found many classical Tibetan vocabulary terms in various readings that no longer existed in modern Tibetan due to extensive language reforms. The meanings of many of the words were challenging to decipher in these texts. Occasionally they baffled even learned scholars like Dungkar La. I had an advantage in interpreting these words because many of the expressions were widely used in the Gyalrong dialect. Here is one related anecdote involving Wang Yao, one of the best-known Tibetologists of Han descent and a professor of Tibetan studies at the Central Nationalities Institute. He was thrilled to discover that *d-myi-g* (དམྱིག) "eye" was used in the Gyalrong dialect. He had initially found this in Dunhuang texts. In modern Tibetan, "eye" was usually simplified as *mig* (མིག) because of language change and reforms.[5] The Gyalrong dialect commonly featured the particle "d-" before a monosyllabic noun. Such usage had disappeared in Lhasa and other Tibetan dialects. The Gyalrong dialect also maintained the sounds of nearly every syllable in a word, as did classical Tibetan. In modern Tibetan, especially in the Lhasa dialect, many of the sounds of a word are reduced, so only the sounds of its key syllables are preserved. For instance, the number 100 (Wylie: *brgya*) is pronounced "gya" in the Lhasa dialect today. However, in Gyalrong, we pronounce it "brgʲa," the exact original pronunciation in classical Tibetan.[6]

When I told Dungkar La about my interest in classical Tibetan, he encouraged me to focus on that research area, adding that he had considered working on this, but his busy schedule prevented it. To further encourage me, he gave me many small cards with classical Tibetan terms he had collected over the years and their sources. Each entry was maintained on one or more of these cards, depending on the number and length of its respective sources. I applied this same method for recordkeeping while expanding my collection of new words, entries, and references until I completed my dictionary of classical Tibetan a decade later, which meant I kept about 20,000 cards.

Tibetan history fascinated me with so many important events and aspects worth investigating that I didn't know where to begin. Dungkar La suggested I identify the topic that intrigued me the most and advised that it would emerge naturally if I continued reading extensively. I greatly benefited from Döndrup Gyel's (1953–1985) guidance in seeking historical subjects. As one of Dungkar La's graduate students,[7] Döndrup Gyel attended classical Tibetan training program courses, especially those taught by Dungkar La,[8] along with two other graduate students, Kelsang Yeshe (1948–) and Chen Qingying (1941–). Our class attended Dungkar La's lectures for graduate students. Moreover, Döndrup Gyel often came to my dormitory room, which I shared with several of his close friends. This led to extensive interactions. We got along well. Döndrup Gyel suggested I work on something that had not been explored or was controversial in Tibetan studies.

I came across a crucial historical debate on the origins of the first Tibetan king of the Yalung Dynasty during the second century BCE. Most accounts traced his lineage back to a royal family in India. This isn't surprising considering India's role as the holy land in the eyes of many Tibetans. However, I found this problematic. There were no records of an Indian kingdom invading Tibet. Additionally, I considered it logically flawed to claim that local Tibetans would make an exiled Indian prince their king. It seemed unlikely that a foreigner without local social and material foundations would be given such an important role. When I told Döndrup Gyel about my doubts, he responded positively, saying it was a great research topic. He had also thought about this and even prepared some relevant materials, which he shared with me. However, although I had his materials and found pertinent other records on my own, I had never written a research paper and was puzzled about how to begin. Döndrup Gyel shared his writing techniques and asked me to write down my rough thoughts first, saying he would help me afterward. After reading my first draft, he said, "You have too many citations, so this is not a research paper. Reduce the number." So I revised it and showed it to him a second time. He said, "It is much better now, but there are some tiny problems," and advised me on how to resolve them. When I showed him my third draft, he declared, "Now it looks great." Next I went to Dungkar La for an opinion. He didn't suggest any changes except that I get the paper published. Ultimately, it became my first published work.[9]

This way, during my study at the Central Nationalities Institute, Döndrup Gyel offered me the most substantial help I'd gotten apart from Dungkar La. However, I was about to complete the two-year program without realizing it. The Tibetan studies program wanted to keep me as a new faculty member and inquired about my interest. I agreed to this proposal, although I was not used to life in Beijing. I agreed for several reasons. I could divorce my wife; I knew she would refuse to move to Beijing. Also, I had just learned how to do research and needed much more intensive training with Dungkar La. However, the Southwest Nationalities Institute refused to release me, accusing the Central Nationalities Institute of stealing their people.

I returned to Chengdu in the summer of 1981, while Döndrup Gyel stayed behind and became a new faculty member in the Tibetan program, though he didn't stay long before returning to Qinghai in 1984. In 1985, Dungkar La returned to Lhasa. I knew he preferred to live there due to the weather and Beijing's lack of butter and *tsampa*. I didn't know why Döndrup Gyel left Beijing, but I guessed it was related to Dungkar La's plan to leave, considering they had a solid teacher-student bond. My return to Chengdu meant losing the opportunity to continue learning from Dungkar La and interacting with Döndrup Gyel.

Still, I got the opportunity to renew my studies with Teacher Samten. As an executive department chair, I invited him to Chengdu to be a guest speaker and lecture in my program several times. During these visits, I would attend the classes and consult him about my questions. I also would meet with him in Ngawa, where he worked during the summer vacation, and stay with him for one to two months, which I did for three or four years. The training I received from him was very similar to what I received from Dungkar La. I would read extensively and prepare my questions before each of our meetings. My readings and questions involved history, logic, language, classical Tibetan, and religion. Just like Dungkar La, Teacher Samten seemed to know almost everything. He answered my questions in an elaborate, precise way. After we met, I would reflect on his replies and suggestions and think and read more before going back to meet him with more questions. Once again, this learning method was very productive, and I benefited tremendously.

Teacher Samten also showed great support for my classical Tibetan dictionary project. He shared the vocabulary he had collected with me, just as Dungkar La did; gave me specific instructions on sources; and suggested additional references and relevant texts. This was helpful, but my project moved at a glacial pace. I had heavy teaching duties and was later asked to be the acting chair of the Nationality Languages Department. These responsibilities were time-consuming. It took me a decade to eventually complete the dictionary. This project also could have gone on forever because of countless classical Tibetan terms. I would frequently find new ones when coming across new texts. Consequently, I grew exhausted and wanted to take a break. Therefore, I decided to get it published, and it came out in 1997.[10] At first, not many people who knew I was working on a dictionary saw much value in it, even with the support of my two teachers, Dungkar La and Teacher Samten. However, I started to hear more positive comments after its publication. Some scholars in the West, such as E. Gene Smith (1936–2010; cofounder of the Tibetan Buddhist Resource Center), an American Tibetologist, knew about this work. Thanks to the dictionary, I was invited to travel abroad for several international Tibetan studies conferences. During the summer of 2018, I was shown a video in which the head of the Karma Kagyü tradition, the Seventeenth Karmapa Orgyen Trinlé Dorjé (born in 1985), complimented this dictionary.

Besides the classical Tibetan dictionary and my other writing projects, training students took much of my time. Even with my limited knowledge, I was trying to become a more qualified teacher. According to Tibetan tradition, masters rarely reject anyone who requests their help. That was how I started to learn from various teachers in Lhasa, in addition to my tutor, and it was also how I became a student of Mugé Samten and Dungkar La. Simultaneously, once a master accepted someone as his student, the master was expected not to withhold any of his knowledge and transmit everything. I was trying to do the same. I never refused when students requested to learn with me and was always available for their questions, discussions, research, and theses. I regularly shared my collected materials when asked, even though some of these works were never returned. As a result, I got along well with students. Some of my former students would come to see me, host me with great hospitality if they heard about my visits where they worked or lived, and sent their regards to me. Those who respected me the most were from Gyalrong.

Southwest Nationalities Institute did not recruit Gyalrong students. There was no systematic Tibetan language education in the local schools since various Gyalrong dialects were often regarded as non-Tibetan languages. After being appointed vice-chair of the Nationality Languages Department, I convinced the department and university to accept a few Gyalrong students annually. In the following years, we admitted dozens of students from Gyalrong. Most would have otherwise had little chance to attend college because the entrance scores required for the Tibetan studies program were generally much lower than those for other regular undergraduate programs. Moreover, because most Gyalrong students had little training in Tibetan before college, I spent a lot of time offering extra lectures and tutorials to help them improve their language skills. Hence, they often developed a special bond with me, and even today, many of these students tell me that I transformed their lives.

I regret to say that I failed to cultivate many qualified students. I trained several graduate students before my retirement, but few had solid Tibetan language and culture foundations. The modern college curriculum and training systems, especially in Tibetan studies, are problematic because they utterly neglect essential techniques in traditional monastic training,[11] including repeated learning of the same texts from different masters, emphasizing memorization and recitation, and reinforcement of learning through debate and logical reasoning. Due to this significant deficiency in the modern education system, even such an erudite scholar and great teacher as Dungkar La failed to produce competent students with comprehensive knowledge of Tibetan literary traditions.

Chapter Thirteen

THE CLOSING AGE OF GIANTS

My teachers, Professor Dungkar Lozang Trinlé (Dungkar La) and Mugé Samten (Teacher Samten), were among the most eminent Tibetologists of our time. Though Döndrup Gyel's academic accomplishments do not compare to those of these two giants, it is fair to say that he is at least a half-giant. More than that, Döndrup Gyel's popularity among Tibetan intellectuals and youth may have exceeded that of these two masters. In terms of their rare talents as well as their spirits of resistance against outdated Tibetan traditions, there is a general tendency to compare Döndrup Gyel to Gendün Chöphel (1903–1951), the most controversial and best-known Tibetan intellectual in the modern era.[1] These three scholars have played an essential role in shaping my academic path. Their rise to prominence marked a luminous era in Tibetan studies, and living Tibetan intellectuals of my generation are situated at the end of this age.

Similarities and differences are evident in the life trajectories and experiences of Dungkar La and Teacher Samten. Both were trained in great Gelugpa monasteries and became the most learned Géshés of their generation. Although their prominence was related to their intelligence and diligence, it is inseparable from the tradition of Tibetan monastic institutions and its unique education system. I received monastic training at Drepung for years, so I had firsthand experience with its supreme learning environment, characterized by the availability of the most learned scholars one could imagine. These two masters' prominent status was also associated with their political destinies since Liberation. Many learned Géshés and lamas fled to India in 1959 or were labeled as the people's enemy, but the CCP recruited both Dungkar La and Teacher Samten to work for the new regime. Dungkar La was assigned to teach at the Central Nationalities Institute, and Teacher Samten acted as a reviewer and editor for the Tibetan translation of Mao's selected works. Even though they could not avoid political struggles during the Cultural Revolution, they were not imprisoned or cut off entirely from their research or teaching.

Dungkar La gained rare access to various archives in this period when he was assigned to catalogue and organize them at the TAR Archives. Meanwhile, Teacher Samten improvised an alternative way to continue teaching. As a counterrevolutionary, he was assigned to making tea for people during his "reform through labor" period. He took advantage of this opportunity to teach his helper, Dornor, by creating special scripts that corresponded to different Tibetan syllables. He drew them with a stick in the dirt as a way to lecture Dornor when others had left for work. The scripts could be brushed away immediately, and even if someone saw them by accident, they were unrecognizable to outsiders because they appeared to be random drawings.[2] Dornor became an accomplished scholar in this unique environment and later a teacher and official at the Sichuan Tibetan School. This school has been one of Sichuan's most important Tibetan language institutes since it was founded in the early 1980s and plays a crucial role in training Tibetan scholars and schoolteachers. Thubten Phuntsok, a professor at the Southwest Nationalities University where I used to teach and a leading scholar in Tibetan studies in China today, was trained there, and Dornor was his teacher. In short, the CCP deemed Dungkar La and Teacher Samten useful thanks to their reputations as erudite scholars, which helped them survive turbulent times. This allowed them to continue their research and teaching after the Cultural Revolution. As a result, they managed to produce essential works for later generations and train a new generation of Tibetan intellectuals, thus playing a significant role in the revival of Tibetan culture and studies during the Reform era.

There are nonetheless some notable differences between these two scholars. Dungkar La had a more thorough understanding of Tibetan history and its relevant texts; Teacher Samten had a broader range of knowledge with expertise in multiple areas, such as astrology, medicine, Sanskrit, poetry, grammar, and Buddhist philosophy. Hence, he was sometimes referred to as the Pandita, a title given to only the most erudite scholars. Even Dungkar La spoke highly of his accomplishments in general, and in Sanskrit in particular, saying that Teacher Samten was among the very few living accomplished Tibetan scholars of Sanskrit.

One may wonder how Teacher Samten gained such a broad spectrum of knowledge. It had a lot to do with the unique tradition of Labrang Monastery, where he was trained. In my view, among the six major Gelugpa monasteries, Labrang had the most comprehensive training system, offering a wide range of subjects for monks, such as astrology, medicine, and Sanskrit, in addition to the usual subjects (five general topics listed in chapter 5). The reason is simple. Labrang was founded the most recently, in 1709, among the other great monasteries, so its founder, the first Jamyang Zhépa, could absorb the best traditions and practices from the other five major Gelugpa monasteries.[3]

In terms of political stances, Dungkar La displayed certain leftist inclinations, which are not as apparent in Teacher Mugé Samten's writings. This largely explains why Dungkar La was chosen to teach at the Central Nationalities Institute twice (1960–65 and 1978–85) and allowed to go abroad and attend international conferences in the 1980s and '90s. Dungkar La's Marxist interpretation of Tibetan history is seen in his famous *On the Relationship Between Religion and State in Tibet*.[4] As this book was written mainly during the Cultural Revolution, he was under tremendous pressure to apply revolutionary overtones by using Marxist-Maoist ideas to critique theocracy in old Tibet. After the Cultural Revolution, this pressure lessened. According to Dungkar La, due to critical reviews from Tibetan intellectuals, especially in monastic circles, he came to see problems with his leftist perspective and revised the original book manuscript substantially in an attempt to neutralize his position. He asked the press to update it, but his request was declined and this revised version was never published. In any case, his change in political position contributed to his losing CCP favor.

A more distinctive difference between these two masters is that Dungkar La was a *tulku* who renounced his monkhood after Liberation, while Teacher Samten was a monk without *tulku* status who maintained celibacy throughout his life. Why does this matter? In the eyes of Tibetans, especially those in the Gelugpa tradition, a monk's renunciation of his celibacy was seen almost as a sin, and it was even worse if a *tulku* did it. Consequently, having renounced this status in his stained past, Dungkar La is mainly seen as a secular scholar and teacher within the CCP system. In contrast, Teacher Samten is a genuine master in religious circles and a Tibetologist straddling state and monastic institutions, so the two teachers cultivated different types of students. Even during the Reform era, Dungkar La's teachings had to be oriented toward the school's agenda, curriculum design, and pedagogy, and the role of ideology and political correctness in its education. To take the subject of Tibetan history as an example, many issues were considered sensitive even after the Cultural Revolution, such as the historical relationship between Tibet and China and the role of religion in Tibetan culture. This put guardrails around Dungkar La's research and teaching. The constraints are evident in *On the Relationship Between Religion and State in Tibet*. Thus, his students were primarily laypeople trained within a secular system, and most went on to work in academic, cultural, and educational spheres.

In comparison, Teacher Mugé Samten's teachings were much less constrained and conducted more traditionally, as had been done in monasteries. He taught predominantly through private tutoring rather than in more public lectures. Students were assigned specific texts or found their texts to read and think about; they would then go and meet with him privately with their questions. Such learning was similar to oral examinations, defenses, and debates. Teacher Samten would question and challenge us to illustrate our points and defend our positions. This process was quite intense, and if students weren't adequately prepared with a deep understanding of the texts, they would be defenseless before the master's questions and would be severely scolded. His scolding wasn't a personal attack on our intelligence but an instructional incentive to push us to think further and inspire our intellectualism. Dungkar La offered private tutoring, but only to a few students, including me, and he rarely scolded his students.

As a result, Teacher Samten trained qualified students, or disciples, in religious and nonreligious spheres. His accomplished students include the above-noted Dornor; Géshé Sherab Gyatso, the Eleventh Panchen Lama's senior tutor; Jampo, one of the tutors and officials at the Advanced Tibetan Buddhist Institute of China in Beijing; Sheldrak, a former employee at Ngawa Prefecture's Editing and Translating Bureau specializing in history and poetry; Tenzin, a specialist in Tibetan medicine; Mönlam, who was proficient in religion and calligraphy; and Samdrup, who specialized in astrology.

Even though longtime close disciples of Teacher Samten accomplished a great deal in their respective fields, many of these names are generally unknown to the public, unlike some of his other students. This odd phenomenon is because nowadays, many so-called Tibetologists do not read or write in Tibetan. Therefore, those who write exclusively or predominantly in Tibetan, such as Teacher Samten's eminent students, are not known to outsiders. Nonetheless, this does little damage to his reputation as an outstanding educator.

In contrast, Dungkar La was marginalized, without the respect and support he deserved during his lifetime. He could have been treated successfully when he was first diagnosed with cancer. However, officials at Tibet University and in Tibet, where he later worked and lived, didn't take his disease seriously and provide timely treatment. He died shortly after. His abrupt death meant his most important work, the *Great Dungkar Tibetan Dictionary,*[5] was not completed. The dictionary currently in print is posthumous. Dungkar La's dictionary is generally considered the most comprehensive and encyclopedic Tibetan dictionary. Each of its entries identifies a key term and has accompanying passages ranging from several lines to several pages, with some nearly as long as a research paper. Every single entry stands on its own as an independent topic. For instance, most people have no clue that the Tibetan calendar is built upon the practice of the "Mongolian Calendar" (Tib. *horda*).[6] Through extensive references, Dungkar La explains how this expression and practice came into being in history. Except for his students, few know that the original plan for the dictionary is not fully seen in the volume in print today. If this dictionary could have come out as originally planned, it would have even more immeasurable value.

As one of his students, I encountered many of the terms during his teachings that were planned for inclusion in the dictionary. Its incompleteness probably is related to Dungkar's belief that the previously mimeographed terms he used for teaching purposes had already been published, so he decided not to include them. It was rumored that some of his writings, including the missing entries, had been stolen by his Han colleagues at the Central Nationalities Institute. However, I would assume that this can't be separated from the officials at Tibet University and in Tibet not attaching much importance to him and his research. In contrast, several other scholars in Tibet enjoyed much stronger official support, such as Chappel Tséten Püntsok (1922–2013; hereafter Chappel) at the Academy of Social Science in Tibet.[7] It is undeniable that he was a great scholar of Tibetan history. Still, most Tibetan scholars would agree that Chappel's contributions are not comparable to Dungkar La's in both scope and depth of the research.

After Dungkar La returned to Lhasa to teach in 1985, he requested an assistant from Tibet University to be assigned to help him with his research, such as typing, organizing, and compiling his dictionary entries and other writings, locating books and archives, and so on. After several petitions, the university eventually assigned someone. Still, the assistants who worked with him part-time were preoccupied with their work at Tibet University and unable to devote themselves entirely to Dungkar La's research. As a consequence, his research was seriously delayed, which he confided to me in 1992 when we both attended the second International Conference on the Tibetan Language at Arcidosso in Italy. At that time, he shared a somewhat uncertain and gloomy vision for his ongoing dictionary project. Unfortunately, as he worried, he could not complete it before his untimely death.

Another great pity is that Dungkar La was unhappy that he encountered and trained only a few students to his satisfaction. However, he did speak highly of one student in Beijing. I first heard about this person from Dungkar La when we met in 1978 in Chengdu. He said he had been hoping to recruit talented students in Tibet (TAR) but had failed to find anyone qualified. However, his new graduate student from Qinghai had shown great potential. According to Dungkar La, this student was so bright that he seemed to have an almost photographic memory for texts he read. Moreover, he also displayed extraordinary talent in poetry and writing. However, he had not been trained in philosophy and logic, which was an obstacle to gaining a deeper understanding of the Tibetan literary tradition. The student he referred to was Döndrup Gyel.

I first met Döndrup Gyel at the Central Nationalities Institute and immediately felt a sense of familiarity. He told me that Dungkar La had informed him I would join the classical Tibetan training program. We got along well, even though others saw him as arrogant and sharp-tongued. In his view, only three of our teachers—Dungkar La, Chöjor La, and Lodor La—were worthy of his respect. He commented that the other teachers, especially the Han Chinese, had a shallow understanding of Tibetan culture and tradition. Oddly, he treated me respectfully, which I said I didn't deserve since I also had limited knowledge of Tibetan culture. He replied, "No. This is not true. You have been through monastic training and have laid a solid foundation in Tibetan studies. You have much more room to grow intellectually. Someone like me is only good enough to play with my pens and produce something superficial."[8]

Some believed that Döndrup Gyel was critical of religion and saw it as a conservative force impeding Tibetan progress and development. He was sometimes accused of blasphemy against Tibetan Buddhism. Our conversations showed that this perspective only partially interprets his real intentions. He had rarely attacked religion directly and was conscious that it is critical to the Tibetan culture and way of life. He took issue with people's superstitions around religion and lamas and did not critique religion itself. According to him, these attitudes are hostile to social change and a forward-looking frame of mind, resulting in Tibetan backwardness and subsequent subjugation by other nationalities such as the Han. Döndrup Gyel hoped to awaken the Tibetan nationality to this ugly reality. Nonetheless, he put too high expectations on himself. He thought his writings could unify the whole Tibetan nationality, especially Tibetan youth, through the common cause of cultural rejuvenation and development. But his urgent calls led to little change in Tibetan society.[9] Quite the contrary, his works and his straightforward and somewhat confrontational style estranged many Tibetan intellectuals and others. Döndrup Gyel became very distressed about this, to the extent that he no longer saw worth in his life, and subsequently died by suicide.[10] Other factors, including his failed marriage and unsatisfactory work environment at a local college in Qinghai (Nationalities Teacher Training School in Chabcha), might have also contributed to his death. Still, I am inclined to believe that it was mainly his awakened vision of the Tibetan nationality's gloomy future that cost him his life.

These stories about Dungkar La and Döndrup Gyel tell us that Tibetan intellectuals were generally not taken seriously in China. Although Dungkar La was given some prominent official titles and displayed certain leftist tendencies, he was a true intellectual and saw his scholarship as the essence of his life. On the surface, people and officials showed great deference to him, but no one bothered to cherish him as the rare gem his students understood him to be. Comparing the official support and social impact of *The Tibetan-Chinese Dictionary* (Tib. *Bod rgya tshig mdzod chen mo*) and *The Great Dungkar Tibetan Dictionary*, we can easily see their disparate treatments. In a way, *The Tibetan-Chinese Dictionary* is better known in China. Despite its scholarly value, it is no more than a reference book, while Dungkar La's dictionary is an encyclopedia of breadth and depth. However, because the central government endorsed *The Tibetan-Chinese Dictionary*, the compilation project gathered tens of the most influential Tibetan scholars, including Dungkar La himself and Teacher Samten. In contrast, Dungkar La's dictionary was completed all on his own. This was not because he didn't want official support but because officials didn't care about the project enough to readily assist him.

While studying with Dungkar La in Beijing, I noticed certain signs of his marginalization. Many of his Han Chinese colleagues in the Tibetan studies program were his former students or had previously sat in on his lectures, but not all treated him with adequate respect. For instance, one Han professor (Professor X hereafter) who had studied with him made a female colleague ask Dungkar La various questions on his behalf because Professor X was a full professor while Dungkar La was an associate professor. This was odd, because in the Tibetan monastic tradition, it is common for individuals to learn from each other across all ranks and positions. Moreover, a rumor circulated that some Han teachers stole Dungkar La's writings through a typist. After completing his papers and chapters, Dungkar La would usually send them to a Han typist who worked for the Nationalities Languages Department. The typist was responsible for typing the Tibetan scripts for all the teachers in the department and would secretly send copies of his writing to several Han teachers who had requested them. We all had a general idea who these "thieves" were, including Professor X. Dungkar La became aware of this eventually. Döndrup Gyel then asked Dungkar La not to send his writings to this typist, which Dungkar La did.

How ironic! On the one hand, these Han teachers, including the prominent Professor X, treated Dungkar La as a font of knowledge, demonstrating that he had an unshakable role in Tibetan studies in China. But on the other hand, his former student Professor X became a full professor before him. The promotion system and the education system as a whole didn't take people like Dungkar La seriously because, in their view, he and other traditional ethnic minority scholars only knew their native language and culture and lacked adequate proficiency in the superior language, namely Chinese.

This isn't to say that Tibetans would treat Dungkar La entirely differently. His students revered him, but Tibetan officials and others showed little regard. The way Tibet University treated him is clear proof. Some Tibetan scholars enjoyed more substantial official endorsements because they had confirmed tangible official titles instead of nominal ones like Dungkar La or because their works strictly followed the Party-state line and were satisfactory for the state's ideological and propaganda purposes. Dungkar La and his works didn't fall into that category. Despite the clear leftist overtones in *On the Relationship Between Religion and State in Tibet*, the text was still classified as a serious scholarly work based on its thorough analyses of historical archives and materials. Dungkar La's works in general, especially his dictionary, fell short of the political significance necessary for special attention as entailed in the Party-state agenda.

Döndrup Gyel's situation appears to have been completely different, but a closer look shows that their fates aren't too dissimilar. Döndrup Gyel indeed had problems. He took a presumptuous stance toward many people, including other famous scholars, and he never tired of making sarcastic remarks about others and even embarrassing them directly. I don't know precisely how his extreme personality came into being. I do know that this personal style and his frustration and anger are inseparable from how our "Han big brothers treat Tibetans." The "Han big brothers" promised a great future for us Tibetans during Liberation, but Tibetan culture was soon labeled feudal, conservative, and backward and was seriously undermined. The situation improved after the Cultural Revolution, but overall, Tibetan culture was still considered inferior despite big Party slogans about ethnic equality and unity. The experiences of our teacher, Dungkar La, at the Central Nationalities Institute evinces the unfavorable circumstances in which Tibetan and other ethnic minority scholars were situated. Even worse, Dungkar La's deep concern about the dilution of Tibetan language education and Tibetan culture in general in China offended the "Han big brothers," who expected him and other Tibetan intellectuals to bow down to the "superior" Han Chinese culture and only express unwavering gratitude to them and to the CCP.

Döndrup Gyel disapproved of the "Han big brothers," especially those in Tibetan studies. Many Han thought he displayed Tibetan nationalistic sentiments too strongly. Consequently, my Han colleagues at the Southwest Nationalities Institute tried to prevent him from coming to teach. I was an acting chair of what was then called the Nationality Languages Department. My colleague Dawa (Nya Dawa Lodrö), a close friend of Döndrup Gyel, and I hoped to hire him, as he had expressed a desire to leave his position in Qinghai. We thought we wouldn't encounter any problems since our institute was short of scholars as talented and renowned as he. We needed someone like him to enhance our Tibetan studies program, which was relatively weak then. However, several Han colleagues of ours, some of whom were former students of the Han Tibetologists in Beijing whom Döndrup Gyel had sneered at, complained about this hiring plan to our department. They claimed that Döndrup Gyel was a heavy drinker, didn't get along with his colleagues due to his overbearing ethnocentric standpoint, and had "loose" sexual relationships. These were formal excuses, but what went unsaid was the actual reason for their objection: they knew Döndrup Gyel would scoff at their limited knowledge of the Tibetan language and culture if he secured a position here. Although the institute was going to drop this hiring plan, I convinced the officials in charge to move forward and subsequently dispatch someone to Döndrup Gyel's school to investigate these accusations. Unfortunately, only two days before this representative arrived, Döndrup Gyel died by suicide.

Döndrup Gyel's suicide is more than a personal tragedy, echoing a pessimistic perspective held by many Tibetans in China about the destiny of the Tibetan language and culture. Since his death, this situation has been further exacerbated. Most of the positive signs of change seen during the Hu Yaobang period in the 1980s are gone.[11] Hu saw the rule and dominance of the TAR by Han officials and cadres at that time as a form of colonialism and proposed returning the TAR to the Tibetans, and consequently ordered two-thirds of the Han employees to leave right away.[12] Now leftist-oriented officials have dominated Greater Tibet and Beijing. The attitude is that Tibetan culture and religion resemble a tumor that should be permanently removed. How would it be possible for Tibetans to practice their religion and develop their culture freely under such circumstances? Since the 2008 unrest, many self-immolation cases have been reported. I wonder if state officials ever considered that their extreme leftist policies, not an external force like the Dalai Lama's instigations, pushed Tibetans to kill themselves radically.

But, what can I do about the situation? I am now at a stage when the King of the Underworld (Tib. Shinjé chögyel) may knock at my door anytime. I had a chance to receive monastic training in Lhasa before Liberation and learn from scholars as great as Dungkar La and Teacher Samten in the 1970s and '80s. Most people with experiences similar to mine are already dead. Although I lack talent, I feel obliged to do something for the Tibetan nationality. Since I am from Gyalrong, I shifted my focus toward my hometown after my retirement. Gyalrong is probably the most Sinicized region in Tibet, so there is a lot for me to do to reintroduce Tibetan and Gyalrong history to the Gyalrongwa.

Chapter Fourteen

THE LAST BREATH

It was not until I was forty-eight years old that I started my academic training at the Central Nationalities Institute. It wasn't until my retirement at the age of sixty-seven that I could free myself from various other duties and devote myself entirely to research. I was eighty-six years old when I began learning to use the computer to type. I am ninety-four now (as of 2023), meaning the first half of my life was wasted. I didn't do anything meaningful or commendable during this period. An academic career has not only given me something worth pursuing but also rejuvenated the second half of my life. Even today, I am still thinking and working. I need to make the best use of my last breaths to face a critical issue that concerns the Gyalrong and the entire Tibetan nationality before the King of the Underworld comes to take me away. If Gyalrong, as Tibetans' geographic and cultural frontier, becomes fully Sinicized, how likely is it that Tibetans in Amdo, Kham, and Central Tibet will be able to resist a similar fate of becoming Han?

Many Gyalrongwa feel good about themselves simply because they believe they know some Chinese language. In juxtaposition, they don't feel ashamed about their limited or nonexistent knowledge of the Tibetan language and culture. Alai (a Gyalrong native and probably the most influential ethnic minority writer in China) even claims that Tibetan is a backward language due to its inability to express complex and modern ideas.[1] How can someone who probably cannot fully recognize even thirty Tibetan

syllables make such an audacious assertion? Tibetan has the most elaborate and comprehensive system of language, grammar, and expressions
one could ever imagine. To provide a simple example, the word "sun" (*nyi
ma*) in Tibetan has more than one hundred alternative expressions that
are applied differently across writing categories and contexts. Overall, such
figures of speech are widely used in Tibetan to avoid monotony and repetition and to enhance the rhythm and elegance of the writing. I don't know
enough languages to make a universal claim. Still, I am confident that the
Tibetan language's figures of speech are much richer and more sophisticated than those in Chinese.

Hence, this Gyalrong celebrity's irresponsible speech reinforces misper-
ceptions about Tibetan culture and language among the Han and Sinicized
Tibetans such as the Gyalrongwa. Alai is not alone. On many occasions, I
have heard Gyalrong officials and others state that Gyalrong has our
native language, which is distinctly different from Tibetan, and that
(written) Tibetan was never widely used in Gyalrong, except among the
monks. But if the Gyalrongwa speak a non-Tibetan language, how could
we have produced vast numbers of great lamas, including at least seven Ganden Tripas, in Tibetan history? There have indeed been many learned
lamas from Mongolia and other nationalities. However, when they begin
speaking Tibetan, most are easily recognized as non-Tibetans by their
strong accent. The Gyalrongwa's situation is quite different. Based on my
own experience, Gyalrong monks learned to understand and speak Tibetan
when we began our travels from Gyalrong to Lhasa over a four-month time
span. Although most of us spoke Tibetan (Lhasa dialect) with an accent, it
was recognized as a native Tibetan accent, not a foreign one.

That Gyalrong dialects have become non-Tibetan languages in the opinion of many Gyalrong officials and people may be based on the lack of
systematic Tibetan language education in Gyalrong schools since Liberation, despite sporadic, temporary attempts at Tibetan language classes here
and there in different Gyalrong regions and at different times. The Gyalrongwa are easily misled by some Han specialists on Gyalrong languages,
for example, Huang Bufan, Sun Hongkai, Jin Peng, etc., as well as a few of
their circle of linguists from Gyalrong proper, such as Lin Xiangrong. They
all claim that Gyalrong dialects are not within the Tibetan language family.[2] None is proficient in contemporary Tibetan, least of all classical Tibetan,
and none except Lin Xiangrong speaks the Gyalrong dialect. How then can

they arrive at this unscientific conclusion based on only "scientific-seeming" linguistic rules rather than actual adequate language skills?

If these linguists acknowledged that many Chinese dialects, nearly incomprehensible to non-native speakers, like Cantonese, Fujian, Suzhou, and others, are independent and non-Chinese languages, I would have to agree with them that Gyalrong dialects are non-Tibetan languages. So why don't they, or other Chinese linguists, treat the Chinese language the same as Tibetan? They must know that the CCP will never permit this. Suppose the pan-Han Chinese identity, built on a shared common language that persists across speakers of various dialects, was seriously questioned. Wouldn't the country risk splitting into many "warring states"? In contrast, linguists find it easy and convenient to bully Tibetans by leaning into our internal divides. If these scholars convince the majority of the Gyalrongwa that Gyalrong dialects are not variants of the Tibetan language, people in Gyalrong might start claiming that they are not part of the Tibetan nationality, as is happening now.

Next, the assertion that only monks use Tibetan in Gyalrong demonstrates those claimants' knowledge of history. Tibetan was the only language used in Gyalrong for official files and other purposes since the creation of the Tibetan script in the seventh century, just as it was in other parts of the Tibetan region. Recently I saw a few letters in Tibetan from the two Jinchuan kings to Qing officials during the Jinchuan Campaigns in the eighteenth century, which are now kept in the Qing Archives in Beijing. The language used in the letters is so elegant and skillful that not many Tibetan scholars today, including even those acclaimed Tibetologists, can compose such excellent writings. It was not until the Qing court implemented a policy known as "substituting chieftains with state-appointed civilian officials" (*gaitu guiliu*) in the wake of these campaigns that Chinese was gradually introduced in Gyalrong, together with Han Chinese immigration. However, only at the end of the Qing era and the beginning of the Republic era did most Gyalrong kings start using Chinese more systematically, including learning Chinese themselves, to better facilitate their contacts and interactions with Han officials and others.

Even so, by the time of Liberation, chieftains and nobles in most of Gyalrong were still taught Tibetan from childhood. Tibetan was the primary language used by the secretaries of various chieftains to keep official records. My former students and I have collected volumes of these official files in Tibetan by various Gyalrong kings during the Qing and Republic eras. I was surprised to find that one of these documents referred to me. When the Okzhi king and Sönamyak magistrate reached an agreement in the 1930s on the status and duties of my parents at Sönamyak after my arrival as their newly recognized *tulku*, the two parties formalized this agreement in writing, which was in Tibetan.[3] The original document is currently kept in the Ngawa Prefecture Archives.

In a nutshell, due to the severe lack of knowledge about Tibetan language, culture, and history, the Gyalrongwa have started to distance themselves from Tibetan identity. Consequently, many have become ashamed of being identified as Tibetans, especially since the 2008 Tibetan unrest. Once by accident, I was shocked to find that my nephew's ID card showed that his nationality was Han. He said, "If I didn't change the nationality on my ID card (from Tibetan to Han), I wouldn't be able to find any odd jobs in Chengdu." I was speechless. I am an insignificant intellectual, and few take scholars like me seriously. However, against the odds, I feel obligated to do something about this situation. Therefore, I decided to focus my work on two areas: promoting Tibetan language education at schools in Gyalrong and compiling books on Gyalrong history and culture based on original Tibetan manuscripts.

Since the 1990s, I have sought official support to introduce Tibetan language education in my hometown, Tsanlha. To be realistic, I proposed that a few hours each week be dedicated to Tibetan language learning at some local schools as a start and as an experiment. However, most Gyalrongwa officials in the local education bureau opposed this, seeing no virtue in Tibetan language classes. My proposal was nonetheless welcomed by many locals who were aware of the significance of Tibetan language to their identity. Thus, some capable and eloquent locals began repeatedly requesting that county officials take action, leading to the county finally approving this plan. Through the prefecture's education bureau, we gained two Tibetan language teachers from nomadic regions to teach at the Mipham township primary school in 1998. They weren't "official teachers" in terms of their status, and their salaries were provided by Trace Foundation.[4] Unexpectedly, these two teachers were soon expelled by local police to "clean up unidentified populations." A few years later, the prefecture's education bureau officially assigned another two Tibetan language teachers to the same primary school. However, it wasn't long before these two teachers left. The school didn't take the Tibetan classes seriously, and only one session of Tibetan class, lasting less than an hour, was arranged per week. Moreover, these teachers were also asked to teach other subjects. I talked to them a couple of times and hoped they would stay on, but they were so frustrated with the situation that they chose to leave.

Supposedly other people were to be assigned to fill their positions, but the county education bureau delayed the hiring process for years. Several older people who had been part of my alliance in establishing Tibetan language education in Tsanlha went to the county education bureau several times to petition its director to assign new teachers to the local school. The director ignored their petition and finally confronted them with, "Tibetan is the Dalai Lama's language. Since you are enthusiastic about promoting this language, have you all been loyal to him?" One of the petitioners called me afterward and said they had decided to stop trying, given the heightened political sensitivities. After that, the situation took a more positive turn when the prefecture Party secretary adopted a more understanding stance toward Tibetan culture. As a result, about five years ago, the prefecture's education bureau sent a new Tibetan language teacher to Mipham. I met him and encouraged him to overcome any difficulties he might face. He expressed determination to hold on to his position. Despite this young teacher's enthusiasm, I understood how difficult the situation could be for him, mainly because a new prefectural Party secretary appeared to be another typical "tough" official in his attitudes and policies toward Tibetans.

Overall, my two decades of efforts to establish Tibetan language education in Tsanlha have largely failed. Fortunately, my mission as a whole has not. To my surprise, what I have been doing has exerted some influence in other Gyalrong regions, such as Rongdrak, Gyelkha, and Barkham. Locals from these places continue to seek me out, ask for my advice on Tibetan language learning, invite me to give talks, and open short-term Tibetan language training programs there.

A second area of focus is my book projects on Gyalrong history and culture. I began collecting manuscripts and works on Gyalrong around the time of my retirement. Most manuscripts and scriptures had been destroyed in Gyalrong during various movements after Liberation, but some survived. I also found other old manuscripts in the 1980s in people's homes in Tsanlha and elsewhere. Few people there have learned to read and write in

Tibetan since Liberation, so these manuscripts were considered prayer scriptures. It turned out that some were records about Gyalrong history and culture. At that time, people were guileless and did not hesitate to show me their surviving manuscripts. They even allowed me to borrow them to photocopy or copy by hand if a photocopier was unavailable. In this way I obtained many vital manuscripts, many of which later became the basis of my edited works. Since the late 1990s, obtaining these manuscripts has become more difficult because people started to believe that these works were cultural relics and were worth money. As a retired professor, I only had a small pension, which was never enough to pay manuscript owners.

This problem was, however, partially resolved by locating many Gyalrong-related records in original Tibetan manuscripts and published works through acquaintances and at different monasteries across historical Gyalrong (see map 2). An unanticipated gain from this is that I have been exposed to many Bön manuscripts that I knew little about. Bön had long been a predominant religion throughout Gyalrong until the Second Jinchuan Campaign (1771–1776).[5] However, due to Bön's connections with the rebel kings, the Qing court ordered the locals to convert to Gelugpa after the military campaigns. Even so, Bön survived in many parts of Gyalrong. Some of the most important manuscripts I have collected so far, like those about the origins and lineages of the Jinchuan kings and connections between Gyalrong and Zhangzhung, were kept in Bön monasteries in historical Gyalrong like Zungchu (Ch. Songpan), where their *tulkus* and abbots have shared some of their collections at my request.

In this way, I have collected hundreds of volumes of Tibetan manuscripts related to Gyalrong history, much more than I expected when I started my work. However, I also had to consider how to make use of them. I had initially considered writing books on Gyalrong history using these manuscripts as foundational material, but after thinking more thoroughly, I dropped the idea. I realized that readers could easily assume that I had made up historical facts, so it would be better to provide the original manuscripts. Considering their vast number, I decided to excerpt the most representative manuscripts for publication. The excerpts are based on major themes, such as the origins of the Gyalrongwa, lineages and accounts of kings, kings' official files, historical events, religious development, language and customs, sacred sites, historical figures, etc. The latest book series I coedited, the *Gyalrong Tibetan History and Culture Series,* came out with

Sichuan Minzu Press in 2017. It comprises ten volumes, each focused on a central theme.[6]

I became more realistic during this process. Many Tibetans, especially the Gyalrongwa, least of all the concerned Han scholars, have limited or nonexistent Tibetan language reading skills, so they cannot comprehend our works if they are in their original Tibetan language versions. I hence saw the necessity of translating Tibetan texts into Chinese. However, organizing this translation and publishing the final products is very expensive. I am retired and have limited social influence, so my publication plans would have encountered severe challenges or been abandoned without the timely sponsorship of the CPPCC of Ngawa Prefecture. The former chair was Gyalrongwa and was interested in my project. More than twenty books have been published, including so-called "internal materials," by the prefectural CPPCC. As an unspoken rule in China, the Party official is seen as the editor-in-chief for most of my CPPCC-sponsored books, even though he has not contributed a single word. However, this is the last thing I care about as long as my books are available. I am grateful for his generous sponsorship and support, worth more than material or money. Since he was a high-ranking official, our book projects encountered fewer barriers, like time spent searching for new manuscripts from monasteries and owners, finding cars for field trips, looking for presses, etc.

In comparison, other officials I have turned to for help in the last decade show little interest in sponsoring our project despite being ethnic Tibetans. Their sole focus is promotion and acquiring more power. The more leftist tendencies they can feign or display (by distancing themselves from Tibetan cultural projects), the more likely they are to advance. The CPPCC chair in question is no exception. However, he knew that he had little chance of "climbing the ladder" because of his age and other factors, so it was no longer necessary for him to demonstrate a leftist stance. Therefore, he wanted to perform good deeds instead and leave a good name for himself.

Even so, I did most of the editing, although we had an editing team that included about ten civil servants and officials, *tulkus*, monks, university lecturers, and others. It has been difficult to secure regular assistants able to stay and work with me for at least several months each year. This kind of work is only part-time for the majority of our team members, especially for the civil servants. Not all of them can be entirely devoted to our book projects, and some have gone as far as to say that they are doing me a personal favor. Who am I doing a favor for? Am I just doing this for my own good? Before I die, I hope to use my last breath to leave something behind for the Gyalrongwa and the Tibetan nationality. Nonetheless, sometimes I feel no more worthy than a beggar, begging for mercy from officials and people to do something worthwhile for their nationality.

This is surely not all of the story. Some say I have made money from my writings. Most people today have little interest in these types of books, especially those on Tibetan and Gyalrong history. Most don't sell well. I've sent many free copies to others. The irony is that those who received them thought these books must not be worth reading because they were free. So I stopped sending free copies. Moreover, plenty of my relatives and other people consider me stupid and closed-minded because they don't see me using my *tulku* status to make money. They've seen other real and fake *tulku*s become wealthy through donations their Han disciples make. On top of that, some Gelugpa *tulku*s refer to me as "Bönpo Lama" because I have used many Bön manuscripts for the book projects. Their deeply ingrained religious biases lead them to ignore the significance of those manuscripts in studying Tibetan history.

These are the realities that I must endure. In the past, I expressed the opinion that Gyalrong, especially my hometown of Tsanlha, would be "finished" within twenty to fifty years, based on my observations of the Gyalrongwa's readiness to relinquish Tibetan and Gyalrong traditions. So many have unquestionably embraced the Han Chinese lifestyle, which emphasizes material gain in this lifetime and acts with little concern for karma and the afterlife. However, I have adopted a more positive perspective in the last few years, seeing the strength of Tibetan culture and many Gyalrongwa's growing awareness of the importance of the Tibetan language and its tradition in their identities. After all, Tibetan civilization has existed for at least several thousand years, if we consider the preceding Zhangzhung civilization. However, the world has not yet fully recognized the contribution of Tibetan civilization to the nonmaterial and spiritual realms. Materially and technologically, humankind has entered a very advanced stage, capable of creating atomic bombs to destroy the whole planet many times over. But science's contributions to the spiritual world are minimal. Scientists are akin to babies when it comes to understanding karma, death, the soul, the afterlife, and our minds. This suggests that Tibetan religion has a unique role in the human future and that Tibetan culture will not perish quickly.

Many Gyalrongwa have also started to see the value of Tibetan culture and traditions to varying degrees. What has happened in Ngawa County in recent years gives hints as to why. Many Tibetans have considered people in this place to be quite Sinicized. However, it has seen the most significant number of self-immolations throughout the Tibetan regions. Unexpectedly, several monks in Gyalrong self-immolated. This indicates that more and more people, including the Gyalrongwa, can no longer turn a blind eye to vanishing Tibetan culture due to tightened Party-state policies toward Tibetan culture and religion. Even though not all Tibetans have taken, or will take, such drastic measures in response to this deplorable situation, increasing numbers, including many of the Gyalrongwa who were once Sinicized, may become determined to defend our cultural and religious traditions. A growing number of people in Gyalrong have become keen to learn the Tibetan language and revive Tibetan culture here. More and more are showing genuine interest in my work in the last few years, in sharp contrast to the general neglect of my earlier efforts.

As I age, I tire more quickly than before, so I want to take a break. However, a break has become a dream. I have done many things, including publishing my updated classical Tibetan dictionary, completing a book comparing Gyalrong dialects and more widely used Tibetan dialects, continuing to train Tibetan language teachers and TV and radio hosts on their pitches and intonations, and so on. Moreover, I continue my role as a teacher by offering private tutoring to people interested in learning Tibetan and doing research.

Lastly, it is time to consider rebuilding Tibetan linguistics. History tells us that Thonmi Sambhota created a Tibetan linguistic system in addition to Tibetan scripts in the seventh century, although his texts on Tibetan linguistics have been lost over the centuries.[7] Certain other Tibetan scholars share my concern that we cannot simply transplant Western linguistics in the way Chinese and Western linguists who work on Tibetan and Gyalrong languages/dialects have done. Instead, we must establish our own system of linguistics based on the Tibetan literary tradition and the characteristics of the Tibetan language. My book project on the relationship between the Gyalrong (Situ) dialect and Tibetan is part of this ambitious project.[8] I wrote a little book and some articles on this topic years ago, but they are not systematic enough to challenge the predominant belief of linguists who classify various Gyalrong dialects as non-Tibetan languages. After I die, a few people might embark on this project. It requires skills in classical Tibetan and different Tibetan-Gyalrong dialects. Unfortunately, I have not encountered many Gyalrongwa or Tibetan scholars who have mastery of all these languages and dialects. Although I have come across several young scholars with great potential in this endeavor, they don't seem interested in such a project. A few prominent Tibetan scholars tell me that if we don't speak out in time, the field of Tibetan language and linguistics will be redefined and dominated by even more linguists who have insufficient skills in both classical and modern Tibetan and Gyalrong dialects, yet assume a prominent role due to their application of so-called scientific (and hence superior) linguistic methods. This is the only and probably final thing I can do for Gyalrong and the Tibetan nationality with my remaining breaths.

NOTES

INTRODUCTION

1. In furthering our understanding of Gyalrong's relationship with Beijing and Lhasa, see Yudru Tsomu's study of a legendary lesser Kham chieftain (Gönpo Namgyel) in the nineteenth century, taken from the local (Sino-Tibetan frontier) political entity's positioning vis-à-vis Beijing and Lhasa. Yudru Tsomu, *The Rise of Gönpo Namgyel in Kham: The Blind Warrior of Nyarong* (Lanham, MD: Lexington Books, 2015). The rise of local Gyalrong chieftains (Jinchuan) in the eighteenth century was also not accidental and must be situated within Gyalrong's marginalized status and the triangular relationships among Beijing, Lhasa, and local chieftains, which share similarities with those of Gönpo Namgyel and Kham. See Alai, *Zhandui: Zhongyu ronghua de tie geda—Yige liangbainian de kangba chuanqi* (Chengdu: Sichuan wenyi chubanshe, 2014).

2. The idea of "Tibetan" (hence Tibetanization) is much more ambiguous than many think. For instance, according to the Gyalrong Kuzhap and most Tibetologists in China I have encountered, Zhangzhung, a pre-Tibetan (Empire) cultural and political entity on the Tibetan Plateau, was an integral part of the long Tibetan history; thus, it is "Tibetan." Therefore, the Gyalrong Kuzhap would argue that Gyalrong had been "Tibetanized" long before the seventh century, starting with the first appearance of Zhangzhung's political and cultural influences in Gyalrong some 4,000 years ago. See the Gyalrong Kuzhap's relevant view of this situation in chapter 1.

3. Based on many old Tibetan manuscripts, Gyalrong is considered part of broader Tibet. The Gyalrong Kuzhap has collected and published many of these original manuscripts, cited below. I discuss Gyalrong's contested Tibetan status in the contemporary context and its broader political and other implications in Jinba Tenzin, *In the Land of the Eastern Queendom: The Politics of Gender and Ethnicity on the*

Sino-Tibetan Border (Seattle; London: University of Washington Press, 2014), and "Seeing Like Borders: Convergence Zone as a Post-Zomian Model," *Current Anthropology* 58, no. 5 (2017): 551–75.

4. The notion of "Sinicization" is seriously challenged in Western academia for its "imperialist" connotations of neglecting the agency and diversity of peoples in the Chinese cultural sphere and neighboring regions. This relates to the growing popularity of the so-called New Qing historians primarily based in North America. They dismiss the validity of the Qing's Sinicization thesis and argue instead for an Inner Asia model of Qing rule. I continue to employ the notion in this book and elsewhere because the idea has become a focus in popular discourse in China. In addition, the Gyalrong Kuzhap uses this concept consistently to express his disapproval toward Gyalrong natives and Tibetans "becoming Han Chinese" in terms of their daily language use (mostly or exclusively Chinese), way of dressing, customs, and especially their "mentality" (the dilution of Gyalrong Tibetan identity).

5. See Jinba Tenzin, "Memory Politics at Work in a Gyalrong Revolt in the Early Twentieth Century," *Cross-Currents: East Asian History and Culture Review* 5, no. 2 (2016): 419–23. Due to the significance of these campaigns in Qing history, many scholars have examined them from diverse angles, such as the Qing's frontier policies and chieftain system, finances and logistics, labor, postwar language, and sociocultural changes. See, for instance, Dan Martin, "Bonpo Canons and Jesuit Cannons: On Sectarian Factors Involved in the Ch'en-Lung Emperor's Second Goldstream Expedition of 1771–1776," *The Tibet Journal* 15, no. 2 (1990): 3–28; Roger Greatrex, "A Brief Introduction to the First Jinchuan War (1747–1749)," in *The History of Tibet: The Medieval Period c. 850–1895*, vol. 2, ed. Alex McKay (London and New York: RoutledgeCurzon, 2003), 615–32; Dai Yingcong, "The Qing State, Merchants, and the Military Labor Force in the Jinchuans," *Late Imperial China* 22, no. 2 (2001): 35–90; Peng Zhiyan, "Qianlong zaiding liangjinchuan zhanzheng gouchen," *The Academic Journal of Tibet Minzu Institute* 25, no. 2 (2004): 22–28; Peng Zhiyan, "Qianlongdi dui daxiao jinchuan tusi gaituguiliu xi," *The Academic Journal of Tibet Minzu Institute* 28, no. 4 (2007): 15–23; Samten G. Karmay, *Feast of the Morning Light: The Eighteenth-Century Wood-Engravings of Shenrab's Life-Stories and the Bon Canon from Gyalrong* (Osaka: National Museum of Ethnology, 2005); Joanna Waley-Cohen, *The Culture of War in China: Empire and the Military Under the Qing Dynasty* (London: I. B. Tauris, 2006); Ulrich Theobald, *War Finance and Logistics in Late Imperial China: A Study of the Second Jinchuan Campaign (1771–1776)* (Leiden: Brill, 2013); Xu Fayan, "Qianlongchao Jinchuan zhanyi yanjiu pingshu," *Studies in Qing History* 4 (2011): 133–42; Xu Fayan, "Diyici Jinchuan zhiyi qiyin chutan qianlongdi suijing chuanbian de nuli," *The Academic Journal of Sichuan University* 5 (2012): 150–60; Ryōsuke Kobayashi, "Shilun Shiba Shiji Houqi Qingchao Dui Kangqu Zhengce De Bianhua," *Journal of Tibetan Studies* 00 (2014): 197–208; Wang Tingyu, "'House,' Illusion or Illumination? The Social Organization and Language of Sichuan Rgyalrong Tibetan" (Ph.D. diss., National Tsing Hua University, Taiwan, 2018).

6. For a discussion of Zhao's reform and later Qing Tibetan frontier policy, see, for instance, Wang Xiuyu, *China's Last Imperial Frontier: Late Qing Expansion in Sichuan's Tibetan Borderlands* (Lanham, MD: Lexington Books, 2011).

7. Most Gyalrong locals I talked to denounce Tibetan rebels for their "riots" and self-immolations or "ungrateful" acts ("ungrateful" to the CCP for "liberating"

Tibetans from the "old" and "dark" system and bringing progress and good life to them). Other Tibetans I interacted with attribute the Gyalrongwa's "betrayal" of the Tibetan nationality and interests to their "inauthentic" Tibetan status and "Sinicization." However, the situation is far more complex. As noted, many Gyalrongwa are ashamed to associate themselves with "treacherous" Gyalrongwa or "inauthentic" Tibetans and choose to neglect or leave behind their Gyalrong identity and past. This is due to multiple factors, not purely out of "allegiance" to the Tibetan cause (religious autonomy, etc.). See an elaborate discussion of this complex situation in Tenzin, *In the Land of the Eastern Queendom* and "Seeing Like Borders."

8. See E. J. Hobsbawm, and T. O. Ranger, *The Invention of Tradition* (Cambridge; New York: Cambridge University Press, 1983). Regarding making an originally fictional Shangri-La-like pure land in southwestern China for tourism and development, see Emily T. Yeh, and Chris Coggins, *Mapping Shangrila: Contested Landscapes in the Sino-Tibetan Borderlands* (Seattle: University of Washington Press, 2014).

9. See, for instance, Charles Lindholm, *Culture and Authenticity* (Malden, MA: Blackwell, 2008).

10. For a discussion of the aristocracy in Tibet and their associated manners and "tastes," see Heidi Fjeld, *Commoners and Nobles: Hereditary Divisions in Tibet* (Copenhagen: NIAS, 2005). See also Tsering Yangdzom, *The Aristocratic Families in Tibetan History:1900–1951* (Beijing: China Intercontinental Press, 2006). Despite being situated in French and Western contexts, a better understanding of Tibetan "high" tastes is possible through a sophisticated discussion of tastes (as an internalized disposition or "habitus") and cultural capital in Pierre Bourdieu, *Outline of a Theory of Practice* (Cambridge; New York: Cambridge University Press, 1977), and *Distinction: A Social Critique of the Judgement of Taste* (Cambridge, MA: Harvard University Press, 1984).

11. The Qing Dynasty (1644–1912) developed a comprehensive system of royal and noble ranks. This was applied generally to the Manchu and Mongols, and the Han were typically excluded. This system came to an end in most parts of the empire at the time of its collapse in 1912. See Evelyn Sakakida Rawski, *The Last Emperors: A Social History of Qing Imperial Institutions* (Berkeley: University of California Press, 1998). However, in the case of Greater Tibet, the Qing acknowledged the unique royal and noble system of different Tibetan regions. In Central Tibet, for example, the Qing formally endorsed the Dalai Lama's role as its spiritual and temporal leader (and the aristocratic system associated with it), while in certain other Tibetan areas, such as Gyalrong, the Qing conferred *tusi* and other titles on local chieftains. This system remained largely intact in many parts of Greater Tibet even after the Qing crumbled and was not fully abolished until the 1950s by the new Communist regime.

12. The system and politics of reincarnation are thoroughly discussed in some recent (and earlier) works, e.g., Peter Schwieger, *The Dalai Lama and the Emperor of China: A Political History of the Tibetan Institution of Reincarnation* (New York: Columbia University Press, 2015); Nicole Willock, "The Revival of the Tulku Institution: Narratives and Practices in Modern China," *Revue D'etudes Tibétaines* 38 (2017): 183–201; Ruth Gamble, *Reincarnation in Tibetan Buddhism: The Third Karmapa and the Invention of a Tradition* (New York: Oxford University Press, 2018); Max

Oidtmann, *Forging the Golden Urn: The Qing Empire and the Politics of Reincarnation in Tibet* (New York: Columbia University Press, 2018). As shown, the reincarnation system is rife with political struggles and manipulations.

13. In the last decade, Tibetan Buddhism has grown into an impressive presence in major Chinese cities, especially in Beijing, China's political, cultural, and economic hub. For the first available systematic book-length study of the spread of Tibetan Buddhism in contemporary China, see Dan Smyer Yü, *The Spread of Tibetan Buddhism in China: Charisma, Money, Enlightenment* (New York: Routledge, 2012). See also Alison Denton Jones, "Contemporary Han Chinese Involvement in Tibetan Buddhism: A Case Study from Nanjing," *Social Compass* 58, no. 4 (2011): 540–53; Zhang Yinong, "Between Nation and Religion: The Sino-Tibetan Buddhist Network in Post-Reform China," *Chinese Sociological Review* 45, no. 1 (2012): 55–69; Joshua Esler, "Tibetan Buddhism and Han Chinese: Superscribing New Meaning on the Tibetan Tradition in Modern Greater China" (Ph.D. diss., University of Western Australia, 2013); Ester Bianchi, "A Religion-Oriented 'Tibet Fever': Tibetan Buddhist Practices Among the Han Chinese in the Contemporary PRC," in *From Mediterranean to Himalaya,* ed. Dramdul and F. Sferra (Beijing: China Tibetology Publishing House, 2014), 347–74; and Jane Caple, "Faith, Generosity, Knowledge and the Buddhist Gift: Moral Discourses on Chinese Patronage of Tibetan Buddhist Monasteries," *Religion Compass* 9, no. 11 (2015): 462–82. For the growing popularity of Tibetan Buddhism among the Han as an outgrowth of its revival and development during the post-Mao era, see Melvyn C. Goldstein and Matthew Kapstein, *Buddhism in Contemporary Tibet: Religious Revival and Cultural Identity* (Berkeley: University of California Press, 1998); Ashild Kolas and Monika P. Thowsen, *On the Margins of Tibet: Cultural Survival on the Sino-Tibetan Frontier* (Seattle; London: University of Washington Press, 2005); Ben Hillman, "Monastic Politics and the Local State in China: Authority and Autonomy in an Ethnically Tibetan Prefecture," *The China Journal* 54 (2005): 29–51; Charlene E. Makley, *The Violence of Liberation: Gender and Tibetan Buddhist Revival in Post-Mao China* (Berkeley: University of California Press, 2007); Koen Wellens, *Religious Revival in the Tibetan Borderlands: The Premi of Southwest China* (Seattle: University of Washington Press, 2010). One of the first comprehensive investigations of nuns' lives and practices in the wake of the Tibetan Buddhist revival is Yasmin Cho, "Politics of Tranquility: Religious Mobilities and Material Engagements of Tibetan Buddhist Nuns in Post-Mao China" (Ph.D. diss., Duke University, 2015). Nonetheless, the spread of Tibetan Buddhism among the Han is not a new or contemporary phenomenon. Instead, it may be seen as a renewal of this historical process and momentum. For a discussion of this process during the Republican era (1912–1949), see Gray Tuttle, *Tibetan Buddhists in the Making of Modern China* (New York: Columbia University Press, 2005); Martino Dibeltulo, "The Revival of Tantrism: Tibetan Buddhism and Modern China" (Ph.D. diss., University of Michigan, 2015); and Wu We, "Indigenization of Tibetan Buddhism in Twentieth-Century China" (Ph.D. diss., Princeton University, 2017).

14. A joke that I have heard from several Han acquaintances, also available on the Internet, goes, "There are 30,000 'free-range' Rinpoche (reincarnate lamas and great masters) in Chaoyang District," a very prosperous district in Beijing. This is cynical and disapproving, given that "free-range" (Ch. *sanyang*) is typically used to

identify freely moving livestock, not people. This highlights Beijing at the heart of Tibetan Buddhist proselytization in China, thanks to the city's role as the country's political and financial center. In addition, it spotlights certain activities among real or fake Tibetan masters and their close disciples and allies, especially their subsequent sexual, monetary, and other scandals that proliferate across Beijing and China, creating suspicions and tensions for one another. One of the best-known recent scandals involves Zhang Tielin, a famous actor who was recognized in 2015 as a reincarnate lama, ironically by another self-proclaimed reincarnate lama, a Han Chinese. Consequently, the Chinese state has begun taking concrete measures to restrain this trend. For instance, it established an online system for the public to check the (in)authenticity of reincarnate lamas (see http://hf.tibet.cn/tibet/pubre source/search.jsp).

15. "Liberation" is a common term used in China to refer to the CCP's takeover of the country or a particular region like Tibet in 1949 or afterward. Tibetans (and others) in China, including the Gyalrong Kuzhap, also use it to identify this historical epoch.

16. See Stevan Harrell, *Ways of Being Ethnic in Southwest China* (Seattle: University of Washington Press, 2001), and Thomas S. Mullaney, *Coming to Terms with the Nation: Ethnic Classification in Modern China* (Berkeley: University of California Press, 2011). See also Mette Halskov Hansen, *Lessons in Being Chinese: Minority Education and Ethnic Identity in Southwest China* (Seattle: University of Washington Press, 1999), and Yang Miaoyan, *Learning to Be Tibetan: The Construction of Ethnic Identity at Minzu University of China* (Lanham, MD: Lexington Books, 2017).

17. See Tenzin, *In the Land of the Eastern Queendom* and "Seeing Like Borders," and Wang , " 'House,' Illusion or Illumination?."

18. Based on posts by Tsering Woeser, a Tibetan dissident writer living in Beijing; the International Campaign for Tibet (https://savetibet.org/tibetan-self-immolations/ #inexile); and other sources (e.g., news), a total of 159 Tibetans in China and in exile had performed self-immolation by March 2022. Forty-six of them (nearly 29 percent) were from Ngawa County, and 64 cases (40 percent) occurred in Ngawa Prefecture as a whole. See Tsering Woeser, *Tibet on Fire: Self-immolations Against Chinese Rule* (London; New York: Verso, 2016). These acts of resistance have also attracted wide attention in Western academia. See Warren W. Smith, *Tibet's Last Stand: The Tibetan Uprising of 2008 and China's Response* (New York: Rowman & Littlefield, 2010); Katia Buffetrille and Françoise Robin, eds., "Tibet Is Burning: Self-Immolation, Ritual or Political Protest?" Special Issue, *Revue D'etudes Tibétaines* 25 (December 2012); Carole Mcgranahan and Ralph Litzinger, "Self-Immolation as Protest in Tibet." Hot Spots, *Fieldsights*, April 9, 2012; Charlene E. Makley, "The Sociopolitical Lives of Dead Bodies: Tibetan Self-Immolation Protest as Mass Media," *Cultural Anthropology* 30, no. 3 (2015): 448–76; Charlene E. Makley, *The Battle for Fortune: State-Led Development, Personhood, and Power Among Tibetans in China* (Ithaca, NY: Cornell University Press, 2018); and John Whalen-Bridge, *Tibet on Fire: Buddhism, Protest, and the Rhetoric of Self-Immolation* (New York: Palgrave Macmillan, 2015). Emily Yeh explores this issue through the state-led development agenda and landscape transformation in Tibet: Emily T. Yeh, *Taming Tibet: Landscape Transformation and the Gift of Chinese Development* (Ithaca, NY: Cornell University Press, 2013). I also discuss the broad

implications of these incidents for the Tibetans and Gyalrongwa in particular, e.g., Tenzin, *In the Land of the Eastern Queendom* and "Seeing Like Borders."

19. Daniel Berounský discusses the lineage of Ngawa chiefs or Megyal kings, including the last king, Palgon Chenle, and the lineage's historical connections with Kirti monastery, briefly of the Gelugpa tradition, in "Kīrti Monastery of Ngawa: Its History and Recent Situation," *Revue D'etudes Tibétaines* 25 (2012): 65–80. According to my local informants, most self-immolated local Tibetans were closely related to this monastery, either as current or former monks or as monastery followers (and/or monks' family members and relatives).

20. For an examination of the destructive consequences to the ecosystem on the Tibetan Plateau through various state-endorsed development projects, see Michael Buckley, *Meltdown in Tibet: China's Reckless Destruction of Ecosystems from the Highlands of Tibet to the Deltas of Asia* (New York: Palgrave Macmillan, 2014).

21. This view is embedded in the Tibetan perspective of nature-culture dynamics, or the idea of dependent arising (all phenomena arise in dependence on one another). As implicated in the notion of the Mandate of Heaven, it is accepted wisdom in Chinese society that particular natural phenomena (such as disasters or rare astral events seen as omens) may signify Heaven's displeasure with certain rulers or human actions and are forewarning of forthcoming grave accidents or political turmoil (e.g., dynasty changes). See, for instance, Zhao Dingxin, "The Mandate of Heaven and Performance Legitimation in Historical and Contemporary China," *American Behavioral Scientist* 53, no. 3 (2009): 416–33, and David W. Pankenier, *Astrology and Cosmology in Early China: Conforming Earth to Heaven* (New York: Cambridge University Press, 2013). Based on this logic, the Sichuan earthquake might be interpreted by the public as a warning from Heaven about Party-state rule and its legitimacy. Oddly, the CCP took advantage of this incident to publicly perform its unchallenged legitimacy (e.g., "benevolent rule") in an extravagant way, both literally and figuratively. See Florian Schneider and Yih-Jye Hwang, "The Sichuan Earthquake and the Heavenly Mandate: Legitimizing Chinese Rule Through Disaster Discourse," *Journal of Contemporary China* 23, no. 88 (2014): 636–56. During the COVID-19 pandemic, a more elaborate performance of legitimate power like this came to life. The CCP and China convey a plain message that the Party-state has significantly outperformed Western and other countries in containing the virus while maintaining social stability and economic growth.

22. In examining several competing accounts about the origins of the Wasi chieftain lineage that are available from the Republican era, Wang Mingke demonstrates that this situation can be understood through two conflicting forms of historical mentalities or historical-cultural trends prevalent in local society, the process of Sinicization and the process of Tibetanization. See Wang Mingke, "Wasi tusi de zuyuan—Yige dui lishi shenhua yu xiangye chua shuo de bianyuan yanjiu," *Lishi renleixue xuekan* 2, no. 1 (2004): 51–88. However, in comparison, Sinicization had become the predominant process by the early twentieth century (and much earlier to a lesser extent). A few works completed from the 1920s to 1940s offer important insight into Han Chinese intellectuals' perspectives on social conditions and cultural changes, as well as the chieftain system in Gyalrong, including the Wasi and Wenchuan. See Zhuang Xueben, *Qiangrong kaocha ji* (Shanghai: Shanghai liangyou tushu gongsi, 1937); Ma Changshou, "Jiarong minzu shehui shi," *Minzuxue*

yanjiu jikan [Collected volumes on nationality studies] 4 (1944); and Li Guangming and Wang Yuanhui, *Chuanxi minsu diaocha ji lu 1929* (Taipei: Zhongyang yanjiuyuan lishi yuyan yanjiusuo, 2004).

23. It is easy to understand, even for first-time foreign visitors, that the extravagant "gratitude campaigns" found all over China are singing the praises of the "almighty" CCP, which they claim has rescued the entire Chinese nation from its semicolonial and semifeudal past and brought great prosperity to people in the post-Mao era. Such campaigns demand even more publicity and propaganda in ethnic minority regions, especially in Tibet and Xinjiang. See, for instance, Yeh, *Taming Tibet*: "Indeed, PRC legitimation of its sovereignty over Tibet has always rested heavily on the presumption of Tibetan gratitude, first for Liberation from the cruel, barbaric, and feudal pre-1950s 'old society' and then, starting in the 1980s, for the bestowal of the gift of development, through the skills brought by Han migrants as well as the provision of large-scale infrastructure and massive subsidies from the government. In this narrative, all but a few radical separatists are grateful for this largesse" (ix).

24. Gyatso's work is illuminating in examining the unique Tibetan *namtar*, especially secret autobiographical tradition, in juxtaposition with biographical writings in a Western context. See Janet Gyatso, *Apparitions of the Self: The Secret Autobiographies of a Tibetan Visionary* (Princeton, NJ: Princeton University Press, 1998). Also see Tsultrim Allione, *Women of Wisdom* (London; Boston: Routledge & Kegan Paul, 1984); and Janice D. Willis, "On the Nature of Rnam-Thar: Early Dge-Lugs-Pa Siddha Biographies," in *Soundings in Tibetan Civilization*, ed. B. A.Aziz and M. Kapstein (Kathmandu: Vajra Publications, 1985), 304–19.

25. The *namtar* (biography) tradition refers to life stories and experiences (e.g., religious teachings) about masters or gurus, often composed by the protagonists' disciples. This common biography type focuses mainly on the accomplishments of the protagonist or master. One of the best-known examples of *namtar* is the biography of Milarepa (eleventh–twelfth centuries), a highly celebrated yogi in Tibetan history. See, for instance, Tsangnyön Heruka, Andrew Quintman, and Donald S. Lopez, Jr., *The Life of Milarepa* (New York: Penguin, 2010) and Andrew Quintman, *The Yogin and the Madman: Reading the Biographical Corpus of Tibet's Great Saint Milarepa* (New York: Columbia University Press, 2014). A *rangnam* (autobiography) is personal experiences or life events such as religious training and teachings, authored by the protagonists. One of the most well-known examples is the autobiography of the Fifth Dalai Lama (1617–1682). See Samten G. Karmay, *The Illusive Play: The Autobiography of the Fifth Dalai Lama* (Chicago: Serindia, 2014). This biography category is often characterized by the author's self-revelations or truth-telling instead of a self-elevation or focus on achievements (as prescribed by the Buddhist notion of "no-self"). A *tokjö* (hagiography) is characterized by extravagant glorification of great deeds of accomplished religious masters and political figures, such as the hagiography of Polhané (1689–1747), an influential political figure and de facto ruler or "king" of Central Tibet in the first half of the eighteenth century. The protagonist is often depicted as an almost unrivaled sacred being deserving absolute tributes and devotion.

26. The three forms of autobiography are outer, inner, and secret (*chi nang sang sum*), targeting different audiences, namely anyone (general readers), people within the

same religious community and lineage (e.g., disciples of the lineage), and those who have received tantric (empowerment) rituals, respectively. One master might create all three forms oriented toward different readerships.

27. See Naktsang Nulo, *My Tibetan Childhood: When Ice Shattered Stone* (Durham, NC: Duke University Press, 2014).

28. Dalai Lama (Bstan'dzin rgya mtsho), *My Land and My People* (New York: McGraw-Hill, 1962); *Freedom in Exile: The Autobiography of the Dalai Lama* (New York: HarperCollins, 1990); *My Spiritual Autobiography* (London: Rider, 2012).

29. Oidtmann, *Forging the Golden Urn*, 61.

30. Gail Hershatter, "Disquiet in the House of Gender," *The Journal of Asian Studies* 71, no. 4 (2012): 873–94.

31. Makley elaborates on how memory politics plays out through the intricate entanglement between "the personal" and "the political" when elder Tibetans recall the violence of the post-Liberation period of social transformation in local (Labrang) society, as well as local people's choices and positioning concerning the new regime and its orchestrated political frenzy. See Charlene E. Makley, "'Speaking Bitterness': Autobiography, History, and Mnemonic Politics on the Sino-Tibetan Frontier," *Comparative Studies in Society and History* 47, no. 1 (2005): 40–78; and *The Violence of Liberation*. Recent publications shed new light on conflicting memories among Tibetans during the Mao era, such as Robert Barnett, Benno Weiner, and Françoise Robin, *Conflicting Memories: Tibetan History Under Mao Retold* (Leiden; Boston: Brill, 2020). For how history and memory among Tibetans in exile are shaped by their experiences, cultural logic, political claims, and international relations, see Carole Mcgranahan, *Arrested Histories: Tibet, the CIA, and Memories of a Forgotten War* (Durham, NC: Duke University Press, 2010); and "Mao in Tibetan Disguise: History, Ethnographic Theory, and Excess," *HAU: Journal of Ethnographic Theory* 2, no. 1 (2012): 213–45.

32. So-called moral decline (a dilution of "traditional" values or virtues, e.g., materialism, utilitarianism, neglect of filial piety, etc.) has characterized the transforming moral landscape in popular discourse in China since the early 1980s, especially at the turn of the twenty-first century. This has produced profound ethical, moral, and psychological repercussions in Chinese society. See Yan Yunxiang, "The Good Samaritan's New Trouble: A Study of the Changing Moral Landscape in Contemporary China," *Social Anthropology* 17, no. 1 (2009): 9–24; and Arthur Kleinman, *Deep China: The Moral Life of the Person: What Anthropology and Psychiatry Tell Us About China Today* (Berkeley: University of California Press, 2011). This state of being sets off popular desires for moral restoration in China. The Gyalrong Kuzhap and many Tibetans believe that Tibetans, especially the younger generation, have been impacted by the wave of moral decline. This situation is vividly reflected in a popular new saying among Tibetans: "Tibetans have become Han; the Han have become demons."

33. For a discussion of sociopolitical changes and ethnocultural transmutation in the Sino-Tibetan borderlands over the last two decades, especially Gyalrong, see Tenzin, *In the Land of the Eastern Queendom* and "Seeing Like Borders." For discussion in a historical context, see Jinba Tenzin, "Memory Politics at Work in a Gyalrong Revolt in the Early Twentieth Century," *Cross-Currents: East Asian History and Culture Review* 5, no. 2 (2016): 408–39.

34. Fiskesjö's article is revealing in showing how "barbaric" non-Han people, or previously "the animal other," were incorporated into the Chinese nation-state by creating a category of "internal others" or ethnic minorities as a foil to the "civilized" Han self in the twentieth century. See Magnus Fiskesjö, "The Animal Other: China's Barbarians and Their Renaming in the Twentieth Century," *Social Text* 29, no. 4 (109) (2011): 57–79.

35. Wang Lixiong sees Tibet's dependent economy as an inevitable consequence of the CCP-enforced agenda of modernization that was external to Tibet and incompatible with the Tibetan way of life. He refers to this external force as a "tumor" in Tibet. See Wang Lixiong, *Tianzang: Xizang de mingyun* (Mississauga, ON: Mingjing chubanshe, 1998), 433–60. This pattern of development models is not exclusive to Central Tibet but also applies to other Tibetan (and more generally to other ethnic minority) regions. However, Central Tibet has received a more significant share of financial and other subsidies. Different works examine the various consequences, e.g., political disempowerment, cultural assimilation, mass Han Chinese migration, economic marginalization, land expropriation, etc. See, for instance, June Teufel Dreyer, "Economic Development in Tibet Under the People's Republic of China," *Journal of Contemporary China* 12, no. 36 (2003): 411–30; Tashi Nyima, "The Chinese Development of Tibet: Lhasa in Transformation," *Forum for Development Studies* 35, no. 2 (2008): 257–77; Yeh, *Taming Tibet*; and Andrew Martin Fischer, *The Disempowered Development of Tibet in China: A Study in the Economics of Marginalization* (Lanham, MD: Lexington Books, 2014).

36. See Benedict Anderson, *Imagined Communities: Reflections on the Origin and Spread of Nationalism* (London; New York: Verso, 1991).

37. Seng ge 'bum, Btsan lha ngag dbang tshul khrims, Tshe dbang, Bstan 'dzin sbyin pa, and Nam mkha' tshul khrims, *Shar rgyal mo tsha ba rong gi lo rgyus dang rig gnas dpe tshogs/Jiarong Zangzu lishi wenhua congshu* (Chengdu: Sichuan minzu chubanshe, 2017).

38. Political correctness is crucial in literary works in China, and this applies even more to Tibetan writers and scholars. However, Tibetan authors do not lack agency or resistance. Their works express concerns about Tibetan cultural survival and political destiny in China in one way or another. See a relevant discussion of sociopolitical contexts in Lauran R. Hartley and Patricia Schiaffini-Vedani, *Modern Tibetan Literature and Social Change* (Durham, NC: Duke University Press, 2008). However, many Tibetan authors in China choose to challenge state narratives outright like "peaceful Liberation" and "development" and "progress" in Tibetan regions. See, for instance, Naktsang, *My Tibetan Childhood*; Woeser, *Tibet on Fire*; Tsering Woeser, *Forbidden Memory: Tibet During the Cultural Revolution* (Lincoln, NE: Potomac Books, 2020). There is surely a political consequence in doing so. For example, Woeser, living in Beijing, is flagged as a dissident writer and under heavy state surveillance.

39. A recent work of the exile genre is Paljor Tsarong, *The Life and Times of George Tsarong of Tibet, 1920–1970: A Lord of the Traditional Tibetan State* (Lanham, MD: Lexington Books, 2021).

40. This, however, does not indicate limited value in the Gyalrong Kuzhap's authored memoir. I recommend interested scholars take a close look at this memoir that focuses more on cultural-historical aspects (including cultural and religious rituals

and customs) and his research (publications). Btsan lha ngag dbang tshul khrims, *Btsan lha ngag dbang tshul khrims rang gis rang gi byung ba brjod pa/Zanla Awang Cuocheng huiyilu* (Lanzhou: Gansu minzu chubanshe, forthcoming).

41. Alai's most celebrated work, *Red Poppies*, is about endless battles among Gyalrong chieftains at a most turbulent time when Gyalrong was soon to be taken over by the CCP. See Alai, *Red Poppies*, trans. H. Goldblatt and S. L.-C. Lin (Boston: Houghton Mifflin, 2002). The book's original Chinese version was released in 1998 and won the Mao Dun Literature Prize, the most influential prize in literature in China, in 2000. Alai is, however, highly critical of Tibetan culture. For instance, in an interview with a Tibetan cultural website, Alai compared Tibetan Buddhism to medieval Christianity regarding its religious monopolies and resistance to modern ideas. Furthermore, in his 2008 interview with CCTV (China's national TV station), he said written Tibetan is a religious language reserved merely for monks with a limited capacity to express ideas (in contrast to the Chinese language's refinement, accuracy, and precision). Consequently, an independent Tibetan literature system has never existed. Most Tibetan intellectuals have dismissed these points of view.

42. James C. Scott, *Weapons of the Weak: Everyday Forms of Peasant Resistance* (New Haven, CT: Yale University Press, 1985).

1. BIRTH AND RECOGNITION

1. Mount Okzhi Kula, referred to as Mount Siguniang in Chinese, constitutes part of the World Heritage site, Sichuan Giant Panda Sanctuaries—Wolong, Mount Siguniang, and Jiajin Mountains.

2. For a "biography" of and ode to Gyalmo Mudo, see Btsan lha ngag dbang tshul khrims, Klu sman, et al., eds., *Rgyal rong yul gyi gnas chen dang dgon khag skor / Jiarong diqu shengdi he siyuan* (Chengdu: Sichuan minzu chubanshe, 2017), 1–55. Regarding Okzhi Kula, see pages 70–90 in the same book.

3. Each *déshok* was usually composed of thirty to forty households.

4. Such deeds are recorded in *Qingshi liezhuan* (清史傳; Biographies of the Qing period) (Biography of Mutaer 木塔爾 in *Biographies No. 120*列传一百二十). Its digital version can be seen at https://ctext.org/wiki.pl?if=gb&chapter=452818&remap=gb (retrieved January 22, 2021). It is also briefly touched upon in Tibetan sources, such as Brag dgon pa dkon mchog bstan pa rab rgyas, *Mdo smad chos 'byung /Amdo zhengjiao shi* (Xining: Qinghai renmin chubanshe, 2017), 1210. A general overview of Gyalrong chieftains', *shoubeis*', and nobles' assistance in and contribution to the Qing's various military campaigns (including consecutive Sönamyak magistrates) since the late nineteenth century can be found in Zhang Xuefeng and Btsan lha ngag dbang tshul khrims, eds., "Qingshilu Zangzu shiliao zai jiarong zangzu huguo weiji," in *Rgyal mo rong gi lo rgyus skor /Jiarong diqu lishi*, ed. Btsan lha ngag dbang tshul khrims, Bstan 'dzin sbyin pa, et al., vol. 3) (Chengdu: Sichuan minzu chubanshe, 2017), 210–39.

5. Gyalrong was dominated by Bön (an indigenous religion in Tibet) until the eighteenth century. Sipa Gyalmo, an important Bön protective deity, was said to reside on and preside over Mount Gyalmo Mudo.

6. For an account of the Gyalrong kings' and people's genealogical origins, especially in relation to Zhangzhung, see Btsan lha ngag dbang tshul khrims, Mtsho sman, et al., eds., *Rgyal mo rong gi lo rgyus skor /Jiarong diqu lishi*, vol. 1 (Chengdu: Sichuan minzu chubanshe, 2017), 1–112.

7. "Situ" (四土) refers to four kingdoms in Barkham, with the most significant number of Situ-dialect speakers across Gyalrong. Although Tsanlha is not part of Situ, the Tsanlha dialect is close to the Situ dialect. Thus, Tsanlha locals tend to see their mother tongue as part of the Situ dialect.

8. Since most locals were killed during and after the battles, the Qing encouraged the Han to immigrate to Tsanlha (Xiao Jinchuan/Maogong) and Chuchen (Da Jinchuan/Jinghua), offering them land, cattle, farming tools, grain, and other subsidies. Soon after this policy was implemented in 1776, it attracted 1,186 Han immigrant households known as "magistrature civilians" (*tunmin*), under the direct jurisdiction of Han magistratures (*hantun*). The Qing recruited 2,596 "magistrature soldiers" (*tunbing*) who oversaw the locals while also cultivating their own allocated lands. Most were Han, but there were also the Gyalrongwa and other indigenous populations (whose ethnicity is now labeled Qiangzu) from Zagu'nao, Baoxian, and Weizhou. These "magistrature soldiers" were administered by native magistrates, and many were gradually integrated into the local Gyalrongwa population. The 1,969 defeated local households were subject to the rule of the heads (magistrates) of native magistratures (*tutun*). See Tenzin Jinba, "Memory Politics at Work in a Gyalrong Revolt in the Early Twentieth Century," *Cross-Currents: East Asian History and Culture Review* 5, no. 2 (2016): 422–23.

9. There were also some Hui Muslims among the "magistrature soldiers," who became the first Hui settlers in the two Jinchuan regions. Accounts of Hui migration to Tsanlha, their livelihood, customs, religion, and relationship with the local Han and Gyalrongwa, are found in Ma Xingyun, "Xiaojin huimin fengtu renqing cexie," in *Xiaojin wenshi ziliao xuanji* 2, ed. Xiaojinxian zhengxie wenshi ziliao gongzuozu (Xiaojin: Xiaojin zhenxie, 1989), 129–42; Cao Shiyong, "Maogong Huihan guanxishi shang de buxing shijian," in *Xiaojin wenshi ziliao xuanji* 3, ed. Xiaojinxian zhengxie wenshi ziliao weiyuanhui (Xiaojin: Xiaojin Zhengxie, 1992), 1–46; and Cao Shiyong, "Xiaojin Huizu yu qingzhensi de lishi he xiankuang," in *Xiaojin wenshi ziliao xuanji* 4, ed. Xiaojinxian zhengxie wenshi ziliao bianweihui (Xiaojin: Xiaojin Zhengxie, 1996), 1–17.

10. The local Gyalrongwa custom of adopting Chinese names can be confusing since it is sometimes difficult to distinguish the ethnic status of local people and many characters in this book merely by their (Chinese) names. To avoid confusion, I explain this status for these characters (especially the Gyalrongwa) when necessary.

11. This Sinicizing trend can also be found in conflicting narratives about the Wasi kings' genealogy within the royal family in the first half of the twentieth century. One line traces back to a migrant Han Chinese origin. See Wang Mingke, "The Origins of Wasi Tusi: A Border Study of Histories, Myths, and Legends," *Lishi Renleixue Xuekan* 2, no. 1 (2004): 51–88.

12. For an extensive discussion of the role of the Gown Brothers in rural Sichuan power structures in the 1940s, see Wang Di, *Violence and Order on the Chengdu Plain: The Story of a Secret Brotherhood in Rural China, 1939–1949* (Stanford, CA: Stanford University Press, 2018). For a discussion of the Gown Brothers' role in the poppy trade

(among other things) in Sichuan's Sino-Tibetan borderlands (Zungchu/Songpan) during the Republican era, see Kang Xiaofei, and Donald Sutton, *Contesting the Yellow Dragon: Ethnicity, Religion, and the State in the Sino-Tibetan Borderland* (Leiden; Boston: Brill, 2016), 123–70 (chapter 3: "Guns, Gold, Gown, and Poppy"). For an extensive discussion of the intertwined relationship between poppies and politics in Sichuan, see Li Xiaoxiong, *Poppies and Politics in China* (Newark: University of Delaware Press, 2009). In his widely acclaimed novel *Red Poppies* (2002), Alai, a Gyalrong native, gives center stage to the role of poppies in the intense struggles between local chieftains/kings in Gyalrong and in the broader politics during the crucial transitional era from Republican to Communist China. A survey of various Gown Brothers factions in Maogong (Tsanlha) in the Republican era can be seen in Ding Xing, "Maogong paoge zuzhi jianshu," in *Aba zangzu zizhizhou wenshi ziliao xuanji*, vol. 3, ed. Xiaojinxian wenshi ziliao weiyuanhui (Xiaojin: Xiaojin Zhengxie, 1992), 86–98.

13. As one of the first seven monks ordained in Tibet, Vairotsana was banished to Gyalrong by anti-Buddhist forces during the reign of King Trisong Detsen in the eighth century. For Vairotsana's activities in Gyalrong, see various biographies collected in Btsan lha ngag dbang tshul khrims, Nam mkha' tshul khrims, et al., eds., *Rgyal mo rong gi lo rgyus skor/Jiarong diqu lishi*, vol. 2 (Chengdu: Sichuan minzu chubanshe, 2017), 154–214.

14. That a female (chieftain/queen) would establish a male *tulku* incarnation lineage is unusual in the Tibetan cultural region. The Gyalrong Kuzhap never had adequate knowledge about why or how this had occurred. This does, however, explain why the later Okzhi kings kept the lineage secret by not officially announcing it, likely in fear of public disapproval.

15. In Tsanlha and other parts of Gyalrong, a basic traditional hierarchical system divides people into nobles (aristocrats) and commoners. The *gyelpo* (king/chieftain) and *shoubei* (magistrate, a Qing-enforced system; close equivalent of *gyelpo*) are placed at the top of the hierarchy. They are followed by *taro* (nobles), but the *taro* include high-rank nobles such as *lönpo* (ministers) and *qianzong* (a rank below magistrate, hence part of the Qing administration; equivalent of *lönpo*) and *khyung ro* (lesser nobles). Among commoners, the descending ranks are *rangzépa* (free peasants), *trepa* (taxpayers), and *khölpa* ("serfs," who are usually those condemned for criminal activities). The king/chieftain and magistrate had exclusive authority to elevate or lower their subjects' status.

16. The activities and influence of Bön and Bön masters and patrons (chieftain/kings) are thoroughly recorded in various volumes of a ten-book series on Gyalrong history and culture (a collection of historical Tibetan texts on Gyalrong and their Chinese translation), such as Btsan lha ngag dbang tshul khrims, *Rgyal mo rong gi lo rgyus skor*, vol. 2.

17. The uprising was led by Zöpa, a low-ranking monk who proclaimed himself emperor and attracted over four thousand participants in Sönamyak, Tsanlha, and other Gyalrong areas. Some of the uprising's agendas and goals contradicted one another. It targeted the Han with the shout of "Crush the Great Han," even though Zöpa's two main henchmen were Han. It invoked the support of a wider Gyalrong community while claiming to avenge Qing oppression since the Jinchuan

Campaigns of the eighteenth century and simultaneously attempting to establish a Qing-branded kingdom. This revolt also targeted foreign influences, as evidenced by the burning of a Catholic church in Danba. Local memories of the Qing's atrocities and subsequent reforms, as well as Gyalrong's "golden past" when it enjoyed full autonomy, catalyzed ethnic and religious tensions. See Tenzin, "Memory Politics at Work in a Gyalrong Revolt in the Early Twentieth Century," 408–39.

18. This arrangement was due to Zungchen Drölma's noble status thanks to her birth to the royal family in Okzhi. In certain circumstances, a noble lady assumes the role of chieftain (queen) or *shoubei* as reflected in the Gyalrong succession system. According to tradition, a chieftain/magistrate's daughter or wife could succeed him after his death as the new chieftain if no direct male heirs—sons or fraternal nephews—were available. This practice is also found in Kham. See Yudru Tsomu, "Women as Chieftains in Modern Kham History," *Inner Asia* 20, no. 1 (2018): 107–31.

19. Gyélek Chödzé literally means "dharma student from the Gyélek household." The Gyalrong Kuzhap is the fourth (incarnation of) Gyélek Chödzé. Gyélek is the household name of the magistrate's family. Chödzé is the official title of the Gyalrong Kuzhap and his predecessors at Drepung Monastery.

20. The Tibetan and traditional Chinese way to count age is one year in addition to one's actual age. The Gyalrong Kuzhap uses the Tibetan way to identify his ages consistently in his own accounts, so I adopt the same method throughout.

2. SPECIAL EDUCATION

1. The Red Army passed through various Tibetan regions in Yunnan, Sichuan, Kham (Xikang), Gansu, and Qinghai between May 1935 and October 1936. In Gyalrong, it established a revolutionary regime for local people known as Gele Desha gongheguo (The Republic of Gele Desha) on November 18, 1935, which came to an end in July 1936. One of the earliest experiments in autonomous regions for ethnic minorities, it was a system of government later formalized in post-1949 Communist China in ethnic minority regions. Some Gyalrong locals joined the Red Army. Sanggyé Yéshé, better known by a Chinese name (Tianbao) that Mao gave him, was one of them. Sanggyé Yéshé became one of the highest-ranking officials of Tibetan nationality in Sichuan from the 1950s to the 1980s. For more on the Red Army's activities in Tibetan areas, especially in Sichuan and Kham (Xikang), see Elliot Sperling, "Red Army's First Encounters with Tibet—Experience on the Long March," *Tibetan Review* 10 (1976): 11–18; and Li Jianglin and Matthew Akester, "Eat the Buddha! Chinese and Tibetan Accounts of the Red Army in Gyalrong and Ngaba 1935–6 and Related Documents (Parts I–IV)," *Blog: War on Tibet: Chinese and Tibetan Documents on the History of the Communist Occupation in English Translation*, May 16, 2012; Harrison E. Salisbury, *The Long March: The Untold Story* (New York: McGraw-Hill, 1985), 231–84; and Sun Shuyun, *The Long March: The True History of Communist China's Founding Myth* (New York: Anchor, 2006), 161–80 (chapter 9: "In Tibetan Lands"). I am indebted to Carole McGranahan for these references in her "Mao in

Tibetan Disguise: History, Ethnography, and Excess," *HAU: Journal of Ethnographic Theory* 2, no. 1 (2012): 213–45. The oral accounts the author collected in Gyalrong tend to have conflicting views about the Red Army. Still, overall, their activities during the Long March were seen as a series of atrocities, as recounted by the Gyalrong Kuzhap here.

2. For the political attitudes of the chieftains/kings and magistrates in Gyalrong and northwestern Sichuan, see Tian Lijun, *Ganwu hongse zhengquan—Ershi shiji qianbanqi zhonggong genjudi zhengquan yanjiu* (Chengdu: Sichuan renmin chubanshe, 2011), 214–45. According to Tian, most of the chieftains/kings and magistrates in Gyalrong and northwestern Sichuan joined the Kuomintang army in battles against the Red Army because the CCP's revolutionary agenda (e.g., land revolution) was unacceptable to these aristocrats and local leaders, who hoped to take advantage of an opportunity to obtain ammunition from the Kuomintang and Chiang Kai-shek to enhance their strength.

3. This stele was built in 1780 by a Qing officer named Yuan Guohuang for his brother, Yuan Guolian, also a Qing officer, who died in action during the Second Jinchuan Campaign.

4. In other parts of Greater Tibet, the term "lama" commonly refers to a *tulku* or a highly learned monk. However, in Tsanlha and some Gyalrong areas, a monk might be called lama if he had stayed and studied in Lhasa for some years.

5. "Gélong" usually refers to a fully ordained monk. However, in Tsanlha and some Gyalrong areas it also refers to a monk who stayed in Lhasa for more than two but fewer than eight years.

6. In Chinese: *Renzhichu, xingbenshan. Xingxiangjin, xixiangyuan.*

7. See Karma Lingpa, Padma Sambhava, and Robert A. F. Thurman, *The Tibetan Book of the Dead: The Great Book of Natural Liberation Through Understanding in the Between* (New York: Bantam, 1994).

3. JUST A KID

1. Firing cannons nine times refers to an elaborate ritual used exclusively to welcome important visitors such as *tulku* and chieftains.

2. The Ngakrampa is a degree from a tantric college in the Gelugpa tradition, specializing in the tantric training. It is sometimes considered an equivalent to the Géshé degree in Buddhist philosophy in the same tradition, focused on the intellectual analysis of Buddhist canons or sutra.

3. A typical interaction for this formal greeting begins with the younger individual "reporting" what has happened to them and their family since their last meeting. This individual then shares where they are going next, and the elder individual repeats the same process. Afterward, they ask each other about various things, such as recent occurrences and news from their respective villages/places. In olden times, geographic barriers and difficult travel made this ritualistic greeting essential to exchange information and learn about the outside world. It is uncommon among today's youth. This Gyalrong custom does not seem to be equally ritualized in other Tibetan regions.

4. ON THE ROAD

1. In one account, the Gyalrong Kuzhap compared the trip from Gyalrong to Lhasa with that from Buryatia and Mongolia to Lhasa, saying that while the former was challenging, it paled in comparison to the latter in terms of the immense distance and extreme hardships encountered. For that reason, the documented pilgrimage to and exploration in Tibet (1899–1902) by Gombojab Tsybikov (1873–1930), a native of Buryatia in Siberia, offers a unique perspective on this long tiring journey, as well as the religious practices and everyday life in Lhasa. See Gombozhab T. Tsybikov, *A Buddhist Pilgrim at the Shrines of Tibet* (Leiden: Brill, 2017).

2. Traditionally, each Gyalrong household was expected to send one son in every generation to the monastery. Thus, it was common for a family to have two monks from two different generations (e.g., uncle and nephew, father and son). Still, some families had two or more monks in one generation, depending on the availability of males.

3. Besides the nomadic Amdo Tibetan and Kham Tibetan dialects, a number of distinctive local dialects are spoken in Gyalrong. Their classification is still under debate among linguists, but most consider them members of the Qiangic branch of the Tibeto-Burman group of the Sino-Tibetan language family, as is the Qiang language. See, for instance, Guillaume Jacques, *Jiarongyu yanjiu* (Beijing: Minzu Chubanshe, 2008). Many of these dialects are barely comprehensible to speakers of other dialects, highlighting the vast cultural diversity within Gyalrong. As noted, Gyalrong was composed of a number of small kingdoms throughout history, reflecting its political complexity. As repercussions of the Jinchuan Campaigns in the eighteenth century intensified, Han immigrants settled in Gyalrong, further contributing to its linguo-cultural landscape. I have extensively studied the effects of this heterogeneity on Gyalrong political and cultural consciousness since the early twentieth century, especially in the last two decades. See Tenzin Jinba, *In the Land of the Eastern Queendom: The Politics of Gender and Ethnicity on the Sino-Tibetan Border* (Seattle; London: University of Washington Press, 2014); "Memory Politics at Work in a Gyalrong Revolt in the Early Twentieth Century," *Cross-Currents: East Asian History and Culture Review* 5, no. 2 (2016): 408–39; "Seeing Like Borders: Convergence Zone as a Post-Zomian Model," *Current Anthropology* 58, no. 5 (2017): 551–75.

4. For Liu Wenhui's rule in Xikang (Kham) and Xikang's role in relation to Central Tibet, Sichuan, and Nanjing under the central Kuomintang government, see James Leibold, "Un-Mapping Republican China's Tibetan Frontier: Politics, Warlordism and Ethnicity along the Kham/Xikang Borderland," *The Chinese Historical Review* 12, no. 2 (2005): 167–201, and Joseph D. Lawson, "Warlord Colonialism: State Fragmentation and Chinese Rule in Kham, 1911–1949," *The Journal of Asian Studies* 72, no. 2 (2013): 299–318. A more comprehensive and multidimensional study of Kham in its transition from the late Qing period can be found in Lawrence Epstein, ed., *Khams Pa Histories: Visions of People, Place and Authority: PIATS 2000, Tibetan Studies, Proceedings of the Ninth Seminar of the International Association for Tibetan Studies, Leiden 2000* (Leiden; Boston: Brill, 2002); Wang Xiuyu, *China's Last Imperial Frontier: Late Qing Expansion in Sichuan's Tibetan Borderlands*

(Lanham, MD: Lexington Books, 2011); Yudru Tsomu, "Taming the Khampas: The Republican Construction of Eastern Tibet," *Modern China* 39, no. 3 (2013): 319–44; Scott Relyea, "Yokes of Gold and Threads of Silk: Sino-Tibetan Competition for Authority in Early Twentieth-Century Kham," *Modern Asian Studies* 49, no. 4 (2015): 963–1009; and Stéphane Gros, ed., *Frontier Tibet: Patterns of Change in the Sino-Tibetan Borderlands* (Amsterdam: Amsterdam University Press, 2019).

5. Since the early eighteenth century, Dartsédo has evolved into a vital commercial hub in Kham and the Sino-Tibetan borderlands. A significant number of firms or local branches of regional and national firms were operated by both Han (from Shaanxi, Sichuan, Yunnan, and elsewhere) and Khampa merchants. Monasteries also became essential actors in commerce. The services and goods they provided included raw and finished goods (herbs, musk, tea, salt, opium, and cotton), transportation, financial capital, currency-remittance services, and so on. They linked to regional and global trading networks, covering vast distances throughout East and Southeast Asia. See C. Patterson Giersch, "The Origins of Disempowered Development in the Tibetan Borderlands," in *Frontier Tibet*, ed. S. Gros (Amsterdam: Amsterdam University Press, 2019), 263–73; Yudru Tsomu, "Guozhuang Trading Houses and Tibetan Middlemen in Dartsédo, the 'Shanghai of Tibet,'" *Cross-Currents: East Asian History and Culture Review* 19 (2016): 71–121; and Patrick Ramzi, "Booze, Tea, Trade and Transport in the Sino-Tibetan Borderlands" (Ph.D. diss., Oxford University, 2011). Christian missionaries were also enmeshed in local economic affairs, including trade. See John Bray, "Trade, Territory, and Missionary Connections in the Sino-Tibetan Borderlands," in *Frontier Tibet*, ed. S. Gros (Amsterdam: Amsterdam University Press, 2019), 151–78.

6. The most important of the three major *tulku* lineages in Kardzé Monastery is the Khangsar Kyapgön. Kyapgön, literally "lord of protection," is an honorary title publicly acknowledging the prestige and significance of a *tulku* lineage, although sometimes used in a looser sense. The Drungsa, a second lineage, was not formally recognized as the Kyapgön but was referred to as the Kyapgön by the head and crew of a caravan on their way to Lhasa.

7. Liu Wenhui was believed to be a devout Tibetan Buddhist who took advantage of his patronage and connections with various Tibetan masters in Kham and Lhasa to enhance his control over Kham. See Liu's own account about the significant role of Tibetan Buddhism in his governance: Liu Wenhui, *Zoudao renmin zhenying de lishi daolu* (Beijing: Sanlian shudian, 2006), 26–27. A general overview is given in Wang Chuan, "Liu Wenhui yu xikang diqu zangchuan fojiaojie guanxi lunshu," *Zhongguo zangxue* 3 (2006): 78–84. Also see Gray Tuttle, *Tibetan Buddhists in the Making of Modern China* (New York: Columbia University Press, 2005), 115, 117, 213. One of the most prominent Tibetan masters with whom Liu had regular contacts was Pabongkhapa. See, for instance, Peter Schwieger, "What Did the Chinese Warlord Liu Wenhui Want from Pha bong kha?," *Revue d'Etudes Tibétaines* 64 (2022): 461–78.

8. Mount Anyé Machen is usually considered the most sacred mountain in the Amdo Tibetan region. This mountain range runs from eastern Qinghai to southern Gansu. However, based on the caravan's travel route, it does not seem very likely that they could see it, even from a distance. But, as this trip took place nearly eight decades ago, the Kuzhap was not so sure whether it was Mount Anyé Machen he saw. Even

so, he remembered clearly the story about Tibetan argali and their said habitats around Anyé Machen. Based on his description, this appears to be a unique subspecies of Tibetan argali.

9. The clashes between the two monasteries are popularly known as the Dargyé-Béri Incident, which started in 1930 and was not officially resolved until 1940. This conflict was entangled in accumulated tensions and struggles among local religious and political forces, the Lhasa Ganden Phodrang government, and the Xikang-Kuomintang regime since the end of the Qing. An overview is in Wang Haibing, *Kangzang diqu de fenzheng yu juezhu*, 1912–1939 (Beijing: shehui kexue wenxian chubanshe, 2012). An investigation of the incident, especially the militarization of Dargyé Monastery, is in Kobayashi Ryōsuke, "Militarisation of Dargyé Monastery: Contested Borders on the Sino-Tibetan Frontier during the Early Twentieth Century," *Cahiers d'Extrême-Asie* 27 (2018): 139–71. For archived historical documents on this dispute (e.g., correspondence, telegrams, treaties, etc.), see Zhongguo di'er lishi dang'an'guan, ed., *Kangzang jng dang'an xuanbian* (Beijing: Zhongguo zangxue chubanshe, 2000).

10. A study of Nalendra's history and Rongtön can be found in David Jackson, *The Early Abbots of 'Phan-Po Na-Lendra: The Vicissitudes of a Great Tibetan Monastery in the 15th Century* (Wien: Arbeitskreis für Tibetische und Buddhistische Studien Universität Wien, 1989). See also a collection of Rongtön's biographies in Btsan lha ngag dbang tshul khrims and Sgrol dkar skyid, eds., *Rgyal rong lo rgyus mi sna grags can skor/Jiarong diqu mingren*, vol. 2 (Chengdu: Sichuan minzu chubanshe, 2017), 156–298.

5. LIFE AT DREPUNG

1. A detailed first-person account of Drepung life and learning is in Lobsang Gyatso, *Memoirs of a Tibetan Lama* (Ithaca, NY: Snow Lion, 1998), 60–210.

2. See Dardo Tulku's biography in Dharmachari Suvajra, *The Wheel and the Diamond: The Life of Dhardo Tulku* (Cambridge, UK: Windhorse, 2004).

3. Arguably, between the fourteenth and eighteenth centuries, Gyalrong become a hub of Bön teachings and influence. Despite the predominant influence of the Gelugpa (and other schools of Tibetan Buddhism) in local society since the late eighteenth century, Bön has survived in much of Gyalrong. See, for instance, Btsan lha ngag dbang tshul khrims, Nam mkha' tshul khrims and Liu Ying, eds., *Rgyal mo rong gi lo rgyus skor/Jiarong diqu lishi* 嘉絨地區歷史 (中冊) [On Gyalrong history], vol. 2 (Chengdu: Sichuan minzu chubanshe, 2017); Samten G. Karmay, *Feast of the Morning Light: The Eighteenth-Century Wood-Engravings of Shenrab's Life-Stories and the Bon Canon from Gyalrong* (Osaka: National Museum of Ethnology, 2005).

4. Pabongkhapa Déchen Nyingpo (1878–1941) was arguably the most influential and controversial Gelugpa master of his time due to his zealous defense of the purity of the Gelugpa teachings, exemplified by his endorsement and elevation of Dorjé Shugden as the main protector of the Gelugpa School, contrary to all other traditions. Divergent views toward the Dorjé Shugden cult have heightened sectarianism in Gelugpa and Tibetan Buddhism in general and among Tibetans in China and the diaspora community. Pabongkhapa resided at the Gyalrong House because he was

recognized as the reincarnation of the abbot of the Pabongkha Hermitage, a Gyalrong native and former resident at the Gyalrong House of Séra Mé College. To learn more about the Dorjé Shugden dispute and the role of Pabongkhapa in it, see Georges Dreyfus, "The Shuk-Den Affair: Origins of a Controversy," *Journal of the International Association of Buddhist Studies* 21, no. 2 (1998): 227–70.

5. On the experiences of Han Chinese monks in Lhasa, see Xing Suzhi, Zhang Jianfei, and Yang Nianqun, *Xueyu qiufa ji: yige hanren lama de koushushi (xiuding ben)* (Beijing: Shenghuo dushu xinzhi sanlian shudian, 2008), 165–218. The practice of Han monks studying in Lhasa was deeply entangled in the dynamic and evolving Sino-Tibetan relations during the Republican era. Tibetan Buddhist masters, Chinese Buddhists, and their disciples played a critical role in this process. One outcome is that the Tibetan Buddhists on both sides significantly contributed to making the modern Chinese nation-state. See Gray Tuttle, *Tibetan Buddhists in the Making of Modern China* (New York: Columbia University Press, 2005). These Han monks came from Manchuria (northeast China), Hebei, Shanxi, Sichuan, Fujian, etc. There is no accurate record of their number, although a rough estimate is no more than a hundred. See Sonam Tsering, "Minguo nianjian (1912~1949) hanzang fojiao wenhua jiaoliu–neidi sengren fucang qiufa," *Xizang yanjiu* 4 (2006): 47.

6. Other colleges and regional houses in Drepung also hosted Han Chinese students, such as Gomang College and Minyag House at Loserling. See, for instance, Xing Suzhi, Zhang Jianfei, and Yang Nianqun , *Xueyu qiufa ji: Yige hanren lama de koushushi (Xiuding Ben)* [Seeking Dharma in the snowland: An Ooal history of a Han Chinese lama (revised edition)] (Beijing: Shenghuo dushu xinzhi sanlian shudian, 2008), 169–70.

7. The biographies of all these important religious figures are collected in Btsan lha ngag dbang tshul khrims, et al., eds., *Rgyal rong lo rgyus mi sna grags can skor/Jiarong diqu mingren*, vols. 1–3 (Chengdu: Sichuan minzu chubanshe, 2017).

8. Short biographies of the seven Ganden Tripas are collected in Btsan lha ngag dbang tshul khrims, Sgrol dkar skyid, and Nam mkha' tshul khrims, eds., *Rgyal rong lo rgyus mi sna grags can skor/Jiarong diqu mingren*, vol. 3 (Chengdu: Sichuan minzu chubanshe, 2017), 188–272. A biography of Lobsang Khyenrab Wangchug can be found in the same volume, 258–67.

9. A native of Dartsédo (part of broader Gyalrong), Dorjé Chöpa pioneered Tibetan Buddhist teachings among Han monks and laypeople. His disciples and patrons included influential warlords and state officials, such as Wu Peifu (1874–1939) and Liu Wenhui. As a result, Dorjé Chöpa became one of the most influential and active Tibetan Buddhist masters in the Han Chinese region by the 1920s and 1930s. See Tuttle, *Tibetan Buddhists in the Making of Modern China*, 84, 86, 114–21, 265 (note 52). Two Tibetan lamas, the Ninth Panchen Lama (1883–1937) and Norlha Qutughtu (1865–1936), remained in exile (as a consequence of political centralization in Central Tibet orchestrated by the Thirteenth Dalai Lama) while also contributing significantly to the spread of Tibetan Buddhism among the Han (see Tuttle, 87–97). With regard to the Panchen Lama's life entangled in Sino-Tibetan relations, see Fabienne Jagou, *The Ninth Panchen Lama (1883–1937): A Life at the Crossroads of Sino-Tibetan Relations* (Paris: École Française d'Extrême, 2011).

10. Another key factor in the delayed Géshé exams was that each monastery in Lhasa had yearly quotas of students to take the exam, especially for the Géshé Lharampa

examination. Some students who were ready in terms of knowledge and financial capacity might have waited years for this opportunity. Those with *tulku* status and "monastic college dharma student" had priority.

11. See Georges Dreyfus, *The Sound of Two Hands Clapping: The Education of a Tibetan Buddhist Monk* (Berkeley: University of California Press, 2003). This book provides an insider's view of monastic education in the Gelugpa tradition and Tibetan Buddhism, especially concerning the significant role of debate.

12. Based on a monastic calendar at Drepung Loseling in 1945, various types of debates were scheduled, e.g., February 1–15 (whole monastery debate), March 1–30 (study break, mixed with the great spring debate sessions), April 11–30 (fourth month-long debate), May 16–June 15 (summer month-long debate), August 1–September 1 (autumn month-long debate), September 16–30 (debate), October 16–30 (debate), and November 16–December 15 (winter debate across all three monasteries). See Gyatso, *Memoirs of a Tibetan Lama*, 84.

13. See Trijang Rinpoche, *The Magical Play of Illusion: The Autobiography of Trijang Rinpoche* (Somerville, MA: Wisdom, 2018).

14. See His Holiness the Dalai Lama, *The Life of My Teacher: A Biography of Kyabjé Ling Rinpoché* (Somerville, MA: Wisdom, 2017).

15. Ronald M. Davidson, *Tibetan Renaissance: Tantric Buddhism in the Rebirth of Tibetan Culture* (New York: Columbia University Press, 2005), discusses the role of tantric or esoteric Buddhism in reconstructing Tibetan religious, cultural, and political institutions from the tenth to thirteenth centuries. See also Martin A. Mills, *Identity, Ritual and State in Tibetan Buddhism: The Foundations of Authority in Gelukpa Monasticism* (London; New York: RoutledgeCurzon, 2003).

16. See Dorji Wangchuk, *The Resolve to Become a Buddha: A Study of the Bodhicitta Concept in Indo-Tibetan Buddhism* (Tokyo: International Institute for Buddhist Studies of the International College for Postgraduate Buddhist Studies, 2007).

6. ON FREEDOM

1. The expulsion occurred in 1947, and the Tsémönling died suddenly the following year. His exile and death were believed to be inseparable from the Tibetan government's retaliation against those with close ties to the Reting.

2. As recounted in Tashi Tsering's autobiography, homosexuality among monks and monastic officials was common. He was a sexual partner to the monk steward of an important official in Lhasa. See Melvyn C. Goldstein, William R. Siebenschuh, and Tsering Tashi, *The Struggle for Modern Tibet: The Autobiography of Tashi Tsering* (Armonk, NY: M. E. Sharpe, 1997), 26–30.

3. The Reting's regency (1934–1941) and his later attempt to regain power (the Reting Conspiracy) were entangled in intricate Sino-Tibetan relations, and intensified internal struggles among various forces in Central Tibet (including a progressive and modern force led by Lungshar Dorjé Tségyel [1880–1938]) as well as volatile international relations (e.g., British encroachment). For more, see Goldstein, Siebenschuh, and Tashi, *The Struggle for Modern Tibet*, 310–66, 464–521.

4. The Reting Rinpoche was later portrayed in Communist China as a "patriotic" (pro-China) religious figure in Tibet against the ultraconservative and pro-British

forces represented by the Taktra clique. The CCP also said Ngawang Gyatso, as the Reting's close ally, was a "patriotic" and anti-imperialist lama. He later held government positions including vice-head of Kardzé Tibetan Autonomous Prefecture and was vice-chair of the Buddhist Association of China from 1950 to 1968. See Zhongguo renmin zhengzhi xieshang huiyi ganzi zangzu zizhizhou weiyuanhui, *Ganzizhou wenshi ziliao xuanji* (Volume 6: Dedication to Ngawang Gyatso) (Kangding: Ganzizhou zhengxie, 1987).

7. RESHUFFLING POWERS

1. See Li Tao, "Yapianyan zai jiarong zangqu de chuanbo," *Xizang minsu* 1 (1994): 39–40. According to the author, in the 1940s, some 90 percent of Gyalrong households cultivated opium, and over 40 percent of the arable land was used exclusively for this purpose.
2. See Ding Xing, "Maogong paoge zuzhi jianshu" [Brief introduction to Maogong Paoge organizations]," in *Aba Zangzu zizhizhou wenshi ziliao xuanji* [Collections of cultural and historical materials in Ngawa Tibetan Autonomous Prefecture], vol. 3, ed. Xiaojinxian wenshi ziliao weiyuanhui [Xiaojin County Committee on Cultural and Historical Materials] (Xiaojin: Xiaojin Zhengxie, 1992), 86–98.
3. Accounts of Tsanlha's Liberation can be found in Shen Yaosheng, *Maogong jiefang jishi* (Chengdu: Chengdu yaxuan yinwu youxian gongsi, 2011); Du Aiguo, *Yiwei zhencha canmou bixia de xueshan caodi Abazhou* (Maerkang: Abazhou zhengxie wenshi he xuexi weiyuanhui, 2011), 31–43; and Zhang Liming, "Maogong jiefang jilüe," in *Xiaojin wenshi ziliao xuanji*, vol. 1, ed. Xiaojinxian zhengxie wenshi ziliao gongzuozu (Xiaojin: Xiaojin zhengxie, 1988), 43–81. For more extensive accounts, primarily from Tibetans, of Liberation and political campaigns during the Mao era in Greater Tibet, see Robert Barnett, Benno Weiner, and Françoise Robin, eds., *Conflicting Memories: Tibetan History Under Mao Retold* (Leiden; Boston: Brill, 2020).
4. An officially organized survey of Jémé's agricultural productivity, relations of production, political system, religion, and customs was conducted from 1958 to 1959. See Zhongguo kexueyuan minzu yanjiusuo/Sichuan shaoshu minzu shehui lishi diaochazu, "Minzhu gaige qian xiaojinxian jiesixiang shehui diaocha," in *Aba zangzu zizhizhou xiao jin, lixian shehui diaocha cailiao* (Beijing/Chengdu: CAS-SEM, 1963), 1–17. An account of Jémé's Liberation is recorded in Shen Yaosheng, *Maogong jiefang jishi*, 297–308.
5. It was said that six to seven thousand people joined the revolt against the PLA, with the Okzhi queen as the nominal leader. For an account of the queen's relationships with the Gown Brothers, Kuomintang, and the CCP, and her revolt against the PLA, see Shen, *Maogong jiefang*, 115–22, 170–74, 210–12, 331–34; Du, *Yiwei zhencha canmou*, 36–42, 194–205; and Zhang, *Maogong jiefang*, 50–65.
6. Men's account of his experience of the Liberation of Maogong can be found in Men Guoliang, "Sanjin Maogong," in *Aba zangzu zizhizhou wenshi ziliao xuanji*, vol. 6 (Maerkang: Abazhou zhengxie wenshi ziliao weiyuanhui, 1987), 1–9.
7. The outcome of this month-long negotiation after the PLA's occupation of Chamdo was the Seventeen Point Agreement. This marked a turning point in Tibetan history, as it formally acknowledged China and the CCP's sovereignty over Central

Tibet. Subsequently, thousands of Han soldiers and civilians were dispatched to Tibet, commonly referred to as the "Peaceful Liberation of Tibet" in CCP discourse. Although the agreement acknowledged the Dalai Lama's status and the existing political system in Tibet, it stirred up tremendous discontent and eventually led to the 1959 revolt and the Dalai Lama's flight to India. See, for instance, A. Tom. Grunfeld, *The Making of Modern Tibet* (Armonk, NY: M. E. Sharpe, 1996), 111–14; Melvyn C. Goldstein, *The Snow Lion and the Dragon: China, Tibet, and the Dalai Lama* (Berkeley: University of California Press, 1997), 41–55.

8. NEW SOCIETY, NEW LIFE

1. For Wang Weizhou's experiences at the institute and his thoughts on education in general, see Wang Rongcheng, Li Ronglan, and Mou Xiong, "Wang Weizhou jiaoyu sixiang tanxi," *Zhonghua wenhua luntan* 12 (2017): 103–14.
2. The Southwest Nationalities Institute, now known as Southwest Nationalities University, was one of the first eight nationalities-style institutes established in the 1950s based on the Soviet model with "Chinese characteristics" (by addressing revolutionary experiences and sociopolitical and ethnic realities in China) to train ethnic minority cadres in Communist-Maoist ideals. Many of these trainees later became principal officials in their respective regions. The regular training programs were interrupted by the Cultural Revolution. From the late 1970s on, these institutes were on their way to becoming full-fledged institutions of higher learning. However, their focus remains on ethnic minority education. In particular, students are trained to become "proper" ethnic minority members, emphasizing identification with CCP agendas (e.g., patriotism, loyalty to the CCP, conscious distancing from ethnonational provincialism, and "separatism" [advocacy of independence]). To learn more about ethnic minority education and especially the Minzu-style institutes, see Gerard A. Postiglione, *China's National Minority Education: Culture, Schooling, and Development* (New York: Falmer Press, 1999); Rebecca Clothey, "Policies for Minority Nationalities in Higher Education: Negotiating National Values and Ethnic Identities," *Comparative Education Review* 49, no. 3 (2005): 389–409; and Yang Miaoyan, *Learning to Be Tibetan: The Construction of Ethnic Identity at Minzu University of China* (Lanham, MD: Lexington Books, 2017). Both the Minzu category and education models have been seriously challenged by Ma Rong, a Peking University professor and a well-known scholar in China on ethnic matters. He advocates "depoliticizing" the Minzu model of ethnicity in China and ending the various Minzu institutes, arguing that they have enhanced ethnic minority people and students' ethnonationalism and distinction, if not separation, from the Han and the nation-state. See Ma Rong: "A New Perspective in Guiding Ethnic Relations in the Twenty-First Century: 'De-politicization' of Ethnicity in China," *Asian Ethnicity* 8, no. 3 (2007): 199–217; "The 'Politicization' and 'Culturization' of Ethnic Groups," *Chinese Sociology and Anthropology* 42, no. 4 (2010): 31–45; "Reflections on the Debate on China's Ethnic Policy: My Reform Proposals and Their Critics," *Asian Ethnicity* 15, no. 2 (2014): 237–46; and "Reconstructing 'Nation' (Minzu) Discourses in China," *International Journal of Anthropology and Ethnology* 1, no. 1 (2017): 1–15.

3. Xikang, as a province, was dissolved officially in September 1955. Most of its original area, including the Kardzé Tibetan Autonomous Prefecture, was merged with Sichuan and the remainder integrated into the TAR.

4. See, for instance, Nick Knight, "Mao Zedong on Contradiction and on Practice: Pre-Liberation Texts," *The China Quarterly* 84 (1980): 641–68.

5. From 1950 to 1966, a number of delegations composed of ethnic minority elites and others were annually invited to visit Beijing and other major cities. Most were invited to attend the May Day (International Labor Day) or National Day parades in Beijing to be inspected by Mao and other top CCP leaders. After the Cultural Revolution, these delegations resumed. This "pilgrimage" to Beijing is referred to as political tourism in Uradyn E. Bulag's "Seeing Like a Minority: Political Tourism and the Struggle for Recognition in China," *Journal of Current Chinese Affairs* 41, no. 4 (2012): 133–58. See also Zhao Zheng, "Xinzhongguo chengli chuqi xikang shaoshu minzu daibiao canguan fangwen neidi shulun," *Zhonggong dangshi yanjiu* 7 (2016): 33–45. Such political tourism was designed to evoke admiration, aspiration, awe, and fear among the ethnic minority delegates.

6. Over 40 percent of the arable land in Gyalrong was used exclusively for growing opium. See Litao, "Yapianyan zai jiarong zangqu de chuanbo" [The spread of opium in Gyalrong Tibetan Region], *Xizang minsu* [Tibetan folklore] 1 (1994): 39. A survey of the Jémé Magistrature (next to Sönamyak) substantiated this claim. See Zhongguo Kexueyuan Minzu Yanjiusuo/Sichuan Shaoshu Minzu Shehui Lishi Diaochazu [Institute of Ethnic Studies, Chinese Academy of Sciences/Sichuan Ethnic Minority Social History Investigation Group], "Minzhu gaige qian xiaojinxian jiesixiang shehui diaocha" [Social survey of Jiesi Township (Jémé) in Xiaojin County before the Democratic Reform], in *Aba zangzu zizhizhou xiao jin, lixian shehui diaocha cailiao* [Social survey materials of Xiaojin and Lixian, Aba Tibetan Autonomous Prefecture] (Beijing/Chengdu: CAS-SEM, 1963) 2.

7. Song Guotai's rise had everything to with the flourishing opium production and trade in Tsanlha, Gyalrong, and beyond. By 1950, Song's power was such that he controlled a major trade route from Tsanlha and Chuchen (Jinchuan) to Guanxian-Chengdu. His rise and subsequent downfall are recorded in Du Aiguo, *Yiwei zhencha canmou bixia de xueshan caodi abazhou* [Snow-capped mountains and grasslands in Aba Prefecture in the portrait of a former PLA scout] (Maerkang: Abazhou zhengxie wenshi he xuexi weiyuanhui, 2011), 167–93.

8. An elaborate account of hunting the three He brothers is given in Shen Yaosheng, *Maogong jiefang jishi* [Documented accounts about Maogong's liberation] (Chengdu: Chengdu yaxuan yinwu youxian gongsi, 2011), 244–61.

9. THE CALM BEFORE THE STORM

1. The newly minted Ngawa Tibetan Autonomous Prefecture's first capital was in Maoxian in 1953, moved to Shuajingsi (T. Lhagyelling) in 1955, and finally moved to Barkham in 1958.

2. United Front work, referred to as one of the CCP's three "magic weapons" (together with "armed struggle" and "Party building"), has played a crucial role in the CCP endeavor to "unite all the forces that can be united" throughout its history. "All the

forces" include a number of political parties outside of the CCP, popularly referred to as the Eight Democratic Parties, e.g., the China Democratic League, China Association for Promoting Democracy, Revolutionary Committee of the Chinese Kuomintang, Chinese Peasants' and Workers' Democratic Party, etc. These parties exist today and constitute the officially proclaimed "system of the multiparty cooperation and political consultation led by the Communist Party of China." Overall, United Front work remains an integral part of the CCP structure, carried out by two major institutions, the United Front Work Department and the CPPCC, at the county and higher levels of government. See Lyman P. Van Slyke, *Enemies and Friends: The United Front in Chinese Communist History* (Stanford, CA: Stanford University Press, 1967); Gerry Groot, *Managing Transitions: The Chinese Communist Party, United Front Work, Corporatism, and Hegemony* (New York: Routledge, 2004); Zhao Taotao and James Leibold, "Ethnic Governance Under Xi Jinping: The Centrality of the United Front Work Department and Its Implications," *Journal of Contemporary China* 29, no. 124 (2020): 487–502.

3. To revisit the notion of political tourism, see Uradyn E. Bulag, "Seeing Like a Minority: Political Tourism and the Struggle for Recognition in China," *Journal of Current Chinese Affairs* 41, no. 4 (2012): 133–58.

4. For a biography of Suo Guanyin, see Ge Ai, "Suo Guanying zhuan," in *Difang shizhi wenji* (Maerkang: Abazhou fangzhi diming bangongshi, 1989), 235–51; Du Aiguo, "Kaiming aiguo gongzai guojia—Ji Zhuokeji tusi Suoguanying," in *Yiwei zhencha canmou bixia de xueshan caodi abazhou* [Snow-capped mountains and grasslands in Aba Prefecture in the portrait of a former PLA scout] (Maerkang: Abazhou zhengxie wenshi he xuexi weiyuanhui, 2011), 248–65; Jiande Dongzhou, *Suo Guanying zhuan* (Maerkang: Maerkang xian zhixie wenshi ziliao weiyuanhui, 1992); and Maerkangxian zhengxie wenshiwei/Aba jiarong wenhua yanjiuhui, *Xueshan tusi wangchao Zhuokeji di shiliudai tusi Suo Guanying zhuan* (Chengdu: Sichuan minzu chubanshe, 2013). For a biography of Dorjé Pasang (Su Yonghe), see Su Xigang, *Wode aba Dorjé Pasang* (Maerkang: Abazhou zhengzhi wenshi he xuexi weiyuanhui, 1995); and Du Aiguo, "Luoye guigen wanjie kefeng—Ji Heishui datouren Su Yonghe," in *Yiwei zhencha canmou*, 284–309. For a biography of Pelgön Trinlé, see Ouerxiao and Ge Zhiyuan, "Huaergong Chenlie zhuan," in *Sichuan jinxiandai renwuzhuan*, vol. 3, ed. Aba zhouzhiban/Ren Yimin (Chengdu: Sichuan renmin chubanshe, 1987), 322–29; and Du Aiguo, "Gangrou xiangfu shenming dayi—Ji caodi zangzu lingxiu renwu huaergong chenglie," in *Yiwei zhencha canmou bixia*, 266–83. Pelgön Trinlé's biography and experiences are portrayed in the memories and accounts of his only living child (a daughter), Gonpo, in Barbara Demick, *Eat the Buddha: Life and Death in a Tibetan Town* (New York: Random House, 2020). This work is also a biography of Gonpo, highlighting her experiences growing up and living in Communist China, and a firsthand and up-to-date account of the current political situation and self-immolations in Ngawa.

5. For the "heroic" history of the Washi kingdom, especially its relationship (e.g., loyalty) to the Qing court and Republican and Communist China, see Zhu Shide, ed., *Shidai zhongzhen zhi Wasi tusi* (Wenchuan: Sichuan Wasi xuanwei shisi xuanwei shishu, 1945); and Wenchuan zhengxie wenshi ziliao weiyuanhui, ed., *Wasi tusi zhuanji/Wenchuanxian wenshi ziliao xuanji*, vol. 4 (Wenchuan: Wenchuan Political Consultative Conference, 1994). As mentioned above, the Gyalrong kings,

including the Wasi kings, assisted and contributed to the Qing's various military campaigns, as described in Zhang Xuefeng and Btsan lhangag dbang tshul khrims, eds., "Qingshilu Zangzu shiliao zai jiarong zangzu huguo weiji" [Gyalrong Tibetans' great achievements in defending the state as recorded in the Tibetan historical materials of the Veritable Records of the Qing], in *Rgyal mo rong gi lo rgyus skor/ Jiarong diqu lishi* [On Gyalrong history], vol. 3, ed. Btsan lha ngag dbang tshul khrims, Bstan 'dzin sbyin pa, Nam mkha' tshul khrims, and Mtsho sman (Chengdu: Sichuan minzu chubanshe, 2017), 210–39.

6. See Lu Zichang and Wang Ankang, "Wo suo zhidao de Maerkang yandu qing-kuang," in *Aba zangzu zizhizhou wenshi ziliao xuanji*, vol. 1 (Maerkang: Abazhou zhengxie wenshi ziliao wei yuanhui, 1984), 131–36.

7. This story is actually widely distributed in Tibetan religio-cultural areas, including among Mongolians.

8. Draktong Chijikmé married a local woman from the noble Naknyo family and gave birth to a daughter. This wife and daughter eventually moved to Shigatse in Central Tibet. The Gyalrong Kuzhap later met his daughter while visiting Shigatse in 1956. As for the Panchen Lama's life experiences implicated in the volatile Sino-Tibetan relationship, see Fabienne Jagou, *The Ninth Panchen Lama (1883–1937): A Life at the Crossroads of Sino-Tibetan Relations* (Paris: École Française D'extrême, 2011).

9. These experiences of Dorjé Pasang are also recounted in his biography, narrated by one of his sons, Su Xigang, *Wode aba Dorjé Pasang* [My father, Dorjé Pasang] (Maerkang: Abazhou zhengzhi wenshi he xuexi weiyuanhui [Cultural-Historical Materials and Study Committee of Aba Prefecture], 1995). This biography seeks to justify, if not glorify, Dorjé Pasang's deeds and political choices. As noted, based on the Gyalrong tradition, Dorjé Pasang was considered to have no "royal blood," and his self-asserted status as the Somang king was widely disputed. Su ignores this controversy, instead celebrating his father's attempt to seize the throne and expand territory and sphere of influence in the name of the king (76–107).

10. See Kui Ge, et al., "Jiefangqian de Aba difang zangjun qingkuang gaiyao," in *Aba zangzu zizhizhou wenshi ziliao xuanji*, vol. 6 (Maerkang: Abazhou zhengxie wen-shi ziliao weiyuanhui, 1987), 94–96. This is an account of Pelgön Trinlé's army structure and military organization among his former subjects.

11. Chiang Kai-shek appointed Zhou Xunyu in 1949 to lead the guerrilla war against the CCP in the border regions of Sichuan, Gansu, Xikang, and Qinghai. Wang Fuxu was the director of General Affairs at the Central Army Military Academy, directing the "Central Military Academy guerrilla training for backbones" (fifth term) in November 1949, which the Okzhi queen attended. He Benchu was one of the right-hand men of Zhou Xunyu. In building alliances with local forces, these officers waged war against the PLA in Maogong (Tsanlha), Jinghua (Chuchen), Heishui (Trochu), Maerkang (Barkham), Ngawa, and other locations in northwestern Sichuan. They finally fled to Ngawa under the protection of Pelgön Trinlé, who was forced to turn them in to the CCP under escalating pressure. See Shen Yaosheng, *Maogong jiefang jishi* [Documented accounts about Maogong's liberation] (Chengdu: Chengdu yaxuan yinwu youxian gongsi, 2011), 19–35; Du Aiguo, *Yiwei zhencha canmou*, 144–66.

12. Based on this account and the Gyalrong Kuzhap's impressions, Li Jingquan attached great importance to the Dalai Lama's visit. But what happened during the Dalai

Lama's return trip to Lhasa via Chengdu in April 1955 shows that this was not the case. Li was absent from the welcome ceremony, which upset the Dalai Lama because the latter had become the deputy director of the People's National Congress, making him a national-level leader. The Dalai Lama had been warmly welcomed by other key leaders including Mao, Liu Shaoqi, the director of the People's National Congress, and Premier Zhou Enlai in Beijing. See a detailed description of this incident in Melvyn C. Goldstein, *A History of Modern Tibet. Volume 2, The Calm Before the Storm, 1951–1955* (Berkeley: University of California Press, 2007), 523–27.

13. Such tensions are captured in Melvyn C. Goldstein, *A History of Modern Tibet. Volume 3, The Storm Clouds Descend, 1955–1957* (Berkeley: University of California Press, 2014). These tensions, as well as accompanying anxieties and uncertainties in Tibet, eventually led to the 1959 Tibetan uprising and the CCP's Democratic Reform. See Melvyn C. Goldstein, *A History of Modern Tibet. Volume 4, In the Eye of the Storm, 1957–1959* (Oakland: University of California Press, 2019); and Liu Xiaoyuan, *To the End of Revolution: The Chinese Communist Party and Tibet, 1949–1959* (New York: Columbia University Press, 2020).

14. Fan Ming was well known for his proactive stance, pushing through an early Democratic Reform that was instrumental in destabilizing Tibet. See, for instance, Goldstein, *A History of Modern Tibet*, 3: 306–34 (chapter 10, "Fan Ming's 'Great Expansion'").

10. THE DEMOCRATIC REFORM

1. Land reform was concurrently seen as the premise, objective, and outcome of the Communist Revolution. Underlying the reform was the idea that equality was achievable by redistributing land and property once owned by the ruling class or landlords in "old China." See, for instance, Isabel Crook and David Crook, *Revolution in a Chinese Village: Ten Mile Inn* (London: Routledge and Kegan Paul, 1959); William Hinton, *Fanshen: A Documentary of Revolution in A Chinese Village* (New York: Monthly Review Press, 2008 [1966]); and Brian James DeMare, *Land Wars: The Story of China's Agrarian Revolution* (Stanford, CA: Stanford University Press, 2019).

2. On the Democratic Reform in Sichuan's ethnic minority regions, including Ngawa and Kardzé Prefectures, see Qin Heping, ed., *Sichuan minzu diqu minzhu gaige ziliaoji* (Beijing: Minzu chubanshe, 2008); and Qin Heping, *Sichuan minzu diqu minzhu gaige yanjiu 20 shiji 50 niandai Sichuan zangqu yiqu de shehui biang* (Beijing: Zhongyang minzu daxue chubanshe, 2011). These two books, especially the first, a collection of various original official reports and document, are a valuable source of reference material in unraveling Reform policies, guidelines, agendas, processes, outcomes, and repercussions (e.g., revolt) in different places of these regions.

3. Most nomadic areas in Ngawa Prefecture are part of the broader Amdo region that spreads north and west across Sichuan, Gansu, and Qinghai. The Democratic Reform was carried out in 1958 in most of the region, and revolts of varying sizes broke out. The year 1958 is seen as a watershed time in Amdo and Tibetan history. See, for instance, Benno Weiner, *The Chinese Revolution on the Tibetan Frontier*

(Ithaca, NY: Cornell University Press, 2020). A vivid portrayal of this resistance and social transition in Amdo is depicted in Nulo Naktsang, *My Tibetan Childhood: When Ice Shattered Stone* (Durham, NC: Duke University Press, 2014).

4. Pelgön Trinlé handed in 31 guns in late August 1958. Thanks to his pioneering role, reportedly 70–80 percent of all the private guns available in Ngawa were handed over to the state within only ten days. See Abaxian renwubu, *Abaxian junshi zhi* (Chengdu: Sichuan daxue chubanshe, 2009), 154.

5. Based on an official report dated February 21, 1959, of the 5,895 households in Ngawa County that had completed the Democratic Reform, the number and percentage of (a) feudal lords, (b) rich peasants-nomads, (c) middle peasants-nomads, (d) poor peasants-nomads and laborers, and (e) others are as follows: (a) 169 (2.86 percent), (b) 225 (3.85 percent), (c) 1,532 (25.98 percent), (d) 3,725 (63.18 percent), and (e) 244 (4.13 percent). See Zhonggong Abaxian gongwei, "Abaxian mingai gongzuo zongjie," in *Sichuan minzu diqu minzhu gaige ziliaoji*, ed. Qin Heping (Beijing: Minzu chubanshe, 2008), 168–69.

6. This monastery was originally founded in 1412 by Rongchen Jaknakpa Gendün Gyeltsen (hereafter Jaknakpa) (1374–1450) from Gyalrong, a disciple of Jé Tsongkhapa, the founder of the Gelugpa. Various biographies of Jaknakpa are collected in Btsan lha, Sgrol dkar skyid, and Nam mkha' tshul khrims, eds., *Rgyal rong lo rgyus mi sna grags can skor/Jiarong diqu mingren* [Historical figures in Gyalrong], vol. 3 (Chengdu: Sichuan minzu chubanshe, 2017), 133–77. It is considered a "mother monastery" (Tib. *magön*; founding monastery with an outgrowth of branches) for a dozen monasteries, including Ngawa Kirti Gönpa, a hub of Tibetan unrest and self-immolations since 2008.

7. Ngawa Prefecture's Tibetan population was 210,000 in the late 1950s. There were over 200 monasteries of different sects and varying sizes, and the total monk population was 15,000. Over 10,000 monks were based in nomadic regions that accounted for over 12 percent of the local Tibetan population. After the Reform, most monks were "persuaded" or forced to return to their respective hometowns and become part of the new socialist labor force. For a detailed description of the reform of Tibetan religious institutions in Ngawa Prefecture, see Qin Heping, *Sichuan minzu diqu minzhu gaige yanjiu*, 317–25. In comparison, based on statistics from 1957, there were 497 monasteries (including nunneries) in Kardzé Prefecture, with 64,000 monks and nuns, who made up about 13 percent of the entire Tibetan population in this region. In Kardzé and Litang, as much as 33 and 31 percent of the local people were monks and nuns, respectively. See Zhang Zhengming, *Ganzi zangqu shehui diaocha ziliao huiji* (Beijing: Quanguo renmin daibiao dahui minzu weiyuanhui bangongshi, 1957), 38. With regard to monks' personal experiences during the Democratic Reform and the Cultural Revolution, especially those involved in revolts and subsequently labeled as "counterrevolutionary," see Shamdo Rinzang, "My Conversation with Akhu Yarphel," in *Conflicting Memories: Tibetan History under Mao Retold*, ed. Robert Barnett, Benno Weiner, and Françoise Robin (Leiden; Boston: Brill, 2020), 334–51. This is only one of many interviews with survivors, including monks and lamas, in the 1950s that were collected in two book-length volumes by Shamdo Rinzang. See Bya mdo rin bzang [Shamdo Rinzang], *Nga'i pha yul dang gzab nyan Nga'i pha yul dang gzab nyan* (unpublished ms., 2008); and

Nga'i pha yul dang zhi ba'i bcings grol (Dharamsala: Bod kyi dgu bcu gsum las 'gul tshogs pa, 2010).

8. For Tséwang Nor's revolt and other revolts in Dzamtang, Ngawa, and other neighboring nomadic regions in Ngawa Prefecture, see Qin Heping, *Sichuan minzu diqu minzhu gaige yanjiu*, 326–38.

11. RIDING THE REVOLUTIONARY TIDES

1. The following works do not necessarily discuss nomads' happiness, but do offer insight into how the Tibetan nomadic livelihood, environment, and social organization contribute to people's notions about well-being or happiness: Gillian G. Tan, *In the Circle of White Stones: Moving Through Seasons with Nomads of Eastern Tibet* (Seattle: University of Washington Press, 2017); Melvyn C. Goldstein and Cynthia M. Beall, *Nomads of Western Tibet: The Survival of a Way of Life* (Berkeley: University of California Press, 1990); and Rinzin Thargyal and Toni Huber, *Nomads of Eastern Tibet: Social Organization and Economy of a Pastoral Estate in the Kingdom of Dege* (Leiden and Boston: Brill, 2007). *In the Circle of White Stones* sketches contemporary nomads' lifestyles in eastern Tibet (Kham), including their relationship with nature and the role of religion in their daily lives. *Nomads of Western Tibet* looks at their way of life and especially their struggle for cultural survival as a nomadic community in western Tibet in the 1980s. *Nomads of Eastern Tibet* portrays the premodern pastoral economy and social organization in eastern Tibet.

2. Often described as the longest epic in the world, the *Epic of King Gesar of Ling* centers on the heroic deeds and numerous battles of the legendary King Gesar. Its plots, structures, episodes, and motifs are diverse and situational and show variation within the region and among narrators. This epic was arguably the most popular form of oral culture in Tibetan cultural spheres until recently, when it has been increasingly replaced by TV and social media access.

3. According to an article by the then Party Secretary of Ngawa Prefecture in 1959, by the second half of 1958, high-level collectives as well as a small number of the people's communes were established in all the prefecture's agricultural areas, with more than 95 percent of local households joining. With the completion of the Democratic Reform in nomad regions at that time, primary collectivization ("mutual aid teams") was established. Some 82 percent of nomad and agricultural households had joined. See Jia Shengcai, "Zai shehui zhuyi daolu shang maijin de Aba zangzu zizhizhou," in *Sichuan minzu diqu minzhu gaige ziliaoji*, ed. Qin Heping (Beijing: Minzu chubanshe, 2008), 250.

4. A variety of factors may explain why specific households had only strong and young cattle left. For instance, the old and infirm cattle were slaughtered for consumption, died from accidents (e.g., wildlife attacks and natural disasters), or had been handed over to the commune in previous rounds.

5. This noble is known as Su Jiabang in Chinese and Sanggyé Bum in Tibetan; he was dispatched by his father, Dorjé Pasang (the ruler of Trochu and the nominal king of Somang), to rule this region on his behalf.

6. The Tenth Panchen Lama was purged after his critiques of CCP officials' progressive and radical agendas in Tibet through what came to be known as the 70,000 Character Petition to Premier Zhou Enlai in 1962. See Robert Barnett, ed., *A Poisoned Arrow: The Secret Report of the 10th Panchen Lama* (London: Tibet Information Network, 1997); and Tsering Shakya, *The Dragon in the Land of Snows: A History of Modern Tibet Since 1947* (New York: Columbia University Press, 1999), 304–18. Although this petition extolled the excellent policies and remarkable achievements of the CCP in Tibet, the Panchen Lama highlighted major mistakes that officials in Tibet made during and after the Democratic Reform, threatening the survival of Tibetan religions and culture as well as a smooth transition in Tibetan society. Mao found such criticism unacceptable. The Panchen Lama was subsequently accused of being a reactionary feudal lord and wanting to restore serfdom and was imprisoned for over a decade. Püntsok Wanggyel cofounded the Tibetan Communist Party in 1939 and later became one of the highest-ranking Tibetan officials in Communist China. Unable to escape destiny, he was labeled a local nationalist, due originally to his disapproval of the more radical policies and agendas in Tibet, especially those by Fan Ming, deputy secretary of the Tibet Work Committee. Consequently, Püntsok Wanggyel was imprisoned in solitary confinement for eighteen years. See Melvyn C. Goldstein, Dawei Sherap, and William R. Siebenschuh, *A Tibetan Revolutionary: The Political Life and Times of Bapa Phüntso Wangye* (Berkeley: University of California Press, 2004); Baba Phuntsok Wangyal, *Witness to Tibet's History*, trans. Tenzin Losel, ed. Jane Perkins (New Delhi: Paljor Publications, 2007).

7. See John Gardner, "Liu Shaoqi and the Cultural Revolution: The Rise and Fall of a Chosen Successor," in *Chinese Politics and the Succession to Mao* (London: Macmillan Education UK, 1982); and Lowell Dittmer, *Liu Shaoqi and the Chinese Cultural Revolution* (Armonk, NY: M. E. Sharpe, 1998).

12. FROM COWSHED TO COLLEGE

1. For factionalism among the Red Guards, see Stanley Rosen, *Red Guard Factionalism and the Cultural Revolution in Guangzhou (Canton)* (Boulder, CO.: Westview Press, 1982); and Andrew G. Walder, "Beijing Red Guard Factionalism: Social Interpretations Reconsidered," *The Journal of Asian Studies* 61, no. 2 (2002): 437–71. For important accounts about the Cultural Revolution in Tibet, including the role of the Tibetan Red Guards, see Melvyn C. Goldstein, Ben Jiao, and Lhundrup Tanzen, *On the Cultural Revolution in Tibet: The Nyemo Incident of 1969* (Berkeley: University of California Press, 2009); and Tsering Woeser, *Forbidden Memory: Tibet During the Cultural Revolution* (Lincoln, NE: Potomac Books, 2020). Also see Tsering Shakya, *The Dragon in the Land of Snows: A History of Modern Tibet Since 1947* (New York: Columbia University Press, 1999), 360–96.

2. Thönmi Sambhota was traditionally believed to have devised the Tibetan script based on Sanskrit scripts after his study in India during the reign of King Songtsen Gampo in the seventh century. He is also said to have composed six texts on Tibetan grammar and linguistics, of which only two survive. However, the authenticity of

this inventor and the script's true origin are hotly debated. See Sam van Schaik, "A New Look at the Tibetan Invention of Writing," in *New Studies of the Old Tibetan Documents: Philology, History and Religion*, ed. Imaeda Yoshiro, Matthew Kapstein, and Tsuguhito Takeuchi (Tokyo: Tokyo University of Foreign Studies, 2011), 45–96.

3. Zhang Yisun, ed., *Bod rgya tshig mdzod chen mo/Zanghan da cidian* (Beijing: Minzu chubanshe, 1985).

4. See Nicole D. Willock, *Lineages of the Literary: Tibetan Buddhist Polymaths of Socialist China* (New York: Columbia University Press, 2021). Mugé Samten and Tséten Zhapdrung wrote autobiographies. See Dmu dge Bsam gtan rgya mtsho [Mugé Samten], "Rtsom pa po rang gi byung ba brjod pa rang gsal A dar sha," in *Rje Dmu dge Bsam gtan rgya mtsho'i gsung 'bum pod dang bo*, vol. 1 (Xining: Mtsho sngon mi rigs dpe skrun khang, 1997); and Tshe tan zhabs drung 'Jigs med rigs pa'i blo gros [Tséten Zhapdrung], "Mnyam med shAkya'i dbang bo'i rjes zhugs pa 'jigs med rigs pa'i blo gros rang gi byung ba brjod pa bden gtam rna ba'i bdud rtsi," in *Mkhas dbang Tshe tan zhabs drung 'Jigs med rigs pa'i blo gros kyi gsung rtsom*, vol. 1, ed. 'Phrin las (Xining: Mtsho sngon mi rigs dpe skrun khang, 1987), 499–801. See also Tashi Dhondup, "A Monastic Scholar Under China's Occupation of Tibet: Muge Samten's (1913–1993) Autobiography and His Role as A Vernacular Intellectual" (M.A. thesis, University of British Columbia, 2019).

5. Based on this discovery, Wang Yao claimed that the Gyalrong dialect was the most representative of classical Tibetan. See Wang Yao, "Zangyu *mig* zi gudu kao—jianlun zangyu shengdiao de fasheng yu fazhan," *Minzu yuwen* 4 (1981): 15–19.

6. The Gyalrong Kuzhap's major works on the Gyalrong dialect and its relationship with classical Tibetan and the Amdo Tibetan dialect (often considered to be relatively closer to classical Tibetan than other major Tibetan dialects) include Btsan lha ngag dbang tshul khrims, *Brda dkrol gser gyi me long/Guzangwen cidian* (Beijing: Minzu chubanshe, 1997); Btsan lha ngag dbang tshul khrims, *A Lexicon of the rGyalrong bTsanlha Dialect: rGyalrong-Chinese-Tibetan*-English (Osaka: National Museum of Ethnology, 2009); and Btsan lha ngag dbang tshul khrims, ed., *rgyal rong yul skad zhib 'jug/ Zangyu jiarong fangyan yanjiu* (Chengdu: Sichuan Minzu chubanshe, 2020).

7. Döndrup Gyel is considered a pioneer in modern Tibetan literature and probably the PRC's most influential and controversial modern Tibetan intellectual. See Pema Bhum, "The Life of Dhondup Gyal: A Shooting Star That Cleaved the Night Sky and Vanished," *Lungta* 9 (1995): 17–29; Tsering Shakya, "The Waterfall and Fragrant Flowers: The Development of Tibetan Literature Since 1950," *Manoa* 12, no. 2 (2000): 28–40; and Nancy G. Lin, "Döndrup Gyel and the Remaking of the Tibetan Ramayana," in *Modern Tibetan Literature and Social Change*, ed. Lauran R. Hartley and Patricia Schiaffini-Vedani (Durham, NC: Duke University Press, 2008), 86–111.

8. Kelsang Yeshe, a native of Lhasa, later became the director of the Tibetan Classics Press in Tibet. Chen Qingyin, a Sichuan native, is often seen as the most influential contemporary Han Chinese Tibetologist in China since Wang Yao. He was the director of the History and Religion Research Division of the China Tibetology Research Center.

9. This was first written as a thesis in Tibetan for the Gyalrong Kuzhap's completion of the classical Tibetan training program. It was subsequently translated into

Chinese for publication with assistance from Zla ba tshe ring. See Btsan lha ngag dbang tshul khrims and Zla ba tshe ring, "Lüeshu zhenzhu lianzhuang de tubo zanpu lingqin," *Xizang yanjiu* 3 (1982): 141–46.

10. Btsan lha ngag dbang tshul khrims, *Brda dkrol gser gyi me long/guzangwen cidian* [The dictionary of classical Tibetan] (Beijing: minzu chubanshe, 1997).

11. For more information on Tibetan monastic education, see Georges Dreyfus, *The Sound of Two Hands Clapping: The Education of a Tibetan Buddhist Monk* (Berkeley: University of California Press, 2003).

13. THE CLOSING AGE OF GIANTS

1. Gedun Chöpel not only publicly celebrated love and sex as basic rights for all people but also relentlessly ridiculed corrupt Tibetan religious and political institutions. See Gedun Chöpel, Jeffrey Hopkins, and Dorje Yudon Yuthok, *Tibetan Arts of Love* (Ithaca, NY: Snow Lion, 1992); and Gedun Chöpel, Donald S. Lopez, and Jinpa Thupten, *The Passion Book: A Tibetan Guide to Love and Sex* (Chicago; London: University of Chicago Press, 2018). See also Irmgard Mengele, *Gedun Chöpel: A Biography of the 20th Century Tibetan Scholar* (Dharamsala, H.P.: Library of Tibetan Works and Archives, 1999); Donald S. Lopez, *The Madman's Middle Way: Reflections on Reality of the Tibetan Monk Gendun Chopel* (Chicago: University of Chicago Press, 2006); and Donald S. Lopez, *Gendun Chopel: Tibet's Modern Visionary* (Boulder, CO: Shambhala, 2018).

2. This ingenuity, improvising religious and literary techniques in a hostile and "progressive" political circumstance like the Cultural Revolution, was recorded in Mugé Samten's biography. For example, he chanted Buddhist prayers along with revolutionary slogans alongside the Red Guards during political struggle sessions. Neither the Chinese nor the Tibetans would acknowledge his chanting because of its improvisational techniques. See Nicole Willock, "Tibetan Buddhist Scholars and the Cultural Revolution: Narratives of Spiritual Achievement and Supporting Tibetan Culture," in *Conflicting Memories: Tibetan History Under Mao Retold*, ed. R. Barnett, Benno Weiner, and Françoise Robin (Leiden; Boston: Brill, 2020), 485–505 (485–86 in particular).

3. See Paul Kocot Nietupski, *Labrang Monastery: A Tibetan Buddhist Community on the Inner Asian Borderlands, 1709–1958* (Lanham, MD: Lexington Books, 2011).

4. Dung dkar, Blo bzang 'phrin las, *Bod kyi chos srid zung 'brel skor bshad pa* (Beijing: Minzu chubanshe, 1981).

5. Dung dkar, Blo bzang 'phrin las, *Dung dkar tshig mdzod chen mo* (Beijing: Zhongguo zangxue chubanshe, 2002).

6. This is part of the entry *losar* in Dung dkar, *Dung dkar tshig mdzod chen mo*, 2001–2002.

7. Chappel Tséten Püntsok is viewed as a founder of "New Tibetan History" in China, defined as a critical Marxist approach and a "politically correct" stance in seeing Tibet as part of China "since ancient times" and thus its history as an integral part of the broader Chinese history. His most celebrated works dispute the historical narratives found in W. D. Shakabpa, *Tibet: A Political History* (New Haven, CT: Yale University Press, 1967). See Chab spel tshe brtan phun tshogs, Nor brang o rgyan,

and Phun tshogs tshe ring, *Bod kyi lo rgyus rags rim g.yu yi phreng ba* (Lhasa: Xizang guji chubanshe, 1996).

8. This quote spotlights Döndrup Gyel's concern about the continuity of Tibetan culture in China, as well as his own and the younger Tibetan generation's related roles. With regard to how this concern is reflected in his works and modern Tibetan literature in general, see Lama Jabb, *Oral and Literary Continuities in Modern Tibetan Literature: The Inescapable Nation* (Lanham, MD: Lexington Books, 2015).

9. Döndrup Gyel's dream of a unified and rejuvenated Tibetan nationality, achieved through a concerted effort among its young generation, is spotlighted in one of his most acclaimed works, *Waterfall of Youth* (*Lang tsho'i rbab chu*): "Our dreams, the dreams the new generation of snowy Tibet, are manifest/Conservatism, cowardice, blind faith, and laziness . . . /These have no place whatsoever in this generation of ours/Backwardness, barbarian, darkness, backward customs . . . /There is no room, whatsoever, for these in our century/Waterfall, O waterfall!/Our mind flows with your movement and/Our blood as well, courses alongside your currents/Although on the path of the future/The twists and turns may be greater than before/Nevertheless, there is no chance for the youth of Tibet to be afraid/We will certainly forge a new path forward/For each and every one of our people." There exist several translated (English) versions. Here I use the translation by Lowell Cook at https://highpeakspureearth.com/poem-waterfall-of-youth-by-dondrup-gyal-in-a-new-translation-by-lowell-cook/ (retrieved February 16, 2021). As to the significance and impact of this work, one comment goes, "The poem was like nothing they had ever read. Not only did it evidence literary innovation, but it contained a bold and nationalistic political statement. The poem fervently appealed to Tibetans to embrace modernism to regenerate their culture and national pride. It beseeched the youth to shake off the past and march proudly towards their future. This boldness in style and politics was characteristic of Dhondup Gyal's writings. For the first time, the possibility emerged that a genuine discourse on Tibetan modernity could occur through the medium of poetry and fiction. At stake were the future direction of Tibet and Tibetan identity in the latter half of the twentieth century. Dhondup Gyal's work was a turning point because, while criticism was unacceptable to the Chinese authorities, he showed that it was nevertheless possible to speak implicitly about the "wound inflicted on the mind of the Tibetans" (bod kyi sems kyi rma), referring to the period under the leadership of the Gang of Four." See Tsering Shakya, "The Waterfall and Fragrant Flowers: The Development of Tibetan Literature Since 1950," *Manoa* 12, no. 2 (2000): 36.

10. Heather Stoddard, "Don grub rgyal (1953–1985): Suicide of a Modern Tibetan Writer and Scholar," in *Proceedings of the 6th Seminar of the International Association for Tibetan Studies*, ed. Per Kvaerne (Oslo: Institute for Comparative Research in Human Culture, 1994), 825–34.

11. Hu Yaobang, the CCP's General Secretary from 1980 to 1987, is known for his liberal approach to Tibetan and ethnic matters in China's diverse political, economic, and cultural spheres. See, for instance, Wang Yao, "Hu Yaobang's visit to Tibet, May 22–31, 1980," in *Resistance and Reform in Tibet*, ed. Robert Barnett and Shirin Akiner (Bloomington: Indiana University Press, 1994), 285–89. During his historical visit to Tibet in 1980, Hu made six major points on the new Tibetan policy on May 29, 1980: 1) Under the unified leadership of the Central Government, the

region's autonomy should be fully exercised; 2) In light of Tibet's seriously difficult situation, the policy of rehabilitation should be firmly implemented to reduce the burden on the masses; 3) Regarding economic issues and policies, Tibet should be treated as a special case and given flexibility according to Tibet's conditions; 4) A substantial portion of subsidies should be used for the development of agriculture, animal husbandry, and the essential needs of the Tibetan people; 5) Under the direction of socialism, Tibet's science, culture, and education systems should be further developed; and 6) The CCP's cadre policy for nationalities should be correctly implemented and Chinese and Tibetan solidarity must be significantly enhanced. This six-point Tibetan policy is requoted from Tseten Wangchuk Sharlho, "China's Reforms in Tibet: Issues and Dilemmas," *Journal of Contemporary China* 1, no. 1 (1992): 38–39.

12. It was hard to believe that the CCP's General Secretary would acknowledge its rule in Tibet as "colonialism." According to the Gyalrong Kuzhap, this shocked him a great deal when he heard about it from Wang Yao (professor of Tibetan Studies at the Central Nationalities Institute, an interpreter for Hu Yaobang during the latter's visit of Tibet in 1980) in Wang's talk with Tibetan students at the institute after he returned to Beijing. In that talk, Wang Yao mentioned that Hu explicitly instructed him not to withhold anything that the latter had said and done in Tibet, including the expression of "colonialism" that Hu used in one of the meetings in Tibet. Hu's overall liberal stance estranged him from many CCP senior leaders, eventually leading to his forced resignation in 1987 after displaying a sympathetic reconciliatory view toward student demonstrations.

14. THE LAST BREATH

1. For example, in an interview with CCTV (China's national TV station), Alai says, "Because Tibetan also has a problem: this language, from the day of its creation to the 1950s, in most cases, is a religious language only used by monks. It is not a language shared by all (Tibetan) people, like a written language that expresses all of our lives. Therefore, its expression is limited. So, if you dig into this writing system, [you will find that] we don't actually have a truly independent literary tradition. Although there may be some literary expression in Buddhist scriptures to make their teachings more vivid, there is no independent literature [in Tibet]." Accessed February 21, 2021, http://news.cntv.cn/program/mianduimian/20100510/105257.shtml.

2. A debate between the Gyalrong Kuzhap and Sun Hongkai (1934–; one of the most senior and renowned linguists on ethnic minority languages in China) occurred in 2017 at a conference on Tibetan linguistics at Nankai University. The Gyalrong Kuzhap claimed that the Gyalrong dialect is part of the Tibetan language family and was supported by most of the Tibetan scholars at the conference, especially Thubten Phuntsok, a professor at the Southwest Nationalities University and one of the most recognized contemporary Tibetologists in China. Professor Thubten Phuntsok went as far as to claim that the Gyalrong dialect should be considered the "mother tongue" (root) of the Tibetan language family because it is the only dialect that preserves classical Tibetan.

3. This agreement is collected in Btsan lha ngag dbang tshul khrims, et al., eds., *Rgyal rong sa khul gyi rgyal po dang yig tshags skor/Jiarong diqu jiebu he wenshu dang'an* (Chengdu: Sichuan minzu chubanshe, 2017), 248–49.
4. Established initially by Andrea E. Soros in 1993, Trace Foundation became a well-known and large-scale organization explicitly dedicated to supporting Tibetan culture, language, education, development, and communities in China.
5. The role of Nyammé Shérap Gyeltsen (1356–1415), a Bön master from Gyalrong (Chuchen) and founder of Menri (a major Bön monastery in Central Tibet), in reviving and spreading Bön in Central Tibet was well known. See a collection of his biographies and teachings in Btsan lha ngag dbang tshul khrims, Sgrol dkar skyid, and Nam mkha' tshul khrims, eds., *Rgyal rong lo rgyus mi sna grags can skor/Jiarong diqu mingren*, vol. 1 (Chengdu: Sichuan minzu chubanshe, 2017), 127–205. Overall, the broader influence of Bön (masters, patrons, and teachings) in/from Gyalrong in the Himalayas and beyond, especially before the Second Jinchuan Campaign, has not been well documented and studied. Some works are emerging to engage with this issue. See Charles Ramble, "The Long Arm of an Eighteenth-Century Bonpo Patron: Gyalrong and Dolpo between the Jinchuan Wars," *Revue d'Etudes Tibétaines* 64 (2022): 447–60.
6. See Seng ge 'bum, Btsan lha ngag dbang tshul khrims, Tsheng dbang, Bstan 'dzin sbyin pa, Nam mkha' tshul khrims, *Shar rgyal mo tsha ba rong gi lo rgyus dang rig gnas dpe tshogs/Jiarong zangzu lishi wenhua congshu* [Gyalrong Tibetan history and culture series] (Chengdu: Sichuan minzu chubanshe, 2017). This book series comprises history, historical figures, holy sites and monasteries, kings and administrative archives, customs, and astrology. Many of these works are cited in this book. The actual chief editor for this extensive series is Btsan lha ngag dbang tshul khrims (Tsanlha Ngawang Tsültrim or the Gyalrong Kuzhap). However, general practice in contemporary China lists the official sponsor as the first author/editor. This explains why Btsan lha ngag dbang tshul khrims's name appears after the particular official who had sponsored the project for years.
7. Thönmi Sambhota was said to have composed six texts on Tibetan grammar/linguistics in total, all but two of which are missing. It is believed that the missing texts included comprehensive works on Tibetan linguistics.
8. Btsan lha ngag dbang tshul khrims, ed., *Rgyal rong yul skad zhib 'jug/Zangyu jiarong fangyan* [Research on Tibetan Gyalrong dialect] (Chengdu: Sichuan minzu chubanshe, 2020).

BIBLIOGRAPHY

Abaxian renwubu 阿壩縣人武部 [Ngawa County People's Armed Forces Department]. *Abaxian junshi zhi* 阿壩縣軍事志 [Ngawa County military history]. Chengdu: Sichuan daxue chubanshe, 2009.

Alai. *Red Poppies*. Trans. H. Goldblatt and S. L.-C. Lin. Boston: Houghton Mifflin, 2002.

Alai 阿來. *Zhandui: Zhongyu ronghua de tie geda—Yige liangbainian de kangba chuanqi* 瞻對: 終於融化的鐵疙瘩, 一個兩百年的康巴傳奇 [Chakdü: The iron knot finally melted—A two-hundred-year legend of the Khampas]. Chengdu: Sichuan wenyi chubanshe, 2014.

Allione, Tsultrim. *Women of Wisdom*. London; Boston: Routledge & Kegan Paul, 1984.

Anderson, Benedict. *Imagined Communities: Reflections on the Origin and Spread of Nationalism*. London; New York: Verso, 1991.

Barnett, Robert, ed. *A Poisoned Arrow: The Secret Report of the 10th Panchen Lama*. London: Tibet Information Network, 1997.

Barnett, Robert, Benno Weiner, and Françoise Robin, eds. *Conflicting Memories: Tibetan History Under Mao Retold*. Leiden; Boston: Brill, 2020.

Berounský, Daniel. "Kīrti Monastery of Ngawa: Its History and Recent Situation." *Revue d'etudes Tibétaines* 25 (2012): 65–80.

Bianchi, Ester. "A Religion-Oriented 'Tibet Fever': Tibetan Buddhist Practices Among the Han Chinese in Contemporary PRC." In *From Mediterranean to Himalaya*, ed. Dramdul and F. Sferra, 347–74. Beijing: China Tibetology Publishing House, 2014.

Booz, Patrick Ramzi. "Tea, Trade and Transport in the Sino-Tibetan Borderlands." Ph.D. diss., Oxford University, 2011.

Bourdieu, Pierre. *Outline of a Theory of Practice*. Cambridge; New York: Cambridge University Press, 1977.

——. *Distinction: A Social Critique of the Judgement of Taste.* Cambridge, MA: Harvard University Press, 1984.

Brag dgon pa, dkon mchog bstan pa rab rgyas. *Mdo smad chos 'byung/Amdo zhengjiao shi* 安多政教史 [Religious history of Amdo]. Xining: Qinghai renmin chubanshe, 2017.

Bray, John. "Trade, Territory, and Missionary Connections in the Sino-Tibetan Borderlands." In *Frontier Tibet: Patterns of Change in the Sino-Tibetan Borderlands*, ed. Stéphane Gros, 151–78. Amsterdam: Amsterdam University Press, 2019.

Btsan lha ngag dbang tshul khrims. *Brda dkrol gser gyi me long/guzangwen cidian* 古藏文辭典 [The dictionary of classical Tibetan]. Beijing: Minzu chubanshe, 1997.

——. *A Lexicon of the Rgyalrong Btsanlha Dialect: Rgyalrong-Chinese-Tibetan-English.* Osaka: National Museum of Ethnology, 2009.

——, ed. *Rgyal rong yul skad zhib 'jug/Zangyu jiarong fangyan* 藏語嘉絨方言研究 [Research on Tibetan Gyalrong dialect]. Chengdu: Sichuan minzu chubanshe, 2020.

——. *Btsan lha ngag dbang tshul khrims rang gis rang gi byung ba brjod pa/Zanla Awang Cuocheng huiyilu* 贊拉·阿旺措成回憶錄 [Memoir of Tsanlha Ngawang Tsültrim]. Lanzhou: Gansu minzu chubanshe, forthcoming.

Btsan lha ngag dbang tshul khrims and Zla ba tshe ring. "Lüeshu zhenzhu lianzhuang de tubo zanpu lingqin" 略述珍珠鍊狀的吐蕃贊普陵寢 [A brief description of the pearl chain-shaped mausoleum of Tibetan kings]. *Xizang yanjiu* 西藏研究 [Tibetan studies] 3 (1982): 141–46.

Btsan lha ngag dbang tshul khrims, Klu sman, and Nam mkha' tshul khrims, eds. *Rgyal rong yul gyi gnas chen dang dgon khag skor/Jiarong diqu shengdi he siyuan* 嘉絨地區聖地和寺院 [Holy sites and monasteries in Gyalrong]. Chengdu: Sichuan minzu chubanshe, 2017.

Btsan lha ngag dbang tshul khrims, Mtsho sman, and Nam mkha' tshul khrims, eds. *Rgyal mo rong gi lo rgyus skor/Jiarong diqu lishi* 嘉絨地區歷史（上冊）[On Gyalrong history], vol. 1. Chengdu: Sichuan minzu chubanshe, 2017.

Btsan lha ngag dbang tshul khrims, Nam mkha' tshul khrims, and Liu Ying, eds. *Rgyal mo rong gi lo rgyus skor/Jiarong diqu lishi* 嘉絨地區歷史（中冊）[On Gyalrong history], vol. 2. Chengdu: Sichuan minzu chubanshe, 2017.

Btsan lha ngag dbang tshul khrims, Bstan 'dzin sbyin pa, Nam mkha' tshul khrims, and Mtsho sman, eds. *Rgyal mo rong gi lo rgyus skor/Jiarong diqu lishi* 嘉絨地區歷史（下冊）[On Gyalrong history], vol. 3. Chengdu: Sichuan minzu chubanshe, 2017.

Btsan lha ngag dbang tshul khrims, Sgrol dkar skyid, and Nam mkha' tshul khrims, eds. *Rgyal rong lo rgyus mi sna grags can skor/Jiarong diqu mingren* 嘉絨地區名人（上冊）[Historical figures in Gyalrong], vol. 1. Chengdu: Sichuan minzu chubanshe, 2017.

Btsan lha ngag dbang tshul khrims and Sgrol dkar skyid, eds. *Rgyal rong lo rgyus mi sna grags can skor/Jiarong diqu mingren* 嘉絨地區名人（中冊）[Historical figures in Gyalrong], vol. 2. Chengdu: Sichuan minzu chubanshe, 2017.

Btsan lha ngag dbang tshul khrims, Sgrol dkar skyid, and Nam mkha' tshul khrims, eds. *Rgyal rong lo rgyus mi sna grags can skor/Jiarong diqu mingren* 嘉絨地區名人（下冊）[Historical figures in Gyalrong], vol. 3. Chengdu: Sichuan minzu chubanshe, 2017.

Btsan lha ngag dbang tshul khrims, TA re skyid, Chos sgron, and Nam mkha' tshul khrims, eds. *Rgyal rong sa khul gyi rgyal po dang yig tshags skor/Jiarong diqu jiebu he wenshu dang'an* 嘉絨地區傑布和文書檔案 [On kings and administrative archives in Gyalrong]. Chengdu: Sichuan minzu chubanshe, 2017.

Buckley, Michael. *Meltdown in Tibet: China's Reckless Destruction of Ecosystems from the Highlands of Tibet to the Deltas of Asia.* New York: Palgrave Macmillan, 2014.

Buffetrille, Katia, and Françoise Robin, eds. "Tibet Is Burning: Self-Immolation, Ritual or Political Protest?" Special Issue, *Revue d'etudes Tibétaines* 25 (December): 2012.

Bulag, Uradyn E. "Seeing Like a Minority: Political Tourism and the Struggle for Recognition in China." *Journal of Current Chinese Affairs* 41, no. 4 (2012): 133–58.

Bya mdo rin bzang [Shamdo Rinzang]. *Nga'i pha yul dang gzab nyan* [My hometown: Listen carefully]. Unpublished ms., 2008.

——. *Nga'i pha yul dang zhi ba'i bcings grol* [My hometown and peaceful liberation]. Dharamsala: Bod kyi dgu bcu gsum las 'gul tshogs pa, 2010.

Cao Shiyong 曹世鏞. "Maogong huihan guanxishi shang de buxing shijian" 懋功回漢關係史上的不幸事件 [An unfortunate incident in the Han-Hui relations in Maogong]. In *Xiaojin wenshi ziliao xuanji* 小金文史資料選輯 [Xiaojin cultural-historical material collections], vol. 3, ed. Xiaojinxian Zhengxie Wenshi Ziliao Bianweihui 小金縣政協文史資料委員會 [Cultural-Historical Materials Editorial Board at Xiaojin County Political Consultative Conference], 1–46. Xiaojin: Xiaojin Zhengxie, 1992.

——. "Xiaojin huizu yu qingzhensi de lishi he xiankuang" 小金回族與清真寺的歷史和現況 [The history and current situation of Xiaojin Hui people and mosques]. In *Xiaojin wenshi ziliao xuanji* 小金文史資料選輯 [Xiaojin cultural-historical material collections], vol. 4, ed. Xiaojinxian Zhengxie Wenshi Ziliao Bianweihui 小金縣政協文史資料委員會 [Cultural-Historical Materials Editorial Board at Xiaojin County Political Consultative Conference], 1–17. Xiaojin: Xiaojin Zhengxie, 1996.

Caple, Jane. "Faith, Generosity, Knowledge and the Buddhist Gift: Moral Discourses on Chinese Patronage of Tibetan Buddhist Monasteries." *Religion Compass* 9, no. 11 (2015): 462–82.

Chab spel tshe brtan phun tshogs 恰白·次旦平措, Nor brang o rgyan 諾章·吳堅, and Phun tshogs tshe ring 平措次仁. *Bod kyi lo rgyus rags rim g.yu yi phreng ba* 西藏通史松石寶串 [General history of Tibet: The precious string of Turquoise]. Lhasa: Xizang guji chubanshe, 1996.

Chen Duxiu 陳獨秀. "Wenxue geming lun" 文學革命論 On literature's revolution. *Xin Qingnian* New youth 2, no. 6 (1917).

Cho, Yasmin. "Politics of Tranquility: Religious Mobilities and Material Engagements of Tibetan Buddhist Nuns in Post-Mao China." Ph.D. diss., Duke University, 2015.

Chöpel, Gedun, Donald S. Lopez, and Thupten Jinpa. *The Passion Book: A Tibetan Guide to Love and Sex.* Chicago; London: University of Chicago Press, 2018.

Chöpel, Gedun, Jeffrey Hopkins, and Dorje Yudon Yuthok. *Tibetan Arts of Love.* Ithaca, NY: Snow Lion, 1992.

Clothey, Rebecca. "Policies for Minority Nationalities in Higher Education: Negotiating National Values and Ethnic Identities." *Comparative Education Review* 49, no. 3 (2005): 389–409.

Crook, Isabel, and David Crook. *Revolution in a Chinese Village, Ten Mile Inn.* London: Routledge and Paul, 1959.

Dalai Lama (His Holiness; Bstan 'dzin rgya mtsho). *My Land and My People.* New York: McGraw-Hill, 1962.

——. *Freedom in Exile: The Autobiography of the Dalai Lama.* New York: HarperCollins, 1990.

——. *My Spiritual Autobiography*. London: Rider, 2012.

——. *The Life of My Teacher: A Biography of Kyabjé Ling Rinpoché*. Somerville, MA: Wisdom, 2017.

Dai, Yingcong. "The Qing State, Merchants, and the Military Labor Force in the Jinchuans." *Late Imperial China* 22, no. 2 (2001): 35–90.

Davidson, Ronald M. *Tibetan Renaissance: Tantric Buddhism in the Rebirth of Tibetan Culture*. New York: Columbia University Press, 2005.

Demare, Brian James. *Land Wars: The Story of China's Agrarian Revolution*. Stanford, CA: Stanford University Press, 2019.

Demick, Barbara. *Eat the Buddha: Life and Death in a Tibetan Town*. New York: Random House, 2020.

Dibeltulo, Martino. "The Revival of Tantrism: Tibetan Buddhism and Modern China." Ph.D. diss., University of Michigan, 2015.

Ding Xing 丁星. "Maogong paoge zuzhi jianshu" 懋功袍哥組織簡述 [Brief introduction to Maogong Paoge organizations]. In *Aba Zangzu zizhizhou wenshi ziliao xuanji* 阿壩藏族自治州文史資料選輯 [Collections of cultural and historical materials in Ngawa Tibetan Autonomous Prefecture], vol. 3, ed. Xiaojinxian wenshi ziliao weiyuanhui 小金縣文史資料委員會 [Xiaojin County Committee on Cultural and Historical Materials], 86–98. Xiaojin: Xiaojin Zhengxie, 1992.

Dittmer, Lowell. *Liu Shaoqi and the Chinese Cultural Revolution*. Armonk, NY: M. E. Sharpe, 1998.

Dmu Dge Bsam Gtan Rgya Mtsho. "Rtsom pa po rang gi byung ba brjod pa rang gsal a dar sha" [The luminous mirror: The author's own autobiography]. In *Rje dmu dge bsam gtan rgya mtsho'i gsung 'bum pod dang bo* [The collected works of Master Mugé Samten Gyatsho, vol. 1]. Xining: Mtsho sngon mi rigs dpe skrun khang, 1997.

Dreyer, June Teufel. "Economic Development in Tibet Under the People's Republic of China." *Journal of Contemporary China* 12, no. 36 (2003): 411–30.

Dreyfus, Georges. "The Shuk-Den Affair: Origins of a Controversy." *Journal of the International Association of Buddhist Studies* 21, no. 2 (1998): 227–70.

——. *The Sound of Two Hands Clapping: The Education of a Tibetan Buddhist Monk*. Berkeley: University of California Press, 2003.

Du Aiguo 都愛國. "Gangrou xiangfu shenming dayi—Ji caodi zangzu lingxiu renwu Huaergong Chenglie" 剛柔相輔深明大義—記草地藏族領袖人物華爾功成烈 [Complementing the rigid and soft, possessing righteousness— Remembering the great achievements of a leader of the nomadic Tibetans, Pelgön Trinlé]. In *Yiwei zhencha canmou bixia de xueshan caodi Abazhou*, 266–83. Maerkang: Abazhou zhengxie wenshi he xuexi weiyuanhui, 2011.

——. "Kaiming aiguo gongzai guojia—Ji zhuokeji tusi suoguanying" 開明愛國功在國家—記卓克基土司索觀瀛 [Open-minded and patriotic, applaudable in his contribution to the ttate—Remembering the Choktsé Chieftain Suo Guanying]. In *Yiwei zhencha canmou bixia de xueshan caodi Abazhou*, 248–65. Maerkang: Abazhou zhengxie wenshi he xuexi weiyuanhui, 2011.

——. "Luoye guigen wanjie kefeng—Ji heishui datouren su yonghe" 落葉歸根晚節可風—記黑水大頭人蘇永和 [Fallen leaves returning to their roots, complementing the restored integrity in his late years—Remembering Su Yonghe, the Chieftain of Trochu]. In *Yiwei zhencha canmou bixia de xueshan caodi abazhou*, 284–309. Maerkang: Abazhou zhengxie wenshi he xuexi weiyuanhui, 2011.

——. *Yiwei zhencha canmou bixia de xueshan caodi abazhou* 一位偵察參謀筆下的雪山草地阿壩州 [Snow-capped mountains and grasslands in Aba Prefecture in the portrait of a former PLA scout]. Maerkang: Abazhou zhengxie wenshi he xuexi weiyuanhui, 2011.

Dung dkar, Blo bzang 'phrin las. *Bod kyi chos srid zung 'brel skor bshad pa* [On the relationship between religion and state in Tibet]. Beijing: minzu chubanshe, 1981.

——. *Dung dkar tshig mdzod chen mo* 東噶藏學大辭典 [The great Dungkar Tibetan dictionary]. Beijing: Zhongguo zangxue chubanshe, 2002.

Epstein, Lawrence, ed. *Khams Pa Histories: Visions of People, Place and Authority: PIATS 2000, Tibetan Studies, Proceedings of the Ninth Seminar of the International Association for Tibetan Studies, Leiden 2000.* Leiden; Boston: Brill, 2002.

Esler, Joshua. "Tibetan Buddhism and Han Chinese: Superscribing New Meaning on the Tibetan Tradition in Modern Greater China." Ph.D. diss., University of Western Australia, 2013.

Fischer, Andrew Martin. *The Disempowered Development of Tibet in China: A Study in the Economics of Marginalization.* Lanham, MD: Lexington Books, 2014.

Fiskesjö, Magnus. "The Animal Other: China's Barbarians and Their Renaming in the Twentieth Century." *Social Text* 29, no. 4 (109) (2011): 57–79.

Fjeld, Heidi. *Commoners and Nobles: Hereditary Divisions in Tibet.* Copenhagen: Nias, 2005.

Gamble, Ruth. *Reincarnation in Tibetan Buddhism: The Third Karmapa and the Invention of a Tradition.* New York: Oxford University Press, 2018.

Gardner, John. "Liu Shaoqi and the Cultural Revolution: The Rise and Fall of a Chosen Successor." *Chinese Politics and the Succession to Mao.* London: Macmillan Education UK, 1982.

Ge Ai 葛艾. "Suo Guanying zhuan" 索观瀛传 [The biography of Suo Guanying]. In *Difang shizhi wenji* 地方史志文集 [Collected Works of Local History], 235–251. Maerkang: Abazhou fangzhi diming bangongshi 阿壩州方志地名辦公室 [The Office of Local Chronicles and Place Names at Aba Prefecture], 1989.

Giersch, C. Patterson. "The Origins of Disempowered Development in the Tibetan Borderlands." In *Frontier Tibet*, ed. S. Gros, 263–73. Amsterdam: Amsterdam University Press, 2019.

Goldstein, Melvyn C. *The Snow Lion and the Dragon: China, Tibet, and the Dalai Lama.* Berkeley: University of California Press, 1997.

——. *A History of Modern Tibet. Volume 2, The Calm Before the Storm, 1951–1955.* Berkeley: University of California Press, 2007.

——. *A History of Modern Tibet. Volume 3, The Storm Clouds Descend, 1955–1957.* Berkeley: University of California Press, 2014.

——. *A History of Modern Tibet. Volume 4, In the Eye of the Storm, 1957–1959.* Oakland: University of California Press, 2019.

Goldstein, Melvyn C., and Cynthia M. Beall. *Nomads of Western Tibet: The Survival of a Way of Life.* Berkeley: University of California Press, 1990.

Goldstein, Melvyn C., and Matthew Kapstein. *Buddhism in Contemporary Tibet: Religious Revival and Cultural Identity.* Berkeley: University of California Press, 1998.

Goldstein, Melvyn C., Dawei Sherap, and William R. Siebenschuh. *A Tibetan Revolutionary: The Political Life and Times of Bapa Phüntso Wangye.* Berkeley: University of California Press, 2004.

Goldstein, Melvyn C., Ben Jiao, and Lhundrup Tanzen. *On the Cultural Revolution in Tibet: The Nyemo Incident of 1969.* Berkeley: University of California Press, 2009.

Goldstein, Melvyn C., William R. Siebenschuh, and Tsering Tashi. *The Struggle for Modern Tibet: The Autobiography of Tashi Tsering.* Armonk, NY: M. E. Sharpe, 1997.

Greatrex, Roger. "A Brief Introduction to the First Jinchuan War (1747–1749)." In *The History of Tibet: The Medieval Period c. 850–1895*, vol. 2, ed. Alex McKay, 615–32. London and New York: RoutledgeCurzon, 2003.

Groot, Gerry. *Managing Transitions: The Chinese Communist Party, United Front Work, Corporatism, and Hegemony.* New York: Routledge, 2004.

Gros, Stéphane, ed. *Frontier Tibet: Patterns of Change in the Sino-Tibetan Borderlands.* Amsterdam: Amsterdam University Press, 2019.

Grunfeld, A. Tom. *The Making of Modern Tibet.* Armonk, NY: M. E. Sharpe, 1996.

Gyatso, Janet. *Apparitions of the Self: The Secret Autobiographies of a Tibetan Visionary.* Princeton, NJ: Princeton University Press, 1998.

Gyatso, Lobsang. *Memoirs of a Tibetan Lama.* Ithaca, NY: Snow Lion, 1998.

Hansen, Mette Halskov. *Lessons in Being Chinese: Minority Education and Ethnic Identity in Southwest China.* Seattle: University of Washington Press, 1999.

Harrell, Stevan. *Ways of Being Ethnic in Southwest China.* Seattle: University of Washington Press, 2001.

Hartley, Lauran R., and Patricia Schiaffini-Vedani. *Modern Tibetan Literature and Social Change.* Durham, NC: Duke University Press, 2008.

Hershatter, Gail. "Disquiet in the House of Gender." *The Journal of Asian Studies* 71, no. 4 (2012): 873–94.

Hillman, Ben. "Monastic Politics and the Local State in China: Authority and Autonomy in an Ethnically Tibetan Prefecture." *The China Journal* 54 (2005): 29–51.

Hinton, William. *Fanshen: A Documentary of Revolution in a Chinese Village.* New York: Monthly Review Press, 2008 [1966].

Hobsbawm, E. J. and T. O. Ranger. *The Invention of Tradition.* Cambridge; New York: Cambridge University Press, 1983.

Jabb, Lama. *Oral and Literary Continuities in Modern Tibetan Literature: The Inescapable Nation.* Lanham, MD: Lexington Books, 2015.

Jackson, David. *The Early Abbots of 'Phan-Po Na-Lendra: The Vicissitudes of a Great Tibetan Monastery in the 15th Century.* Wien: Arbeitskreis für Tibetische und Buddhistische Studien Universität Wien, 1989.

Jacques, Guillaume. *Jiarongyu Yanjiu* 嘉戎研究 [A study on the Rgyalrong Language]. Beijing: minzu chubanshe, 2008.

Jagou, Fabienne. *The Ninth Panchen Lama (1883–1937): A Life at the Crossroads of Sino-Tibetan Relations.* Paris: École Française D'extrême, 2011.

Jia Shengcai 賈生採. "Zai shehui zhuyi daolu shang maijin de Aba zangzu zizhizhou" 在社會主義道路上邁進的阿壩藏族自治州[Ngawa Tibetan Autonomous Prefecture marching on the road of socialism]. In *Sichuan minzu diqu minzhu gaige ziliaoji* 四川民族地區民主改革資料集 [A collection of materials on the democratic reform in ethnic minority regions in Sichuan], ed. Qin Heping 秦和平, 250–55. Beijing: Minzu chubanshe, 2008.

Jiande Dongzhou 建德·東周. *Suo Guanying zhuan* 索觀瀛傳 [The biography of Suo Guanying]. Maerkang: Maerkang xian zhixie wenshi ziliao weiyuanhui 馬爾康縣政

協文史資料委員會 [Cultural-Historical Materials Committee at Maerkang County Political Consultative Conference], 1992.

Jones, Alison Denton. "Contemporary Han Chinese Involvement in Tibetan Buddhism: A Case Study from Nanjing." *Social Compass* 58, no. 4 (2011): 540–53.

Kang, Xiaofei, and Donald Sutton. *Contesting the Yellow Dragon: Ethnicity, Religion, and the State in the Sino-Tibetan Borderland.* Leiden; Boston: Brill, 2016.

Karma Lingpa, Padma Sambhava, and Robert A. F. Thurman. *The Tibetan Book of the Dead: The Great Book of Natural Liberation Through Understanding in the Between.* New York: Bantam, 1994.

Karmay, Samten G. *Feast of the Morning Light: The Eighteenth-Century Wood-Engravings of Shenrab's Life-Stories and the Bon Canon from Gyalrong.* Osaka: National Museum of Ethnology, 2005.

——. *The Autobiography of the Fifth Dalai Lama.* Chicago: Serindia, 2014.

Kleinman, Arthur. *Deep China: The Moral Life of the Person: What Anthropology and Psychiatry Tell Us About China Today.* Berkeley: University of California Press, 2011.

Knight, Nick. "Mao Zedong's on Contradiction and on Practice: Pre-Liberation Texts." *The China Quarterly* 84 (1980): 641–68.

Kolas, Ashild, and Monika P. Thowsen. *On the Margins of Tibet: Cultural Survival on the Sino-Tibetan Frontier.* Seattle; London: University of Washington Press, 2005.

Kui Ge 虧戈, Gaerge 嘎爾戈, Ouzhou 歐周, and Jiamucuo 甲木措. "Jiefangqian de Aba difang zangjun qingkuang gaiyao" 解放前的阿壩地方藏軍情況概要 [A summary of the Tibetan army in Ngawa before Liberation]. In *Aba zangzu zizhizhou wenshi ziliao xuanji* 阿壩藏族自治州文史資料選輯 [Collections of cultural and historical materials in Ngawa Tibetan Autonomous Prefecture], vol. 6, 94–96. Maerkang: Abazhou zhengxie wenshi ziliao weiyuanhui 阿壩州政協文史資料委員會 [Cultural-Historical Materials Committee at Aba Prefecture Political Consultative Conference], 1987.

Leibold, James. "Un-Mapping Republican China's Tibetan Frontier: Politics, Warlord-ism and Ethnicity Along the Kham/Xikang Borderland." *The Chinese Historical Review* 12, no. 2 (2005): 167–201.

Li Guangming 黎光明 and Wang Yuanhui 王元輝. *Chuanxi minsu diaocha ji lu 1929* 川西民俗調查記錄 1929 [Survey records of folk customs in Western Sichuan in 1929. Taipei: Zhongyang yanjiuyuan lishi yuyan yanjiusuo, 2004.

Li, Jianglin, and Matthew Akester. "Eat the Buddha! Chinese and Tibetan Accounts of the Red Army in Gyalrong and Ngaba 1935–6 and Related Documents (Parts I–IV)." *Blog: War on Tibet: Chinese and Tibetan Documents on the History of the Communist Occupation in English Translation,* May 16, 2012.

Li, Xiaoxiong. *Poppies and Politics in China: Sichuan Province, 1840s to 1940s.* Newark: University of Delaware Press, 2009.

Lin, Nancy G. "Döndrup Gyel and the Remaking of the Tibetan Ramayana." In *Modern Tibetan Literature and Social Change,* ed. Lauran R. Hartley and Patricia, 86–111. Durham, NC: Duke University Press, 2008.

Lindholm, Charles. *Culture and Authenticity.* Malden, MA: Blackwell, 2008.

Litao 李濤. "Yapianyan zai jiarong zangqu de chuanbo" 鴉片煙在嘉絨藏區的傳播 [The spread of opium in Gyalrong Tibetan Region]. *Xizang minsu* 西藏民俗 [Tibetan folk-lore] 1 (1994): 39–40.

Liu Wenhu i 劉文輝. *Zoudao renmin zhenying de lishi daolu* 走到人民陣營的歷史道路 [Take the historical path of the people's camp]. Beijing: Sanlian shudian, 1979.

Liu, Xiaoyuan. *To the End of Revolution: The Chinese Communist Party and Tibet, 1949–1959.* New York: Columbia University Press, 2020.

Lopez, Donald S. *The Madman's Middle Way: Reflections on Reality of the Tibetan Monk Gendun Chopel.* Chicago: University of Chicago Press, 2006.

——. *Gendun Chopel: Tibet's Modern Visionary.* Boulder, CO: Shambhala, 2018.

Lu Zichang 路梓常 and Wang Ankang 王安康. "Wo suo zhidao de maerkang yandu" qingkuang" 我所知道的馬爾康煙毒情況 [What I know about Malkang's toxic opium]. In *Aba zangzu zizhizhou wenshi ziliao xuanji* 阿壩藏族自治州文史資料選輯 [Collections of cultural and historical materials in Ngawa Tibetan Autonomous Prefecture], vol. 1, 131–36. Maerkang: Abazhou zhengxie wenshi ziliao wei yuanhui 阿壩州政協文史資料委員會 [Cultural-Historical Materials Committee at Aba Prefecture Political Consultative Conference], 1984.

Ma Changshou 馬長壽. "Jiarong minzu shehui shi" 嘉戎民族社會史 [Social history of the Gyalrong people]." *Minzuxue yanjiu jikan* 民族學研究集刊 [Collected volumes on nationality studies] 4 (1944).

Ma, Rong. "A New Perspective in Guiding Ethnic Relations in the Twenty-First Century: 'De-Politicization' of Ethnicity in China." *Asian Ethnicity* 8, no. 3 (2007): 199–217.

——. "The 'Politicization' and 'Culturization' of Ethnic Groups." *Chinese Sociology and Anthropology* 42, no. 4 (2010): 31–45.

——. "Reflections on the Debate on China's Ethnic Policy: My Reform Proposals and Their Critics." *Asian Ethnicity* 15, no. 2 (2014): 237–46.

——. "Reconstructing 'Nation' (Minzu) Discourses in China." *International Journal of Anthropology and Ethnology* 1, no. 1 (2017): 1–15.

Ma Xingyun 馬興雲. "Xiaojin huimin fengtu renqing cexie 小金回民風土人情側寫 [Profile of Xiaojin Hui People's Custom]." In *Xiaojin wenshi ziliao xuanji* 小金文史资料选辑 [Xiaojin cultural-historical material collections], vol. 2, ed. Xiaojinxian zhengxie wenshi ziliao gongzuozu 小金县政协文史资料工作组 [Cultural-Historical Materials Working Group at Xiaojin County Political Consultative Conference], 129–42. Xiaojin: Xiaojin zhenxie, 1989.

Maerkangxian zhengxie wenshiwei/Aba jiarong wenhua yanjiuhui 馬爾康縣政協文史委/阿壩嘉絨文化研究會 [Cultural-Historical Materials Committee at Maerkang County Political Consultative Conference and the Association of Gyalrong Cultural Studies]. *Xueshan tusi wangchao zhuokeji di shiliudai tusi suo guanying zhuan* 雪山土司王朝—卓克基第十六代土司索觀瀛傳 [The dynasty of a snow mountain chieftain—The biography of Suo Guanying, the sixteenth king of Choktsé]. Chengdu: Sichuan minzu chubanshe, 2013.

Makley, Charlene E. "'Speaking Bitterness': Autobiography, History, and Mnemonic Politics on the Sino-Tibetan Frontier." *Comparative Studies in Society and History* 47, no. 1 (2005): 40–78.

——. *The Violence of Liberation: Gender and Tibetan Buddhist Revival in Post-Mao China.* Berkeley: University of California Press, 2007.

——. "The Sociopolitical Lives of Dead Bodies: Tibetan Self-Immolation Protest as Mass Media." *Cultural Anthropology* 30, no. 3 (2015): 448–76.

——. *The Battle for Fortune: State-Led Development, Personhood, and Power Among Tibetans in China*. Ithaca, NY: Cornell University Press, 2018.

Martin, Dan. "Bonpo Canons and Jesuit Cannons: On Sectarian Factors Involved in the Ch'en-Lung Emperor's Second Goldstream Expedition of 1771–1776." *The Tibet Journal* 15, no. 2 (1990): 3–28.

McGranahan, Carole. *Arrested Histories: Tibet, the CIA, and Memories of a Forgotten War*. Durham, NC: Duke University Press, 2010.

——. "Mao in Tibetan Disguise: History, Ethnographic Theory, and Excess." *HAU: Journal of Ethnographic Theory* 2, no. 1 (2012): 213–45.

McGranahan, Carole, and Ralph Litzinger. "Self-Immolation as Protest in Tibet." *Hot Spots, Fieldsights*, April 9, 2012. https://Culanth.Org/Fieldsights/Series/Self -Immolation-as-Protest-in-Tibet.

Men Guoliang 門國樑. "Sanjin Maogong" 三進懋功 [Entering Maogong three times]. In *Aba zangzu zizhizhou wenshi ziliao xuanji* 阿壩藏族自治州文史資料選輯 [Collections of cultural and historical materials in Ngawa Tibetan Autonomous Prefecture], vol. 6, 1–9. Maerkang: Abazhou zhengxie wenshi ziliao weiyuanhui 阿壩州政協文史資料委員會[Cultural-Historical Materials Committee at Aba Prefecture Political Consultative Conference], 1987.

Mengele, Irmgard. *Gedun Chöpel: A Biography of the 20th-Century Tibetan Scholar*. Dharamsala, H.P.: Library of Tibetan Works and Archives, 1999.

Mills, Martin A. *Identity, Ritual and State in Tibetan Buddhism: The Foundations of Authority in Gelukpa Monasticism*. London; New York: Routledge, 2003.

Mullaney, Thomas S. *Coming to Terms with the Nation: Ethnic Classification in Modern China*. Berkeley: University of California Press, 2011.

Naktsang, Nulo. *My Tibetan Childhood: When Ice Shattered Stone*. Durham, NC: Duke University Press, 2014.

Nietupski, Paul Kocot. *Labrang Monastery: A Tibetan Buddhist Community on the Inner Asian Borderlands, 1709–1958*. Lanham, MD: Lexington Books, 2011.

Nyima, Tashi. "The Chinese Development of Tibet: Lhasa in Transformation." *Forum for Development Studies* 35, no. 2 (2008): 257–77.

Oidtmann, Max. *Forging the Golden Urn: The Qing Empire and the Politics of Reincarnation in Tibet*. New York: Columbia University Press, 2018.

Ouerxiao 歐爾孝 and Ge Zhiyuan 葛志遠. "Huaergong Chenlie zhuan" 華爾功臣烈傳 [Biography of Pelgön Trinlé]. In *Sichuan jinxiandai renwuzhuan* 四川近現代人物傳 [Modern and Contemporary Figures in Sichuan], vol. 3, ed. Aba zhouzhiban/ Ren Yimin 阿壩州志辦/任一民, 322–29. Chengdu: Sichuan renmin chubanshe, 1987.

Pankenier, David W. *Astrology and Cosmology in Early China: Conforming Earth to Heaven*. New York: Cambridge University Press, 2013.

Pema Bhum. "The Life of Dhondup Gyal: A Shooting Star That Cleaved the Night Sky and Vanished." *Lungta* 9 (1995): 17–29.

Peng Zhiyan 彭陟焱. "Qianlong zaiding liangjinchuan zhanzheng gouchen" 乾隆再定兩金川戰爭鉤沉 [Anecdotes on Qianlong's re-subjugation of the two Jinchuans]. *The Academic Journal of Tibet Minzu Institute* 25, no. 2 (2004): 22–28.

——. "Qianlongdi dui daxiao jinchuan tusi gaituguiliu xi" 乾隆帝對大小金川土司改土歸流析 [An investigation of the Qianlong's policy of substituting chieftains with state-appointed civilian officials]." *The Academic Journal of Tibet Minzu Institute* 28, no. 4 (2007): 15–23.

Postiglione, Gerard A. *China's National Minority Education: Culture, Schooling, and Development*. New York: Falmer Press, 1999.

Qin Heping 秦和平, ed. *Sichuan minzu diqu minzhu gaige ziliaoji* 四川民族地區民主改革資料集 [A collection of materials on the democratic reform in ethnic minority regions in Sichuan]. Beijing: Minzu chubanshe, 2008.

——. *Sichuan minzu diqu minzhu gaige yanjiu 20 shiji 50 niandai sichuan zangqu yiqu de shehui bianqe* 四川民族地區民主改革研究: 20世紀50年代四川藏區彝區的社會變革 [A study of the democratic reform in ethnic minority regions in Sichuan—Social transition in Sichuan's Tibetan and Qi People regions in the 1950s]. Beijing: Zhongyang minzu daxue chubanshe, 2011.

Quintman, Andrew. *The Yogin and the Madman: Reading the Biographical Corpus of Tibet's Great Saint Milarepa*. New York: Columbia University Press, 2014.

Ramble, Charles. "The Long Arm of an Eighteenth-Century Bonpo Patron: Gyalrong and Dolpo Between the Jinchuan Wars." *Revue d'Etudes Tibétaines* 64 (Juillet 2022): 447–60.

Rawski, Evelyn Sakakida. *The Last Emperors: A Social History of Qing Imperial Institutions*. Berkeley: University of California Press, 1998.

Relyea, Scott. "Yokes of Gold and Threads of Silk: Sino-Tibetan Competition for Authority in Early Twentieth-Century Kham." *Modern Asian Studies* 49, no. 4 (2015): 963–1009.

Rinzang, Shamdo. "My Conversation with Akhu Yarphel." In *Conflicting Memories: Tibetan History Under Mao Retold*, ed. R. Barnett, Benno Weiner, and Françoise Robin, 334–51. Leiden; Boston: Brill, 2020.

Rosen, Stanley. *Red Guard Factionalism and the Cultural Revolution in Guangzhou (Canton)*. Boulder, CO: Westview Press, 1982.

Ryōsuke, Kobayashi. "Shilun Shiba Shiji Houqi Qingchao Dui Kangqu Zhengce De Bianhua [The new policies of the Qing toward the Khams region during the late eighteenth century]." *Journal of Tibetan Studies* 00 (2014): 197–208.

——. "Militarisation of Dargyé Monastery: Contested Borders on the Sino-Tibetan Frontier During the Early Twentieth Century." *Cahiers D'extrême-Asie* 27 (2018): 139–71.

Salisbury, Harrison E. *The Long March: The Untold Story*. New York: McGraw-Hill, 1985.

Schneider, Florian, and Yih-Jye Hwang. "The Sichuan Earthquake and the Heavenly Mandate: Legitimizing Chinese Rule Through Disaster Discourse." *Journal of Contemporary China* 23, no. 88 (2014): 636–56.

Schwieger, Peter. *The Dalai Lama and the Emperor of China: A Political History of the Tibetan Institution of Reincarnation*. New York: Columbia University Press, 2015.

——. "What Did the Chinese Warlord Liu Wenhui Want from Pha bong kha?" *Revue d'Etudes Tibétaines* 64 (2022): 461–78.

Scott, James C. *Weapons of the Weak: Everyday Forms of Peasant Resistance*. New Haven, CT: Yale University Press, 1985.

Seng ge 'bum, Btsan lha ngag dbang tshul khrims, Tsheng dbang, Bstan 'dzin sbyin pa, Nam mkha' tshul khrims. *Shar rgyal mo tsha ba rong gi lo rgyus dang rig gnas dpe tshogs/Jiarong zangzu lishi wenhua congshu* 嘉絨藏族歷史文化叢書 [Gyalrong Tibetan history and culture series]. Chengdu: Sichuan minzu chubanshe, 2017.

Shakabpa, W. D. *Tibet: A Political History.* New Haven, CT: Yale University Press, 1967.

Shakya, Tsering. *The Dragon in the Land of Snows: A History of Modern Tibet Since 1947.* New York: Columbia University Press, 1999.

——. "The Waterfall and Fragrant Flowers: The Development of Tibetan Literature Since 1950." *Manoa* 12, no. 2 (2000): 28–40.

Sharlho, Tseten Wangchuk. "China's Reforms in Tibet: Issues and Dilemmas." *Journal of Contemporary China* 1, no. 1 (1992): 34–60.

Shen Yaosheng 沈堯生. *Maogong jiefang jishi* 懋功解放紀實 [Documented accounts about Maogong's liberation]. Chengdu: Chengdu yaxuan yinwu youxian gongsi, 2011.

Smith, Warren W. *Tibet's Last Stand: The Tibetan Uprising of 2008 and China's Response.* New York: Rowman & Littlefield, 2010.

Smyer Yü, Dan. *The Spread of Tibetan Buddhism in China: Charisma, Money, Enlightenment.* New York: Routledge, 2012.

Sonam Tsering 索南才讓. "Minguo nianjian (1912~1949) hanzang fojiao wenhua jiaoliu—Neidi sengren fuzang qiufa" 民國年間（1912~1949年）漢藏佛教文化交流—內地僧人赴藏求法 [Cultural exchanges between Han and Tibetan Buddhism—Inland monks traveled to Tibet for Dharma seeking]. *Xizang yanjiu* 西藏研究 [Tibetan studies] 4 (2006): 44–50.

Sperling, Elliot. "Red Army's First Encounters with Tibet—Experiences on the Long March." *Tibetan Review* 10 (1976): 11–18.

Stoddard, Heather. "Don Grub Rgyal (1953–1985): Suicide of a Modern Tibetan Writer and Scholar." In *Proceedings of the 6th Seminar of the International Association for Tibetan Studies,* ed. Per Kvaerne, 825–34. Oslo: Institute for Comparative Research in Human Culture, 1994.

Su Xigang 蘇希剛. *Wode aba Dorjé Pasang* 我的阿爸多吉巴桑 [My father, Dorjé Pasang]. Maerkang: Abazhou zhengzhi wenshi he xuexi weiyuanhui 阿壩州政治文史和學習委員會 [Cultural-Historical Materials and Study Committee of Aba Prefecture], 1995.

Sun, Shuyun. *The Long March: The True History of Communist China's Founding Myth.* New York: Anchor, 2006.

Suvajra, Dharmachari. *The Wheel and the Diamond: The Life of Dhardo Tulku.* Cambridge, UK: Windhorse, 2004.

Tan, Gillian G. *In the Circle of White Stones: Moving Through Seasons with Nomads of Eastern Tibet.* Seattle: University of Washington Press, 2017.

Tashi, Dhondup. "A Monastic Scholar Under China's Occupation of Tibet: Muge Samten's (1913–1993) Autobiography and His Role as a Vernacular Intellectual." M.A. thesis, University of British Columbia, 2019.

Tenzin, Jinba. *In the Land of the Eastern Queendom: The Politics of Gender and Ethnicity on the Sino-Tibetan Border.* Seattle; London: University of Washington Press, 2014.

——. "Memory Politics at Work in a Gyalrong Revolt in the Early Twentieth Century." *Cross-Currents: East Asian History and Culture Review* 5, no. 2 (2016): 408–39.

——. "Seeing Like Borders: Convergence Zone as a Post-Zomian Model." *Current Anthropology* 58, no. 5 (2017): 551–75.

Thargyal, Rinzin, and Toni Huber. *Nomads of Eastern Tibet: Social Organization and Economy of a Pastoral Estate in the Kingdom of Dege*. Leiden; Boston: Brill, 2007.

Theobald, Ulrich. *War Finance and Logistics in Late Imperial China: A Study of the Second Jinchuan Campaign (1771–1776)*. Leiden: Brill, 2013.

Tian Lijun 田利軍. *Ganwu hongse zhengquan—Ershi shiji qianbanqi zhonggong genjudi zhengquan yanjiu* 感悟紅色政權—20世紀前半期中共根據地政權研究 [Making sense of the red regime—A study of the CCP's revolutionary bases in the first half of the twentieth century]. Chengdu: Sichuan renmin chubanshe, 2011.

Trijang Rinpoche. *The Magical Play of Illusion: The Autobiography of Trijang Rinpoche*. Somerville, MA: Wisdom, 2018.

Tsangnyön Heruka, Andrew Quintman, and Donald S. Lopez, Jr. *The Life of Milarepa*. New York: Penguin, 2010.

Tsarong Paljor. *The Life and Times of George Tsarong of Tibet, 1920–1970: A Lord of the Traditional Tibetan State*. Lanham, MD: Lexington Books, 2021.

Tshe tan zhabs drung 'jigs med rigs pa'i blo gros. "Mnyam med shakya'i dbang bo'i rjes zhugs pa 'jigs med rigs pa'i blo gros rang gi byung ba brjod pa bden gtam rna ba'i bdud rtsi" [Truthful discourse, acoustic ambrosia: The life story of 'Jigs Med Rigs Pa'i Blo Gros, himself a disciple of the powerful, matchless Shākya]." In *Mkhas dbang tshe tan zhabs drung 'jigs med rigs pa'i blo gros kyi gsung rtsom* [The collected works of the scholar tshe tan zhabs drung 'jigs med rigs pa'i blo gros], vol. 1, ed. 'Phrin las, 499–801. Xining: Mtsho sngon mi rigs dpe skrun khang, 1987.

Tsybikov, Gombozhab T. *A Buddhist Pilgrim at the Shrines of Tibet*. Leiden: Brill, 2017.

Tuttle, Gray. *Tibetan Buddhists in the Making of Modern China*. New York: Columbia University Press, 2005.

van Schaik, Sam. "A New Look at the Tibetan Invention of Writing." In *New Studies of the Old Tibetan Documents: Philology, History and Religion*, ed. Imaeda Yoshiro, Matthew Kapstein, and Tsuguhito Takeuchi, 45–96. Tokyo: Tokyo University of Foreign Studies, 2011.

Van Slyke, Lyman P. *Enemies and Friends: The United Front in Chinese Communist History*. Stanford, CA: Stanford University Press, 1967.

Walder, Andrew G. "Beijing Red Guard Factionalism: Social Interpretations Reconsidered." *The Journal of Asian Studies* 61, no. 2 (2002): 437–71.

Waley-Cohen, Joanna. *The Culture of War in China: Empire and the Military Under the Qing Dynasty*. London: I. B. Tauris, 2006.

Wang Chuan 王川. "Liu Wenhui yu xikang diqu zangchuan fojiao jie guanxi lunshu" 劉文輝與西康地區藏傳佛教界關係論述 [On the relationship between Liu Wenhui and the Tibetan Buddhist circle in Xikang]. *Zhongguo Zangxue* 中國藏學 [China tibetology] 3 (2006): 78–84.

Wang, Di. *Violence and Order on the Chengdu Plain: The Story of a Secret Brotherhood in Rural China, 1939–1949*. Stanford, CA: Stanford University Press, 2018.

Wang Haibing 王海兵. *Kangzang diqu de fenzheng yu juezhu* 康藏地區的紛爭與角逐 (1912–1939) [Disputes and rivalry in Kham and Tibet, 1912–1939]. Beijing: Shehui Kexue Wenxian chubanshe, 2012.

Wang Lixiong. *Tianzang: Xizang de mingyun* [Sky burial: The fate of Tibet]. Mississauga, Ont.: Mingjing chubanshe, 1998.

Wang Mingke 王明珂. "Wasi tusi de zuyuan—Yige dui lishi shenhua yu xiangye chua shuo de bianyuan yanjiu" 瓦寺土司的祖源——一個對歷史、神話與鄉野傳說的邊緣研究

[The origins of Wasi Tusi: A border study of histories, myths, and legends]." *Lishi renleixue xuekan* 歷史人類學學刊 [Journal of history and anthropology] 2, no. 1 (2004): 51–88.

Wang Rongcheng 王榮成, Li Ronglan 李蓉蘭, and Mou Xiong 牟雄. "Wang Weizhou jiaoyu sixiang tanxi" 王維舟教育思想探析 [An analysis of Wang Weizhou's educational thoughts]." *Zhonghua wenhua luntan* 中華文化論壇 [Forum on Chinese culture] 12 (2017): 103–14.

Wang Tingyu. " 'House,' Illusion or Illumination? The Social Organization and Language of Sichuan Rgyalrong Tibetan." Ph.D. diss., National Tsing Hua University, Taiwan, 2018.

Wang Yao 王堯. "Zangyu mig zi gudu kao—jianlun zangyu shengdiao de fasheng yu fazhan 藏語 mig 字" 古讀考—兼論藏語聲調的發生與發展 [An investigation of the ancient reading of the Tibetan word mig—Also on the occurrence and development of Tibetan tones]. *Minzu yuwen* 民族語文 [National languages] 4 (1981): 15–19.

——. "Hu Yaobang's Visit to Tibet, May 22–31, 1980." In *Resistance and Reform in Tibet*, ed. Robert Barnett and Shirin Akiner, 285–89. Bloomington: Indiana University Press, 1994.

Wang, Xiuyu. *China's Last Imperial Frontier: Late Qing Expansion in Sichuan's Tibetan Borderlands*. Lanham, MD: Lexington Books, 2011.

Wangchuk, Dorji. *The Resolve to Become a Buddha: A Study of the Bodhicitta Concept in Indo-Tibetan Buddhism*. Tokyo: International Institute for Buddhist Studies of the International College for Postgraduate Buddhist Studies, 2007.

Wangyal, Baba Phuntsok. *Witness to Tibet's History*. Trans. Tenzin Losel. Ed. Jane Perkins. New Delhi: Paljor Publications, 2007.

Weiner, Benno. *The Chinese Revolution on the Tibetan Frontier*. Ithaca, NY: Cornell University Press, 2020.

Wellens, Koen. *Religious Revival in the Tibetan Borderlands: The Premi of Southwest China*. Seattle: University of Washington Press, 2010.

Wenchuan zhengxie wenshi ziliao weiyuanhui 汶川縣政協文史資料委員會 [Cultural-Historical Materials Committee at Wenchuan County Political Consultative Conference], ed. *Wasi tusi zhuanji* 瓦寺土司專輯/*Wenchuanxian wenshi ziliao xuanji* (4) 汶川縣文史資料選輯 [Wasi Tusi album/Wenchuan cultural-historical material collections, vol. 4]. Wenchuan: Wenchuan zhengxie, 1994.

Whalen-Bridge, John. *Tibet on Fire: Buddhism, Protest, and the Rhetoric of Self-Immolation*. New York: Palgrave Macmillan, 2015.

Willis, Janice D. "On the Nature of Rnam-Thar: Early Dge-Lugs-Pa Siddha Biographies." In *Soundings in Tibetan Civilization* (Kathmandu), ed. B. A. Aziz and M. Kapstein, 304–19. Kathmandu: Vajra Publications, 1985.

Willock, Nicole. "The Revival of the Tulku Institution: Narratives and Practices in Modern China." *Revue d'etudes Tibétaines* 38 (2017): 183–201.

——. "Tibetan Buddhist Scholars and the Cultural Revolution: Narratives of Spiritual Achievement and Supporting Tibetan Culture." In *Conflicting Memories: Tibetan History Under Mao Retold*, ed. R. Barnett, Benno Weiner, and Françoise Robin, 485–505. Leiden; Boston: Brill, 2020.

——. *Lineages of the Literary: Tibetan Buddhist Polymaths of Socialist China*. New York: Columbia University Press, 2021.

Woeser, Tsering. *Tibet on Fire: Self-Immolations Against Chinese Rule*. Trans. K. Carrico. London; New York: Verso, 2016.

——. *Forbidden Memory: Tibet During the Cultural Revolution*. Lincoln, NE: Potomac Books, 2020.

Wu, We. "Indigenization of Tibetan Buddhism in Twentieth-Century China". Ph.D. diss., Princeton University, 2017.

Xing Suzhi 邢肅芝, Zhang Jianfei 張建飛, and Yang Nianqun 楊念群. *Xueyu Qiufa ji: Yige hanren lama de koushushi (Xiuding Ben)* 雪域求法記：一個漢人喇嘛的口述史 (修訂本) [Seeking Dharma in the snowland: An oral history of a Han Chinese lama (revised edition)]. Beijing: Shenghuo dushu xinzhi sanlian shudian, 2008.

Xu Fayan 徐法言. "Qianlongchao Jinchuan zhanyi yanjiu pingshu" 乾隆朝金川戰役研究評述 [An overview of research on the Jinchuan Campaigns]. *Studies in Qing History* 4 (2011): 133–42.

——. "Diyici Jinchuan zhiyi qiyin chutan qianlongdi suijing chuanbian de nuli 第一次金川之役起因初探——乾隆帝綏靖川邊的努力 [An investigation of the cause of the first Jinchuan Campaign: Emperor Qianlong's efforts to subdue and pacify the Sichuan frontiers]." *The Academic Journal of Sichuan University* 5 (2012): 150–60.

Yang, Miaoyan. *Learning to Be Tibetan: The Construction of Ethnic Identity at Minzu University of China*. Lanham, MD: Lexington Books, 2017.

Yangdzom, Tsering. *The Aristocratic Families in Tibetan History: 1900–1951*. Beijing: China Intercontinental Press, 2006.

Yeh, Emily T. *Taming Tibet: Landscape Transformation and the Gift of Chinese Development*. Ithaca, NY: Cornell University Press, 2013.

Yeh, Emily T., and Chris Coggins. *Mapping Shangrila: Contested Landscapes in the Sino-Tibetan Borderlands*. Seattle: University of Washington Press, 2014.

Yudru, Tsomu. "Taming the Khampas: The Republican Construction of Eastern Tibet." *Modern China* 39, no. 3 (2013): 319–44.

——. *The Rise of Gönpo Namgyel in Kham: The Blind Warrior of Nyarong*. Lanham, MD: Lexington Books, 2015.

——. "Guozhuang Trading Houses and Tibetan Middlemen in Dartsedo, the 'Shanghai of Tibet.'" *Cross-Currents: East Asian History and Culture Review* 19 (2016): 71–121.

——. "Women as Chieftains in Modern Kham History." *Inner Asia* 20, no. 1 (2018): 107–31.

Zhang Liming 張理明. "Maogong jiefang jilüe" 懋功解放記略 [A brief account of thelLiberation of Maogong]. In *Xiaojin wenshi ziliao xuanji* 小金文史資料選輯 [Xiaojin cultural-historical material collections], vol. 1, ed. Xiaojinxian zhengxie wenshi ziliao gongzuozu 小金縣政協文史資料工作組 [Cultural-Historical Materials Working Group at Xiaojin County Political Consultative Conference], 43–81. Xiaojin: Xiaojin zhengxie, 1988.

Zhang Xuefeng 張學鳳, and Btsan lha ngag dbang tshul khrims, eds. "Qingshilu zangzu shiliao zai jiarong zangzu huguo weiji 《清實錄藏族史料》載嘉絨藏族護國偉績 [Gyalrong Tibetans' great achievements in defending the state as recorded in the Tibetan historical materials of the veritable records of the Qing]." In *Rgyal mo rong gi lo rgyus skor/Jiarong diqu lishi* 嘉絨地區歷史（下冊）[On Gyalrong history], vol. 3, ed. Btsan lha ngag dbang tshul khrims, Bstan 'dzin sbyin pa, Nam mkha' tshul khrims, and Mtsho sman, 210–39. Chengdu: Sichuan minzu chubanshe, 2017.

Zhang Yinong. "Between Nation and Religion: The Sino-Tibetan Buddhist Network in Post-Reform China." *Chinese Sociological Review* 45, no. 1 (2012): 55–69.

Zhang Yisun 張怡蓀, ed. *Bod rgya tshig mdzod chen mo/Zanghan da cidian* 藏漢大辭典 [The Tibetan-Chinese general dictionary]. Beijing: minzu chubanshe, 1985.

Zhang Zhengming 張正明, ed. *Ganzi zangqu shehui diaocha ziliao huiji* 甘孜藏區社會調查資料匯輯 [A collection of social survey data in Kardzé Tibetan Area]. Beijing: Quanguo renmin daibiao dahui minzu weiyuanhui bangongshi 全國人民代表大會民族委員會辦公室 [National People's Congress Nationality Committee office], 1957.

Zhao, Dingxin. "The Mandate of Heaven and Performance Legitimation in Historical and Contemporary China." *American Behavioral Scientist* 53, no. 3 (2009): 416–33.

Zhao, Taotao, and James Leibold. "Ethnic Governance Under Xi Jinping: The Centrality of the United Front Work Department and Its Implications." *Journal of Contemporary China* 29, no. 124 (2020): 487–502.

Zhao Zheng 趙崢. "Xinzhongguo chengli chuqi xikang shaoshu minzu daibiao canguan fangwen neidi shulun" 新中國成立初期西康少數民族代表參觀訪問內地述論 [On the visit of representatives of ethnic minorities from Xikang to the mainland in the early days of the rounding of New China]." *Zhonggong dangshi yanjiu* 中共黨史研究 [CCP history studies] 07 (2016): 33–45.

Zhonggong Abaxian gongwei 中共阿壩縣工委 [The CCP Ngawa Work Committee]. "Abaxian mingai gongzuo zongjie" 阿壩縣民改工作總結 [A summary of the democratic reform in Ngawa]." In *Sichuan minzu diqu minzhu gaige ziliaoji* 四川民族地區民主改革資料集 [A collection of materials on the democratic reform in ethnic minority regions in Sichuan], ed. Qin Heping 秦和平, 168–83. Beijing: minzu chubanshe, 2008.

Zhongguo di'er lishi dang'an'guan 中國第二歷史檔案館, ed. *Kangzang jiufeng dang'an xuanbian* 康藏糾紛檔案選編 [Selected archives on Kham-Tibet dispute]. Beijing: Zhongguo zangxue chubanshe, 2000.

Zhongguo Kexueyuan Minzu Yanjiusuo/Sichuan Shaoshu Minzu Shehui Lishi Diaochazu 中國科學院民族研究所/四川少數民族社會歷史調查組 [Institute of Ethnic Studies, Chinese Academy of Sciences/Sichuan Ethnic Minority Social History Investigation Group; abbr., CAS-SEM]. "Minzhu gaige qian xiaojinxian jiesixiang shehui diaocha" 民主改革前小金縣結思鄉社會調查 [Social survey of Jiesi Township (Jémé) in Xiaojin County before the democratic reform]. In *Aba zangzu zizhizhou xiao jin, lixian shehui diaocha cailiao* 阿壩藏族自治州小金、理縣社會調查 [Social survey materials of Xiaojin and Lixian, Aba Tibetan Autonomous Prefecture], 1–17. Beijing/Chengdu: CAS-SEM, 1963.

Zhongguo renmin zhengzhi xieshang huiyi ganzi zangzu zizhizhou weiyuanhui 中國人民政治協商會議甘孜藏族自治州委員會 [Kardzé Tibetan Autonomous Prefecture Committee of the Chinese People's Political Consultative Conference]. *Ganzizhou wenshi ziliao xuanji* 甘孜州文史資料選輯 [Selected collections of cultural and historical materials of Kardzé Prefecture] (Volume 6: Dedication to Ngawang Gyatso). Kangding: Ganzizhou zhengxie, 1987.

Zhu Shide 祝世德, ed. *Shidai zhongzhen zhi wasi tusi* 世代忠貞之瓦寺土司 [The chieftains of the Wasi for generations of loyalty]. Wenchuan: Sichuan wasi xuanweishisi xuanwei shishu 四川瓦寺宣慰使司宣慰史署 [History Division of the Sichuan Wasi Xuanwei Cheiftaincy], 1945.

Zhuang Xueben. *Qiangrong kaocha ji* [Field investigation of Qiang and Rong people]. Shanghai: Shanghai liangyou tushu gongsi, 1937.

INDEX

disrupted by, 190; nomad connections and, 176; Red Guards, 180, 187, 188, 250n2; survival skills during, 55; "Three Giants" of Ngawa and, 183; Tibetan language skills honed during, 187–88

CYLC (Communist Youth League of China), 131, 138, 154, 169

Dalai Lama, 2, 7, 223n11; Fifth, 13, 84, 227n25; Twelfth, 84; Thirteenth, 87, 238n9

Dalai Lama, Fourteenth (present), 3, 18, 104, 153, 208, 244–45n12; assistant tutors to, 85, 93, 94, 105, 151, 153; autobiographies of, 13; Chengdu visit (1954), 149–52; flight to India (1959), 147; principal tutor to, 94; selection of, 77, 103; United Front and, 149

Damdo Monastery, 70–71

Damzhung, 69

Dardo Tulku, 68, 81

Dargyé-Béri Incident, 237n9

Dargyé Monastery, 77, 237n9

Dartsédo, 69, 70, 83, 236n5

Dartso (wife of Suo Guokun), 140, 142–43

death and souls, 50, 92, 217; intermediate stage between life and death, 51–54; King of the Underworld (Tib. Shinjé chögyel), 208, 210

debates, 89–93, 97, 239nn11–12

Dedrug lineage (Gyalrong Khutuktu), 84, 104

Dedrug Residence, 78, 79, 100

Dedrug Rinpoche (Gyalrong Khutuktu), 78–79, 81, 87, 100, 154

Dégé, 69

Dégé Sé (Dégé prince), 130

delusion (Tib. timuk), as "poison," 96

Democratic Reform (late 1950s), 10, 22, 134, 174, 245nn13–14; CCP policy to provoke revolts, 163, 170; class categories and, 159–60, 246n5; Dalai Lama as obstacle to, 147; expectations of, 136; gun confiscation and, 158, 246n4; land reform and, 156; Makeup

Movement, 167; "mutual-aid teams" (Ch. huzhu zu), 173, 247n3; out-transfer of local elites and, 158–59; rebellions against, 163–64; study/struggle sessions, 159–63

Deng Xiaoping, 125

Deng Xihou, 114, 115, 120, 145

Denpa kingdom, 141

Deyang College, 94

Döndrup Gyel, 194, 195–96, 204–5, 206, 249n7; death of, 15, 205, 208; popularity of, 198; undermined by Han colleagues at Southwest Nationalities Institute, 207–8; Waterfall of Youth [Lang tsho'i rbab chu], 251n9

Dorjé Chöpa, Lama, 85, 86, 238n9

Dorjé Den Monastery, 153

Dorjé Pasang (a.k.a. Su Yonghe), 138, 140, 141, 244n9, 247n5; CCP distrust of, 143–44; Cultural Revolution and, 183; flight to India, 147, 155; Kuomintang and, 146, 157; power struggles of, 145–46; throne assumed by force, 144, 146

Dorjé Shugden, 237n4

Dornor (helper to Dungkar La), 200, 202

Drakgo, 69, 71

Drakgo Gön Monastery, 71

Draktong Chijikmé, 144, 244n8

Drepung Monastery (Lhasa), 36, 67, 126, 153, 199, 233n19; admission procedure at, 80–81; Dalai Lama's visit to, 150; debates at, 89–93, 97, 239n12; empowerment rituals at, 95; teacher-student relationship at, 93–94. See also Gyalrong House; Loserling College

Druktar, 32–33

Dungkar La (Dungkar Lozang Trinlé), 15, 190–93, 195–97, 209; classical Tibetan dictionary project and, 196; Cultural Revolution and, 200; deficiencies of modern education system and, 198; as eminent Tibetologist, 198; The Great Dungkar Tibetan Dictionary, 203, 206;